CLASSIC MOVIE MONSTERS

by
DONALD F. GLUT

with an Introduction
by
Curt Siodmak

The Scarecrow Press, Inc.
Metuchen, N.J. & London
1978

Cover illustration, of Lon Chaney's Phantom of the Opera, by Linda L. Glut.

Library of Congress Cataloging in Publication Data

Glut, Donald F
    Classic movie monsters.

    Includes index.
    1.   Horror films--History and criticism. I.   Title.
PN1995.9.H6G57   791.43'7   77-16014
ISBN 0-8108-1049-2

To my wife Lindagray,

who would probably refuse
an expense-paid trip to Skull Island
or the Black Lagoon

TABLE OF CONTENTS

Acknowledgments   vii

Preface   ix

"The Wolf Man" by Way of Introduction
    (by Curt Siodmak)   xiii

I   When the Wolf Man Prowls   1

II   The Dual Horror of Dr. Jekyll   68

III   The Invisible Man and Co.   130

IV   The Curse of the Mummy   162

V   Quasimodo of Notre Dame   204

VI   The Phantoms of the Opera   230

VII   The Creature--Monster of the Fifties   257

VIII   His Majesty, King Kong   282

IX   Godzilla, the New King   374

Index   413

v

ACKNOWLEDGMENTS

The author sincerely thanks the following contributors to this book:

Toria Aiken and M. J. Campbell of the Los Angeles Public Library; Dave Allen; Dick Andersen; Rick Baker; Bruce Barbour; Steve Barkett; Calvin Thomas Beck, author of the excellent Heroes of the Horrors; John Berg; Paul Blaisdell; Dennis and Sandy Billows; Robert Bloch; Ronald V. Borst; Larry Brill and Joe Kane of The Monster Times; Larry Byrd; the late Lon Chaney, Jr.; Bob and Sody Clampett; Frederick S. Clarke, publisher/editor of Cinefantastique; Gerry Conway; the late Merian C. Cooper; Ray Craig; Jim Danforth; Walter J. Daugherty; Maurine Dawson; Mark Evanier; the late Victor Fabian; Philip José Farmer; Mark Frank, publisher/editor of Photon; Luis Gasca; Julia Glut, my mother who took me to see so many monster movies when I was too young to go alone; Lindagray Glut, who is not impressed that I graduated from USC in the same auditorium in which Carl Denham once exhibited the "Eighth Wonder of the World"; Orville Goldner and George E. Turner, authors of The Making of King Kong; Brenda Gray; Bob Greenberg; Ray Harryhausen; Jan Henderson; Saki Hijiri; Eric Hoffman; Larry Ivie; Heather Johnson; Marvin Jones; Mark Kausler, possibly the world's greatest authority on animated cartoons; David Kinoshita of Toho International; Paul Klug; Allen G. Kracalik; John Landis; Mike Lefebvre of L/C Distributors of home movies (PO Box 6263, Santa Ana, CA 92706); Christopher Lee; David M. Massaro; Norman Maurer of Hanna-Barbera Productions; Mark McGee; Don Megowan; Doug Moench; Wayne Moretti; Norbert Novotny; Darlyne O'Brien; Gus Ocosta of Columbia Pictures; Randy (R. J.) Robertson; Bill Rotsler; Jesse Santos; Scott Shaw; Curt Siodmak; Ferenc (not to be confused with "Ferenk") Solyomi; Adam Spektor; Dan Spiegle; Ray Dennis Steckler; Jim Steranko, publisher/editor of Mediascene; the late Glenn Strange; Roy Thomas; James Warren of Warren Publishing Company; Len Wein; Tom Werner; Bongo Wolf; Marv Wolf-

man; Jim Wnoroski; and the staff of the Margaret Herrick
Library of the Academy of Motion Picture Arts and Sciences.

Special thanks go to Forrest J Ackerman (editor of
Famous Monsters of Filmland); Ralph Costantino (the monster expert of Lorain, Ohio); Jim Harmon (author of The
Great Radio Heroes, The Great Radio Comedians and Jim
Harmon's Nostalgia Catalogue); Ron Haydock (author of Deer-
stalker! Holmes and Watson on Screen [Scarecrow Press,
1977] and editor of King of the Monsters and the E-Go Collectors Series magazines); and Bill Warren (author, historian,
book reviewer). They are monster hunters all, who were
always prompt in reporting to this writer the latest news,
however earth-shaking or trivial, about the Wolf Man, Godzilla or the rest of the infamous horde.

And a most monstrous thanks to Donald G. Willis, au-
thor of Horror and Science Fiction Films: A Checklist
(Scarecrow Press, 1972), and to Walt Lee, author of the
Reference Guide to Fantastic Films (available from Chelsea-
Lee Books, PO Box 66273, Los Angeles, CA 90066), whose
Kong-sized masses of titles, dates and credits were invalu-
able in the preparation of this book.

To everyone, including those contributors I may have
missed, my wholehearted thanks.

PREFACE

There was hardly a time in my life when I wasn't hooked on monsters.

I suppose my childhood in Chicago, from the middle 1940s through the early 1950s, was typical enough. Superman, Lionel trains and Roy Rogers, Hopalong Cassidy and Gene Autry were always uppermost in my mind as they were with most kids during those innocent years. Somehow, though, I also developed a fascination with skeletons (probably after the first time my mother took me down to Chicago's Field Museum of Natural History) and astronomy (following a trip to the Adler Planetarium, within walking distance of the Museum).

Skeletons and celestial bodies. I would draw them at every opportunity. I recall my doctor's nurse giving me a chart depicting a human skeleton, a real prize that I still have in my possession. And I remember spending hours drawing what I considered at the time to be accurate maps of the entire universe!

Naturally, stories and movies involving skeletons began to interest me as much as the action packed adventures of Hoppy or the Man of Steel. Most of these productions were either eerie mysteries or horror. Perhaps I wasn't yet old enough for the horror kind because I recall becoming frightened by such scary characters as Margaret Hamilton's Witch in The Wizard of Oz and the ghost (played by Charles Middleton) in Strangler of the Swamp when it first played on Chicago television.

There were also less terrifying outlets for my interest in outer space and the planets. During the early fifties "Tom Corbett, Space Cadet," "Captain Video" and "Space Patrol" were filling our television screen with glimpses into the future and wondrous visions of extraterrestrial travel and life. My interest in skeletons was evolving into a more spe-

ix

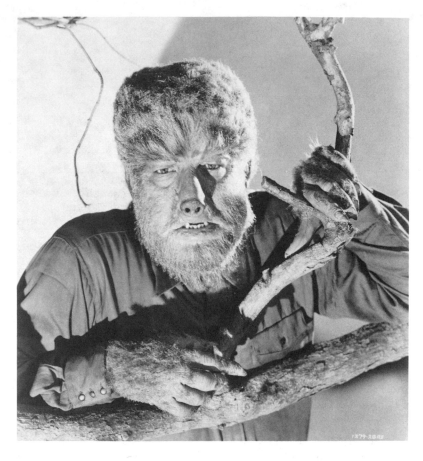

Lon Chaney, Jr., as the most famous werewolf of all, in
Frankenstein Meets the Wolf Man (Universal, 1943).

cific interest in fossil bones and I was thoroughly delighted
when prehistoric monsters began to lumber and slither through
the worlds of Corbett, Captain Video, and Buzz Corry and
Cadet Happy of the Space Patrol. One episode of an early
1950s Saturday morning show, "Rod Brown of the Rocket
Rangers," even had a friendly chimpanzee growing to King
Kong proportions. At the time, however, I knew little of the
famous simian who met his death atop the Empire State Building.

After a while, I sought out every dinosaur movie to play in Chicago, either in theatres or on television. There were great ones like The Beast from 20,000 Fathoms (which I saw for the first of many times at a drive-in), with Ray Harryhausen's special effects totally baffling me. On television there was the spectacle of the original One Million B.C. (the first motion picture I recall ever seeing on TV). I'd begun to hear tales of a movie called King Kong, in which a giant gorilla lived behind a colossal wall in a world of dinosaurs. My fascination with prehistoric monsters was developing into one with monsters in general.

As my interest waxed I was gradually transforming, without the need of a full moon or Dr. Jekyll's potion, into a monster movie fan.

I was thrilled in 1953 to see the impressive posters advertising a rerelease of Mighty Joe Young and totally transfixed three years later when I finally saw a revival of the first (and best) King Kong. After Kong's plunge from his skyscraper roost, I was certain his screen adventure could never be topped. In many ways I was right.

Then, though I'd read of werewolves often enough in the horror comic books so popular during the early 1950s, I saw my first motion picture incarnation of that variety of beast in The Werewolf, a Columbia picture of 1956. I remember hearing my friends talk about a character called the Wolf Man who had appeared in a movie called, incredible as it sounded, Abbott and Costello Meet Frankenstein. And when I saw my first two Frankenstein movies in 1956, House of Frankenstein and House of Dracula, I discovered the real Wolf Man for myself--and tried unsuccessfully to reconcile him with the character in the Columbia film.

Before 1956 I had not seen any of Universal's "Mummy" films, though I'd seen the newspaper ads; and a classmate had described with near mouth-frothing detail how the bandaged monster emerged from the swamp in The Mummy's Curse. My first exposure to the Mummy was, thankfully, in the Boris Karloff picture, The Mummy. It was part three of a triple bill, the first two-thirds being the above-mentioned House of Frankenstein and House of Dracula.

December 7 may have had historical meaning for other people in 1957, but for me and a few other monster-craving friends in Chicago it meant the day we'd long been awaiting.

That was the Saturday that Shock Theater premiered on local station WBKB-TV at 10:00 p.m. Shock Theater began running the newly available "Shock Package" of Universal horror movies. The second week the original Wolf Man was scheduled, followed by Night Monster, a motion picture that we had to sit through until the next week's more promising film, The Mummy. Before long The Invisible Man was removing his bandages to reveal "nothing" in our living rooms. And, of course, there were all the sequels.

Like other monster movie fanatics, I did my active part to approach their shadowy world. Scrapbooks, amateur monster movies, story writing, trying to capture grisly likenesses in artwork, instigating fan clubs (like the AFL, standing for the American Fiend League)--I did them all. Before I bought the first issue of the world's original monster magazine, Famous Monsters of Filmland, I was certain that publisher Jim Warren and editor Forry Ackerman had had printed only a few copies for themselves, one for me, and a couple extra for friends. However, through FM (as that magazine is affectionately known) I learned that there were other monster buffs out there--thousands of them. It is for them (and myself) that I've written this book.

I've tried to cover the nine greatest monsters and fiends of the movies--the Wolf Man, Dr. Jekyll (and his alter ego Mr. Hyde), the Invisible Man, the Mummy, the Hunchback of Notre Dame, the Phantom of the Opera, the Creature from the Black Lagoon, King Kong, and Godzilla--along with their monstrous kith and kin. Conspicuously absent from these pages are the Frankenstein Monster and Count Dracula. Aficionados of these perhaps most infamous horrors of all, I refer to my earlier books, The Frankenstein Legend: A Tribute to Mary Shelley and Boris Karloff (1973) and The Dracula Book (1975), both published by Scarecrow Press. But the rest of the brood is here, howling at the moon, reaching with crumbling fingers for the throat of a violator of the tomb and struggling to the last against the weapons of Mankind--the Classic Movie Monsters.

Donald F. Glut
January 1977

Curt Siodmak

By Way of Introduction:

THE WOLF MAN

Even a man who's pure in heart
And says his prayers by night,
May become a wolf when the wolfbane blooms
And the autumn moon is bright.

I made up that ditty when I wrote The Wolf Man for
Universal Pictures in 1941. The title came from Boris Karloff, who never played the Wolf Man. I gave the monster a
name: Larry Talbot. Now film historians believe that my
four-liner was taken from German folklore and that Larry
Talbot's name also is part of European horror history.
That's how film history is being made.

Walter Evans, a professor in the English department
at Augusta College in Georgia, gave a lecture on popular
tragedy, which explains the basic impact of horror stories
and movies on the public. He talked about Aristotle's Poetics
and The Wolf Man. His dissertation compares the Wolf Man
to the construction of Aristotelian tragedy. Reading his
learned lecture, I acquired a word unknown to me: hamartia.
In ancient Greek tragedy hamartia means an error in judgment resulting from a defect in the character of a tragic
hero. According to Dr. Evans, Aristotle notes that his hero
does not come into his misfortune because of badness or ras-
cality, but through some inequity or positive fault. The better monster movies invariably tend to echo this element of
hamartia to which Aristotle gave much prominence in his
study of classical tragedy. The Universal studio writers (I
was one of them) who hacked out the scripts for so many
film monster movies were, one assumes, largely ignorant
of Aristotle's Poetics (one would assume right in my case),
but like Aristotle and those of whom he wrote, these script
writers had a finely-tuned sense of the inner dynamics of
powerful popular art.

The Athenian noble watching a semi-religious dramatic performance and the modern teenager looking at a monster movie demand a protagonist who bears some moral responsibility for the suffering and terror to which he and his community will be committed. The Western cowboy hero, the Detective, the Secret Agent are almost invariably blameless. The protagonist in a monster movie, however, like the hero in a classical tragedy, has, through some character flaw or error of judgment, helped create or release the monster which he must now aid or exorcise.

In Nosferatu, a German horror story of the early 1920s, a young real estate agent must seek out the vampire whom he helped to locate in urban Germany.   Henry Frankenstein must destroy the Monster he created.   Carl Denham must help track down the monster ape he kidnapped from Skull Island.   Dr. Jekyll must destroy Mr. Hyde.

Why hamartia in monster movies?   The best reason perhaps is that it cements the vital link of identification between both protagonist and monster; the identification is most rich, complete and profound, however, when the monster and protagonist are themselves (as in The Wolf Man) causally linked through the creator's ethical responsibility for the created.

The Wolf Man figure shares certain significant features with the great characters of Sophoclean tragedy, Oedipus and Antigone, and seems to conform to Aristotle's analysis.   Like Oedipus, Larry Talbot must wrestle with a personal fate in which destiny and his own character have conspired to destroy him.   Like Oedipus, Talbot is driven to self-recognition so horrible that he views the possibility of death as a blessing.   Like Antigone, the Wolf Man provides a double tragedy, that of the passionately self-destructive younger person and the older father figure whose fatally shortsighted commitment to discipline and personal authority requires the tragic death of the younger.   As in a Sophoclean tragedy, The Wolf Man yields much of its structure and meaning to an Aristotelian analysis of the tragic character, the tragic flaw, reversal, recognition and catharsis.

It is just as well that we writers do not always know what we are writing and that we simply work with our techniques and our emotions, which seem to lead, sometimes, the right way.   Written thirty-five years ago, The Wolf Man still plays on television in prime time.   Something basically

CURT SIODMAK

right must be propping up that original story. It might be
that the story follows the Aristotelian laws. But knowing
those laws, as Dr. Evans does so well, would certainly in-
hibit the imagination of such a writer as myself.

I remember that I was given the title and a deadline:
seven weeks for the screenplay. I was told the cast: Lon
Chaney, Jr., Claude Rains, Madame Ouspenskaya, Warren
William, Bela Lugosi, Ralph Bellamy and a very pretty
actress whose greatest talent was a most terrifying scream,
Evelyn Ankers from Australia. The picture, I was told,
should be in the range of $180,000. My salary was $400 a
week, no percentages of course, and I only had
twenty-four-hour, cut-off employment. When the picture
made its first million, the producer got a $10,000 bonus,

the director a diamond ring for his wife, and I got fired,
since I wanted $25 more for my next job.   Per week, of
course.   I was told to get my raises outside.   Universal
then would pay too.   That was the policy of the motion picture industry.

I invented a name for Dracula: Count Alucard, Dracula spelled backwards.   It stuck.   Now the name is part of
Hungarian folklore.   History is made behind the typewriter.

But the history of horror movies also has its frightening cycle.   The popularity of horror films and current historical trends are interrelated.   Horror stories and horror
movies are safety valves for human anxieties.   During World
War Two there was a renaissance of the Frankenstein, Wolf
Man and Invisible Man stories.   That trend lasted until the
war's end.   Though the cloud of the horrors of war permeated
our everyday lives, motion pictures of heroic soldiers mow-
ing down hordes of enemies only increased anxieties, since
everybody knew that one machine gun couldn't liquidate five
thousand Nazis and that fathers and sons were in the battle-
line facing death.   But abstract horror movies--the Monster
kidnapping the fair lady, the Wolf Man anxiously watching
the moon which could change him into a murderous beast--
were highly successful thrillers.   Their horrors were de-
tached from reality.   When the audience left the theatre they
knew they had seen a fantasy.

The day the war ended, the bottom of the horror
movie industry fell out.   Even Germany, having shed the
Nazi spirit, liked only "Schnultzen," insipid love stories,
all sugar and spice.   Horror pictures couldn't even be given
away.   In the United States the musicals and comedies had
their heydays.   Then, with Truman's cold war policy, with
Russian and American atom bombs and other apocalyptic
weapons against which there was no defense, horror pictures
returned in quantity.   They peaked in the early 1950s with
the election of Eisenhower and with the cold war abated for
a time.   Then, they again faded away.   But with the Kennedy,
Johnson and later administrations and renewed world tensions,
the horror movie cycle returned.   Again the world's acceler-
ating insecurity tried to find release in horror films and horror novels.   As the danger for humanity increased even more
with sophisticated weaponry, so the theme of horror pictures
grew in magnitude.   Disaster pictures like The Towering Inferno and Earthquake tried to top each other; the mental horror films like Rosemary's Baby, The Exorcist, and The Omen

presented stories of devilish possession as though the world were ruled by Satan and humans had no power. Violence on the screen and in books became standard for those minds which saw mankind as racing toward the seemingly inescapable holocaust prophesied in the Bible. The "Club of Rome," the "Institute of a New World Order" of St. John's University (Jamaica, N.Y.), and sociologists all over the world try in vain to warn the world of its dash toward destruction. Lectures by members of the "Institute of a New World Order" are shown on television at 6:30 a.m. and thus one of the most important programs of our time is hidden from the public. Motion pictures and stories devoted to horror mirror those warnings in cosmic dimensions--wars among galaxies, flying saucers, attacks by giant monsters, visitors from outer space trying to alert the earth to a coming holocaust. Mankind, like the dinosaur, seems to have its span of life on this globe.

Horror stories and movies of anxiety are here to stay until the world's tensions diminish. To a writer's mind, global catastrophy might accelerate the world's quest for a solution to its problems. All this sounds rather grim. It is. Many great minds work on plans of how to rearrange the world we live in without fright and fears. The blueprint of the continuation is being worked on. Does mankind have the will to carry it out?

When the monsters die for good, the world might have died with them. Or we might have found a way to live together with a sense of social justice and ecological stability.

> The way you walk is thorny
> through no fault of your own.
> For as the rain enters the soil
> and evil enters the sea,
> so tears run to their predestined end.
> Your suffering is over.
> Now find peace for eternity, my son.

Brave words, intoned by a former star of the Moscow Art Theater, Mme. Maria Ouspenskaya, over the Wolf Man's body.

They were not his final epitaph. He was revived many times. That leaves hopes for the world.

German-born Curt (or Kurt) Siodmak has long been associated with
science fiction, horror and fantasy films. A real-life reporter in
Germany, his attempt to interview director Fritz Lang got him a
part as an extra in Lang's 1926 science-fiction masterpiece Metropolis. While still in his homeland in 1932, Siodmak, with Walter
Reisch, wrote the screenplay for the film F. P. 1 antwortet nicht
("Floating Platform 1 Does Not Answer"), which was seen in the
United States as simply F. P. 1. He adapted the novel Der Tunnel,
by Bernard Kellerman, for the British film The Trans-Atlantic
Tunnel in 1935. In 1937, Siodmak came to Hollywood, where he
amassed a great number of screen credits, many of the films he
wrote or directed having fantastic content.

Among such screen-writing credits are Her Jungle Love (1938),
The Invisible Man Returns, The Invisible Woman, The Ape, and
Black Friday (all 1940), The Wolf Man (1941), The Invisible Agent
(1942), Son of Dracula, I Walked with a Zombie, and Frankenstein
Meets the Wolf Man (all 1943), House of Frankenstein and The Cli-
max (both 1944), The Beast with Five Fingers (1946), Tarzan's
Magic Fountain (1949), Riders to the Stars (1954), The Creature
with the Atom Brain (1955), Earth vs. the Flying Saucers (1956)
and the German Sherlock Holmes und das Halsband des Todes
("Sherlock Holmes and the Deadly Necklace," 1962).

Siodmak wrote and directed Bride of the Gorilla (1951), The Mag-
netic Monster (1953), Curucu, Beast of the Amazon (1956), and
Love Slaves of the Amazon (1957). In 1958 he turned to television
and directed "The Face in the Tombstone Mirror," the pilot episode of the unsold "Tales of Frankenstein" series. Four years
later he directed several episodes of another unsold series, "No.
13 Demon Street," which were released as a feature-length film
entitled The Devil's Messenger.

Perhaps the most famous of all the prolific writers' stories is the
1942 novel Donovan's Brain, about a scientist who keeps alive the
brain of a financial genius. The story was adapted to other media,
including a two-part radio version by Orson Welles for the CBS
series "Suspense" during the 1940s. Three motion pictures were
made from the story, The Lady and the Monster (Republic 1944),
Donovan's Brain (United Artists 1953) and the German Ein Toter
sucht seiner Mörder ("A Dead Man Seeks His Murderer"), seen in
America as The Brain (Governor 1962). There have also been
countless stories, comic book tales, radio and television dramas
and motion pictures about living brains, all owing their existence
to the Siodmak original. In 1968, Siodmak wrote a sequel to Donovan's Brain entitled Hauser's Memory. It became a Universal
television movie in 1970.

WHEN THE WOLF MAN PROWLS

Lawrence Talbot had sufficient reason to fear the rising of the full moon. The moon's rays acted as a catalyst upon his rugged, husky body. Talbot's sad face twitched as the cool beams struck him. His face darkened, his nose elongating to resemble that of an animal. Teeth lengthened into fangs, hair grew profusely until his face and body were covered with coarse, reddish brown fur. What had once been hands and feet were now the claws of a monstrous human wolf. Within Talbot's brain was the mind of a savage beast.

Throwing back his shaggy head, the Wolf Man howled at the gleaming moon.

The image of the Wolf Man, the tragic werewolf character peerlessly portrayed by Lon Chaney, Jr., set the standard for the motion picture werewolf. Amid a list of other werewolf films which appeared during the 1940s, it was the Wolf Man who dominated over the entire pack. The character, both as the werewolf and the sinister Lawrence Talbot, has through the performance of Chaney achieved a classic status among his monstrous peers and managed to endure upon the screen through a series of five authorized motion pictures. He was unleashed before the public in The Wolf Man, a film made by Universal Pictures in 1941.

The Wolf Man was not Universal's first venture into screen lycanthropy. Universal released two werewolf movies before the monsters' howls even became audible. The first of these silent film entries was The Werewolf (Bison, 1913), directed by Henry McRae. The story was not in the European setting which has come to be associated with the werewolf legend. Rather, it was based upon a Navajo Indian legend in which a human being (via a simple camera dissolve) was transformed into a complete wolf. In this case, the werewolf was female, the daughter of an Indian witch, who

lures white men to their deaths. Universal followed the motion picture with The White Wolf (Nestor, 1914). Again the
story was based upon Indian lore, with a wolf caught in a
trap metamorphosing into a quite human medicine man.

In 1932, with Universal Pictures already into their
first sound era horror films cycle (which commenced with
Dracula and Frankenstein in 1931), the studio announced its
return to the subject of the werewolf. Boris Karloff, then
a popular screen villain after his portrayal of the Monster
in Frankenstein, was to star in a picture called, prophetical-
ly, The Wolf Man. The picture was not made--at least as a
Karloff vehicle. There years later Universal's WereWolf of
London (known in Canada as Unholy Hour) became the first
major screen treatment of the lycanthropy theme and was
based on the British version of the werewolf legend, wherein
a full moon is necessary for the man-to-beast transformation.

Actually, the full moon is a rare requirement in actual
mythology and legend for the transformation of werewolves.
The "authentic" werewolf (founded in folklore rather than in
fiction) is, basically, a living person (as opposed to the re-
suscitated corpse which becomes the vampire) who is able to
change shape to become a wolf or hybrid creature of human
being and wolf and who, once in this altered state, is driven
to commit acts of violence in the fashion of his namesake.
Oftentimes, rather than undergoing an actual physical metamorphosis, the human spirit is transferred to the body of a
wolf to prowl and hunt down victims while the human body
remains in a comatose state.

The werewolf legend can be traced back as far as ancient Greece with the first extant piece of werewolf fiction
appearing in the Satyricon by Petronius. Yet the werewolf
image that managed to find a permanent den on the motion
picture screen was that which originated in Europe. Traditionally the wolf has been regarded as an almost demonic
predator in Europe with its chilling howl suggesting the cry
of some restless spirit. Thus it was the wolf that impressed
itself upon the superstitious mind when a creature required
inventing that best expressed the acknowledged animal nature
of man.*

---

*The cultures of the world are rich in lycanthropic beliefs,
with various predacious beasts acting as surrogates for West-
erners' familiar wolf. In Africa, which has no wolves,

The standard werewolf (which means, literally, "man wolf") of legend can easily be identified in his human form. His eyebrows are straight and meet over the nose; ears are flat and oftentimes pointed; the fingernails are pointed and sharp and sometimes the fourth finger is as long as the middle; frequently the person is betrayed by a particular "wolfishness" or hairiness. Thus, when choosing our friends, we should take note of these physical traits and act accordingly.

The werewolf usually transforms into a complete wolf, though a larger and more ferocious one. If a known were-wolf exhibited no external signs of such a transformation, it was sometimes assumed that his hair grew inside his body (in which event he was often cut open by his executioners in hopes of exposing him for the monster he presumably was). The actual transformation can be accomplished through sorcery, drinking water from a wolf's footprint, wearing a girdle made of wolf skin, eating a wolf's brains or the flesh of a rabid wolf, drinking from a stream used by wolves and a number of other ways. Though most of the werewolves of folklore become such by their own volition, a smaller percentage (like most of the werewolves of films) transform involuntarily, through such agents as the curses of French priests.

Some werewolves of tradition can cure themselves by such practices as abstaining from human flesh for a period of nine years, shedding three drops of blood while in wolf form, and being called by their Christian names three times. Usually, however, the werewolf is either unwilling to be cured or unavailable. In such cases the creature must be killed, usually through hanging or being burned alive. Bullets will often end the monster's life, though in certain parts of France, England and Scotland the bullet must be fashioned from silver. Fire obviously offered a more thorough (and inexpensive) destruction of the monster.

The film WereWolf of London (Universal, 1935) drew upon the concept of the involuntary, moon-transformed version of the legendary creature. The hapless werewolf of the title is actually an English floriculturist named Dr. Glendon,

(continued) were-lions, were-jackals, were-leopards, were-crocodiles and other formidable were-beasts are believed to exist; India has its were-tiger and in Scandinavia and Russia the were-bear is as feared as the werewolf itself.

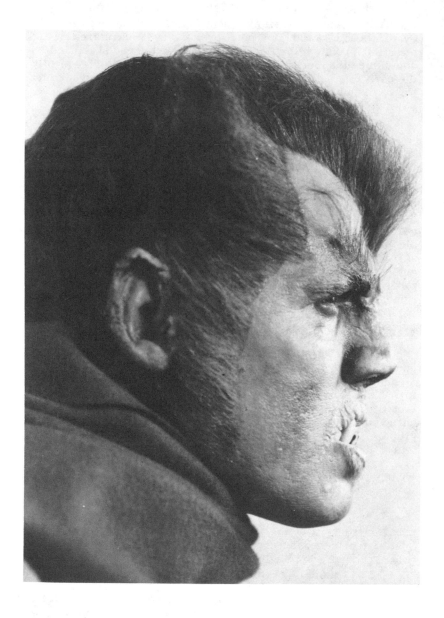

Henry Hull in the first major lycanthrope film, WereWolf of
London (Universal, 1935).

played by Henry Hull.   Glendon is in Tibet searching for a
mysterious plant called the Mariphasa lumina lupina, a flower that blooms only under the light of a full moon.   While
on this expedition, Glendon is attacked by a snarling werewolf.   The scientist survives the attack, only wounded, and
returns to London with the coveted mariphasa.

Upon his return, Glendon is visited by a mysterious
Oriental doctor named Yogami (played by Warner Oland,
famous for his portrayals of Dr. Fu Manchu and Charlie
Chan) who claims they already met in Tibet while on a similar mission.   Dr. Yogami speaks to the nonbelieving Glendon of werewolves; that the lupine curse is passed by the
werewolf's bite to its victim and that the only antidote to
the transformation is the mariphasa.   There is something
distressing in the way Yogami claims to know of two cases
of werewolfry in London today.   When Glendon refuses to
give the plant to Yogami, the Oriental warns: "Remember
this, Dr. Glendon.   The werewolf instinctively seeks to kill
the thing it loves best.   Unless this rare flower is used tonight, the werewolf must kill at least one victim every
night. "

Later that night, Glendon looks at his hands and observes wolflike hair growing from his palms.   Rushing outside, the scientist passes a series of pillars, and every time
we see his face between them it has undergone another stage
of the terrible change.   His teeth become animal-like fangs,
his ears grow pointed, hair appears profusely from a widow's peak above the bridge of his canine nose and on the
top of his head.   Then donning a hat, cloak and scarf, the
WereWolf of London, as if in imitation of the nefarious Mr.
Hyde, stalks out into the fog.

Henry Hull's werewolf make-up was created by Jack
Pierce, who was responsible for all of Universal's monsters.
Originally, Pierce had planned a more shaggy version of the
WereWolf of London, something more on the order of the
later Wolf Man.   But the make-up, in its final incarnation,
was modified.   A number of reasons have been given for this
alteration, one being that the "Wolf Man" version seemed
too gruesome for the public tastes of 1935, the others being
that actor Hull either found the make-up too uncomfortable
or concealing or that its application required too much time.
Nevertheless, the WereWolf of London was considered quite
frightening in its day and has, despite the popularity of the
Wolf Man character, lost little of its impact.   (As late as

1957 a Chicago theatre booked WereWolf of London on a
double bill with Universal's Murders in the Rue Morgue, a
Bela Lugosi film based on the Edgar Allan Poe story, and
advertised them as "adults only.")

That night the London streets are alive with the cries
of a wolf as the monster that had been Dr. Glendon claims
its first victims. The following day, Glendon, fearing what
might happen when the moon rises, takes temporary lodging
above a tavern. When one of the women there peeks
through his key hole she witnesses the awesome change.

This time there was no cheating as when Henry Hull
walked behind the pillars. First his face darkened, an effect accomplished by first covering the actor's face with a
make-up sensitive only to certain colors of light. When filters were removed and the make-up registered before the
camera lens, the face seemed to darken. Then Pierce created a series of make-ups, each more lupine than the previous one. With a locked-down camera and dissolves (by
special effects wizard John P. Fulton) bridging the cuts between the various make-ups, Henry Hull transformed into
the WereWolf of London, not only to the amazement of the
nosey woman in the tavern, but for audiences as well.

Realizing what he has become, Glendon prays for salvation, but the transformation comes again. He frees a
wolf "brother" from its cage in the zoo and continues to
hunt down human victims. Yogami sneaks into Glendon's
laboratory in order to steal the precious mariphasa. But
the human Glendon discovers him, accuses him of being the
werewolf (which had actually been played by stuntman Alex
Chivra) he met in the mountains of Tibet, and, after a furious struggle, chokes him to death. Afterwards, Glendon
orders his servant to lock him inside a tower and not let
him out despite his cries. Once again the moonlight bathes
him and his features distort into the wolfish lycanthrope.
Lisa (Valerie Hobson), Glendon's wife, and her lover Paul
Ames (Lester Matthews) arrive below. Now governed by the
rule that the werewolf kills the one he loves most, the monster crashes through the window to claim his victim. Ames
attempts to stop the creature with his walking stick, but the
werewolf is soon pursuing his wife up the stairs. Only a
bullet (not a silver one in this film) fired by the Chief of
Scotland Yard brings down the man-beast. In 1935 it was
not unusual to see a talking werewolf on the screen (the
complete animal personality of the snarling Wolf Man having

not yet been established) and his dying words are: "Thanks
for the bullet. It was the only way. In a few moments now
I shall know if all this had to be." His life ended, the
WereWolf of London undergoes one final transformation,
leaving the lifeless and peaceful body of Dr. Glendon. (In
1976 this final scene from Werewolf of London was shown
and then recreated on Don Adams' Screen Test on NBC-TV.)

Stuart Walker directed WereWolf of London with the
taste that was characteristic of all the old Universal horror
films, with lots of atmospheric fog to cover the true horrors
that were left mostly to the viewer's imagination. Although
the film is rather slow in comparison to the more action-
packed Wolf Man films of the next decade and though the
image of Hull's cloaked and articulate lycanthrope is jarring
to audiences familiar mostly with the Chaney, Jr., characterization, WereWolf of London remains a classic, yet a
most definite precursor to The Wolf Man of 1941.

ENTER LAWRENCE TALBOT

The Wolf Man was intended as an "A" production to
celebrate Universal's tenth year in the successful production
of horror films. Originally the film was to be called Destiny; then the studio decided to give it the more commercial
title, "The Wolf Man."

By 1941 the title, "The Wolf Man," was not original.
There was a novel by Alfred Machard titled Der schwarze
Mann ("The Dark Man"), which was published in an English
edition by Edward J. Clode, New York, in 1925 as The Wolf
Man (The Were-Wolf). But the "wolf man" of this story
was more of a bogeyman intended to frighten children and hardly
inspired the 1941 Universal film. A German film, Le Loup
garou ("The Werewolf"), was made in 1932 based on this novel.

Reliance-Mutual made a silent film called The Wolf
Man in 1915 which apparently did not include a werewolf in
the storyline. In 1918, Polifilms released The Wolf Man,
a picture that may or may not have boasted a lycanthropic
monster. Two movies entitled The Wolf Man were made in
1924, one from Sunset Productions starring J. B. Warner
(but apparently no werewolf), the other from Fox, directed
by Edmund Mortimer and starring John Gilbert as a kindly
gentleman who becomes a vicious brute when under the influence of alcohol.

Curt Siodmak, who created the Wolf Man, based his excellent screenplay upon authentic werewolf legends. The film was to be allotted an impressive budget, a good portion of which went to an all-star cast headed by former Dracula, Bela Lugosi. But although Bela Lugosi did appear in the film as a werewolf, it was a younger man who won the role of Lawrence Talbot. Lon Chaney, Jr., had introduced a youthful image to horror movie fans familiar with the older Boris Karloff and Bela Lugosi with the Universal film Man Made Monster, made earlier in 1941. Not only was Chaney a viable commodity, because of his father's name and reputation, he also had a youthful appeal and considerable acting talent. Chaney's performances often brought out tragedy and aroused the sympathy of his audience, surely necessary for the hapless human side of Lawrence Talbot. He was a big man, six feet tall and husky enough to convey the strength of a superhumanly powerful werewolf. In short, Lon Chaney, Jr., was the perfect choice to portray the Wolf Man.

Lon Chaney, Jr., was born Creighton Tull Chaney in Oklahoma City on February 10, 1906. His birth was premature and he would have died had not the doctor who delivered him rushed to the nearby Belle Isle Lake to submerge him in the cold water. Creighton was a teenager when he first mentioned to his father that he too would like to be an actor. But his father refused to aid him in following such a career and promptly transferred him from Hollywood High School to a less influential business school. Consequently, Creighton left school, got married and settled down to a career at a waterheater company, starting as a boilermaker and eventually getting promoted to secretary. Not until Lon Chaney, Sr., died in 1930 did his son turn to the movies for a career.

Refusing to change his name to Lon Chaney, Jr. (which would have boosted his value at the box office), Creighton appeared in a number of motion pictures that hardly advanced his career. In 1937, starving, Creighton finally submitted to the name change and signed a contract as Lon Chaney, Jr., with RKO. His first important role, however, did not come until 1939 when he played the simple-minded giant Lennie in the United Artists production of John Steinbeck's Of Mice and Men. As Lennie, Chaney drew praise from the severest critics. His powerful performance had made him an actor of the first class and Universal Pictures, recognizing his potential as a second Man of a Thousand Faces, signed him on to resume his father's career. The

Studio photograph showing Bela the Gypsy (Bela Lugosi) menaced by Lawrence Talbot (Lon Chaney, Jr.) in The Wolf Man
(Universal, 1941).

Lennie influence was indeed potent; most of Chaney's subsequent roles, from the Man Made Monster and Wolf Man
right on through the final parts he played before dying from
a number of ailments on Friday the 13th, 1973, would betray the influence of the Steinbeck character.

    Other notable actors in The Wolf Man were Claude
Rains as Sir John Talbot, Universal horror films queen
Evelyn Ankers as the love interest, and Ralph Bellamy,
Warren William, Patric Knowles, Madame Maria Ouspenskaya and, in a small yet important role, Bela Lugosi.
Ample funds went into the construction of sets, including the
interiors of the impressive Talbot Castle, and the gloomy
fog-shrouded forests and graveyards which perpetuated the
gothic atmosphere so much a part of the Universal horror

productions.   Hans J. Salter composed a musical score
which conveyed both eerieness and action and which became
a veritable Wolf Man's "theme," used repeatedly in later
motion pictures.   The Wolf Man certainly had the ingredients to become a worthy successor to the studio's earlier
Frankenstein and Dracula classics.

The Wolf Man opens with young Lawrence Talbot returning to his home, Talbot Castle, in Wales.   Later, Talbot visits the nearby village, wandering into an antique shop
attracted by its proprietress, Gwen Conliffe (Evelyn Ankers).
She shows him an interesting cane with a silver top in the
form of a wolf's head and a five-pointed star.   (Actually
this cane head was made by the Universal prop department
from balsa wood, but it appeared authentic on screen.)   The
pentagram, Gwen explains, is the sign of the werewolf, a
beast-man which figures into a popular verse (actually written by Siodmak):

> Even a man who's pure at heart
> And says his prayers by night,
> May become a wolf when the wolfbane blooms
> And the autumn moon is bright.

According to legend, says Gwen, the werewolf can see the
pentagram in the hand of his next victim.   (Although the
pentagram does have occult significance, its association in
this context with the werewolf legend was entirely an invention of Siodmak.)

At night Talbot takes Gwen and her girlfriend Jennie
(Fay Helm) to visit a nearby Gypsy camp.   Wolfbane, the
plant associated with werewolves in this film (but not in legend) grows in the misty woods.   At the camp a Gypsy
named Bela (Lugosi) tells Jennie's fortune but is horrified
to see the pentagram materialize in her palm.   Bela warns
her to flee for her life.

Talbot and Gwen react to the sound of Jennie's scream
and see her being slain by a growling wolf.   Heroically, Talbot rushes upon the great beast, swinging his silver-headed
cane until the great canine lay lifeless before him.   Actually,
Chaney had little reason to fear the beast he was struggling
with, for offscreen the animal was his own German shepherd!

Perhaps the real appeal of the Wolf Man character is
in our empathy for Lawrence Talbot.   Talbot's downfall is

not due to some inherent tragic flaw but to Fate.   The horrors that are to befall him are the result of an act of heroism in which he placed his own life in jeopardy to attempt
to save that of a friend.

Apparently bitten by the beast, Talbot is taken to his
ancestral castle.   In the morning he discovers a pentagram-
shaped wound on his chest and is informed by Sir John that
Bela the fortune teller was found beaten to death with the
conspicuous wolf's-head cane lying nearby.   Of course, Talbot insists that it was a wolf he killed and not a man.   Then
the horror begins for the young Englishman: Talbot is intimidated into leaving his own church (actually a set left
over from the Chaney, Sr. , silent film, The Hunchback of
Notre Dame) as heads and eyes turn and gawk at the apparent murderer.   His own dog takes a mysterious dislike
to him.   And the figure of a wolf that pops up among the
targets of a Gypsy camp shooting gallery instills a sudden
horror in Talbot. *

When Talbot finally confronts Bela's mother, the ancient Gypsy Queen Maleva (Madame Maria Ouspenskaya), she
tells him that her son was a werewolf and that "whoever is
bitten by a werewolf and lives becomes a werewolf himself. "
Maleva gives Talbot a charm with the sign of the pentagram
to break the spell.   Later, Talbot gives the charm to Gwen
for protection when the Gypsies hastily pack their things to
leave the area--with the explanation, "There's a werewolf in
camp!"

Talbot now believes the Gypsy Queen's words.   Racing back to Talbot Castle, he removes his jacket, shoes and
socks.   A peculiarity of The Wolf Man is that, though the
"autumn moon" is mentioned in the werewolf poem, no full
moon is ever discussed, not to mention shown, within the
course of the film.   The implication exists, however, and
Talbot in the apparent moonlight experiences the weird and
painful feelings that now take command of his body.   In a
medium close shot we see (through a series of dissolves)
his feet transforming into those of a human monster, becoming hairier and hairier; the camera then pans with the shaggy
feet as the Wolf Man stalks out into the night.

---

*Scenes of Chaney wrestling a bear in the Gypsy camp have
been excised from prints of The Wolf Man circulated for
television.

The transformation complete, Lon Chaney, Jr., begins his werewolf career in <u>The Wolf Man</u> (Universal, 1941).

   Director George Waggner was careful not to reveal too much of the character, keeping the Wolf Man in the shadows of night throughout the entire film. Only briefly do we glimpse the face in the moonlight, surely not enough to study the hairy countenance. Thus, Waggner retained a certain mysterious quality about the character which was lost in the later sequels.

For the Wolf Man, Jack Pierce was finally able to
adapt to Chaney the lycanthrope make-up originally intended
for Henry Hull in WereWolf of London. Pierce based his
Wolf Man creation upon descriptions of the semi-human version he had read in old European writings. Working from a
life mask of Chaney, the make-up wizard created a rubber
"appliance" in the shape of a lupine nose. A thick wig of
yak hair, more hair covering most of the face, and a set
of fangs were also utilized. The fangs were only slightly
longer than Chaney's own teeth, set over his own lower ca-
nines; Universal always maintained its own standards of
taste, with blood and actually sharp fangs a rarity in that
studio's films. Chaney was also given a pair of hairy claws
and feet while a dark brown shirt and pair of trousers finished the Wolf Man's appearance. The entire guise required
five hours of application time. Prowling the foggy, moonlit
graveyard, the Wolf Man, now clad entirely in dark brown
(having mysteriously gotten into his brown shirt after transforming while wearing a white T-shirt), attacks and kills a
gravedigger, his howl issuing through the town and alerting
its residents to the presence of a wolf. In the morning Talbot awakens with a pentagram-shaped wound on his chest and
to see the tracks of a wolf leading from his open bedroom
window to his bed. When he goes downstairs he learns of
the murder of the gravedigger and of the trail of wolf prints
which lead from the murder scene to the castle.

That night, the Wolf Man prowls again, only to be
caught in one of the traps that the police have set for the
supposed animal. Unconscious, the monster transforms back
to Talbot in another close-up of his feet and is saved from
the police by the maternal Maleva. Painfully reaching the
antique shop, Talbot beholds the pentagram in Gwen's hand.
Now thoroughly convinced that he has inherited the lupine
curse and can only be stopped by a silver weapon, Talbot
returns to his family's castle where his father, in order to
prove that his son's terror is unfounded, straps him to a
chair and locks the room. Before Sir John leaves to aid
the police in hunting down what they assume to be an ordinary wolf, Larry begs him to take along the silver-handled
cane.

The climax of The Wolf Man occurs upon the moor-
like grounds near Talbot Castle. Ignoring the warning of
Maleva that she must avoid meeting Larry, Gwen searches
him out in the fog, only to confront the bloodthirsty Wolf
Man. Before the monster can fully attack her, Sir John

arrives. Swinging the cane frantically, Sir John beats the beast until it crumples to the ground, battered and dying. Incredulously the elder Talbot sees the features of the Wolf Man metamorphose into the peaceful countenance of his son, while Maleva delivers the eulogy she had previously spoken over the corpse of Bela: "The way you walked was thorny, through no fault of your own. But as the rain enters the soil, the river enters the sea, so tears surround your pre-destined end. Your suffering is over, my son. Now you will find peace." Moments later the wolf hunters arrive to find the Gypsy woman and Sir John Talbot regarding the still form of Larry. The official police story will be that the wolf attacked Gwen, Larry came to the rescue, and in the darkness Sir John accidentally killed his heroic son.

The facial transformation came to be one of the more anticipated scenes in the subsequent Wolf Man films, although it was featured only once in this first of the series. Years later, Chaney described the shooting of these scenes: "The day we did the transformations I came in at 2:00 A.M. When I hit that position they would take little nails and drive them through the skin at the edge of my fingers, on both hands, so that I wouldn't move them anymore. While I was in this position they would build a plaster cast on the back of my head. Then they would take the drapes from behind me and starch them, and while they were drying them, they would take the camera and weigh it down with one ton, so that it wouldn't quiver when people walked. They had tar-gets for my eyes up there. Then, while I'm still in this po-sition, they would shoot five or ten frames of film in the camera. They'd take the film out and send it to the lab. While it was there, the make-up man would come and take the whole thing off my face and put on a new one, only less. I'm still immobile. When the film came back from the lab they'd put it back in the camera and then they'd check me. They'd say, 'Your eyes have moved a little bit, move them to the right ...' then they'd roll it again and shoot another ten frames. Well, we did twenty-one changes of make-up and it took twenty-two hours. I won't discuss about the bathroom."

The Wolf Man remains the definitive werewolf film and is, in the opinion of this writer, the best. Certainly it set the standard and style for most non-Wolf Man lycanthrope films to follow. For Chaney, The Wolf Man (Man Made Monster notwithstanding) was the actual beginning of his ca-reer as the successor to his father. When asked toward the

end of his career which of his more than 130 film roles he
found creatively most satisfying, he responded, "I guess it
was the Wolf Man ... since at that time it was totally new.
The makeup took ... almost as long as the Frankenstein
Monster.   But the studio received more mail for me during
that period than any other star ..." ["An Interview with
Lon Chaney, Jr.," Castle of Frankenstein no. 10 (February
1966), p. 26].   Equally important, Universal realized that,
just as Count Dracula was a name character more popular
than any mundane vampire, so had the specifically christened
Wolf Man transcended the status of simple werewolf.   The
studio rushed Chaney, now a horror films star of the same
league as Karloff and Lugosi, into The Ghost of Frankenstein (1942), wherein the youthful actor essayed the role of
the Monster.   Posters advertizing the new Frankenstein
movie boasted that it starred the "sensational creator of the
Wolf Man."   Chaney's next horror characterization was the
role of Kharis in The Mummy's Tomb that same year, but
it was the Wolf Man that his ardent fans wanted to see again
on the screen.

        The Wolf Man was probably not intended to spark a
series.   Yet, considering the profits Universal raked in
from their sequel films starring Frankenstein's Monster and
Count Dracula, in the 1943 production of Frankenstein Meets
the Wolf Man, directed by Roy William Neill, it was inevitable.

        By this time audiences were no longer frightened by
the lumbering creation of Frankenstein who had sent faint-
hearted adults fleeing into theatre lobbies when first unveiled
back in 1931.   This was a new era of horror films designed
more to thrill than to scare.   Also, the studio had exhausted
all its creative resources in infusing new life into the Frankenstein Monster character.   Reduced to a lumbering automaton, the once celebrated Monster was forced to step backwards and let the newer and fresher Wolf Man prowl in
the moonbeam spotlight.

        The Wolf Man was the real star of Frankenstein
Meets the Wolf Man and remained consistent with his initial
screen appearance, thanks to the scripting of his creator
Curt Siodmak once again.   The new film opened with the violation of Lawrence Talbot's (Chaney again) tomb by a pair
of grave-robbers.   During these early scenes we learn what
had happened between the two films.   Sir John, having "accidentally" slain his son, died of grief shortly afterwards.
Lawrence Stewart Talbot had been entombed wearing a

valuable ring, which is the reason for the grave-robbers'
presence in the family crypt.   When Lawrence Talbot's coffin is opened, his body is discovered in a perfect state of
preservation and covered with dried wolfbane plants.   One of
the ghouls recites the old poem, substituting "moon is full
and bright" for "autumn moon is bright. " Coincidentally,
the full moon is shining into the crypt and bathing the corpse
of Talbot.   In a beautifully atmospheric scene and one suitably terrifying in 1943, Talbot's hand grasps one of the
thieves and pulls him toward the coffin with an unbreakable
grip.   A fire results from a dropped lantern and the Wolf
Man, who was either revived by the moonbeams or never
truly dead at all, is on the prowl again.

Talbot is, about a month later, discovered unconscious in a street of the town of Cardiff.   Reviving in the
Queen's Hospital, Talbot spends the next night in horror as
he sees the full moon rise outside his window.   For the
first time, audiences were treated to a well-lit transformation scene wherein Chaney's face, without the obstruction of
shadow and mist, metamorphosed into that of the Wolf Man.
There was no longer any need for mystery.   The make-up
had already been established and the Wolf Man, now Universal's second most popular character (Frankenstein's Monster
still had more box office appeal), would be seen from that
moment onward in full view.

The Wolf Man kills a constable in the town and then
returns to the hospital.   He confesses his crime and his
werewolf condition to Dr. Frank Mannering (Patric Knowles),
an English scientist who refuses to accept his story.   Mannering confines his obviously mad patient in a straightjacket,
but that night, again under the influence of the full moon,
Talbot literally chews himself free.

Some time later, the human Talbot locates old Maleva
(Ouspenskaya) and expresses his desire to be truly dead.
Maleva tells him that only Dr. Ludwig Frankenstein knows
that secret.   They will venture to the town of Vasaria for
Frankenstein's help.   In Vasaria the pair learns that the
scientist is dead (having perished in the flames at the climax of The Ghost of Frankenstein).   Despairing, Talbot
again sees the full moon rise.   In an unusual scene, he
dashes through the woods with his face only half transformed.
Soon, the completely changed Wolf Man kills a child and
arouses the wrath of the villagers who pursue him through
the hillsides and into the ruins of the Frankenstein castle.

The Frankenstein Monster (Bela Lugosi) and the werewolf (Lon Chaney, Jr.) clash in Universal's first multi-monster production, Frankenstein Meets the Wolf Man (1943).

Wounded from a rifle bullet, the Wolf Man backs inside the
ruins and drops through the crumbling floor into a subterranean chamber of ice.   Reviving in the morning, the human
Talbot finds the weakened Frankenstein Monster (Bela Lugosi)
frozen in the ice and frees the creature, hoping that he can
reveal the notes and journals containing the secrets of life
and death.

Incognito as "Mr. Taylor," Talbot meets the daughter
of Dr. Frankenstein, Baroness Elsa (Ilona Massey), in hopes
of securing her father's notes.   During the festival of the
new wine, Mannering, who has tracked Talbot all the way
from England by his series of moonlight killings, attempts
to take him back to the hospital as a homicidal murderer.
When the Frankenstein Monster wanders into the town, he
and Talbot escape in a wagon to the ruined castle.

Mannering, accompanied by Elsa and Maleva, follow
Talbot to the ruins.   There the Baroness produces her father's notes, the Secrets of Life and Death, which inspire
Mannering not only to save the Wolf Man but to also destroy
the Monster for all time.   Mannering's plan, dictated by
Frankenstein's writings, is to drain off both Talbot's and
the Monster's energy, leaving them lifeless shells.   In the
end, however, Mannering realizes that he cannot destroy
Frankenstein's creation and reverses the connection.   As
both Talbot and the Monster lie strapped to platforms in the
rebuilt Frankenstein laboratory, the apparatus crackles with
electrical life.   Fully recharged, the Monster breaks his
bonds and for no apparent reason stalks toward Elsa and
bears her up on his powerful arms.   Meanwhile, another
month having passed, the full moon has risen and the Wolf
Man snaps his own bonds with ease.   The Wolf Man leaps
upon the Monster as the giant stalks up a flight of stairs,
pulling him down backwards and beginning the battle that
most people in the audience had paid their War-rationed
money to see.   The two famous horrors tear at one another,
with the Wolf Man leaping off any high place at his disposal
and the Monster tossing the heavy machinery.   Mannering
and Elsa escape as an irate villager blows up a nearby dam,
drowning the battling monsters in a torrent of water.

Frankenstein Meets the Wolf Man was a good action
film which established the tone of Universal's subsequent
horror films.   Unlike Frankenstein's Monster and Dracula,
the Wolf Man would always be played by Lon Chaney, Jr.,
although the name "Wolf Man" would never again appear in

the title of one of the sequels.   (The story of "Frankenstein
Meets the Wolf Man" was published in prose form in the
March 1943 issue of Movie Story magazine.   Later issues of
this and Screen Romances published similar stories based on
the Wolf Man films House of Dracula and Abbott and Costello
Meet Frankenstein.   Scenes from the film Frankenstein Meets
the Wolf Man were later included in an episode of the Universal television series "The Munsters," in the 1969 television special, "The Wolf Men," and as a visual example
for Forrest J Ackerman's appearance on "To Tell the Truth.")

In 1944, Universal Pictures implied that a werewolf
or similar creature was prowling the misty fields of Canada
in the Sherlock Holmes film, The Scarlet Claw, directed by
Roy William Neill.   But this glowing horror was climacti-
cally exposed as a disguised and very human murderer by
the incomparable Sherlock Holmes (Basil Rathbone).   Werewolf fans felt cheated with The Scarlet Claw and were pleased
to know that their favorite authentic werewolf, the Wolf Man,
would return in a movie tentatively called The Devil's Brood
to be made that same year.

Since the public had already been spoiled with the
meeting of two infamous horrors, Universal sought to top itself by introducing five into The Devil's Brood--not only the
unsinkable Frankenstein Monster and Wolf Man, but also
Count Dracula, a Mad Doctor and a Quasimodo-type Hunchback.   Before the film's release the title was changed to
the more commercial House of Frankenstein.   The movie
was directed by Erle C. Kenton.   Edward T. Lowe wrote
the script from Curt Siodmak's story.

House of Frankenstein is really the story of Dr. Gus-
tav Niemann (Boris Karloff, in his return to the Frankenstein series after leaving it in 1939 with the completion of
Son of Frankenstein) as he escapes from prison with a hunchback named Daniel (J. Carrol Naish) and formulates a plan
to avenge himself on the men who had sent him to prison.
Niemann's plan involves Count Dracula (John Carradine) and,
after he discovers them both frozen beneath the ice of the
Frankenstein castle, the Monster (Glenn Strange) and the
Wolf Man as well.

The Wolf Man (House of Frankenstein being the first
and only film in which a character referred to him specifically by that name) thaws out on a slab of ice and transforms back into Lawrence Talbot.   In a reversal of what

had taken place in the last film, Dr. Niemann promises to
build Talbot a new brain and lift his werewolf curse if Talbot helps him find the Frankenstein records for his experiments. After locating the records, the three characters,
along with the beautiful Gypsy girl Ilonka (Elena Verdugo),
whom Daniel had rescued from a sadistic Gypsy leader,
journey to Niemann's estate. Ilonka takes an immediate
liking to Talbot but is puzzled over his strange melancholic
personality. Daniel hopes that Niemann will utilize his mad
scientist skills to transplant his brain into the perfect body
of Talbot. But Niemann has other plans. After capturing
two of his former enemies, Niemann threatens the one
named Strauss (Michael Mark): "As for you, Strauss, I'm
going to give you the brain of the Wolf Man, so that all
your waking hours will be spent in untold agony awaiting the
full of the moon, which will change you ... into a werewolf!"
Actually, Niemann's threat was not entirely sound; all his
cerebral legerdemain would accomplish is the transferring
of Talbot's consciousness, along with his werewolf curse,
into another corporeal shell. As for Talbot's body, Dr.
Niemann considers it the perfect home for the Monster's
brain.

     Already jealous of Ilonka's affection for Talbot, and
now finding that all the murders and other unpleasantries
done for his master Dr. Niemann were in vain, Daniel reveals the Wolf Man's tragic secret to the Gypsy girl. When
the full moon rises and she sees him rush out into the night
in search of victims, she decides to confront him with his
problem the next morning. Again, Talbot hears the folk
verse and again there was a change from the original text,
"... a wolf" now becoming "... a werewolf." She says (in
a new bit of screen mythology) there is only one way to kill
a werewolf. Now the act required not only a silver bullet,
but one "fired by the hand of one who loves him enough to
understand." Afterwards, Ilonka surreptitiously fashions a
silver bullet from a Gypsy charm.

     The following night, with a full moon on the rise,
Talbot tries to force Niemann into operating. But the mad
doctor is too concerned with reviving the Frankenstein Monster. And Talbot cannot harm Niemann for fear of eliminating his only source of salvation. Returning to his room,
Talbot again experiences "the tortures of the damned" and
prowls outside, finding his next victim to be Ilonka. The
Wolf Man attacks her as she fires the silver bullet. We
see the hairy wolf feet transform into those of a man.

Revived from suspended animation, the Wolf Man (Lon
Chaney, Jr.) attacks the Gypsy girl Ilonka (Elena Verdugo)
in House of Frankenstein (Universal, 1944).

There is a faint smile upon Talbot's peaceful face as Ilonka falls to die upon the corpse of the man she loved.

House of Frankenstein climaxes with the predictable villagers storming the Niemann estate in search of the were-wolf but finding instead the Frankenstein Monster. Daniel, who turns his anger upon Niemann because he could have averted the death of Ilonka, is killed by the Monster. Then, pursued by the torch-wielding villagers, the Monster carries his master into the forest, only to sink beneath a quicksand pool.

Apparently the writers were already exhausting the possibilities of the Wolf Man character. There is but a minimum of on-screen footage allotted the character in his hirsute state--one scene of him supine in the ice chamber, one in which he runs out into the night to seek his first victim, and finally one when he transforms and then has his fatal encounter with Ilonka. At least his appearances, brief though they were, were not anticlimactic, as they were to be in the next film in the series, House of Dracula, which was again directed by Kenton and released in 1945. By the time of House of Dracula, writer Edward T. Lowe realized that all three series (Frankenstein, Wolf Man and Dracula) had grown stale and it was time for a merciful end.

The focal point in House of Dracula is Dr. Edelmann (Onslow Stevens) who, though advertised on the posters as another Mad Doctor, is shown to be a kindly scientist who happens to live in a castle and own a lot of Frankenstein-type laboratory equipment. He is assisted by another token hunchback to maintain the five-monster quota of House of Frankenstein, this time an otherwise beautiful nurse named Nina (Jane Adams).

The budget of House of Dracula was noticeably cheaper than House of Frankenstein, with most of the action taking place within Edelmann's eerie-looking castle and with lots of stock footage from earlier Universal Frankenstein movies. While Dracula (Carradine) comes to Edelmann to be cured of his "affliction," so does Lawrence Talbot, who miraculously survived the supposedly fatal bullet of the previous film. Continuity between movies was no longer so important as long as this last, serious, "Wolf Man" film could be rushed out before the public's interest had been thoroughly extinguished. Chaney appeared in House of Dracula sporting a small mustache, probably to maintain

the image of himself established by Universal's series of
"Inner Sanctum" pictures. (Based on the popular Blue network radio series "Inner Sanctum," these psychological horror films consisted of six Chaney vehicles: Calling Dr.
Death (1943), Dead Man's Eyes, The Frozen Ghost, and
Weird Woman (all 1944), and Pillow of Death and Strange
Confession (both 1945). The "Inner Sanctum" movies presented Chaney sans monster make-ups and afforded him the
opportunity to demonstrate more of his acting ability.) As
always, the sad face and dark clothes remained, in House
of Dracula, consistent with the previous Wolf Man entries.

        Finding that Dr. Edelmann is too busy to help him,
Talbot gives himself up to Inspector Holtz (the perennial
Lionel Atwill) and is promptly locked in the town jail.   When
Edelmann and his attractive nurse Miliza (Martha O'Driscoll)
are summoned by Holtz, Talbot confesses his predicament
from behind bars.   Naturally the scientifically-minded Edelmann at first disavows the existence of werewolves.   As the
full moon casts its light into the cell, however, and Talbot
changes into the shaggy Wolf Man, Edelmann promises to
help him.

        House of Dracula provided scientific explanations for
both the vampire and werewolf. In Talbot's case, according
to Edelmann, his transformations are attributable to both a
pressure on his brain and to a moon-induced self-hypnosis
which literally causes his hair and teeth to grow.   The fact
that he had been attacked by Bela the Gypsy never entered
Edelmann's thinking. (Was Bela also afflicted by such pressure and suggestion?) Universal approved of the inconsis-
tency. After all, if any new angles could be applied to the
dying characters, they might be considered good.

        Edelmann hopes to relieve the pressure by means of
a special kind of mold he has been growing in the laboratory.   Theoretically, the mold will soften Talbot's cranium
and in this way inevitably cure him.   The scientist also
hopes to straighten Nina's crooked back by this process.
The only problem is that the mold does not yet exist in sufficient quantity.

        Fearing the rising of the next full moon, Talbot at-
tempts suicide by leaping off the cliffside and into the crashing sea.   Feeling responsible, Edelmann is lowered by a
harness in the hopes that Talbot still lives in one of the
caves below.   The moon has already reached its peak when

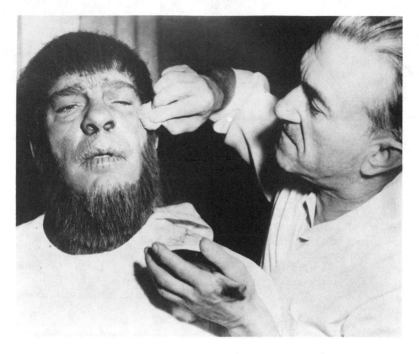

Make-up artist Jack Pierce transforms Lon Chaney, Jr., into the Wolf Man for the film House of Dracula (Universal,
1945).

Edelmann enters the cave.   There he is attacked by the Wolf
Man during the creature's only other appearance in the film.
Before the werewolf can kill his would-be savior, he transforms back into a guilty Talbot.   Actually, the cave provides the answer to Edelmann's dilemma.   Its atmosphere
is best suited for the growing of the mold and boasts a long-
forgotten stairway up into the castle.   Also, the cave harbors the skeleton of Dr. Niemann and the still living, though
barely, body of the Frankenstein Monster (Glenn Strange).

During the course of events, Edelmann's blood becomes contaminated with that of Dracula.   After the scientist destroys Dracula by sunlight, he becomes a kind of
Jekyll and Hyde.   (If the studio had considered this possibility a bit more, they might have advertised six monsters
in House of Dracula to top the House of Frankenstein's five.)
While in his human state, Edelmann manages to give Talbot

The Wolfman (Lon Chancy, Jr.) attacks Dr. Edelmann (Onslow Stevens) in the werewolf's last serious film, House of
Dracula (Universal, 1945).

his operation.   The scientist warns Talbot that any blow to
his head might undo all the work he had done, thereby providing an "out" by which the Wolf Man character might be
revived for yet another film.   Cautiously, Talbot steps beneath the light of the rising full moon and discovers that
Edelmann has indeed accomplished his miracle.   There is
no transformation and he and Miliza embrace.

     During the climax of the film, the "Hyde" personality
of Edelmann overtakes him.   The Mad Doctor strangles Nina
and unleashes the revived Frankenstein Monster as Holtz
and a mob of the ubiquitous villagers enter the laboratory.
After the doctor slays the inspector, Talbot retrieves Holtz'
pistol and is forced to shoot the stalking Edelmann.   There

is a final confrontation between Talbot and the Frankenstein
monster before the patchwork creature crashes into some
flammable chemicals to become trapped in the burning, col-
lapsing building. (Since many of these shots were lifted
from the earlier Ghost of Frankenstein it was essentially
Chaney fleeing from Chaney.) As the cured Lawrence Talbot and his beloved Miliza flee the holocaust, it truly appeared as if the Wolf Man had howled at his last full moon,
and was gone forever.

      In Italy House of Dracula was given the title La casa
degli orrori ("The House of Horrors"). The Wolf Man sequence from House of Dracula was carefully edited to eliminate all reference to the Frankenstein Monster for The Wolfman's Cure, a home-movie edition released by Castle Films.

      Scenes from some of the Universal werewolf movies
were included in two short films made by Cortlandt B.
Hull's Troc Film Corporation. Rendezvous (1973) showed
scenes from WereWolf of London and Wolf Man footage from
The Wolf Man and House of Frankenstein. A followup film,
Revenge of Rendezvous (1975), featured Wolf Man scenes
from House of Dracula. The selected scenes were backed
by popular songs.

      The year following House of Dracula's release, Uni-
versal made another attempt to film a werewolf story. Returning to the earlier WereWolf of London idea, the studio
released a film with a similar title and with the opposite
sex the apparent victim of a lycanthropic curse. She-Wolf
of London (1946; released in England as The Curse of the
Allenbys) starred June Lockhart as Phyllis Allenby, who believes that she suffers from the legendary Allenby Curse.
As a child, Phyllis had dreams about running wild with a
wolf pack. Now dogs snap and growl at her. Rumors of a
werewolf persist as victims are found apparently clawed to
death by a mysterious beast-woman who skulks through the
countryside in a hooded cloak. Poor Phyllis awakens from
periods of unconsciousness with blood on her hands. Had
the She-Wolf of the title actually proven to be real, perhaps
so boring a film as this might have been saved. Instead,
although the series of wolf murders points toward Phyllis
as the culprit, the real killer is exposed as her aunt (Sara
Haden), an insane opportunist whose werewolf "claw" was
actually (as in The Scarlet Claw) a garden tool. She-Wolf
of London, with a more than ample budget, was set at the
turn of the century and utilized some of the old Talbot

Castle sets from The Wolf Man.   Jean Yarbrough directed a
few excellent scenes of the She-Wolf stalking her victims
through the typically Universal fog.   But the picture generated zero excitement, failing to "deliver the goods."   Apparently the scenes of werewolves in the film were laughed
off as at least passé; Universal issued a statement that the
werewolf theme had reached its culmination.

But the original Wolf Man was not, in fact, gone forever.   If he could survive a silver-headed cane, a battle
with the Frankenstein Monster during a raging flood, and a
well-aimed silver bullet, he could also survive Dr. Edel-
man's questionable operation.   Somewhere during the next
few years he must have bumped his head on a door at least
once to undo what the scientist had done.   Thus, when Universal Pictures became Universal-International, a project
entitled The Brain of Frankenstein got underway.   The film
was to spoof the old horror films and pit Frankenstein's
Monster, Count Dracula and his son, the Mummy, the Invisible Man and, of course, the Wolf Man against comics
Bud Abbott and Lou Costello.   Perhaps this element of comedy was the one element needed to infuse new life into the
old characters.   Eventually the Mummy and Dracula's offspring were dropped and the movie was released in 1948
under the more obvious title, Abbott and Costello Meet
Frankenstein.   [In England, Meet the Ghosts and Abbott and
Costello Meet the Ghosts; in France, Abbott et Costello
contre Frankenstein and Deux Nigauds contre Frankenstein
("Two Simpletons Against Frankenstein"); in Belgium, Abbott
et Costello et les monstres ("... and the Monsters"); and
in Germany, Mein Gott, Frankenstein ("My God, Frankenstein")].

Returning to his role of the Wolf Man in this film, a
noticeably older Chaney was saved some of the discomforts
of the role by make-up chief Bud Westmore and his assistant Jack Kevan.   Chaney's face was already scarred from
his heavy make-ups from earlier films.   Kevan devised a
Wolf Man mask that not only provided the actor with some
comfort (as much as might be afforded with a confining rub-
ber-based mask under the grueling studio lights), but permitted him to register some facial expressions.

Director Charles T. Barton realized that those fans
who remembered with love the old Universal horrors would
be outraged if their beloved characters were lampooned.
The monsters were, therefore, handled with care--and for

the most part in all sobriety. Abbott and Costello Meet
Frankenstein emerged as an almost logical example of what
would occur if the comedy team did encounter Frankenstein's
Monster, the Wolf Man and Dracula.   Remove Abbott and
Costello and a legitimate horror plot remains.   Technically
it was one of the best (if not the best) film in the entire
Frankenstein/Dracula/Wolf Man series.   For Abbott and
Costello the film remains among their funniest.

Bud Abbott and Lou Costello portrayed Chick Young
and Wilbur Brown respectively, two shipping clerks who are
in charge of delivering the remains of Frankenstein's Monster (Strange) and Dracula (Bela Lugosi) to McDougal's
House of Horrors, a wax museum in Florida.   Wilbur receives a mysterious call from London, a man named Lawrence Talbot telling him that he believes Dracula is alive
and plans to revive the Monster.   Before Talbot can complete his message the full moon rises and he is once again
in the streets as the non-cured Wolf Man.

Dracula wants to create the perfect slave by giving
Wilbur's simple brain to the Monster.   Talbot finally arrives
from England, having pursued Dracula and the Monster all
across Europe.   In a hotel room, Talbot gives Wilbur the
key and warns him not to unlock his door no matter what he
hears.   What follows is a series of mishaps as Wilbur enters
Talbot's room, never noticing the Wolf Man as he attempts
to grab him from behind but always fails miserably, tripping
over furniture while only inches away from the corpulent
shipping clerk.

At a masquerade party, Talbot tries to warn the
Americans that the man in the Dracula costume is not wearing a costume.   In the locker room, Chick dons a werewolf
mask which arouses Talbot to shake him violently.   That
night Talbot again becomes the Wolf Man and makes another
attempt to sink his fangs into the naive Wilbur.   When the
Wolf Man gets stuck in some foliage, Wilbur, believing him
to be Chick in his mask, kicks him and pulls out some of
his hair.   Later, having failed to kill Wilbur, the Wolf Man
attacks McDougal (Frank Ferguson) who has been attempting
to track down his missing wax museum exhibits.   (What was
never explained is why McDougal, who survives the Wolf
Man's attack, does not become a werewolf himself.)

The final scenes of Abbott and Costello Meet Frankenstein are set in Dracula's island castle, where the King of

Lon Chaney, Jr.'s final appearance as Lawrence Talbot was
in the horror films spoof Abbott and Costello Meet Frankenstein (Universal-International, 1948).

Vampires is about to have Wilbur's brain transplanted into
the Monster's skull thanks to the surgical skills of the vampiric Sandra Mornay (Lenore Aubert).   It is Talbot who
charges through the crackling laboratory to free Wilbur of
his restraining straps when he notices the full moon outside.
In a marvelously funny scene, Wilbur's eyes gawk at Talbot's now hairy hands; then the camera pans up to the growling face of the Wolf Man.   What follows is a contest between
the Wolf Man and Dracula with the yelling Wilbur the prize.
The Wolf Man pursues Dracula out of the room, leaving
Wilbur to the Frankenstein Monster!   After the two fiends
battle each other from room to room, Dracula transforms

into a bat while the Wolf Man leaps at the winged creature, seizing it and plunging into the rapids far below.

Both Wilbur and Chick are chased by the Frankenstein Monster until he burns to death on a flaming pier. A cameo "appearance" by the Invisible Man (Vincent Price) climaxed this most excellent of all horror film spoofs.

Scenes from Abbott and Costello Meet Frankenstein later appeared in The World of Abbott and Costello (Universal 1965), Il vicino di casa (an Italian film by Luigi Cozzi which has been noted in English as "The Man Upstairs," early 1970s), and in the television specials "Hey, Hey, Hey--It's Fat Albert" and "The Wolf Men" (both 1969), the latter a documentary about men who handle wolves.

The Wolf Man, a durable character in the 1940s, proved his commercial viability even three decades later, for in 1976 Universal Pictures announced a color remake called WOLFMAN, to be scripted by Wolf Mankowitz.

THE "WOLF MAN" STRIKES AGAIN

Universal Pictures owned the copyright on the Wolf Man character.   That did not, however, stop other film companies from using the character in their own productions. Oftentimes an unnamed werewolf appeared alongside such characters as the Frankenstein Monster and Dracula; in such cases it would be safe to assume that these lycanthropes were intended to represent the Wolf Man incognito while simultaneously avoiding any entanglements with Universal's legal department.

A character called Wolfman and sporting a wolf's head menaced Daffy Duck in the 1946 Warner Brothers color cartoon The Great Piggybank Robbery, directed by Bob Clampett.   In 1953 a werewolf apparently supposed to be the Wolf Man appeared along with the Mummy and Frankenstein Monster in the Egyptian horror comedy Haram Alek ("Shame on You"), directed by Issa Karama.   The House on Bare Mountain (Olympic International Films, 1962), directed by R. Lee Frost, was the first theatrically released "nudie" to feature a Wolf Man, although there have been reports of an untitled "stag" film featuring the character.   The movie [also known as Night on Bare Mountain and, in Belgium, as La Colline des desirs ("The Hill of Desires")] was made

in color and featured a real werewolf at a party crashed by
a fake Dracula and Frankenstein Monster.   Jack Pierce recreated his Wolf Man make-up for the 1963 color version of
Beauty and the Beast from United Artists.   Mark Damon
played the Beast who, in this reworking of the classic fairy
tale, is actually a werewolf who transforms at sunset.
Bikini Beach (American International, 1964), a color movie
directed by William Asher, featured in a brief poolroom sequence Val Warren in a Don Post Wolf Man mask enacting
the role of a werewolf.   Warren had won this appearance by
disguising himself as a werewolf for a make-up contest
sponsored by Famous Monsters of Filmland magazine.   John
Andrews wore a Post Wolf Man mask for his appearance in
Orgy of the Dead (Astra, 1966), a color nudie directed by
Edward J. Wood.   The werewolf, a living mummy, and the
menacing "Prince of Darkness" harass a young couple during
a night of the full moon.   (A novel, Orgy of the Dead, written by the film's scriptor Edward D. Wood, Jr. , was published by Greenleaf Classics in 1966.)   A more family-
oriented film, Mad Monster Party? was made in color in
1967 by Arthur Rankin, Jr. , and released by Embassy Pictures.   Miles Bass directed this children's film with animated puppets representing the world's most famous horrors.
Baron Boris von Frankenstein (Karloff's voice) creates a new
explosive and invites such characters as the Werewolf, Dracula, Dr. Jekyll, the Hunchback, the Mummy, the Invisible
Man and a "Black Lagoon"-like creature to a celebration.
The Werewolf appeared in Gypsy garb and in an effective
scene tracked the hero and heroine through the forest.
(There was also a record album of Mad Monster Party? released by RCA and a comic book adaptation of the film issued by Dell Comics in 1967.)   "Mad, Mad, Mad Monsters, "
a cartoon sequel to Mad Monster Party?, brought all these
infamous creatures to the television screen on September 23,
1972.   Now the Werewolf was also shown in his human form
of "Ron Chanley."   The Wolf Man, the Frankenstein Monster,
the Mummy and other legendary horrors inhabited a realm
called the Netherworld in Apple Films' color production of
Son of Dracula [originally announced as Count Down and
later re-released as Young Dracula] in 1973.   Freddie Francis directed the tongue-in-cheek picture.   Blood, a Joseph
Kent Presentation made in color in 1974 and directed by
Andy Milligan, was an unbelievably bad English film set in
1899 involving the marriage of Larry Talbot's son and
Dracula's daughter, played respectively by Allan Berendt
and Hope Stransbury.   Together they journey back to America, hoping to cure themselves of their individual curses by,

of all things, the use of flesh-eating plants. The Wolf Man
(actually Berendt in a novelty shop mask) perishes in a fire
set by the landlord's wife after Talbot had fallen in love with
their daughter. That same year Dick and the Demons, a
pornographic horror comedy featuring the Wolf Man and other
familiar monsters, was announced (but never filmed) by Jim
Wnoroski.

     Mexico, where low-budget horror films are made un-
abashedly in imitation of the old Universal productions, has
contributed a number of poor quality Wolf Man entries. El
castillo de los monstruos ("The Castle of the Monsters"),
directed by Julian Soler in 1957 for Producciones Sotomayor,
starred Mexican comic Clavillazo and actress Evangelina
Elizondo. Clavillazo played a handyman in the castle of a
mad scientist who has created his own versions of the Wolf
Man, Frankenstein Monster, Dracula, the Mummy and the
Creature from the Black Lagoon, with a gorilla added to
this gruesome roster.

     The services of an aging, overweight Lon Chaney, Jr.,
were enlisted South of the Border for La casa del terror
("The House of Terror"), made by Clasa Mohme and Azteca
in 1959 and released the next year. The picture was directed by Gilberto Martínez Solares who also wrote one of
the most fatuous scripts in horror movie history. Mercifully the film was a comedy and its only redeemable quality
was the fact that Chaney was, in a way, reviving two of his
old Universal roles at once. Chaney portrayed an Egyptian
mummy which is shipped to a wax museum operated by another mad scientist. The mummy is restored to life via
blood transfusions and the doctor's Frankensteinian laboratory apparatus. If that were not fantastic enough for the
plotline, the mummy is then cleaned off and now appears to
be an old Lawrence Talbot, dark shirt and all. Unlikely
though it is, the revived mummy was a werewolf in earlier
centuries and now, when the full moon rises, the transformations commence anew. Once the mummy aspects of the
picture were bypassed, Chaney recreated his old Wolf Man
role as best he could. Locked in a jail cell, he sees the
full moon shining through the barred window. As in more
glorious days past, Chaney's face begins to twitch as a
Mexican attempt at the Jack Pierce make-up appears on his
face. After a new brain is transplanted into the "Wolf
Man's" skull, the monster breaks out of its cell to menace
Mexican comedian Tin Tan and the city as well. In the final scenes the werewolf climbs a skyscraper with his victim

An Egyptian mummy-turned-werewolf (Lon Chaney, Jr.) in
the Mexican film La casa del terror (1959), re-edited and
released in 1964 in the United States as Face of the Screaming Werewolf.

---

slung over one shoulder but soon falls to an awful (and merciful for the audience) death below.   La casa del terror was
re-edited by Jerry Warren to eliminate most of the intention-
al comedy and given an American release in 1964 as Face
of the Screaming Werewolf.

The Wolf Man returned along with "Frankestein" [al-
so, variously, Frankestain] and the Dracula-style "Vampiro" in
Frankestein, el Vampiro y Compañía "Frankestein, the Vampire

and Company"), a 1961 comedy directed by Benito Alazraki
for Cinematográfica Calderón. The picture was a shameless
(and unauthorized) Mexican remake of Abbott and Costello
Meet Frankenstein with comedians Paco and Agapito playing
the roles of the express agents. As per the original, the
Wolf Man (el Hombre Lobo) is trying to track down the
bodies of Frankestein and the Vampire and destroy them before they can be restored to life. Naturally he fails. During a fiesta he transforms into his lycanthropic other self
and later crashes into the laboratory as the Vampire is about
to give Frankestein Agapito's simple brain. The Wolf Man
and Vampire fight each other until both are destroyed in a
fire.

In 1970 the Wolf Man appeared on Mexican theatre
screens as a lifeless dummy, along with Dracula and Frankenstein Monster figures, in the color film La señora muerte
("Madame Death"), which was directed by Jaime Salvador
for Filmica Vergara. Three years later a living Wolf Man
joined such familiar horrors indigenous to American screens
as Dracula, the Frankenstein Monster, Mr. Hyde, the Mummy and an undistinguished gorilla for the comedy Chabelo y
Pepito contra los monstruos ("Chabelo and Pepito vs. the
Monsters"), made in color for a younger audience.

The Wolf Man has come to be associated with Santo
and the Blue Demon, two of Mexico's most popular masked
wrestlers who lead fantasy lives on the screen as crime-
fighting superheroes. A wax Wolf Man figure stood in the
background of the 1963 Filmadora Panamericana movie Santo
en el museo de cera ("Santo in the Wax Museum"). The
film was directed by Alfonso Corona Blake. It was released
to American television under the misleading title Samson in
the Wax Museum. In 1969 "el Hombre Lobo" encountered
both Santo and Blue Demon: Santo y Blue Demon contra los
monstruos ("Santo and Blue Demon vs. the Monsters") [also
known as Santo contra los monstruos de Frankenstein] was
made in color by Cinematográfica and directed by Gilberto
Martínez Solares. Bruno Halder (Carlos Ancira) is revived
from the dead and, after creating an evil duplicate of the
heroic Blue Demon, proceeds to revive the bodies of the
Wolf Man, the Mummy, the Vampire, Cyclops, an alien
humanoid and another Mexican version of the Frankenstein
Monster. The fake Blue Demon then leads the monsters,
including the Wolf Man (an actor sporting an incredibly in-
ept werewolf make-up), to carry out Halder's evil plans.
In one amusing sequence, Santo is in the wrestling arena

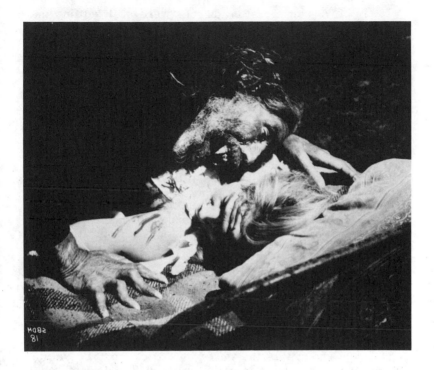

"El Hombre Lobo," a Mexican version of the Wolf Man, was but one of the creatures to battle the masked heroes of <u>Santo y Blue Demon contra los monstruos</u> (1969).

---

when the monsters enter the ring and engage him in battle.* The film climaxes as Santo and the real Blue Demon fight against the monsters, with Halder's grotesque minions perishing in an explosion.

---

*This scene parallels a similar one in the earlier film <u>El Santo contra las mujeres vampiras</u> ("Santo vs. the Vampire Women"), made in 1961 by Alfonso Corona Panamericana and directed by Alfonso Corona Blake. In this picture Santo is fighting a masked wrestler in the ring who is finally unmasked as a werewolf. If that were not enough for Santo to handle, the werewolf then transforms into a vampire bat and flies away! The film plays on American television as <u>Samson vs. the Vampire Women</u>.

By 1973 both wrestling heroes were still battling the
Wolf Man in Calderón's Santo y Blue Demon contra Dracula
y el Hombre Lobo ("Santo and Blue Demon vs. Dracula and
the Wolf Man"). The movie was shot in color and directed
by Miguel M. Delgado. Both Count Dracula and the Wolf
Man (herewith given the human identity of "Rufus") are revived when Professor Cristaldi's blood is spilled onto their
skeletons, both having been imported in coffins from Transylvania. Both monsters are to be used by a villain named
Eric against the family of the professor. Eric hopes that
Rufus will court Cristaldi's daughter Laura and then kill her
when the full moon rises. Eventually the Wolf Man creates
several more werewolves which battle both wrestling heroes.
In the final conflict Santo and Blue Demon kick the Wolf Man
and Dracula into a pit of stakes, their impaled corpses then
vanishing. At least the Wolf Man make-up in this film--
still indebted to the Universal character for inspiration--was
an improvement over its Mexican predecessors.

Amateur films about the Wolf Man are always popular among youthful movie makers who are impressed by the
character and tempted to recreate the Jack Pierce make-up
and duplicate John Fulton's transformation scenes. Les
Ghouls (1959) was an Abbott and Costello Meet Frankenstein
style film make by Gary Friedrich, Roy Thomas and John
Short, with Thomas as the werewolf. Dick Andersen made
his own Wolf Man story in color, entitled The Lycanthrope
(1963): after a number of grisly murders are committed in
a Chicago apartment building, a police captain and a medical
criminologist discover the killer to be Talbot the Wolf Man
(Ron Graham). Before the monster can slay a teenage girl,
the captain whacks him to death with a silver-headed cane.
Three years later Andersen made Terror Is a Man for Columbia College, with Rick Goodbar as the Wolf Man, now
plaguing the Canadian north woods. The beast is finally
chased through the hills by hunters and shot to death.

Haunted Tomb was a semi-professional Wolf Man film,
scripted by Ron Haydock and intended for marketing through
his magazine Fantastic Monsters of the Films in 1964. Bob
Burns was to play the Wolf Man who, with a witch, terror-
izes a young couple forced to take shelter in a haunted house.
The film was never completed. The Terror of New York
City (1972) was made in color by the Madison Square Boys
Club, with Andy Galbo as the Wolf Man.

I must plead guilty to having made a series of amateur Wolf Man movies during my younger days. The color

Return of the Wolfman (1957) pitted the hairy monster (Wayne Moretti) against both Dracula and the Frankenstein Monster, with the werewolf destroying his two foes. In The Teenage Frankenstein (1959) the Wolf Man (Victor Fabian) is intimidated into aiding Dr. Frankenstein in the assembling of another monster and eventually battles the original Frankenstein creature while the castle explodes. The Wolf Man came back in the person of this writer in The Slave of the Vampire (1959) to break free of his master Dracula and stake him after a long battle. The character returned, again played by the author, for a cameo in the color Monster Rumble (1961). His final appearance in this series was in the color serial The Adventures of the Spirit (1963) in which he was played both by Bob Burns and myself. In Chapter Two, "Fangs of Death," the Wolf Man attacks the Spirit but is killed in the followup episode by the comic book hero Captain America, wielding the actual cane head made for Universal's The Wolf Man.

Television was a logical medium for the Wolf Man to prowl with the culmination of the Universal film series. In 1950, Lon Chaney, Jr., along with Glenn Strange as the Frankenstein Monster and Bela Lugosi as Dracula, menaced Bud Abbott and Lou Costello once again on "The Colgate Comedy Hour." Chaney's final appearance as the Wolf Man was also for television, in the "Lizard's Leg and Owlet's Wing" episode of the CBS series "Route 66" in 1962. Chaney, along with Boris Karloff and Peter Lorre, hold a meeting at Chicago's O'Hare Inn to determine whether or not modern-day audiences are still afraid of the old classic monsters. Wearing a Wolf Man make-up patterned by Ben Lane after the Universal character, Chaney tries in vain to frighten a young secretary and finally begins to cry over his failure. In the final sequence, the Wolf Man, Lorre, and the Frankenstein Monster (Karloff) triumphantly succeed in scaring a group of secretaries, at the same time bringing some pleasant memories back to horror film buffs.

"Dark Shadows" (ABC-TV), a daytime gothic serial produced by Dan Curtis, adapted the Wolf Man character to its multi-monster storyline in 1969. Don Briscoe played Chris Jennings who, in moonlit nights (along with ancestor Quentin Collins, played during a long flashback by David Selby) transformed into a Talbot-style werewolf courtesy of an excellent make-up by Vincent Loscalzo and the stuntwork of Alex Stevens (who actually wore the guise). The "Dark Shadows" plotline heavily borrowed elements from The Wolf

Man (the Gypsy curse, Siodmak's poem, the pentagram on the palm, the silver-headed cane) and WereWolf of London (the antidote plant that blooms under moonlight). After numerous attacks, confinements and attempts by writer Sam Hall to bring new innovations to the character (after a while bringing about the transformations even in broad daylight), the werewolf of "Dark Shadows" was written out of the plot without so much as a howl. During the height of "Dark Shadows" popularity, the Quentin Collins werewolf continued to snarl and prowl in a series of comic books published by Western Publishing Company (Gold Key Comics) and novels issued by Paperback Library.

New blood was pumped into the Wolf Man character in 1976. Bruce the Wolfman (played by Buck Kartalion) joined Count Dracula and the Frankenstein Monster as the lead characters of "Monster Squad," an NBC children's series filmed by D'Angelo Productions. The trio of horror favorites are wax dummies by day, but at sunset a computer brings them to life to atone for their evil careers by enacting the roles of crime fighters. Now the Wolfman is something of a weird pet who uses his claws to scale walls in the battle against such unlikely villains as a living mummy, an astrologer who uses an atom bomb to make his earthquake prediction come true, and a witch who transforms the monsters into two-dimensional cut-outs.

The Wolf Man's television career also included such programs as "Get Smart," "The Munsters," "The Kopykats" (Rich Little as the character), "Sinister Cinema" (Los Angeles), "Shock Theatre" (Indianapolis and San Antonio, the latter featuring Bob Burns), and "The Hilarious House of Frightenstein" (Billy Van simultaneously imitating the Wolf Man and rock music personality Wolfman Jack--a popular radio, television and film personality of the 1960s and 1970s, who recorded his own album Wolfman Jack for the Wooden Nickel record company in 1972. The album included his theme song, "Hey Wolfman."

Other programs featuring the Wolf Man were "The Monkees," "The Ghost Busters," "The Funny Side," "The Sonny and Cher Comedy Hour" and "The Mouse Factory," the animated cartoon series "Tom Slick," "Abbott and Costello," "Scooby Doo--Where Are You?" and "The Groovie Goolies." "Wolfie," the hip Wolf Man type character of "The Groovie Goolies," also appeared with the other Goolies on the followup shows "Sabrina, The Teenage Witch," "Uncle Croc's Block" and

in the 1972 "Saturday Superstar Movie" entitled "Porky Pig
and Daffy Duck Meet the Groovie Goolies. " This latter appearance had the Goolies appear as flesh and blood characters in one sequence. The popular Groovie Goolies also
were the subjects of masks, costumes, coloring books and
dolls.

Television specials like "Wayne and Shuster Take an
Affectionate Look at the Monsters" (Canada; includes scenes
from the Universal horror films), "Lights! Camera! Marty!,"
"The Horror Hall of Fame--A Monster Salute," "What Are
the Loch Ness and Other Monsters All About?" and "Halleluja, Horrorwood" (Los Angeles; with Jack Deleon as the
Wolf Man); and television commercials for Binaca breath
freshener, Baby Ruth candy bars, and Post Sugar Crisp and
Alpha Bits cereals, all also featured Wolf Man themes.

Personal appearances of the Wolf Man have not been
infrequent. When Abbott and Costello Meet Frankenstein was
in its original release, Lon Chaney, Jr. , appeared as the
Wolf Man with Glenn Strange and Bela Lugosi recreating
their roles in theatres across the country that booked the
film in 1948. Larry M. Byrd impersonated the Wolf Man
in a make-up of his own for a 1963 Halloween show at
Leavenworth, Kansas. Byrd transformed into the character
in a cage, then escaped. In 1965 another Wolf Man, joined
by such familiar horrors as Mr. Hyde, were played by actors wearing Don Post rubber masks on a supermarket tour
to promote the new line of masks.

I'm Sorry, The Bridge Is Out, You'll Have to Spend
the Night was a musical comedy which opened on April 28,
1970, at the Coronet Theatre in Hollywood. Bob Benveniste
played the effeminate Gypsy Prince "Rex" Talbot, alias the
Wolf Man. Talbot's mother Mom Talbot believes that the
only double cure (of the werewolf curse and his dislike for
girls) for Rex is a few hours with the play's attractive heroine. Unfortunately all the other bizarre characters in the
musical have their own designs on the young woman. Rex
must settle for the scientific knowhow of Dr. Frankenstein
who finally comes forth with the two-fold cure. I'm Sorry,
The Bridge Is Out... was directed by Maurine Dawson and
almost became a Halloween television special that same year.
The play was written by Sheldon Allman and Bob Pickett.

The Wolf Man character was adapted to two plays in
1974. "Frankenstein Slept Here," by Tim Kelly, included

such horrors as Baroness Frankenstein, a descendant of Dr.
Jekyll, Vampira, Medusa, the Mummy, a Phantom Bride,
insane Igor, the Invisible Man and the Werewolf, all of
whom now live posing as servants in a castle owned by an
unsuspecting society matron. The menacing Werewolf is
eventually selected to be the matron's latest husband.
"Thursday Meets the Wolfman," a combination "Dragnet" and
monster spoof by Willard Sims, involved a search for a killer in Swampville, U.S.A. The murders are eventually explained as accidents while the Wolfman is exposed as botanist
Percy Fish. While searching for rare plant specimens in
the bog, Percy had been attacked by a werewolf that had escaped from a nearby movie studio. Before killing the beast
with a shovel, Percy was bitten, the results manifesting
themselves on the next moonlit night. Both plays were intended to be performed by high school dramatic groups.

Werewolves have established themselves as an important sub-genre in the body of horror literature; yet the celebrated Wolf Man himself has only rarely found his way into
prose. The Beast with the Red Hands, by Sidney Stuart,
was published in 1973 as part of Popular Library's "Frankenstein Horror Series" of novels. A superhumanly strong
woman strangler creates a wave of panic and also a horror
craze at a motion picture theatre. The theatre revives such
classics as WereWolf of London, Frankenstein, The Mummy,
Dracula, The Spencer Tracy Dr. Jekyll and Mr. Hyde, The
Island of Dr. Moreau and its most popular film The Wolf
Man, all of which are affectionately described. The Wolf
Man, Dracula, Frankenstein's Monster, Jack the Ripper and
the Phantom of the Opera all figured into the Brazilian
novel As Máscaras do pavor ("Masquerade of Fear"), by
"Vincent Lugosi, (R. F. Lucchetti)," published in 1974.

The Wolf Man's career in short stories was slightly
more prolific. "Silver Threats Among the Gold," by Peter
Wang and Spencer Strong (Forrest J Ackerman), was published in Famous Monsters of Filmland no. 23 (June 1963).
Tom Adams, who had inherited the werewolf curse from the
bite of the last Talbot, travels via time machine to 1863
Texas, where he is promptly shot by the Lone Ranger's
silver bullets. "Litter to a Werewolf," by K. Vazau Virlup (Ackerman; the nom de plume is Esperanto for "Pseudo
Man-Wolf"), in Famous Monsters no. 25 (October 1963),
was supposedly a letter written by Larry Talbot, Jr., to
his father, describing his new life at a Transylvanian university. In "Blood Relatives," Famous Monsters no. 29

(July 1964), by Alan B. Greene, the Wolf Man meets a female of his own species. All three of these stories appeared
in the Famous Monsters series "These Were Their Lives."
Robert Bloch's story "The Plot Is the Thing," published in
The Magazine of Fantasy and Science Fiction (July 1966),
concerned a movie buff who gets a lobotomy and becomes
part of a world where Lawrence Talbot and the WereWolf of
London are living beings. And in "Hard Times," a story
written by Sonora Morrow and published in the December
1974 issue of Ellery Queen's Mystery Magazine, Dracula and
a character apparently representing the Wolf Man bemoan the
violence in the modern day world of the 1970s.

Strangely, the coarse Wolf Man has also managed to
infiltrate poetry, such as Howard Moss' affectionate "Horror
Movie," published in Harper's Bazaar. The Wolf Man, the
Mummy, Jekyll and Hyde, Dracula, Frankenstein's Monster
and the Mole People all appeared in "A Nightmare," a poem
by Brad Johnson published on the fan page of Famous Monsters of Filmland no. 102 (October 1973). "Nine Hairy Horrors," a fan poem by Bruce Freedberg, appeared in Famous
Monsters no. 104 (January 1974).

Although the Wolf Man has inspired literally countless
imitations in the graphic story medium, a very small percentage of comic book tales have actually featured that character. A take-off on the Wolf Man appeared in National
Periodical Publications' Superman's Pal Jimmy Olsen no. 44
(April 1960), entitled "The Wolf-Man of Metropolis." Cub
newspaper reporter Olsen drinks a bottle of "ye wolfman potion" and, as a result, becomes a werewolf on nights of the
full moon. Only the kiss of a beautiful maiden will break
the spell and when that seems unlikely mighty Supergirl secretly comes to Jimmy's rescue.

Jimmy Olsen resumed his Wolf-Man identity in several later stories. A more conventional Wolf-Man menaced
the young reporter in Jimmy Olsen no. 142 (October 1971),
"The Man from Transilvane!" In this story, written, drawn
and edited by Jack Kirby, Superman rescues Olsen from the
attacking "Lupek," the Wolf-Man. In the followup issue
(November 1971), "Genocide Spray!," Lupek and his monster
cohorts are exposed as inhabitants of the miniature planet
Transilvane who were affected by a heavy dosage of terran
horror movies. National spoofed the Wolf Man in the 83rd
issue of The Adventures of Jerry Lewis (July-August 1964),
in the tale "Scared Silly!" written by Arnold Drake with art

by Bob Oksner. Here called "Dog-Boy," the Wolf Man character, along with take-offs on Frankenstein's Monster and
Dracula, are really disguised gangsters who cause grief for
Lewis as well as their horror movie counterparts. An almost identical threesome of monsters appeared, via the
same writer and artist, in "Super-Hip, the Sickest Super-
Hero of 'em All" in The Adventures of Bob Hope no. 95
(October-November 1965). Now a chemistry instructor
called Professor Heinrich von Wolf-Man, the character went
on to co-star in almost three years worth of Bob Hope comic
books.

The Wolf Man, no longer wanted by the motion picture industry, joined his friends the Phantom of the Opera,
the Invisible Man and other horrors in an old monsters'
home in "The Ogre's Ode," published in the debut issue of
Bats (November 1961), from the Archie comics group. The
story was written by George Gladir and drawn by Orlando
Busino. The WolfMan, a comic book from Dell Publishing
Company purporting to be based on the Universal film, was
dated June-August 1963. The cover, depicting a spectral
Chaney Wolf Man, and the notice that the book was copyrighted by Universal Pictures were misleading. Instead of
a Lawrence Talbot type werewolf, the lead character of the
story was a villain named Vorcla, a man with lupine features and the power to control wolves. Vorcla is finally
impaled through the back with a silver-handled cane while
readers expecting a traditional Wolf Man tale felt cheated
out of the 12 cents cover price. The Wolf Man, Creature
from the Black Lagoon, Phantom of the Opera and other
movie horrors lurked out of retirement to perform in a musical stage show in "Mannie Get Your Ghoul," Mad no. 85
(March 1964), written by Jack Rickard and illustrated by
Frank Jacobs.

The Wolfman became the star of a series of Brazilian comic books Almanaque Lobisomem, published during
the late 1960s by Gráfica Editôra Penteado. "The Frankenstein Gang," in Harvey Publications' Richie Rich Vault of
Mystery no. 2 (January 1975), presented what appeared to
be the ghosts of the Wolf Man, Frankenstein Monster and
Dracula. But the monsters were really only costumed
gangsters trying to tunnel into a bank. An incredibly poor
"Wolfman" story was published in the fourth issue (September 1975) of Mayfair Publications' Quasimodo's Monster
Magazine. Talbot changes into the Wolfman, doing little
more than seeking out victims in this pointless imitation of

an "underground" comic strip.   An authentic "underground"
comic book The Legend of the Wolfman, published in 1976
by Wolfman Comix in cooperation with Rose Press, and written and drawn by Armando and Joana Zegri, was an even
cruder variation on the character.   The barely intelligible
story had the Wolfman, a "spirit of the night," materialize
into the world of 1960s-style hippies.

The sounds of the Wolf Man have been heard on numerous phonograph records.   The music from the House of
Frankenstein film was included on the album Themes from
Horror Movies (Coral, 1960), by Dick Jacobs.   Excerpts
from the soundtracks of The Wolf Man and House of Frankenstein became available on An Evening with Boris Karloff
and His Friends (Decca, 1967), with connecting script written for Karloff by Forrest J Ackerman.

Carl Bonafede recorded a "Werewolf" rock 'n' roll
record during the 1950s.   A few years later another "Werewolf" (Dolton) was an instrumental recorded by the Frantics,
opening with the Wolf Man poem only slightly altered and
embellished with snarls and howls.   (The back side "No
Werewolf" was the number sans narration and sound effects.)
The Dark Shadows album (Philips, 1969) included a werewolf
theme, "Night of the Pentagram."   In 1957, John Zacherle
recorded "Dinner with Drac" (Cameo) featuring the Wolf
Man.   But Bobby "Boris" Pickett and the Crypt-Kickers
maintain the distinction of recording the greatest number of
Wolf Man oriented numbers.   The Original Monster Mash
featured Pickett's "Wolfbane," "Monster Minuet," "Monster
Motion" and the very popular "Monster Mash," all utilizing
the Wolf Man character.   "Monster Mash" was later recorded by other artists.   Zacherly (formerly John Zacherle)
brought out his own Monster Mash album, his own single
record of the song, and also included the number on another
album called Rock-o-Rama, vol. 2 (ABKCO).   "Monster
Mash" also appeared on Beach Boys Concert (Capitol), by
the Beach Boys; Tadpoles (Imperial), by the Bonzo Dog
Band; Nova ... Sounds of the Stars (London), by Sounds Galactic; Monster Mash (Peter Pan Industries), which also included the song "Dinner with Drac"; and another Bobby Pickett album, All American Hits (Parrot).

Pickett also released a Christmas single "Monster's
Holiday" which was later rerecorded in an extremely rare
version by Lon Chaney, Jr. , in 1965, climaxed by an audio
recreation of his Wolf Man transformation.   No relation to

the Pickett tune, (It's a) Monster's Holiday (Capitol, 1974)
was an album opening with the title song by Buck Owens and
the Buckeroos, and including Frankenstein's Monster, Dracula and the Hunchback.   And the Wolf Man howled on "Personality Crisis," recorded on the New York Dolls (Mercury,
1973) album starring the titled group.

Children of the Night, a rock group consisting of performers impersonating the Wolf Man, Jekyll and Hyde, Mummy, Count Dracula, Igor the Hunchback and Frankenstein's
Monster, recorded the album Dinner with Drac! (Pickwick
International Productions) in 1976.   Selections on the album
were "Dinner with Drac," "The Invitation," "Monster Time,"
"The Wolfman," "The Mummy," "Transylvania," "The Bat,"
"The Arrival," "Little Green Riding Hood," "Dracula's Undying Love" and "Dinner Is Served." Richie Stevens wrote
the dialogue pieces between the various songs.   A possible
television show featuring Children of the Night was announced
in 1974.

The Wolf Man, Mummy, Hunchback, Dracula and
Frankenstein Monster figured into Bill Cosby's "9th St.
Bridge" nightclub routine and was included on his comedy
album Revenge (Warner Brothers Records; when this same
cut was later included on the album The Best of Bill Cosby
[Warner Brothers-Seven Arts Records], its title was changed
to "Old Weird Harold").   In 1975 the Wolf Man and his
monstrous cohorts all underwent changes, so as not to violate Universal's copyrights, for a Power Records (Peter
Pan) dramatic album called A Story of Dracula, Frankenstein and the Wolfman [the album jacket also gave as the
title both A Story of Dracula, the Wolfman and Frankenstein
and A Story of Dracula, Werewolf, Frankenstein].   The title
was misleading.   Among the changes in the "Wolfman" character was an apparent sex change operation, for both werewolves in the story are female.   Attacked by a werewolf
(actually the Gypsy queen Maleva) in 1883, the beautiful fiancée of young Baron Frankenstein becomes a werewolf herself.   After a battle of the two werewolves in which Maleva
is killed, the female "Wolfman" survives the fire in Castle
Dracula with a possible cure in her future.   Included was
the uncredited Siodmak poem--again.   Contained in the album was a beautifully illustrated comic strip of the story
drawn by Neal Adams.

Not until the early 1960s and on through the 1970s
did Universal realize the potential of the Wolf Man as a

source of revenue.   The last authorized Wolf Man movie had
been filmed in 1948.   But, through the release of the Universal Pictures "Shock Package" of 1930s and 1940s horror
and mystery films, The Wolf Man and its sequels invaded
television and were discovered by a new, mostly young audience.

It was only a matter of a few years before the most
popular werewolf of all could be purchased and brought into
the home in the form of licensed merchandise.   There were
enough Wolf Man looseleaf binders, beach towels, lamps,
decals, Colorforms sets and other items to please the most
critical junior lycanthrope.   The Wolf Man became an exhibit in various wax museums by the early 1960s and his
image was even utilized in the advertisements for Esquire
Socks, the newspaper Grit and the Trust Company of Colum-
bus, Ohio.   In 1941 no one at Universal Pictures ever
dreamed that the Wolf Man would become so commercially
viable almost twenty years later.

Though the Wolf Man was based upon the werewolf
legend, the specific character who howled and mauled through
the Universal horror films was invented for the movies.
Once on screen, Lawrence Talbot set down the rules for
most of the Wolf Man's successors.   Few of them, though
they did their best to emulate their inspiration, were in the
same league.

EL HOMBRE LOBO

The original Wolf Man had retired from the screen
after his misadventure with Abbott and Costello.   But his
tradition was resumed, albeit on a less prestigious level, in
Spain twenty years later.   In 1968 a new Wolfman bared his
fangs and howled at the full moon, this time in full color.
This Spanish werewolf, or hombre lobo, would become the
tragic protagonist of more films than even the prolific
Lawrence Talbot.   His human identity was Waldemar Daninsky and he transformed for the first time in the Maxper production La marca del Hombre Lobo ("The Mark of the Wolfman"), directed by Enrique L. Equiluz.

Waldemar Daninsky was the creation of Paul Naschy,
a former architect turned actor and writer.   Naschy, stout
and muscular, achieved stardom in Spain with La marca del
Hombre Lobo and would go on to portray an assortment of

mummies, hunchbacks, ghouls, zombies, and even the cele-
brated Jack the Ripper and Count Dracula. But it was as
Daninsky the Wolfman that Naschy became a kind of Spanish
Lon Chaney.

Writing his own screenplay for La marca del Hombre
Lobo under his real name, Jacinto Molina, Naschy tailored
the character to meet the requirements of an action story.
The portrayal required little in the way of actual dramatics
but a maximum of grimacing, snarling, crouching, running,
leaping and attacking, with Naschy channeling all of his en-
ergies into the role.

Perhaps La marca del Hombre Lobo was the most
ambitious werewolf epic of all. The picture was shot on a
sizable budget in 70mm, stereophonic sound and a polaroid
three-dimensional process. While the Wolfman's growls
were heard from one side of the theatre to the other, his
claws would lash out at the viewers who watched his actions
from behind their 3-D glasses. Not content with showcasing
his Wolfman in a simple tale of a moon-crossed lycanthrope,
Naschy included in his story yet another werewolf along with
a pair of vampires, presumably Dracula and his wife.
Waldemar Daninsky was unleashed to the public in spectacular fashion.

Two gypsies seek refuge from a storm in the old
Wolfstein castle and find the tomb of a man whose corpse
has been impaled with a silver dagger. The corpse is that
of Wolfstein who, in a previous century, had been executed
for his crimes as a werewolf. The Gypsies steal the valuable dagger, thereby freeing Wolfstein from his grave--the
robbers' lives are terminated shortly thereafter.

With Wolfstein at large in the village, his descendant
Waldemar Daninsky joins the hunt to destroy him. It is
Waldemar who encounters the beast-man and buries another
silver dagger in his heart, but not before (à la Lawrence
Talbot) suffering the monster's bite. When the next full
moon rises, Daninsky sweats and snarls and rips at his
shirt in what might remain the most energetic (and noisy)
werewolf transformation in the history of the genre. After
a few dissolves resulting in a standard werewolf make-up,
the dark-shirted Wolfman scrambles out to claim his initial
victims.

Daninsky's only hope seems to be in the arrival of
an alleged scientist named Dr. Mialhoff, who is actually the

vampire Count Dracula. But rather than attempt to effect a
cure for Daninsky, Mialoff and his wife Wandessa plan to
use him in their service of Satan. Further complicating
poor Daninsky's troubles, the vampires have resurrected
Wolfstein once again. Both werewolves are chained to the
wall of the subterranean laboratory when the full moon rises,
only to break their metal bonds and engage in a spectacular
battle, the first movie fight between two such creatures.
The Daninsky Wolfman, not surprisingly, slays his ancestor.

During the final minutes of the film, Daninsky's
friend Rudolfo stakes Wandessa through the breast, while
Mialhoff entrances Hyacinth, whom both Daninsky and Rudolfo love. There is yet another battle of the monsters,
with the vampire bursting aflame, before el Hombre Lobo
is shot to death by silver bullets.

For audiences satisfied with comic-book plots, La
marca del Hombre Lobo was indeed spectacular fare. The
film boasted some excellent camera work which made full
use of the atmospheric sets and action for the 3-D process.
An interesting fact is that when the picture was bought in
1970 for American release by Independent-International, that
company had already promised a number of theatres to deliver a film entitled Blood of Frankenstein. Since the
film was not yet in production Independent-International still
owed theatres a film including the words "blood" and Frankenstein" in its title. The solution to Independent-International's problem lay in the recently acquired La marca. A
prologue was added to the Spanish film showing, through a
series of paintings by artist Gray Morrow, the scientist
Frankenstein, allegedly having suffered the werewolf curse,
transforming into the lycanthropic Wolfstein. The title in
America was now the misleading Frankenstein's Bloody Terror. Only the theatre owners who exhibited the picture did
not feel cheated. (The originally intended Blood of Frankenstein did go into production in 1971 as The Blood Seekers
and was released the following year as Dracula vs. Frankenstein.)

In Spain La marca del Hombre Lobo received a tremendous reception while Paul Naschy had suddenly become
that country's top horror films draw. (In Germany it became variously Der Wolfsmensche des Dr. Dracula, Die
Vampire des Dr. Dracula ("The Wolfman... " and "The Vampire of Dr. Dracula"), and Toten Augen des Dr. Dracula
("Dead Eyes of Dr. Dracula"); in Belgium, Dracula en de

Werewolf ("Dracula and the Werewolf") and Hell's Creatures;
in Spain alternately as El Hombre Lobo; and in Southeast
Asia as The Wolfman of Count Dracula.) Like the American
Wolf Man, the Daninsky werewolf was too popular to remain
dead, despite the silver bullets that had been pumped into
his body. He returned from the dead in La noche del Hombre Lobo ("The Night of the Wolfman"), a Spanish and
French co-production made in 1968 by Kinfilms and directed
by René Govar. In color like all the Daninsky werewolf
films, this second entry of the series was made on a mark-
edly cheaper budget than La marca del Hombre Lobo and
written by "Molina." In La noche del Hombre Lobo Waldemar Daninsky goes to a scientist friend named Dr. Bradoch
in the hope of finding a cure for his werewolf condition.
Instead, Bradoch uses the werewolf to kill off the people
who disgraced him because of his strange experiments. As
might be expected, the Wolfman eventually kills his would-
be master.

Naschy's third outing as Waldemar Daninsky was in
El hombre que vino de Ummo ("The Man Who Came from
Ummo"), which was directed by Tulio Demicheli and released in 1970 by Jaime Prades/Eichberg Film/International
Jaguar. The Spanish/West German/Italian co-production not
only resurrected the Wolfman, but also versions of the
Frankenstein Monster, Count Dracula and the Mummy. This
was the House of Frankenstein of the series, borrowing
heavily from that film's storyline with a generous heaping
from Frankenstein Meets the Wolf Man. To avoid any copyright infringement problems with Universal's lawyers, the
Frankenstein name was changed to "Franksella" and Dracula
became, once again, Mialhoff when the movie played on
American television as Assignment Terror. The film was
shown in Great Britain as Dracula vs. Frankenstein (not to
be confused with the Independent-International picture), in
Spain as Los monstruos del terror ("The Monsters of Terror"), in Mexico as Operación Terror, and in Germany as
Dracula jagt Frankenstein ("Dracula Hunts Frankenstein").

The premise of El hombre que vino de Ummo was a
common cliché to science fiction fans. Ummo is a dying
planet and the only hope of its population's salvation is a
mass migration to Earth. Naturally this necessitates the
elimination of our world's current populace, which becomes
the task of an Ummo scientist (played by Michael Rennie)
and his female colleague. The two alien scientists hope to
conquer the Earth people through the creatures of human

superstition, hardly a practical scheme in the 1970s considering the fact that unleashing such horrors as Frankenstein's
Monster and the Mummy would hardly be a threat of global
proportions.

In a direct steal from House of Frankenstein, the
staked remains of Dracula are revived after being exhibited
at a carnival. Waldemar's tomb is opened and the silver
bullets extracted (with death now being permanent only if administered by a woman who loves the werewolf enough to
die for him). Chained to a wall, Daninsky, with Naschy
scowling and going through his usual girations, breaks free
and attacks a couple of young women. Later the human
Daninsky, promised a serum that will cure him, accompanies
the aliens to Egypt where the Living Mummy is brought out
of its tomb and put under their control. Finally the Frankenstein Monster is revived and "tested" by the aliens by attacking Daninsky.

The picture climaxes with a series of battles. After
Dracula is staked by a secret agent (played by Craig Hill),
the Wolfman, who never realizes the promised cure, battles
the Mummy to the final death, then attacks the Frankenstein
Monster in a fight scene that could only have been staged
after a study of Frankenstein Meets the Wolf Man. During
the not unexpected laboratory fire that results from the
battle, the Wolf Man kills the Monster, only to be shot by
the woman who has come to love him. As in House of
Frankenstein, the girl perishes as a result of the werewolf's
final aggressive act. When the castle finally explodes audiences feel as if they had seen it all before, only better.

By the fourth film in the Daninsky series La furia
del Hombre Lobo ("The Fury of the Wolfman") in 1970,
Naschy had apparently given up on maintaining any kind of
strict continuity from one picture to the next. The only
really consistent factor in the subsequent films of the series
was the Daninsky character himself. Naschy seems to have
ignored the fact that an absence of continuity in a series de-
tracts from the credibility of the continuing character and
that audiences generally resent such "tampering" with the
Wolfman they had come to know.

La furia del Hombre Lobo was a Spanish production
made by Maxper and directed by José María Zabalza. The
storyline set the picture apart from the previous Daninsky
film, borrowing heavily from WereWolf of London and

misinterpreting one of the trappings from The Wolf Man (i. e. ,
the mark of the pentagram is shown as a pentagon).   Daninsky (first name "Walter" in the English-dubbed version) is a
member of an expedition to Tibet where he is attacked, like
Dr. Glendon in the Universal film, by a werewolf.   The
wounded Daninsky is saved by some Sherpas who give him a
parchment that informs him of what will happen beneath the
next full moon.   Back in civilization Daninsky seeks aid
from a female scientist who is the daughter of the infamous
Dr. Helmut Wolfstein (no connection with the Wolfstein of
La marca del Hombre Lobo), a combination neurologist and
mad scientist who experimented in order to control human
minds.   But since Daninsky once spurned her love, the
vengeful woman scientist uses him for her own ends.   Chain-
ing him to a wall, she whips him after the transformation,
then sends him out to attack the woman he married in her
stead, thereby making her into a werewolf.   By now it
seemed obvious that Naschy was no longer as enthusiastic
about the role as he was in La marca del Hombre Lobo.
He leisurely walked about in his werewolf make-up as if
Daninsky's human mind still motivated the shaggy creature
he had become.   The most exciting footage in the picture
consisted of mismatching scenes of the lively werewolf running about and attacking his victims from La marca del
Hombre Lobo.   Silver bullets end not only Daninsky's life
once again but also a dull entry to the series.

La noche de Walpurgis ("Walpurgis Night") was a
Spanish/West German team-up made in 1970 by Plata Films
and directed by Leon Klimovsky.   This latest Daninsky film
crossed-over with the historical vampiress Countess Elizabeth Báthory.   Naschy, along with collaborator Hans Munkell,
did, in fact, maintain some degree of continuity between this
film and La furia del Hombre Lobo.   A police surgeon dis-
inters Daninsky's body to perform an autopsy.   But he could
have picked a more opportune time to extract the silver bullets; it is a night of the full moon!   The revived Wolfman
slays the surgeon and his aide.

Two young girls, Elvire and Genevieve (played by
Gaby Fuchs and Barbara Cappell), working on a doctorate
thesis, search for the grave of Countess Wandesa de Nadasdy.   The Countess, the students are determined to prove,
retained her youth and beauty by drinking the blood of vir-
gins.   The Countess was impaled by a silver cross which
Waldemar Daninsky hopes will end his Wolfman curse.   After providing Elvire and Genevieve with the hospitality of

Lycanthrope Waldemar Daninsky (Paul Naschy) is stabbed with a silver crucifix in the Spanish/West German film La noche de Walpurgis (1968), released in the United States as The Werewolf vs. the Vampire Woman.

his house, he accompanies them to the tomb.   The Countess is revived when the crucifix is removed and some of Gene- vieve's blood drops onto the corpse.   After Genevieve is made into a vampire and attacks Elvire, Daninsky rams a stake through her heart.   When Elvire becomes Wandesa's intended sacrificial victim to Satan, the Wolfman attacks the vampiress, tearing out her throat, while the only human

being in the group impales the transformed Daninsky with
the cross that might have been his salvation.

La noche de Walpurgis was titled The Werewolf vs.
the Vampire Woman for distribution in the United States.
In France the movie became Dans les griffes de Dracula
("In the Claws of Dracula"), in Belgium, La Nuit des loups-
garous ("Night of the Werewolves"), in Great Britain, Sha-
dow of the Werewolf, and in Germany Nacht der Vampire
("Night of the Vampire").   The picture is also known as
The Werewolf's Shadow.

Guild-Hartford Publishing Co. issued a novel, The
Werewolf vs. the Vampire Woman, by Arthur N. Scram, in
1972.   The story was revamped to become a sex comedy.
Now "Waldo" the werewolf and Wandesa de Nadasdy travel
to Hollywood to play roles in a horror film but end up killing one another, Waldo using a silver stiletto and the vampiress the standard silver bullets.

Daninsky's problems were augmented in the 1971 production of Dr. Jekyll and the Werewolf, a Spanish effort
from Arturo González, directed once again by Klimovsky.
Waldemar Daninsky saves a young woman named Justine
from a mugger and discovers that she is in love with the
grandson of the famous Dr. Jekyll.   Young Jekyll has re-
discovered the formula by which his grandfather changed into the evil Mr. Hyde.   Trying the formula on Daninsky, the
scientist succeeds in finally curing him of his affliction.
But Sandra, Jekyll's assistant, jealous of the scientist's success, has increased Daninsky's dosage so that the former
werewolf now metamorphoses into a new incarnation of Hyde
and is soon perpetrating acts of violence and crime.

Yet another origin to the Daninsky werewolf curse
was presented in El retorno de Walpurgis ("The Return of
Walpurgis") in 1973.   The film removed the Wolfman character from the time period which existed in his earlier adventures, opening in the 16th century.   Irineus Daninsky
(Naschy, who is fond of playing dual roles in many of his
non-Wolfman horror movies), a notorious Polish inquisitor,
invades Transylvania and condemns Princess Elizabeth
Báthory to be burned at the stake.   Before she dies the
princess curses both Irineous and his descendants.

In 1900, Waldemar Daninsky has inherited his ancestor's curse and creates a wave of horror in the Carpathian

Mountains.   Though the villagers believe the murders to be
the work of an insane killer, Daninsky's pregnant wife learns
the truth about her husband.   Finally she kills him, using
the series' alternate to silver bullets, a silver crucifix which
she jabs into his heart.   Yet even with Daninsky dead the
woman wonders if her unborn child will also inherit the
curse.

     For several years, Waldemar Daninsky remained in
limbo, until returning to prowl once more in the 1976 film
The Werewolf and the Yeti, in which he meets the legendary
Abominable Snowman of the Himalayas.   The 1977 title Night
of the Howling Beast, starring Paul Naschy, may also be
part of the "Hombre Lobo" series.

     The quality of the Spanish Wolfman pictures varies;
La marca del Hombre Lobo is certainly exciting and extravagant, while such lesser efforts as La furia del Hombre Lobo
are dull and wanting for a greater production budget.   None
of the films can be considered good cinema.   Yet the series
has been a successful one.   In terms of the number of films
to his credit, Waldemar Daninsky has even been more successful than his precursor Lawrence Talbot.

THE REST OF THE PACK

     Werewolves have become almost as familiar on the
screen as they have in the pages of horror fiction.   In 1923
a French silent film entitled Le Loup-garou featured a werewolf who had suffered the curse of a priest he murdered and
who was eventually dispatched by a bolt of lightning.   The
picture starred Jean Marau and Madeleine Guitty.

     Even with the debut of Universal's Wolf Man, other
less popular lycanthropes prowled the motion picture screen.
Another French picture Le Loup des Malveneurs ("The Wolf
of the Malveneurs") was directed by Guillaume Radot and
released in 1942, one year after The Wolf Man premiered
in the United States.   Reginald de Malveneur is haunted by
the belief that an ancestor was a werewolf.

     Producers Releasing Corporation (PRC), in an attempt
to profit from the success of The Wolf Man, issued its own
werewolf movie in 1942.   The Mad Monster was a ludicrous
effort directed on a cheap budget by Sam Newfield and is so
outrageously naive and unintentionally humorous that it is a

delight to watch. George Zucco portrayed a mad scientist
who creates a werewolf throwback from a Lennie-type handyman played by Glenn Strange, later to portray the Monster
in House of Frankenstein and its followup pictures. Through
Zucco's injections of wolf blood, and a few camera dissolves
(unusual, in that dissolves were usually done in the film
laboratory), Strange sprouted facial hair and a set of elongated canine teeth that protruded over his lower lip.

"The make-up took eight hours to put on," Glenn
Strange revealed to me in 1965. "I lay flat on my back;
I'd take a breath while they shot one scene. And the make-
up man [Harry Ross] would change the hair and so on, and
I'd hold my breath and just lay perfectly still. They'd
shoot another scene and change the make-up. They had the
camera right straight over me, shooting right down on my
face."

By day, the handyman continues his loveable, dull-
witted existence. But under the influence of the mad doctor,
he transforms into the "Mad Monster" to stalk through the
fog and murder his master's enemies. Not surprisingly,
the werewolf finally breaks free of his master and kills him
before suffering fatal bullet wounds.

After the release of The Mad Monster, Glenn Strange
was kidded by an actor friend. He recalls, "Lon Chaney
said to me, 'What are you trying to do? Lennie in Of Mice
and Men?' And I said, 'Well, I haven't seen the thing.'
Then, of course, Broderick Crawford did it on the stage
before Lon, the same way. There's just one way to do a
Lennie, and that's just a big 'Da... Da....' You can't do
it any other way."

The most prestigious werewolf film of 1942 was The
Undying Monster from 20th Century-Fox, directed by John
Brahm. (It was released in Britain as The Hammond Mystery.) Based on Jessie Douglas Kerruish's novel, The Undying Monster is a remarkable combination of mystery and
horror which has been overshadowed through the years by
the more popular Wolf Man pictures. Actor Bramwell
Fletcher, who went mad in The Mummy of 1932, set the
mood of the film with his opening narration: "Hammond
Hall, at the turn of the century, when the age-old mystery
of the Hammond monster was at last revealed to all England. That mystery, which although by 1900 had become a
legend, was indeed a tragedy and constant threat to the

Two years before playing the Frankenstein Monster, Glenn
Strange portrayed a werewolf in The Mad Monster (PRC,
1942).

---

lives of all the seemingly doomed members of the House of
Hammond. ''

     Scotland Yard begins an investigation into the latest
murder on the Hammond Hall moors. During the investigation, the legend is told of an ancestral Hammond who, by
giving his soul to the devil, lives eternally through human
sacrifices. In a cellar tomb, the grave of Sir Reginald
Hammond, a crusader, is found along with the statue of a

monstrous wolf and an inscription reminiscent of the poem
from The Wolf Man:

> When stars are bright on a frosty night,
> Beware thy bane, on the rocky lane.

A piece of incriminating hair is revealed to be that of a wolf.
During the climax of the picture, the Hammond monster
stalks through the halls, always in shadow so that its features are not clearly visible.   After abducting his female
victim (played by Heather Angel), the werewolf climbs to the
top of a cliff where he is killed by a policeman's bullet.   In
a unique scene for a werewolf movie, the transformation was
accomplished not by a series of dissolves and make-up
changes, but rather by use of a traveling matte, a process
by which the monster's face was later added to the finished
piece of film.   The mystery is finally resolved by the expo-
sition of the human face of Oliver Hammond (John Howard),
who had inherited his ancestor's werewolf curse.

Columbia Pictures contributed four werewolf films
during the 1940s and 1950s, three of which owed their style
to the Lawrence Talbot features.   The Return of the Vampire
(1943) was Columbia's blatant imitation of the Universal horror films of the Forties and might well have been titled
Dracula Meets the Wolf Man had those characters not fallen
under the latter studio's copyrights.   The atmosphere, direction (by Lew Landers), music and even the casting were
obviously inspired by those which characterized the Universal
movies.   Husky actor Matt Willis was almost certainly selected for his role of werewolf Andreas Obry because of his
physical resemblance to Lon Chaney, Jr.

In 1918, a werewolf enters a crypt to summon his
vampire master Armand Tessla (Bela Lugosi).   Unlike his
Wolf Man inspiration, Andreas can also speak (and throw
punches like a prizefighter).   Later, when Tessla's grave is
discovered and a metal pike is driven through his heart,
Andreas feels the pain tear through his own heart and regains his human appearance.   During the German blitzkrieg
over two decades later, the pike is removed and Andreas,
who has been cured of his werewolf affliction, is summoned
to resume his bloody career.   The plot of The Return of
the Vampire was hardly original, based upon the cliché horror theme of master commanding monster slave.   The ending, in which Tessla reveals to the hairy Andreas that the
werewolf has exhausted his usefulness, was predictable.

Touching a discarded crucifix, the werewolf again regains
his humanity and destroys his former master by dragging
him into the sunlight and impaling his heart with a spike.

Two werewolf films were released by Columbia in
1944; Cry of the Werewolf (which went into production as
Daughter of the Werewolf), directed by Henry Levin, was
not a direct imitation of the Wolf Man pictures. This time
the werewolf assumed the shape of a complete wolf; it was
also female. Nina Foch portrayed a Gypsy who inherits the
werewolf curse from her dead mother. The transformation
scenes were unsatisfying as Ms. Foch simply stooped forward as the picture dissolved to that of a snarling beast.
The cursed werewolf is finally shot to death. That same
year Columbia brought a more conventional "Wolf Man" to
the screen in the Three Stooges comedy short Idle Roomers,
directed by Del Lord. Lupe the Wolf Man (Duke York), as
the beast-man is called, escapes from his cage in a hotel
room (how the monster ever passed the registration desk is
never explained). Lupe becomes enraged whenever he hears
music and, not surprisingly, he hears plenty when he encounters Stooges Moe Howard, Curly Howard and Larry Fine
until all four motley characters shoot up through the roof in
a runaway elevator.

The Werewolf, a Columbia film of 1956 directed by
Fred F. Sears, brought the Wolf Man style werewolf into
the realm of science fiction. Steven Ritch played the sympathetic Duncan Marsh, an accident victim who is given a serum by a pair of scientists and promptly turns into a werewolf. Actually the scientists were benign enough; they had
been trying to find a cure for radiation poisoning. But they
should have had more foresight than to use the blood of a
wolf in their scientific tinkerings. The Werewolf was produced by Sam Katzman, known for his cheaply made "B"
films and serials that always brought money into the box
offices. No doubt Katzman was little aware of the actual
fine quality into which The Werewolf was developing during
its production. Though by no means a classic, the film
does include two satisfyingly terrifying scenes. In one scene,
after the two scientists have tracked Marsh to a mine, he
transforms in the dim light with eyes almost ablaze and glis-
tening fangs dripping saliva. Later, after the human Marsh
has been placed in a jail cell, the scientists discover him
in the werewolf condition, leering from the shadows. The
monster proceeds to tear his creators apart in the darkness
of his cell. Escaping jail, the werewolf is tracked through

The "wolfman" legend was revived in the 1950s and given a
scientific origin in The Werewolf (Columbia, 1956), starring
Steven Ritch.

---

the brightly lit snow (spawned by science, Marsh needs no
full moon to transform) until he reaches a dam, where he
is shot to death by the posse that is pursuing him.

Scientists created another lycanthropic monster in an
American International picture of 1957 which went into production under the rather traditional title of Blood of the
Werewolf. But the 1950s was an era of rock 'n' roll and
leather-jacketed teenagers. Thus the film was released
under the incredible title of I Was a Teenage Werewolf.
Produced by Herman Cohen and directed by Gene Fowler,

Jr., the low-budget thriller is not actually as bad as legend
has branded it.   There are some nicely photographed scenes
and the production values are far more impressive than those
of some of the films that followed in this newly created sub-
genre (such as the atrocious I Was a Teenage Frankenstein,
also produced by Cohen and released later that year).   In
the role of Tony Rivers, alias the Teenage Werewolf, was a
newcomer to the screen, young Michael Landon, who today
speaks only rarely of this role which brought him to stardom.

Tony Rivers is a temperamental, moody high school
student, prone to violence at the slightest provocation.   An
analyst, Dr. Alfred Brandon (Whit Bissell), cooperates with
the school in trying to help Tony.   Brandon, however, plans
to save humanity by regressing them back to a more primitive stage in their evolution.   By a combination of hypnosis,
suggestion and drugs, the unbalanced scientist reverts Tony
back into his former wolf life (a state of existence which
would have raised the eyebrow of Darwin had he still lived).
During one of the film's better scenes Tony watches a shapely coed practicing her gymnastics when the school bell sounds
and brings on the werewolf metamorphosis (again obviating
the need for a full moon).   From her point of view as she
hangs from the gymnasium's parallel bars we see the in-
verted image of the approaching werewolf, foam bubbling about
the protruding upper fangs.   The Teenage Werewolf is soon
tracked through the woods where he fights and kills a vicious
German Shepherd.   Dr. Brandon and his assistant are photographing the final transformation of their creation when the
hairy-faced teenager kills them both, after which he is shot
down by the police.   As with Duncan Marsh in The Werewolf, the Teenage Werewolf did not require expensive silver
bullets to be killed.

Though Herman Cohen never made an actual sequel
to I Was a Teenage Werewolf (scenes from which were used
in Columbia's 1973 Let the Good Times Roll), he did produce
How to Make a Monster in 1958, directed by Herbert L.
Strock and, in a way, featuring both the Teenage Werewolf
and Teenage Frankenstein.   (A one-page comic strip based
on the film was made available to help publicize it upon
first release.)   The titles of the film are superimposed over
the hand of an artist who is sketching the countenance of the
Teenage Werewolf.   The story begins as actor "Larry Drake,"
the Teenage Werewolf (played by Gary Clarke), is being led
across the American International backlot by make-up artist
Pete Crummond (played by Robert H. Harris).   The studio

Michael Landon achieved movie stardom with his portrayal
of another science-spawned horror in I Was a Teenage Werewolf (American International, 1957).

is in the process of filming its last horror film, Werewolf
Meets Frankenstein (with Gary Conway recreating his role
from I Was a Teenage Frankenstein), after which it will go
into the production of musicals. A few shots of the prelude
to the battle of the teenage monsters are taken. Afterwards,
realizing that his career will end in concert with AIP's
cessation of horror films, Crummond embarks on an insane
scheme of revenge. Mixing a secret ingredient into his
make-up materials, he thereby forces the two youthful actors
to obey him explicitly. As one of the studio executives
watches footage of the Teenage Werewolf in a private screening room, Larry, made-up as the character, attacks him
from behind and kills him. Crummond eventually burns to
death in his home, which is decorated with the actual heads
of his former make-up subjects.

This writer must plead guilty to having made a series
of amateur Teenage Werewolf movies and playing the character in most of them. Because of their inclusion in various
film lists, I will cite them here. The Teenage Werewolf
was the first; in it the title character is created through the
hypnosis of the weird Dr. Macabre and finally falls from a
garage roof to his apparent death. In Return of the Teenage
Werewolf (in color) the amnesic character fights a teenage
gang before getting run down by a car in an alley. The lycanthrope returns from the grave in The Teenage Frankenstein Meets the Teenage Werewolf (also in color) with Paul
Klug in the werewolf role to drown after battling the juvenile
Monster during a forest fire. Revenge of the Teenage Werewolf had the creature again attacking greasy-haired teenagers
before being staked and then shot to death in another alley.
All four films were made in 1959. The series ended with
the color Monster Rumble (1961) in which the Teenage Werewolf (Tom Werner) hopes to be cured by the Teenage Dracula but succeeds only in being an even match against the
Teenage Frankenstein, battling while the vampire's castle
explodes.

What many horror films aficionados hail as a greater
excursion into werewolf lore than even The Wolf Man is the
Hammer Films color production of The Curse of the Werewolf (1961), which was directed by Terence Fisher and released by Universal. Based on Guy Endore's famous novel
The Werewolf of Paris* (1933), it concerns Bertrand Caillet,

---

*Endore's novel was actually based upon a real-life Sergeant
Bertrand, who was responsible for opening a number of

the son of a cursed stranger and a serving girl who grows up with a hunger for human flesh and a taste for blood. Bertrand hunts the streets of Paris, taking women as his mistresses and then violating them werewolf style. The Curse of the Werewolf was originally to be titled The Werewolf of Paris (also announced as The Wolfman) but the title was changed, probably to accommodate the story's shift of location to 18th-century Spain. The film was made on a modest budget but gave the illusion of a more expensive production thanks to lavish color and sets designed to convey a feeling of opulence.

The Curse of the Werewolf chronicles the career of a werewolf from birth to death. Leon is the offspring of an unkempt beggar, who spends his final years leading a dog's life in the dungeon of a sadistic marques, and a mute servant girl whom the beastlike beggarman rapes. Contributing to young Leon's predestined downfall is the fact that he is born on Christmas Eve, a day upon which werewolves are born. Leon's fate seems to be sealed when lightning crashes overhead and the waters of his baptismal font boil and reflect the stone face of an overhead gargoyle.

At the age of six, Leon sees hair sprouting from the palms of his hands. Sheep are being attacked by an apparent wolf and after the beast is shot, bullets are taken from the body of the boy. Not until Leon becomes an adult (played by Oliver Reed) does the werewolf curse become fully actualized. The make-up designed by Hammer's Roy Ashton remains one of the finest ever to be preserved on film. Ashton built up Reed's face and trimmed it with grayish hair, the same color as the fur of the timber wolf. Unfortunately Hammer Films did not, as usual, go in for special optical effects, leaving audiences in want of an onscreen transformation from man to monster.

(continued) graves and desecrating the corpses in 1849. Bertrand was identified as the perpetrator of the crimes when he fell prey to a trap setup by the police in one of the graveyards. Leaving behind a trail of blood and some fragments of his uniform, Bertrand was traced to the 74th regiment of the army. He confessed to the crimes, explaining that a compulsion to violate the dead would overcome him, after which he would slip into a coma. Sergeant Bertrand's punishment was no silver bullet but a year in prison. During his trial, Bertrand gained a reputation as "The Vampire."

The Curse of the Werewolf (Hammer, 1961), starring Oliver Reed, here menacing Yvonne Romain, is considered to be one of the finest excursions into screen lycanthropy.

Briefly, Leon manages to fight off the curse, his temporary antidote being the love of a woman who stays with him while the moon remains full. But screen werewolves are never entitled to so happy an ending. Instead, Leon is jailed for the murders committed by his werewolf identity. When the full moon rises, Leon becomes a gray-furred, hairy-chested werewolf, rips off the barred cell door with supernatural strength, and escapes outside to the rooftops. With a last vestige of humanity, the man-wolf begs his adopted father to fire the silver bullet which he had made from a crucifix. Mortally wounded, the monster plummets to the street below. Strangely the ending of The Curse of the Werewolf does not permit Leon to resume his human form--an unexpected departure from the standard werewolf movie.

The Curse of the Werewolf was adapted to the comic strip format by writer Gary Gerani and artist Carlos Garzon and published in the 8th issue of The Monster Times (May 10, 1972); and by Steve Moore and artist John Bolton in The House of Hammer no. 10 (January, 1978).

The same year that The Curse of the Werewolf thrilled audiences the Italian/Austrian film Lycanthropus (released in the United States as Werewolf in a Girls' Dormitory) lulled them to sleep. The werewolf character sported a modicum of make-up, most of it in the form of shaggy eyebrows and a set of fangs. The picture was directed by Paolo Huesch for the Royal Film Company and featured a chained werewolf who escapes to prey upon the students at a corrective school for girls. (The picture is known in Austria as Bei Vollmond Mord ["Murder with a Full Moon"], in England as I Married a Werewolf, and in France as both Le Monstre au filles and Le Lycanthrope. The picture is also known as Ghoul in a Girls' Dormitory, Monster Among the Girls and The Ghoul in School, the latter named after the song included in the English language version.)

Legendary Circe transformed a group of men into werewolves in the Italian color adventure Hercules vs. Maciste in the Vale of Woe (1962). Mexican wrestling hero Blue Demon battled a werewolf in his first movie El Demonio Azul, which was made in 1963 and released the next year. Werewolves were prolific in 1964: in Principle Productions' Devil Wolf of Shadow Mountain, directed by Gary Kent, an authentic werewolf tradition was brought to the screen. U.S. Cavalry trooper Aven Hunter (Johnny Cardoz) inadvertently becomes a werewolf after drinking from a wolf's paw print. The film climaxes with the firing of the inevitable silver bullet. Amicus' color production of Dr. Terror's House of Horrors, directed by Freddie Francis, included an effective segment in which a werewolf is freed from his tomb. A witch uses her powers to change men into human wolves in yet another Italian muscleman "epic, " Hercules, Prisoner of Evil (also known as Terror of the Kirghiz), directed in color by Antonio Margheriti for Royal Sodifilm.

Lon Chaney, Jr. , returned to the werewolf theme in 1965 in House of the Black Death (which was originally announced as The Widderburn Horror and went into production as Night of the Beast), a dull, cheaply-made Taurus film directed by Harold Daniels. Chaney did not play the werewolf, however, but rather a warlock with horns and a cloven hoof like the Devil. That same year saw the Mexican La loba ("The She-Wolf"), which went into production as Los horrores del Bosque Negro ("The Horrors of the Black Forest"), directed by Rafael Baledon for Sotomayor. It starred Kitty de Hoyos as a female werewolf with fangs, a long mane and shaggy body hair. Also that year a werewolf appeared in Monsters Crash Pajama Party, a color mini-feature (45 minutes) from Brandon films.

El charro del los calaveros ("The Rider of the Skulls") was made in 1966 in Mexico. The Mexican film, directed by Alfredo Salazar, was actually a Western, pitting a masked cowboy hero against vampires, headless horsemen and were-wolves. Dr. Terror's Gallery of Horrors, an imitation of Dr. Terror's House of Horrors made by Dora Corporation-Borealis Enterprises and released by American General, was an amateurish picture directed by David L. Hewitt. "Count Alucard," one of the film's segments, recreated the opening scenes from Bram Stoker's novel Dracula--with one basic exception. Harker, who comes to Transylvania to visit the vampire Count, happens to be a werewolf who, in a climax frequently used in comic book stories, attacks "Alucard" to eliminate the competition. Dr. Terror's Gallery of Horrors went into filming as the abbreviated Gallery of Horrors. It was later reissued to theatres as The Blood Suckers and to television as the less obvious Return from the Past.

A dummy werewolf made a cameo appearance in the color comedy Hillbillys in a Haunted House (shot under the title Ghost Party), a Woolner Brothers picture directed by Jean Yarbrough. The appearance is significant only in that Lon Chaney, Jr., was one of the stars of the picture.

In 1969 the King of Vampires changed a man into a werewolf via hypnosis in the ignominiously poor Dracula (The Dirty Old Man), made in color by Whit Boyd Productions and directed by William Edwards. An MGM spoof The Maltese Bippy was released in color that year and included a dream sequence in which comedian Dick Martin transforms into a werewolf. Norman Panama directed. (Before the picture's release it was known by such titles as The Strange Case of ... !#*%?, The Incredible Werewolf Murders and Who Killed Cock Rubin?) An entire pack of werewolves battle a flock of vampires before being destroyed in an earth-quake, in the ludicrous Tore ng Diyablo ("Tower of the Devil"), based on Nela Morales' serial appearing in Lagim Komiks and filmed in the Philippines with direction by Lauro

Pacheo.   Also in 1969 Robert Dix played a werewolf named
Johnny in Blood of Dracula's Castle (known on television as
simply Dracula's Castle), a color picture directed by Al
Adamson and Jean Hewitt.   Johnny does almost as much
killing while in human form as he does under the full moon
on the pretext of learning the secret of immortality from
Count and Countess Dracula in their Mojave Desert castle.
Blood of Dracula's Castle was made by the A & E Film
Corporation and released by Crown-International.

        Nympho Werewolf was a Portuguese effort made about
1970.   The following year a scientist attempted to cure his
crippled son and ended up with a young werewolf instead in
the Brazilian movie O homem lôbo ("The Wolf Man").   The
color film was written, directed and edited by Rafaello
Rossi for Pinheiro-Filmes.   One of the most preposterous
titles since I Was a Teenage Werewolf was the youth-oriented
Werewolves on Wheels, a Southstreet color production directed by Michel Levesque and released in 1971 by Fanfare.
After an encounter with a Satanist cult, two members of a
motorcycle gang are changed into werewolves.   Both werewolves are destroyed by fire, one of them (played by Stephen
Oliver) fleeing on his motorcycle when the flames strike.
The same year Lon Chaney, Jr., wore a werewolf mask for
a scene in Independent-International's Dracula vs. Frankenstein, in color, directed by Al Adamson.

        The early 1970s continued to thrust werewolves onto
the screen.   Moon of the Wolf (1972) was a television movie
made in color by Filmways and aired on the ABC network.
Based on the novel of the same title by Leslie H. Whitten,
the film was a whodunit, or rather "who-is-it," wherein a
werewolf plagues the bayou country.   Daniel Petrie directed
and Bradford Dillman played the werewolf, who is not exposed until the picture's final scenes.   The werewolf make-
up by William and Tom Tuttle was simple and somewhat disappointing.   The Rats Are Coming! The Werewolves Are
Here!, with one of the most unusual titles in werewolf film
history, was made that same year by the British Mishkin
Company.   Andy Milligan wrote, directed and shot this tale
of a family of werewolves and a female relative who raises
man-eating rodents in 19th-century England.   With the Water-
gate scandals hot in the news, The Werewolf of Washington
(1973) from Milco Productions had a ready audience.   The
plot is just barely more unbelievable than what was really
happening in Washington.   Dean Stockwell played Jack Whit-
tier, an American reporter who, after being bitten by a

werewolf in Budapest with the usual results, brings his deadly curse into the White House and, before his death, passes
it on to the President. The Boy Who Cried Werewolf (Universal, 1973), was made in color and directed by Nathan H.
Juran.   Again the werewolf (played by Kerwin Mathews in a
make-up by Tom Burman) is the result of the attack of another lycanthropic beast.   The novelty of this film is the
application of the old "boy who cried wolf" theme to the
werewolf as he unsuccessfully tries to tell what has happened to his unfortunate father.   Amicus' 1974 color production
of The Beast Must Die, directed by Paul Annett, combined
the werewolf legend with elements borrowed from Agatha
Christie's Ten Little Indians and Richard Connell's story
"The Most Dangerous Game. " The story is that of a group
of people trapped at an isolated estate.   One of them is a
werewolf and victim-to-be of a jaded big game hunter.   As
the potential suspects are gradually killed by the beast (a
complete wolf, or actually a disguised German shepherd) it
became the audience's task to guess the monster's human
identity.   Viewers were given a thirty-second "Werewolf
Break" to reach their decisions.

Peter Cushing, who starred in The Beast Must Die,
returned as Professor Cantaflanque in Tyburn's lycanthrope
film of 1974, Legend of the Werewolf, directed in color by
Freddie Francis.   The story was based upon two earlier
projects, the announced but never filmed Plague of the Werewolves and John Elder's Wolf Boy.   During the late 19th
century, wolves attack a band of Russian refugees and carry
off an infant boy who grows up in the woods as one of the
pack.   Later he is captured and put on exhibit as a freak,
only to escape to Paris where, as an adult (played by David
Rintoul) he becomes a murderous werewolf.   Unlike most
motion picture werewolves, this one can talk.   The werewolf make-up was created by Roy Ashton, patterning it after
the one he designed for Hammer's Curse of the Werewolf
thirteen years earlier.

Obviously the werewolf has become a permanent ingredient to the horror film genre and will continue to prowl
in search of human victims, usually when the moon beams
large and full.   His situation is not unique, however, as he
transforms from normal human being into monstrous beast.
A similar misfortune also befell the unfortunate Dr. Henry
Jekyll.

II

THE DUAL HORROR OF DR. JEKYLL

The most frequently filmed horror story of all time remains The Strange Case of Dr. Jekyll and Mr. Hyde (or simply Dr. Jekyll and Mr. Hyde as it is popularly known today), Robert Louis Stevenson's classic short novel about the dual nature of Man. Indeed the story has probably been adapted to the motion picture screen more often than any other piece of literature of any genre. The concept of a man unleashing another personality that has lain dormant within him has, in fact, become a part of our everyday language. The mere change in a person's mood is enough to prompt some comment about his being a regular "Jekyll and Hyde."

Like the ill-fated Lawrence Talbot of decades later, Dr. Henry Jekyll unleashed his bestial personality by undergoing a literal physical transformation. But while Talbot's metamorphosis from man to Wolf Man occurred via a Gypsy curse stemming from an heroic act, Dr. Henry Jekyll's distortion into the evil Mr. Edward Hyde was spurred by the scientist's own curiosity, experimentation and a desire to be something else. He was, in a sense, like Victor Frankenstein literally becoming the Monster that he had created.

Robert Louis Stevenson (1850-1894) was born into a strict Calvinist family in Victorian Scotland. Throughout his early life he had been taught to resist the temptations of the flesh and was also reminded of the duality of man's nature. Young Robert's subsequent revolt against the Calvinistic teachings created hostilities between him and his family, especially his father. Though his father had intended that Robert take up his own profession of lighthouse engineer, the young Stevenson further rebelled by studying law, after which he pursued a literary career and an education at Edinburgh University.

At Edinburgh, Stevenson not only went against his family and Calvinism but against the whole Victorian system. There he succumbed to some of his more Bohemian instincts. He wore his hair long, dressed the way he chose and caroused in an atmosphere of "Seamen, chimney sweeps and thieves." Yet his Calvinistic upbringing had left its indelible mark. Stevenson's free-thinking lifestyle was still dampened by a deep-rooted sense of morality and an obsession with evil. Edward Hyde was developing in the womb of Stevenson's imagination.

It was Stevenson's conviction that every human being is possessed of a dual nature, one motivated by goodness and righteousness, the other by the baser instincts of Man the savage or animal. These personalities co-exist and are in constant opposition, with Man's more positive qualities fighting to suppress his more primitive instincts. Yet it is this evil side of Man's personality that permits him unbridled freedom and pleasure, unrestricted by conscience and guilt. Stevenson was unable to enjoy the wild abandonment of his Bohemian lifestyle without recriminations from his own conscience. But Henry Jekyll would succeed in that area where Stevenson himself had failed, by discovering the potion that would release the waiting Mr. Hyde.

Prior to the story of Dr. Jekyll and Mr. Hyde, Stevenson had explored the possibilities of man's dual nature. In his play Deacon Brodie; or, The Double Life, co-authored with the poet William Ernest Henley, he told the story of the cabinetmaker who made Stevenson's own chest of drawers when Robert was a child. By night Brodie changed from an upstanding citizen to an unscrupulous burglar. In his short story "Markheim," Stevenson told of a murderer and thief who meets and is convinced by his own alter ego to go legitimate and surrender to the authorities. Unlike Deacon Brodie, Markheim's other identity was a separate entity altogether. Mr. Hyde would also be a distinct character from his other self, Dr. Jekyll, but, like Brodie, the evil nature would literally emerge from the good like twin faces on the same coin.

For Jekyll the catalyst for releasing his Hyde personality was the laboratory, while Stevenson would discover the nefarious character lurking in the shadows of a nightmare. In 1885, Stevenson was living in the seaside resort of Bournemouth, England, melancholic over financial and health problems (he was suffering from tuberculosis at the time) and

his insomnia. To compound his depression, Stevenson had
been attempting to augment his dwindling capital by "trying
to write a story ... to find a body, a vehicle, for that
strong sense of man's double being which must at times
come in upon and overwhelm the mind of every thinking
creature. "

On one fateful night, after Stevenson finally managed
to get to sleep, he was moved by a nocturnal experience of
which he later wrote: "... for two days I went about rack-
ing my brains for a plot of any sort; and on the second night
I dreamed the scene at the window, and a scene, afterward
split in two, in which Hyde, pursued for some crime, took
the powder and underwent the change in the presence of his
pursuers. All the rest was made awake, and consciously.... "

When Stevenson was aroused from his restless sleep
by his wife, he complained, "Why did you wake me? I was
dreaming of a fine bogey tale. "

Immediately, almost entranced, Stevenson began to
write down what he remembered from the dream as the
morning sun began to rise. The author wrote the story of
a man with a dual nature as a straight horror story. But
several days later Stevenson's wife read the first draft and
complained that it was simply a "shilling shocker" or a
"crawler" and that 'he had treated it simply as a story,
whereas it was in reality an allegory. " Stevenson fought
verbally with the woman, then agreed with her critique.
Dramatically he hurled the manuscript into the fire and began his serious revision of the tale. Within three days his
first draft rewrite was completed. Several weeks later the
allegorical Strange Case of Dr. Jekyll and Mr. Hyde was
ready for publication. It was issued in January, 1886.

The Strange Case of Dr. Jekyll and Mr. Hyde was
originally written as a mystery story. Today's audiences
are well aware of the dual-identity protagonist of the story,
yet the relationship between Henry Jekyll and Mr. Hyde
proved to be a startling revelation to readers back in 1886.
The story begins with Mr. Utterson, a lawyer, and his distant kinsman Richard Enfield, a man-about-town, discussing
a singular event that the latter had witnessed. Enfield relates how a small, brutish man had trampled an eight-year-
old girl, then paid her parents a sizable sum of money not
to have him arrested. Soon thereafter, Dr. Henry Jekyll,
a handsome distinguished, middle-aged citizen, visits Utterson

and requests that he change his last will and testament so
that, in the event of the doctor's disappearance, all of his
possessions are to become the property of his "friend and
benefactor Edward Hyde." Though Utterson is against the
altering of the will and knows nothing of this mysterious Edward Hyde, he complies with Jekyll's wishes. Determined
to find Jekyll's alleged benefactor, Utterson vows, "If he be
Mr. Hyde ... I shall be Mr. Seek."

Patrolling the city by night, Utterson finally encounters Hyde, whom he now knows to be the man who had
knocked down the child.

> Mr. Hyde was pale and dwarfish, he gave an im-
> pression of deformity without any namable malfor-
> mation, he had a displeasing smile, he had borne
> himself to the lawyer with a sort of murderous
> mixture of timidity and boldness, and he spoke
> with a husky, whispering, and somewhat broken
> voice: all these were points against him, but not
> all of these together could explain the hitherto un-
> known disgust, loathing, and fear with which Mr.
> Utterson regarded him. 'There must be something
> else,' said the perplexed gentleman. 'There is
> something more, if only I could find a name for it.
> God bless me, the man seems hardly human!
> Something troglodytic, shall we say? or can it be
> the old story of Dr. Fell? or is it the mere radi-
> ance of a foul soul that thus transpires through,
> and transfigures its clay continent? The last, I
> think; for oh, my poor old Harry Jekyll, if I ever
> read Satan's signature on a face it is on that of
> your new friend.'

A year later Mr. Hyde commits his first murder,
breaking his cane in half as he clubs to death the distinguished
Sir Danvers Carew, another of Utterson's clients. An eye-
witness description of the killer brings Scotland Yard Inspector Newcomen to Hyde's sleazy residence in Soho, finding
there the other half of the murder weapon. Edward Hyde is
now a wanted man and soon vanishes from public life. Shortly after Jekyll's return from a self-imposed seclusion, his
friend Dr. Lanyon ages considerably after having a shock
from which he claims there can be no recovery. Furthermore, Lanyon wishes to hear no mention of the name of
Henry Jekyll. Soon Dr. Lanyon is dead. When Utterson
later visits Henry Jekyll's home, the doctor confesses that
he has severed all association with Edward Hyde.

In a chapter entitled "Incident at the Window," Stevenson relates one of the images manifested in his nightmare. Utterson and Enfield are walking by Jekyll's house when they perceive the doctor sitting by a window. Jekyll is cordial to the pair until his smile is suddenly replaced by "an expression of such abject terror and despair as froze the very blood of the two gentlemen below." The mystery is far from solved. Jekyll has barracaded himself inside his laboratory and tells Utterson to leave the house. Poole produces a letter written by Jekyll to a chemical wholesaler stating that their last sample was useless for his own purpose. When Utterson recognizes the voice from the laboratory as that of Hyde, he smashes down the door with an ax, fearing that the fiend has harmed or murdered the good doctor. Inside the laboratory Utterson and Poole find only the corpse of Edward Hyde with Jekyll nowhere to be seen. Hyde has committed suicide as evidenced by the crushed vial in his lifeless hand. To further complicate the situation Hyde is wearing Jekyll's larger, ill-fitting clothes.

Readers were still not aware of Jekyll's double personality. In a second part of the novel, "Dr. Lanyon's Narrative," a desperate and wanted Edward Hyde visits Jekyll's friend Dr. Lanyon to procure some chemicals from Jekyll's own laboratory. Lanyon gives the man what he needs, then observes:

> He thanked me with a smiling nod, measured out a few minims of the red tincture and added one of the powders. The mixture, which was at first of a reddish hue, began, in proportion as the crystals melted, to brighten in color, to effervesce audibly, and to throw off small fumes of vapor. Suddenly and at the same moment, the ebullition ceased and the compound changed to a dark purple, which faded again more slowly to a watery green. Hyde begs Lanyon to leave the room, but the doctor refuses.

> He put the glass to his lips, and drank at one gulp. A cry followed; he reeled, staggered, clutched at the table, and held on, staring with injected eyes, gasping with open mouth; and, as I looked, there came, I thought, a change; he seemed to swell; his face became suddenly black, and the features seemed to melt and alter--and the next moment I had sprung to my feet and

> leaped back against the wall, my arm raised to
> shield me from that prodigy, my mind submerged
> in terror.
>   'Oh, God!' I screamed, and 'Oh, God!' again
> and again; for there before my eyes--pale and
> shaken, and half fainting, and groping before him
> with his hands, like a man restored from death--
> there stood Henry Jekyll!

The final denouement occurs in the final section of
Stevenson's unusually structured book "Henry Jekyll's Full
Statement of the Case." Jekyll reveals his discovery "that
man is not truly one, but truly two." His own life had
evolved according to the dictates of his moral nature, even
though he fantasized about succumbing to life's baser temptations. He had begun to consider the possibility of separat-
ing his two identities. "If each, I told myself, could but be
housed in separate identities, life would be relieved of all
that was unbearable; the unjust might go his way, delivered
from the aspirations and remorse of his more upright twin;
and the just could walk steadfastly and securely on his upward path, doing the good things in which he found his
pleasure, and no longer exposed to disgrace and penitence
by the hands of this extraneous evil."

In his laboratory Henry Jekyll discovered the chemical means to free his evil side and experimented upon himself; thus was born Edward Hyde, a name which Stevenson
perhaps chose to mean "hide," both in the sense of the
flesh, which the Calvinist considered a source of temptation
and evil, and to imply something clandestine.

> Again, in the course of my life, which had been,
> after all, nine-tenths of a life of effort, virtue,
> and control, it had been much less exercised and
> much less exhausted. And hence, I think, it came
> about that Edward Hyde was so much smaller,
> slighter, and younger than Henry Jekyll. Even as
> good shone upon the countenance of the one, evil
> was written broadly and plainly on the face of the
> other. Evil besides (which I must still believe to
> be the lethal side of man) had left on that body an
> imprint of deformity and decay. And yet when I
> looked upon that ugly idol in the glass, I was con-
> scious of no repugnance, rather of a leap of wel-
> come.

Upon downing another batch of the same concoction, Hyde reverted back to his normal identity of Henry Jekyll. To his dismay Jekyll thereby discovered that his experiment did not, as originally anticipated, separate man into two new personalities, one evil and the other entirely noble and good. There were only Edward Hyde, whose ugliness reflected the corruptness of his spirit, and the Henry Jekyll that had always existed--the composite man who had for so long lived the life of the nineteenth-century English gentleman while simultaneously suppressing his hidden desires for a more sensuous existence. "Hence, although I had now two characters as well as two appearances, one was wholly evil, and the other was still the old Henry Jekyll, that incongruous compound of whose reformation and improvement I had already learned to despair. The movement was thus wholly toward the worse."

Carefully Henry Jekyll established his Edward Hyde identity. As Hyde he partook of the undignified pleasures that society had begrudged of his handsome counterpart. Hyde's villainies surely outraged the respectable doctor; but Jekyll had managed to rationalize these acts as the perpetrations of another man altogether. Yet even though Stevenson had rebelled against his Calvinistic upbringing, the doctrines that his former religion had engrained in his mind determined his novel's outcome. Once Henry Jekyll willfully unleashed his baser side and accepted the pleasures enjoyed by Hyde, the doctor was damned. The evil personality had gradually superseded the good, growing in strength as Jekyll weakened. In his despairing narrative Jekyll describes the horror of realizing that the drug was no longer required to bring about the changes. He had gone to bed as Jekyll and awakened as Hyde.

For two months Jekyll had refused to take the drug, resolving that Hyde would never again show his evil face and therefore having an opportunity of salvation. Still, as if not believing his own vow, Jekyll had maintained Hyde's Soho apartment and the fiend's smaller clothing, and finally, like an alcoholic or narcotics addict, Jekyll could not resist the temptation to become Hyde once again; and this decision proved to be his downfall. After his thrill murder of Sir Danvers Carew, he discovered that it now required a double dosage of the potion to become Jekyll. Moreover, while it was originally Jekyll who was the normal identity, now it was Hyde. Jekyll had become the other self who would exist only during the short intervals of time following the

consumption of the drug. When Jekyll did appear it was in
the image of a weary man beyond his years. Jekyll's ultimate horror had become not the gallows but the mere concept of being Hyde.

With Hyde unable to appear in public for fear of arrest, he sent Poole out to secure the proper chemicals
needed to bring back Jekyll. But an impurity in the chemicals which brought on the transformations had been eliminated by the druggists and Jekyll had just quaffed the final
drops of what remained of his potion. With a half hour remaining before Hyde was to return forever, Dr. Henry Jekyll
wrote down his full confession and swallowed the fatal poison,
destroying a monster at the expense of his own life.

As a projection of Stevenson himself, Henry Jekyll
sought to enjoy the forbidden pleasures of a life denied by
both an era and a religion. Yet in the final scene of his
story Stevenson's moral upbringing wins out. The demonic
side of Jekyll rises from his body as if to claim his soul
for damnation and it is in the shape of Edward Hyde that his
corpse is discovered.

The Strange Case of Dr. Jekyll and Mr. Hyde established Stevenson's fame and financial security. The book was
enthusiastically received by a public who regarded it as both
a satire of contemporary society and a thriller, while clergy-
men preached its message from the pulpit. The book rapid-
ly went into numerous editions (over 40,000 copies were sold
the first six months), anxiously bought and read by a public
who realized through Stevenson's narrative that the evil Hyde
character exists not only within Henry Jekyll but in everyone.
In 1888, Stevenson wrote, "If your morals make you dreary,
depend upon it they are wrong. I do not say 'give them up,'
for they may be all you have; but conceal them like a vice,
lest they should spoil the lives of better and simpler people."

RICHARD MANSFIELD AND MR. HYDE

With The Strange Case of Dr. Jekyll and Mr. Hyde
in publication for only a year, the story was already a theatrical property. Thomas Russell Sullivan adapted it to the
stage in his play Dr. Jekyll and Mr. Hyde in 1887 (and
sometimes himself played Gabriel Utterson). Starring in
the dual role of Jekyll and Hyde was thirty-year-old matinee
idol Richard Mansfield who would eventually become identified

with the part after twenty years of performances. The play
opened at the Boston Museum on May 9 to an astonished
audience who gasped incredulously as Mansfield twisted and
grimaced, becoming the evil Mr. Hyde on stage and in full
view.

"That night in the third act where, as Jekyll, I
grasped the potion, swallowed it, writhed in the awful agony
of transformation and rose pale and erect, the visualized
embodiment of Hyde--," Mansfield later wrote, "an ague of
apprehension seized me and I suffered a lifetime in the silence in which the curtain fell. In another instant I realized
that silence was a tribute of awe and terror, inspired by the
reality of the scene, for through the canvas screen came a
muffled roar which was the sweetest sound I ever heard in
my life, and I breathed again."

Sullivan rearranged Stevenson's plot, its convoluted
structure too confusing for a stage presentation. This first
theatrical version of Dr. Jekyll and Mr. Hyde was presented
in a linear style, as though all of the scenes from Stevenson's novel were snipped apart and reorganized, eliminating
the need of flashbacks. Sullivan also added a romantic interest for Henry Jekyll in the person of Alice, daughter of
the vicar, the Reverend Edward Leigh. It was Sullivan's
version of the story that later became the basis for most of
the film adaptations that would follow in the decades to
come.

The story opens with the Reverend Leigh (and not
Richard Enfield as in the novel) describing to Utterson how
he saw Hyde trampling the young girl in the street. The
story progresses with Utterson revealing to the Vicar how
Jekyll has made this Hyde his sole heir and how the doctor
has been dabbling in "unscientific balderdash." Later in the
garden Jekyll explains to Alice about the duality of man and
that it is indeed a blessed person who can control both his
good and evil natures. The audience who may have been
mystified over the events of the Stevenson novel are informed of Jekyll's duplicity immediately as he tells them in
an aside, "My God! I feel the change approaching. I must
go at once to my cabinet."

Jekyll never reaches his room. He drops his cane
and coat and complains, "Too late--too late!," writhing in
agony as his hair falls across his eyes and his body twists
into a dwarfish shape. When he turns to face Alice his

Richard Mansfield (shown appropriately in a double exposure) was the first actor to play the dual role of Dr. Jekyll and Mr. Hyde on stage (beginning in 1887).

features are contorted into the visage of Edward Hyde. Alice
calls to her beloved Jekyll for help but receives only Hyde's
snarl in reply, "Don't call him--I hate him--I'll kill him if
he comes!" The Vicar comes to Alice's rescue only to be
thrashed to death by Hyde's cane.

The play then follows according to Stevenson's story
as arranged by Sullivan. Jekyll, seeing a vision of Hyde
going to the gallows, determines to forsake Alice and to
confess everything to Lanyon in the event that the Hyde personality overpowers him against his will. Eventually, after
his transformation before Lanyon (which results in Lanyon's
death by shock), Jekyll barricades himself within his cabinet.
When Alice calls upon him he downs the last of his drug so
that it will be Jekyll and not Hyde that receives her. After
she forgives him for whatever transgressions he may have
committed, he talks her into leaving, then alone drops to
his knees. "O God," he prays, "look into my heart and for-
give my sins; You were right--I was wrong to tempt You!
Ah, I must pray--pray to keep away the demon."

But the transformation is already beginning. Hearing
Utterson outside demanding that he be let in, Jekyll takes
the poison, exclaiming before he dies and Utterson and
Poole, the butler, make their entrance, "They're going to
take me to the gallows--but Hyde won't die on the gallows--
he-he-he-he-ha! I've killed two people already--here goes
for the third--Jekyll--I've always told you I'd kill him."

Mansfield had his rivals in the contest for most not-
able Jekyll-Hyde. Oscar Dane wrote his own Dr. Jekyll and
Mr. Hyde play, which toured Missouri, luring in the customers with his advertised boast that Hyde "must be kept
chained in a box car en route and in the theater."

But Mansfield found his greatest headaches in maintaining his stage image of Jekyll and Hyde in the person of
Daniel E. Bandmann, a German-American actor. In 1888,
Bandmann portrayed the most grotesque Hyde ever seen on
the stage in an unauthorized version of Dr. Jekyll and Mr.
Hyde, which he based upon the Mansfield drama. It played
in New York and later moved to London, where Mansfield
was scheduled to open his original version one month later.
Mansfield was outraged and immediately set off for London,
determined to outfox his rival by opening on August 4. Yet
even while Mansfield feverishly rehearsed his cast he fell
victim to another upstaging. Just ten miles from London on

July 26, actor-manager Howard Pool beat both Mansfield
and Bandmann with a rushed-out version of his own Dr.
Jekyll and Mr. Hyde. Mansfield fumed. But Pool's version
of the story was indirectly denounced by Robert Louis Stevenson himself who proclaimed the Mansfield play alone to be
the "real McCoy." Mansfield's frustrations were alleviated
by the rave reviews garnered by his performance and by the
Bandmann version's flop.

Yet Mansfield's greatest rival was not any actor in
his own interpretation of the Jekyll and Hyde role but a real-
life monster who literally brought an end to the play in London. In 1888 one of history's most fiendish killers, Jack
the Ripper was stalking the foggy streets of Whitechapel
Editorials and public opinion blamed the existence of criminals like the Ripper upon such popular forms of entertainment as crime novels and theatrical melodrama (much as
today's crime and violence are conveniently blamed upon
television, motion pictures and comic books). Mansfield
was pressured into closing down his Dr. Jekyll and Mr. Hyde
in October, 1888, after a ten-week run at the Lyceum Theatre.

The Daily Telegraph reported: "Mr. Richard Mansfield has determined to abandon the 'creepy drama,' evident-
ly beloved in America, in favor of wholesome comedy. The
murderous Hyde will peer round the drawing-room windows
and leap at his victim's throat for the last time during the
forthcoming week.... Experience has taught this clever
young actor that there is no taste in London just now for
horrors on the stage. There is quite sufficient to make us
shudder out of doors."

Mansfield's last performance of Dr. Jekyll and Mr.
Hyde at the Lyceum was a benefit show; its proceeds went
to establish a night shelter for the East End's homeless
poor.

Despite Mansfield's success with the Sullivan play,
new dramas of the story were still surfacing. "Countless
dramatic versions of J&H have been presented through the
years, in opera houses, tent shows, airdomes & the greatest
legitimate theaters in the country. It was even adapted as
a brief thrill-skit for vaudeville" ['Dr. Jekyll & Mr. Hyde,"
Famous Monsters of Filmland no. 34 (August 1965), p. 44].
Dr. Jekyll and Mr. Hyde which played the Union Hall, Boston, in 1894. Luella Forepaugh and George F. Fish

presented their four-act Dr. Jekyll and Mr. Hyde play
in 1897, theirs concerned with the more sensational as-
pects of the story.   By 1908, the year after Mansfield's
death, the show opened in Chicago.   An 1898 version of Dr.
Jekyll and Mr. Hyde, by Charles Leonard Fletcher, played
Boston's Bowdoin Square Theatre.   The same year Edwin
Tanner wrote and starred in a new Dr. Jekyll and Mr. Hyde
at the Grand Opera House in Wilkes Barre, Pennsylvania.
In 1899, J. Comyne Carr's drama of Dr. Jekyll and Mr.
Hyde played the Lyceum Theatre in London, with Sir Henry
Irving enacting the starring roles in one of his most success-
ful performances.   Toledo's Lyceum Theatre launched its
own Dr. Jekyll and Mr. Hyde in 1906, adapted by Eugene
Thomas and starring Thomas E. Shea.   John Kellard wrote
his own play called The Strange Case of Dr. Jekyll and Mr.
Hyde which was presented in 1923.   There was also a
Dr. Jekyll and Mr. Hyde by Lena Ashwell and Roger
Pocock, which played London's "Q" Theatre, the date un-
known.

    Richard Abbott's three-act play Dr. Jekyll and Mr.
Hyde (1941) remained reasonably faithful to Stevenson, even
quoting dialogue from the novel.   Abbott expanded Jekyll's
romance by establishing a triangle between him, Diana Carew (daughter of Sir Danvers), and Richard Enfield, while
also substituting housekeeper Pauline and maidservant Connie
for butler Poole.   Sir Danvers objects to the engagement of
his daughter to the considerably older Jekyll.   Thus, when
Jekyll becomes Hyde and murders Sir Danvers Carew, his
motive is clearly the man's opposition to the upcoming marriage.   All the action in the play takes place within Dr.
Jekyll's London home with the actual appearances of Hyde
reduced to a bare minimum, his more brutal actions occur-
ring off stage.   Abbott describes the manner in which Hyde
should be presented:

        He seems to be short of stature, as he walks
        or stands in a crouching position.   He shuffles
        along, dragging his feet on the ground.   His arms
        and hands appear to be crooked, as though partial-
        ly paralyzed.   He wears no make-up, his face
        being pale.   Covering his entire body, under which
        the attire of Jekyll is worn, except for the coat, is
        a long, over-sized frock coat which hangs on his
        body like a loose gown.   The back of the coat is
        padded to give him a hunchback effect.   The collar
        is turned up around his neck.   The coat is old and

dirty.   On his head he wears a torn and battered
black felt hat.   Inside the brim of the hat is sewed
long strands of hair that hangs down over his face,
ears and neck.   Coming from the front of the
theatre or from an advantageous position back stage,
a small green spotlight covers his face at all times.
This, in addition to his facial expressions of rage,
hatred and fiendishness, will give the proper effect
of horror.   He speaks in a jerky, rasping voice.

In the final scene, a white-haired, sickly Jekyll takes
the fatal poison, dying in the form of the benevolent doctor
instead of (as Stevenson wrote it) the grotesque Edward Hyde.

Not only Mr. Hyde, but also the Hunchback of Notre
Dame, the Mummy, Frankenstein's Monster and Count Dracula haunted various city streets and motion picture theatres in
1958 to promote the release of a Twentieth Century-Fox science fiction movie called The Fly.   The next year a pale-
faced Hyde with bushy eyebrows and blacked-out teeth appeared on the Grand-Guignol stage in Paris, committing such
heinous acts as slitting the throats of beautiful young women.
Dr. Jekyll and His Weird Show was a live stage presentation
in Chicago during the late 1950s or early 1960s.

Other plays based on Stevenson's novel include Dr.
Jekyll and Mr. Hyde in Harlem, which opened in New York
in 1964, and Frankenstein Slept Here (1974).   This latter
play included the character Jacqueline Hyde, a descendant
of the infamous doctor, who, while masquerading as a maid
at Castle Frankenstein, involuntarily changes into a female
Hyde.

DOUBLE FEATURE

Stevenson's novel has been adapted to the motion picture medium a truly astounding number of times.   It has
been rumored that the first in a seemingly endless list of
movies directly based upon the classic was a Dr. Jekyll and
Mr. Hyde filmed as early as 1897.   But since, at this time,
there is no way of confirming that film's existence, we must
consider the first Dr. Jekyll and Mr. Hyde as that made in
1908 by the Selig Polyscope Company.   The film (which is
also known as The Modern Dr. Jekyll) was made as a result
of Col. William Selig's attendance at a Chicago presentation
of the Forepaugh and Fish play.   Selig compacted the story

into a single reel and utilized the actors from the play in
his Chicago studio. So concerned was Selig with presenting
a facsimile of a stage play on film that he opened his picture with a rising curtain. Jekyll is shown in a church garden courting Alice the Vicar's daughter. Then, seized by
his addiction to his transformation drug, Jekyll becomes Mr.
Hyde, writhing and contorting (while the unbilled actor pulled
down a matted wig over his brow and eyes) and savagely attacking the woman he loves. When her father tries to save
Alice from the fiend, Hyde delightedly kills him, then slips
away to resume his Jekyll identity. In the climax of this
short film, Hyde, haunted by a vision of the gallows, takes
the fatal poison, simultaneously killing his hated Jekyll personality.

The silent years of the motion picture yielded an incredible crop of films based on Stevenson's tale. Den
Skaebnesvangre Opfindelse (also known as Dr. Jekyll and
Mr. Hyde or just Jekyll and Hyde) was a Danish version
filmed in 1909 by Nordisk and released in 1910. The picture followed the Stevenson novel more closely than the play
did. August Blom wrote and directed the movie in which
Dr. Jekyll's experiences prove to be only a dream. The
film featured Alwin Neuss as Jekyll and Hyde. A British
version, The Duality of Man (Wrench, 1910), portrayed
Hyde as a criminal who robs a gambling den, then is chased
by the police to his home where he again becomes his normal self. When Jekyll's fiancée Hilda and her father approach the man, he becomes Hyde once more. While Hilda
watches, Hyde kills her father, then, as the police enter
the room, drinks the deadly poison.

One of the more popular of the early silents based
on Stevenson's novel was Thanhouser's Dr. Jekyll and Mr.
Hyde (1912), which Lucius Henderson directed. The picture
was shot in New Rochelle, N.Y., and remains to date the
oldest filmed version of the story extant. James Cruze portrayed Dr. Jekyll while his wife Marguerite Snow was his
leading lady, identified only as the "Minister's daughter."
The plot again was adapted from the Mansfield play, with
Dr. Jekyll discovering his identity-changing drug, courting
the clergyman's daughter, attacking her and her father, and
discovering that he has used up the last of his potion and
will remain Hyde forever. Again Hyde takes the potion and
it is in that form that his corpse is found when a policeman
batters down his study door with an ax.

Harry Benham (shown here) played only Hyde to James
Cruze's Jekyll in the silent Dr. Jekyll and Mr. Hyde (Thanhouser, 1912).

Cruze's Jekyll was played with dignity and restraint,
his hair symbolically white. His Hyde, however, was a
scuttling cripple, with clawing fingers, fangs and a mop of
equally symbolic black hair. Impressive camera dissolves
melted one character into the other. Strangely, not all of
Hyde's scenes were enacted by Cruze; at times the evil side
of Jekyll's personality featured actor Harry Benham.

"As Cruze & I were the same size," Benham recalls,
"we could wear the same clothes & wig but we did not use
the same set of false teeth! We had separate sets, which
we kept attached with the same powdered mastic that denture
wearers use today. What I remember most about the making of the picture is that we were constantly changing clothes,

after about every scene" ["Out of Hyding," Famous Monsters
of Filmland no. 25 (October 1963), p. 75].

King Baggot, Universal's biggest box office draw in
1913, assumed the dual role that year for the Studio's Dr.
Jekyll and Mr. Hyde, relying on greasepaint, crepe hair and
camera dissolves instead of the theatre's facial contortions
to simulate the transformations. Baggot also directed the
picture. Two other versions of the story were also screened
that year. The British Kinemacolor Company made its own
Dr. Jekyll and Mr. Hyde as the first of all color horror
movies. Vitascope's Dr. Jekyll and Mr. Hyde of that year
was directed by Max Mack and starred Albert Basserman.

By 1914 the Stevenson novel had lost none of its
screen potential. The Starlight motion picture company made
it into a comedy that year while Warner Features also filmed
the story for laughs in the satiric Dr. Jekyll and Mr. Hyde
Done to a Frazzle. Universal issued another (or rereleased
the 1913) version of Dr. Jekyll and Mr. Hyde in 1915. That
same year Jerold T. Hevener both directed and starred in
the Lubin comedy Horrible Hyde, playing an actor in the
Hyde role who goes about frightening people; and Paul Scardon played Satan out to claim an evildoer's soul in Vitagraph's Miss Jekyll and Madame Hyde, directed by Charles
L. Gaskill, the film having nothing to do with Stevenson's
story except the title. Movies entitled Dr. Jekyll and Ma-
dam Hyde and simply Dr. Jekyll may have been made in
1917.

The best year for Dr. Jekyll during his silent movie
cycle is undoubtedly 1920, when five motion pictures based
on Stevenson's story emerged. Arrow Film Corporation's
Dr. Jekyll and Mr. Hyde, starring Hank Mann, and Aywon's
When Quackel Did Hyde, starring Charlie Joy, were comedies soon forgotten, overshadowed by the year's more prestigious offerings.

Der Januskopf: Eine Tragödie am Rande der Wirklichkeit ("Janus-Faced: A Tragedy on the Border of Reality") [also known as The Head of Janus, Love's Mockery
and the more familiar Dr. Jekyll and Mr. Hyde] was a
German version directed by F. W. Murnau, one of the
great expressionists of the German cinema, for the Lipow
company. The production was unauthorized and royalties to
Stevenson were eschewed, the result being that Hans Janowitz altered the plot somewhat and changed the names of

Jekyll and Hyde to Dr. Warren and Mr. O'Connor. (Murnau similarly altered the proper names for his 1925 horror
classic Nosferatu, his filmed plagiarism of Bram Stoker's
Dracula.)

Instead of the standard drug, the catalyst for Dr. Warren (played by Conrad Veidt) to transform into the evil Mr.
O'Connor is a bust of Janus, a Roman god with two faces,
one human and the other that of a satyr. As O'Connor, the
doctor becomes possessed by the statue and commits such
heinous crimes as murdering a small girl and forcing his
own fiancée to a Whitechapel house of prostitution. The ending of the film is almost the same as Stevenson's, with the
self-poisoned Warren grasping the Janus bust as he dies.
(In the role of Warren's butler was an actor who had not
yet become prominent in horror films, Bela Lugosi.)

If one were to single out the classic silent film of
Dr. Jekyll and Mr. Hyde it could only be the Paramount
version of 1920, produced by Adolph Zukor, directed by
John S. Robertson and starring thespian John Barrymore in
the title roles. The film was set in Stevenson's time, the
late nineteenth century, and successfully brought a Grand
Guignol mood to the screen. Clara S. Beranger's screenplay was based on both the Stevenson novel and the Mansfield play and even utilized the sinister Lord Henry (played
with serpentine suavity by Brandon Hurst) character from
Oscar Wilde's story The Picture of Dorian Gray, to become
Jekyll's mentor and evil influence, Sir George Carewe. It
is at a dinner that Carewe suggests to Dr. Jekyll the possibilities of man living according to the dictates of his baser
instincts, unhampered by society's restrictions. (Even some
of the character's dialogue was borrowed from the Wilde
novel.)

John Barrymore (1882-1942) was a handsome matinee
idol and excellent pantomimist who loved to portray grotesque
and bizarre characters. His classic good looks had earned
him the title of the Great Profile and Barrymore delighted
in nothing more than distorting his handsome features through
facial contortions and heavy make-up. Dr. Jekyll and Mr.
Hyde was his thirteenth motion picture and the first in which
he appeared in fright make-up. But though he relied upon
an ugly disguise and camera dissolves to enact the change-
overs from Jekyll to Hyde, he also, being a stage performer, returned to the original transformation technique pioneered
by Richard Mansfield.

Henry Jekyll stands alone in his laboratory, eyeing
the drug concoction that had been influenced by Carewe.
Then in a typically theatrical Barrymore gesture he downs
the drink. Jekyll's body jerks, his hair flopping about, his
face twisting into a false face of pain and finally an evil
leer of delight. It was Barrymore hamming to the hilt, to
his delight and that of the audience, as he, like Mansfield,
distorted his handsome features into Hyde without the use of
camera trickery. Here Robertson's direction is crafty indeed. For even while Barrymore climaxes his tour de
force by maintaining his hideous expression, the director
cuts to a close shot of his hand dissolving into the spider-
like hand of Edward Hyde. The next shot is of Barrymore
in full Hyde make-up, accentuated by a rather pointed head
and dark greasepaint shading. The total effect is remark-
able--and the rumor of Barrymore's becoming Hyde without
any trick photography or fright make-up in this initial transformation scene continues to be perpetuated. (So delighted
was Barrymore with his transformation scene and his Hyde
make-up that he virtually reenacted the role in Don Juan
(1926) and used the make-up as the basis for his Captain
Ahab portrayal in The Sea Beast (1926), a version of Mel-
ville's Moby Dick.)

Barrymore portrayed his Mr. Hyde as a human spider, intimating an arachnid with his pointed head, talon-
like fingers, bent legs that scuttle him along. In one amazing scene Jekyll sleeps in his four-poster bed as an enormous ghostly spider crawls in with him, stares closely into
his face then dissolves into his body, bringing on the now involuntary change-over to Hyde. The scene is usually accepted by movie buffs as a simple superimposition utilizing
a real, albeit magnified, arachnid. But upon close inspec-
tion we can see the lengths to which Barrymore would go in
creating one of his bizarre characterizations. Though the
spider scene is brief and though the stunt has gone uncredited,
it is actually Barrymore himself, his leering face made-up
as Mr. Hyde, who climbs into bed wearing the cumbersome
outfit of a man-sized spider!

The Beranger story introduced other elements which
would become established ingredients in future filmed adaptations of the story. Every transformation from Jekyll into
Hyde brings on a decisively more hideous manifestation of
his other self. It is as Hyde that he maintains a relationship with a sultry dancer, Miss Gina (played by Nita Naldi),
while Jekyll's romantic interests lie with a young beauty of

The screen's classic silent version of Dr. Jekyll and Mr. Hyde (Paramount, 1920), starred John Barrymore (right) in the dual role, here shown with Louis Wolheim.

---

more respectable reputation, Carewe's daughter Millicent (Martha Mansfield). While Jekyll's relationship with Millicent remains romantic and platonic, Hyde's with Gina is undeniably perverted, the results showing themselves in Hyde's gradual physical deterioration while his mistress slowly loses all signs of health and energy.

Toward the end of the film, Sir George Carewe comes to Jekyll's laboratory where he sees the tortured face of Jekyll become that of a grinning Hyde. As Carewe flees into an alley, Hyde hobbles after him, and for his knowledge, there clubs him to death. Later, Millicent begs to see

Jekyll in his laboratory.   But as he touches the doorknob
his hand becomes the withered claw of Hyde.   Jekyll takes
the poison, after which his most horrendous Hyde manifestation of all limps to the door to claim Millicent to satiate
his licentious cravings.   As he attacks her, the traditional
poison takes effect and Beranger's final innovation to the
Stevenson classic is shown in close-up: Hyde's features dissolve into the Great Profile of a Henry Jekyll at peace.
Barrymore's fans could exit the theatre with a lingering
image of their handsome matinee idol shot from its most
flattering angle, while Stevenson's conception of Jekyll going
to the grave in the damning form of Hyde was destroyed by
a more happy Hollywood ending.   Now Jekyll's death has
redeemed him of his crimes as Hyde and his presumption
for seeking to bring out that character in the first place.
This final transformation back to Henry Jekyll (and its implied salvation) established a precedent for most Jekyll and
Hyde films to follow and would be the catharsis demanded
by audiences empathizing with the unfortunate scientist.   To
viewers with consciences unfettered by Calvinistic beliefs,
Jekyll had suffered enough in life, his final act of self-
sacrifice redeeming him from an afterlife burning in Hell.

Surprisingly, another Dr. Jekyll and Mr. Hyde movie
was released at the same time that the Paramount version
was first thrilling its theatre audiences.   Louis B. Mayer's
Pioneer production of Dr. Jekyll and Mr. Hyde was a shoddy
attempt to capitalize on the Paramount version.   Mayer was
able to make his film because of a copyright technicality,
but he safely (and cheaply) set it in modern day New York
to avoid a possible lawsuit from Zukor.   The film was so
cheap and so technically poor in fact, that the director wisely chose not to list his name in the credits.   The star of
the film, however, along with the other performers in the
film, did receive credit.   Sheldon Lewis, a familiar menace
to fans of the silent movie serials, played Dr. Jekyll and a
Mr. Hyde that seemed almost a carbon copy of his Clutching
Hand characterization in the Pearl White chapterplay The Exploits of Elaine (1914-15).

Dr. Jekyll transforms into a rather seedy looking Mr.
Hyde through a simple and inexpensive cutaway to the butler,
accompanied by a subtitle that damns him as "An Apostle of
Hell!" Sporting fangs, scraggy hair, and wearing a dark
coat and a pulled-down hat, Hyde skulks through the city,
fingers wringing and clutching at the air, performing such
outrages as purse-snatching in the tenement district.   Hyde

is finally given the police third-degree, tossed into jail, and strapped into the electric chair. His only salvation is a plot device that had become a cliché quite early during the silent films era: Jekyll awakens from a dream in his own easy chair, exclaiming, "I believe in God! I have a soul--" then the picture ended and rightfully slipped into obscurity. In 1929, Sheldon Lewis recreated his dual role in a short subject made in sound, titled simply Dr. Jekyll and Mr. Hyde.

By 1925, with John Barrymore's Dr. Jekyll and Mr. Hyde firmly established in the public's memory, there was little reason to make another (and inferior) movie version of the story. Take-offs were still being filmed, however. Before teaming up with Oliver Hardy, comedian Stan Laurel spoofed the Barrymore classic in Standard Cinema Corporation's Dr. Pyckle and Mr. Pride. The short subject was filmed on the same exterior sets where, two years earlier, Lon Chaney loped about in The Hunchback of Notre Dame. In a comical recreation of Barrymore's Hyde characterization, Laurel's Mr. Pride was an impish prankster who dashed through the streets tweaking the noses and kicking the pants seats of innocent bystanders, prancing about with the "scissors jump" for which the comedian was famous. Possibly Standard filmed one other spoof that year, simply titled Dr. Jekyll and Mr. Hyde, but until the arrival of the talking motion picture, Stevenson's characters otherwise retired from the screen.

With the added dimension of sound, Paramount, in 1931, began production of its remake of the John Barrymore silent classic and by 1932 had in release a new Dr. Jekyll and Mr. Hyde which is considered by most film buffs to be the greatest motion picture adaptation of the story. The film's release was perfectly timed, riding on the success of Universal's Dracula and Frankenstein, which had ushered in a new wave of horror pictures. But the first sound Dr. Jekyll and Mr. Hyde was not simply part of the craze; Paramount poured a handsome budget into the picture, the end result being one of the true classics of the early 1930s.

Dr. Jekyll and Mr. Hyde was directed by Rouben Mamoulian, a prominent stage director who relocated to the motion picture medium in the late 1920s. Mamoulian was known as an experimentalist and would introduce such ideas into Dr. Jekyll and Mr. Hyde as voice-over dialogue to reveal a character's thoughts, dissolves with one scene directly relating to the next, and diagonal split screens with the

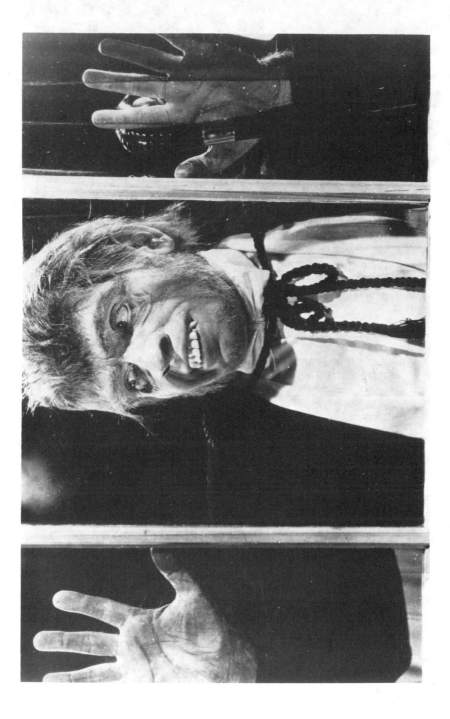

character in one shot indirectly interacting with the character in the other shot.

Mamoulian had been fascinated by both the Mansfield
play and Barrymore's movie. Paramount had intended to
star Irving Pichel, that studio's equivalent of Boris Karloff,
in this latest Dr. Jekyll and Mr. Hyde, but Mamoulian ob-
jected on the grounds that the actor could only play the evil
personality. It was Mamoulian who demanded that the role
be given to the younger Fredric March, a light comedian
and romantic leading man whose resemblance to John Barrymore was certainly a plus factor in his acquiring the role.
The studio executives ridiculed Mamoulian's choice but
sobered considerably when the director threatened that either
Paramount take both him and March--or neither. Paramount
grudgingly agreed with no later regrets; March won that
year's Academy Award for best actor.

Mamoulian embellished upon Stevenson's attempt at
audience identification with the Jekyll and Hyde characters.
He used the moving camera to open his picture through the
eyes of Dr. Henry Jekyll (pronounced "Jee-kyl" in this version). The audience literally becomes the character as the
camera (cinematography by Karl Struss) moves from a pipe
organ, through Jekyll's home and outside, down a London
street and into a great hall of an English university, filled
with students and colleagues with other characters speaking
directly at us. When the camera finally cuts to an objective
shot of Jekyll the effect has already been achieved.

While Stevenson's Dr. Jekyll was mainly concerned
with a hedonistic (though not explicitly sexual) motive for becoming Hyde, Mamoulian's was more humanitarian. "Now,
if these two selves could be separated from each other,"
Jekyll lectures to his audience, "how much better the good
in us might be, what heights it might scale; and the so-called
evil, once liberated, would fulfill itself and trouble us no
more. I believe the day is not far off when this separation
will be possible. In my experiments I have found that certain chemicals have the power--..."

Mamoulian injected a sexuality into the story that had
been missing (save for Hyde's attacks on his fiancée) from
the earlier screen adaptations and only intimated in the

Opposite: Fredric March won an Academy Award for his
performance in Paramount's 1932 remake, Dr. Jekyll and
Mr. Hyde.

Barrymore picture. Jekyll rescues a likable prostitute
named Champaign Ivy Pierson (Miriam Hopkins), whose
bruised knee he attends to and who exhibits a strong attraction for the proper English doctor. But Jekyll is engaged
to an equally proper Muriel Carew (Rose Hobart), the daughter of pompous Brigadier-General Carew (Halliwell Hobbes).
Though Jekyll desires Muriel now, the stuffy general refuses
to grant them a marriage in the immediate future. One
night the frustrated Jekyll locks his laboratory door, mixes
his experimental drug and brings the steaming flask to his
lips.

Mamoulian had become enthralled by the legendary
change-overs performed before live audiences by Richard
Mansfield. But Mamoulian's transformations would be superior, changing Fredric March with as little facial contortions and grunting as possible and without the need of any
observable camera cuts or dissolves. As we again become
the character, Jekyll sees his image transform in a mirror,
his face gradually darkening with unsightly lines and shadows. The tension of the scene is heightened by the ampli-
fied thumping of Mamoulian's own heartbeat on the soundtrack. To this day the director refuses to divulge his "secret" concerning the methods behind this scene; yet the mechanics can be deduced by anyone with a basic knowledge of
film lighting and the use of filters. March's features darkened as a series of red filters were removed from the
lights, allowing his already applied red make-up (which
photographed in blacks and grays but was unseen with the
filters yet in place) to show.

The half-transformed Jekyll drops behind his work
table, where he is tormented by conflicting images, including the image of General Carew telling him that his desire
for an earlier marriage is "positively indecent" and by a
lingering memory of Ivy's leg dangling erotically. When
Jekyll next looks into the mirror his hair is almost gorilla-
like, his brow slopes and an evil smile shows upon a leering mouth filled with oversized teeth. "Free!" says Hyde
in triumph.

While Barrymore's Hyde was based upon the spider,
March's can be traced back to an earlier period in mankind's
history. "Mr. Hyde is the exact replica of the Neanderthal
Man," Mamoulian revealed, "so he's our ancestor. We
were that once. The struggle or dilemma is not between
evil and good, it's between the sophisticated, spiritual self

in man and his animal, primeval instincts" [Thomas, Bill,
"Mamoulian: On His Dr. Jekyll and Mr. Hyde," Cinefantastique no. 3 (summer 1971), p. 37].

About the make-up, March later remarked: "For six
weeks I had to arrive at the studio each morning at 6 a. m. ,
so that Wally Westmore could spend four hours building
pieces on my nose and cheeks, sticking fangs in my mouth,
and pushing cotton wool up my nostrils. "

For some of the transformation scenes, March sat in
a chair while the camera roved about to reveal the changes
in various parts of his body. Cameraman Karl Struss later
said: "I can see the makeup man now. He squatted in back
of Fredric wherever he was seated, and while we were
photographing one part of the body, he reached around, put
the false teeth in and then disappeared. Or when we did
another part of the body, he'd put the hair on the arms.
The camera would swing back quickly to Fredric's face
while he inserted fingernails. Then back to the hands again
while a wig went on his head, and so on. Four different
wigs were used, and a number of sets of different length
fingernails. "

After the first transformation, Poole the butler (Edgar Norton) rushes to his master's locked laboratory door
to investigate the strange voice he hears: When the door
opens, however, it is Jekyll who appears before him, saying that his friend "Hyde" just left by the rear entrance.
Again Jekyll goes to Muriel in hopes of speeding up their
marriage. When Muriel and her father leave England for a
while, Jekyll again takes the drug, becoming a slightly more
apish Mr. Hyde.

This Neanderthal interpretation of Hyde baptizes himself by rushing outside and lifting his face to the rain, ex-
hilarated by the sensation that an umbrella-carrying Jekyll
would never intentionally experience. Hyde ventures into
the Soho district where he patronizes a music hall, intimi-
dating the customers and the hired help by his ugliness,
pranks and general aura of evil. There he meets Ivy who
is singing for the customers. Hyde fascinates her at first
with his declaration of love. Soon he and Ivy are sharing
a Soho apartment. Each subsequent transformation brings
out a more physically revolting Hyde and Ivy suffers accordingly. At last she goes to Dr. Jekyll and when he sees the
whip marks on Ivy's back the doctor promises that Hyde
will never menace her again.

Jekyll maintains his problem until the fateful day on which the general is to announce his and Muriel's engagement at dinner. On his way, Jekyll pauses in the park, sitting on a bench to watch a nightingale. In a beautifully symbolic scene the bird is attacked by a hungry cat, the violent scene immediately triggering the metamorphosis sans the drug. Hunched over, more bestial in appearance than ever, the apish Hyde returns to Ivy. When he mimmicks some of the verbal exchange between her and Jekyll, Ivy cannot understand how he could have overheard. Hyde gloats, "I am Jekyll!" Then in a blasphemy of an expression of love, he leads her down against the bed, saying mockingly, "There, my sweet. There, my dove. There, my little bride," and strangles her--below the frame of the film, while the camera holds on a statue of an angel and his lover in an amorous embrace. Hyde then escapes from the apartment, performing en route some incredible simian acrobatics (done by a stunt double).

As per the standard movie version of the story, Hyde confronts Lanyon (Holmes Herbert) for the chemicals procured from Jekyll's laboratory (the Utterson character having been eliminated from the plot). Promising Lanyon that he will sever his engagement to Muriel, Jekyll goes to her but becomes an even more deteriorated Hyde. He attacks her and is forced to kill her father (as in the Mansfield play), breaking his cane and leaving behind the evidence that brings Lanyon and the police to Jekyll's laboratory. Jekyll has already regained his human appearance. But when Lanyon points him out as the killer he changes into Hyde before everyone's incredulous eyes.

This final incarnation of Hyde is the most grotesque of all, which pleased the horror buffs but was hardly faithful to Stevenson. The Hyde of the novel always maintained an overall semblance of humanity. The Fredric March Mr. Hyde, howver, was an inhuman monster who even in his earliest stages could not have gone through even the thickest of London fogs without attracting undue attention.

After a final chase through the laboratory, Hyde climbs upon a shelf and prepares to leap, knife clutched in hairy hand, atop his pursuers. But a detective's bullet brings him down. On the floor Hyde transforms back into Dr. Henry Jekyll in a recreation of John Barrymore's final scene, close-up, profile and all.

Perhaps it is fitting that in this definitive screen treatment of Dr. Jekyll and Mr. Hyde, R. L. Stevenson, a nephew of Robert Louis Stevenson, appeared in a role, though a small and uncredited one.

Scenes from Mamoulian's Dr. Jekyll and Mr. Hyde appeared in Rendezvous (1973) and Revenge of Rendezvous (1975) and, along with shots from the Spencer Tracy version and a non-Jekyll and Hyde cartoon with Donald Duck purported to be in a Hyde characterization, in an untitled promotional film made by the Hollywood Center for the Visual Arts in 1970.

The spoofs were still coming: Universal made Dr Jekyll's Hide the same year that the Mamoulian film was released, no doubt to capitalize on the prestigious Paramount feature. This short subject was produced, written and directed by Albert De Mond and was made up of footage from the studio's 1915 Dr. Jekyll and Mr. Hyde. Four years later, 20th Century-Fox's Sing, Baby, Sing, directed by Sidney Lanfield, included a Jekyll and Hyde vaudeville routine.

It was in 1941 that the Mamoulian Dr. Jekyll and Mr. Hyde virtually disappeared after a decision by Metro-Goldwyn-Mayer to remake the film. There was no real reason to remake the classic at this early stage, less than a decade following the Paramount picture's initial release. Nevertheless MGM launched their own Dr. Jekyll and Mr. Hyde, produced and directed by Victor Fleming, and to ensure that no competition would result from its predecessor, the Mamoulian film was bought up and stored away, presumably never to be screened again.

Uncredited as such, MGM's Dr. Jekyll and Mr. Hyde is a carbon copy of the Paramount version, though the emphasis was on the psychological aspects of the story rather than on the brutal appearance of Hyde. The dual title role was played by Spencer Tracy (replacing the studio's original choice of Robert Donat) who was, in the opinion of many reviewers, simply unsuited for the role. As Henry Jekyll, unlike Barrymore and March before him, Tracy was not handsome enough; and as Hyde his make-up (by Jack Dawn), though looking quite unlike Tracy, especially during the latter part of the film, was not sufficiently grotesque. While the changes from March's Jekyll to his Hyde were in the extreme, some viewers saw little difference between Tracy's

characters.   When Somerset Maugham visited the set of Dr.
Jekyll and Mr. Hyde he said of Tracy, "Which one is he
now, Jekyll or Hyde?"

Lana Turner was originally slated to portray the
singer/prostitute saved by Jekyll and then victimized by
Hyde, while the doctor's fiancée was to be played by Ingrid
Bergman.   Once on the set, however, Turner and Bergman
decided that they had been miscast into each other's parts
and swapped, with positive results.   As Ivy, Ms. Bergman
shone in one of her finest screen performances and though
the picture has its detractors, rarely is her work in it ever
criticized.

To recap the plot of the 1941 Dr. Jekyll and Mr.
Hyde would be fruitless, similar as it is to the Paramount
film.   The innovations include the Freudian montage by
Peter Ballbusch, with such imagery as a wild-eyed Edward
Hyde whipping a team of horses which metamorphose into
the nude figures of the two women in his composite life.
Fleming utilized the polka sung by Ivy in the music hall to
advantage also.   She is singing it when Hyde first sees her
and stops abruptly upon her first notice of the evil-looking
man.   Later, as Jekyll strolls through the park whistling a
tune, it suddenly becomes Ivy's polka melody, which then
brings on the transformation to Hyde.

Jekyll's last transformation occurs while trying desperately to convince the police that he is not the Hyde character they have been pursuing; then he is shot while attempting an escape, dying on the floor in the by-now familiar
death scene, changing back to Jekyll in profile close-up.

While MGM's Dr. Jekyll and Mr. Hyde lacks the
energy and experimentalism of its Paramount inspiration,
the film is directed in a slick style lacking in the Mamoulian version.   Seen today the Dr. Jekyll and Mr. Hyde of
1932 appears dated, with March's first Hyde appearance often arousing laughter for its unintentional resemblance to
a comedian of two decades later, Jerry Lewis.   While
March's Hyde could be accepted on the street as a human
being by only the most gullible or poor-sighted passers-by,
Tracy's is more in keeping with Stevenson's character.
Nevertheless, Tracy's performance in the dual role got him
his only bad reviews.   The picture itself, however, holds
up by modern standards and is a classic in its own right.

The Paramount Dr. Jekyll and Mr. Hyde was finally resurrected from the MGM storage vaults in 1967, though the picture had been severely edited down to a shorter length in order to get more theatre plays per booking. Among the missing sequences (totaling about sixteen minutes) was the crucial scene in the park where the attacking cat arouses the Hyde personality in Jekyll. Now Jekyll seems to under-go the change-over for no logical reason, seeing as he does no more than the singing nightingale. Also missing were Jekyll's opening scenes at the organ and his home, a scene of his convincing a crippled child that she can walk and all the footage between the first and second transformations.

With MGM's Dr. Jekyll and Mr. Hyde in prominence, Stevenson's story was laid to rest in the United States. The Jekyll and Hyde characters were at least intimated in House of Dracula (Universal, 1945) in the person of Dr. Edelmann (Onslow Stevens), the advertised "Mad Doctor" of the picture. Edelmann's blood is contaminated by that of Count Dracula, transforming him into a kind of living vampire obviously in-spired by Tracy's performance as Hyde. A montage sequence showing various horror images is superimposed over his change-over. And Edelmann's later intimidation and murder of a hired man betrays its origins in Tracy's psychological performance. Perhaps if not for MGM's copyright Mr. Hyde might have been added to House of Dracula's boasted list of Dracula, Frankenstein's Monster, Wolf Man, Hunchback and Mad Doctor.

International, a Canadian film company, made a short subject, Gentleman Jekyll and Driver Hyde, in 1950, but this was only a film about safe driving. An authentic new ver-sion of the Stevenson novel was filmed in Argentina the next year. El hombre y la bestia ("The Man and the Beast") [also known as El extraño caso del hombre y la bestia ("The Strange Case of ... "), El sensacional y extraño caso del hombre y la bestia ("The Sensational and ... "), and Dr. Yekyll [sic]; in Italy the title is Il dottor Jekyll] was made by Sono and starred Mario Soffici, whose face darkened as Hyde, teeth lengthened and fingernails grew long and sharp. Soffici also directed the picture, playing the Hyde role for pathos, which was certainly an unusual interpretation. Both Jekyll and Hyde are tormented creatures, with the latter detesting his newly acquired freedom. El hombre y la bestia is an impressive addition to the Jekyll and Hyde myth-ology; one scene in particular is a standout. Jekyll is flee-ing through a subway tunnel when a train passes him by, its lighted windows reflecting upon his face, each flash revealing another stage of his changing visage.

Columbia Pictures thought it better to leave the original Dr. Jekyll to MGM and concentrate upon his offspring for The Son of Dr. Jekyll (apparently also known as The Second Face of Dr. Jekyll), which was directed by Seymour Friedman and released in 1951. Louis Hayward, a handsome former star of swashbuckler films, played the title character. Stevenson, of course, never had Jekyll marry or have children. But script-writer Edward Huebsch* found a solution to the problem: Hayward (as "Edward Jekyll") apparently is the illegitimate son of Jekyll in his Edward Hyde identity. To pay a minor tribute to an earlier film treatment of The Strange Case of Dr. Jekyll and Mr. Hyde, Hayward brought to the 1951 movie the actual swordcane once owned by John Barrymore and inscribed "Dr. Jekyll." The cane was a souvenir from the 1920 Paramount Dr. Jekyll and Mr. Hyde.

After murdering his mistress, Mr. Hyde, pursued by a mob, flees to his laboratory where he mixes the drug that will change him back into Dr. Jekyll. The laboratory soon becomes a raging conflagration and soon his Jekyll self leaps from a burning window to his death. His baby Edward is then salvaged from Hyde's Soho apartment by Jekyll's friends Dr. Curtis Lanyon (Alexander Knox) and solicitor John Utterson (Lester Matthews).

Years later, Lanyon is in charge of the Jekyll estate. Edward (Hayward), now a young man, has been ousted from medical school because of his own strange theories. When Edward learns of his bizarre heritage from Lanyon, he postpones his marriage to Lynn (Jody Lawrence) until he can prove that his father was actually a humanitarian whose sinister actions were prompted by a drug and whose formula might help people by releasing their inhibitions. Restoring his father's laboratory, Edward takes the fateful potion (to which Lanyon had secretly added an ingredient of his own) and transforms into a ruddy-faced, sharp-toothed version of Hyde.

---

*Huebsch was one of the Hollywood personalities to be blacklisted as a "Communist" during the Red Scare of the 1950s. Out of the United States when the controversy about him arose, when he returned Huebsch discovered that his name had been removed from the credits of The Son of Dr. Jekyll.

Clay Campbell created Hayward's Hyde make-up. The black-and-white film did not reveal the use of the red and white greasepaint that was already on Hayward's face at the beginning of the transformation. The change-over was done the same way that Mamoulian first erased the handsome features of Fredric March--by the use of filters. A red filter hid the already applied Hyde make-up at the opening of the scene; when the red filter was replaced by a blue one Hayward's Hyde features were recorded by the camera.

But Campbell's make-up was only briefly utilized in The Son of Dr. Jekyll. Hayward was never shown wearing it again. In an effort to exonerate his deceased father, Edward demonstrates the experiment before the authorities but, without Lanyon's added chemical, fails dismally. But soon Hyde is apparently loose in London again, beating a young boy nearly to death. Edward is arrested for the new Hyde crimes and charged to Lanyon's sanitarium, from which he eventually escapes.

The audience, as well as Edward, becomes aware that he is not Hyde when the youthful Jekyll sees the real fiend slipping out of his father's old Soho apartment after murdering the woman living there. Jekyll finally deduces that Lanyon is the cause of his problems and finds him in his father's laboratory, burning a copy of Henry Jekyll's notes. Lanyon, holding a gun on Edward, admits that he faked the new Hyde appearances by masquerading as the fiend in order to discredit Edward and claim the Jekyll estate for himself. After a final battle between Edward and Lanyon in the burning laboratory, the latter tries to escape. The crowd, seeing Lanyon's bruised and soiled face, believes him to be the monster Hyde. While Edward escapes, Lanyon is forced back into the burning building to die in a sequence not unlike that at the picture's opening.

In 1953 the original Stevenson story was adapted to the screen once again: Shado Kalo ("Black and White") was an Indian version directed by Amal Bose. That same year the Three Stooges faced a mad scientist called Dr. Jekyll, armed with a hypodermic needle, in the 3-D Columbia short subject Spooks, produced and directed by Jules White. (A home movie edition of this comedy was retitled Tails of Horror.)

Comedians Bud Abbott and Lou Costello had a more ambitious adventure with the Stevenson characters in the

spoof Abbott and Costello Meet Dr. Jekyll and Mr. Hyde
(Universal International, 1953), which Charles Lamont directed.   (In France the film was called Deux Nigauds contre
le Dr. Jekyll et Mr. Hyde--"Two Simpletons vs. Dr. Jekyll
and Mr. Hyde. ") This was the second time Karloff met Universal's star comics on screen (the first being in the 1949
Abbott and Costello Meet the Killer: Boris Karloff) and,
surprisingly, his only association with the Jekyll and Hyde
characters.   The original story for the film, then called Dr.
Jekyll and Mrs. Hyde, written by Sidney Fields, was later
rewritten by Grant Garrett; the two shared the screen credit.

    Abbott and Costello played Slim and Tubby, respec-
tively, a pair of American police detectives studying English
crime-fighting methods in turn-of-the-century London, where
a monster called Hyde is enjoying a reign of terror.   Slim
and Tubby meet the ingratiating Dr. Jekyll (Karloff), who in
this picture is nearly as fiendish as Hyde.   Jekyll has been
experimenting in transferring character traits in animals
and human beings and soon takes the drug which changes him
into the monstrous Hyde.   This newest version of Hyde was
a werewolf type of character, with a shaggy face, sharp
teeth and an animalistic growl to match.

    Karloff was already sixty-six years old when he made
Abbott and Costello Meet Dr. Jekyll and Mr. Hyde and could
certainly not be expected to perform the athletic stunts required of the Hyde role.   Studio make-up chief Bud Westmore
designed a Hyde mask which could be worn by Universal's
utility stuntman Edwin (Eddie) Parker, who became the more
energetic character after the transformation scenes.   The
change-overs themselves were accomplished with a series
of make-ups and a number of camera dissolves much in accordance with the Wolf Man metamorphoses executed by John
P. Fulton during the 1940s.

    Secretly in love with his ward Vicky Edwards (Helen
Westcott), Jekyll plans to murder her fiancé, a reporter
named Bruce Adams (Craig Stevens).   When Tubby miraculously captures Hyde, the monster becomes Jekyll again,
yet no one will believe that Jekyll is indeed the fiend.   After a fruitless investigation of Jekyll's house, Tubby inadvertently drinks a potion which transforms him into a
Costello-sized mouse with an amusing sequence following,
set in an English pub.

    The humor of Abbott and Costello Meet Dr. Jekyll
and Mr. Hyde peaked toward the end when Tubby falls onto

Boris Karloff (right) played Dr. Jekyll but most of Hyde's scenes were performed by stuntman Eddie Parker (left) in Abbott and Costello Meet Dr. Jekyll and Mr. Hyde (Universal International, 1953).

a hypodermic needle loaded with Jekyll's serum and later
transforms into a portly Hyde.   A frantic chase follows,
with Adams and his men pursuing the real monster and Slim
and associates following the horrible Tubby.   London is in
a turmoil as Tubby rampages through the city while the genuine Hyde escapes to his home to claim Vicky.   In a last
effort to avoid capture as Adams and his men enter the
house, Hyde exits through a window.   But when the vine he
grasps snaps, he falls to his death on the pavement.   Before Tubby regains his normal appearance he bites four
policemen and an inspector (Reginald Denny), all of whom become Hyde monsters and chase the two Americans outside
to end one of Abbott and Costello's funnier and more atmospheric horror film parodies.

    Another of Jekyll's heretofore unknown family mem-
bers surfaced in the incredibly low-budgeted Daughter of Dr.
Jekyll, Allied Artists' dubious contribution to the mythos in
1957.   The picture, which was directed without style by
Edgar G. Ulmer, was the most unorthodox treatment of the
Stevenson theme yet.   Now Dr. Jekyll was supposedly a
werewolf who rose vampire-like from his coffin at night to
drink human blood.   If that were not confusing enough, he
was allegedly pursued by an angry mob to his tomb where,
Dracula style, he was destroyed by a stake driven through
his heart!

    Janet Smith (Gloria Talbot), accompanied by her fi-
ancé George Hastings (John Agar, the star of many 1950s
and 1960s horror and science fiction movies), arrives in
England to claim an inheritance from a father she never
knew.   Her former guardian Dr. Lomas (Arthur Shields)
tries to discourage their marriage by the revelation that
her father was Dr. Jekyll and was suspected of being the
werewolf Mr. Hyde.   Lomas' dim-witted servant Jacob (John
Dierkes, who played a Jekyll's zombie-like assistant in the
Abbott and Costello picture) loses no time in spreading the
news of Janet's arrival through the village, precipitating
murmurs that she is the reincarnation of her father's bestial self.   After a new wave of werewolf murders begins in
the area, Janet is convinced that she becomes the creature
after nightfall.   But Hastings, peering through a window,
discovers Lomas hypnotizing the young woman, after which
he becomes the hairy-faced monster so long attributed to
her father.   Hastings stops Janet from hanging herself in an
attempt to end the Jekyll curse forever, while, in typical
horror films tradition, the werewolf is chased into a cave

by villagers and dispatched with a wooden stake through his
heart.   If the storyline of Daughter of Dr. Jekyll were not
preposterous enough, the final shot in the picture shows the
Hyde werewolf alive and grinning.   After we are informed
that the monster will never again prowl the night, Hyde turns
toward the audience and replies, "Are you sure?   Ha, ha,
ha, ha, ha...."

When Daughter of Dr. Jekyll's 71-minute running
time proved too short for television, some of the frames
were double-printed to stretch out the action, while Janet's
nightmare sequence was augmented by stock footage from
Allied Artists' Frankenstein 1970, made in 1958.   Strangely,
the Frankenstein Monster of the one film became the Mr.
Hyde of the other.

The film Attack of the Puppet People [also called Six
Inches Tall and The Fantastic Puppet People] (American International Pictures, 1957), produced, written and directed
by Bert I. Gordon (who also created the special effects), included a marionette sequence in which a puppet Jekyll turns
into Mr. Hyde.   The following year Herman Cohen's British
production Horrors of the Black Museum, directed by Arthur
Crabtree and released in color by AIP, starred Michael
Gough as a lunatic journalist who transforms his assistant
into a hideous, swollen-faced murderer by injecting him
with Dr. Jekyll's serum, kept among the grim treasures in
London's Black Museum of crime.   An actual new version
of Stevenson's story also emerged from England in 1959,
The Ugly Duckling, a Hammer film directed by Lance Comfort.   The film was a comedy and introduced yet another of
the original doctor's descendants, also named Henry Jekyll.
The new Henry (Bernard Bresslaw) rediscovers his infamous
grandfather's secret, changing himself into the supremely
confident Teddy Hyde, a jewel thief and the terror of the
dance-hall circuit.   Hammer tried a serious version of the
Stevenson classic the next year, with The Two Faces of Dr.
Jekyll, directed in color by Terence Fisher and released in
the United States by AIP in 1961 as the nondescript House of
Fright.   (Also known as Jekyll's Inferno and the traditional
Dr. Jekyll and Mr. Hyde, the picture was reinstated as The
Two Faces of Dr. Jekyll when it was shown in America on
network television.)   Screenwriter Wolf Mankowitz rewrote
Stevenson quite extensively for this one, making Dr. Jekyll
(Paul Massie) an elderly, bearded and overly dull character,
so dull in fact that his wife Kitty (Dawn Addams) takes on
handsome gambler Paul Allen (Christopher Lee) as her lover.

Hyde, on the other hand, is a youthful, virile and inexplicably beardless bon vivant who, in his new identity, frequents
the Can Can and the gaming rooms.   Later, as Jekyll again
becomes Hyde, the sadist has a brief affair with a beautiful
snake dancer and actually begins to finance Paul's affair with
Kitty by paying some of his bad gambling debts.   Soon Hyde
has seduced Jekyll's wife and is frequenting the opium dens
and other lower haunts of London.   Finally, unable to satisfy his wife as Hyde, Jekyll resolves to remain his more
colorful personality.   He disposes of his rival Paul by sending him to Maria's python; but after Paul is crushed to death
an hysterical Kitty throws herself off the balcony and through
a glass dome.   Hyde's final criminal act is the murder of
Maria.   In desperation, Hyde returns to the laboratory to
become Jekyll once again--but the mirrors reflect the evil
face of Hyde.   The character's career ends in a courtroom
where an aged and exhausted Jekyll weeps while announcing
his supposed triumph over Hyde.

   The Two Faces of Dr. Jekyll was not one of Hammer's more successful enterprises, partially due to a bland
script and the audience's unwillingness to accept a handsome Hyde.   Terence Fisher proposes, "There was not one
redeeming character in The Two Faces of Dr. Jekyll.   Only
one person had any semblance of good in him and that was
Jekyll's friend who said, for God's sake be careful about
what you're doing.   And he didn't do much stopping.   They
were basically a shoddy lot, weren't they?   Jekyll, who allowed himself to become shoddy.   Chris Lee, who was
shoddy.   A wife who was no good anyway.   God--raped by
her reconstructed husband!   It was an exercise, rightly or
wrongly, badly done or well done, in evil.   You didn't have
a single character in that story who was worth tuppence
ha'penny" [Ringel, Harry, "Terence Fisher: Underling,"
Cinefantastique, vol. 4, no. 3 (fall 1975), p. 24-6].

   Il mio amico, Jekyll ("My Friend, Jekyll"), also
known as My Friend, Dr. Jekyll and My Pal, Dr. Jekyll,
was an Italian comedy of 1960, made by MG and directed
by Marino Girolami.   Inventing a machine that can transfer
his mind into other bodies, an ugly professor becomes handsome for a while but ends his career trapped in the body of
a chimpanzee.   The Scarab (originally announced as Fantastique) was intended for filming in 1961 by Jack H. Harris,
with Jim Harmon writing the screenplay.   Harmon's treatment crossed over a number of famous characters in turn-
of-the-century London, including Dr. Jekyll, to have been

played by Lon Chaney, Jr. Jekyll, who had only begun the
experiments that would eventually release Mr. Hyde, would
have aided Dr. Victor Frankenstein in tracking down a monstrous insect had the film ever gone into production.

Jerry Lewis directed and starred in his comedy version of the Stevenson tale The Nutty Professor in 1962. The
color Paramount movie was originally announced as the more
descriptive Dr. Jerkyll and Mr. Hyde and was first released
to theatres in 1963. In one of his better motion pictures
since splitting with Dean Martin, Lewis portrayed professor
Julius Kelp, a buck-toothed, awkward wash-out of a character, who teaches chemistry and looks amorously upon a
pretty coed (played by Stella Stevens). Kelp invents a chemical potion, drinks it and, in a sequence effective enough to
be included in a serious version of the story, twists, con-
torts and transforms into a black-maned creature who, with
the camera mounted at a high angle, pulls himself out of
the school laboratory. When next we see the "horror" that
Kelp has become it is in the person of Buddy Love, a handsome, sophisticated, and malicious playboy. When Love enters a nightclub, he literally commands everyone's attention,
on the dance floor or behind the piano, with every woman
present swooning. Though physically normal, Buddy Love is
an image of horror to compete with Stevenson's own Edward
Hyde, especially as his influence draws to him the women
that would never have given Professor Kelp a single romantic
look. Kelp's high-pitched, nasal voice escapes from Love's
mouth in an amusing scene with the latter doing his best to
conceal his secret from the coed; still, it is the homely
Kelp that she inevitably loves, the more normal appearing
Buddy Love vanishing into the limbo occupied by most screen
Mr. Hydes. Jerry Lewis and Bill Richmond collaborated on
the script.

Mr. Hyde was a wax museum exhibit in Santo en el
museo de cera in 1963, but it was in 1964 that Dr. Jekyll
and his evil alter ego became associated with at least four
movie titles. Paramount spoofed its own Fredric March
film in the color Paris When It Sizzles (which went into production as The Girl Who Stole the Eiffel Tower) when, in a
camera shot, Mel Ferrer transformed into Mr. Hyde. The
picture was directed by Richard Quine. Ensign Pulver (Warner Brothers) lifted scenes from Warner's 1936 film The
Walking Dead, added new black-and-white footage of a mad
doctor working the laboratory apparatus, and called it
"Young Dr. Jekyll Meets Frankenstein," a film within a film
that a ship captain relentlessly screens for his crew.

The Italian Dottor Jekyll, directed by Guardamagna and starring Franco Andrei, returned to the Fredric March film for inspiration.   But the Spanish/Austrian co-production El secreto del Doctor Orloff ("The Secret of Orloff"), directed by Jesus Franco, was actually not about Stevenson's characters but rather a human robot.   Nevertheless it was erroneously also known as The Brides of Dr. Jekyll and Mistresses of Dr. Jekyll.

The year 1965 virtually ignored Stevenson's characters, the one project based on the theme being Allied Artists' proposed but never filmed comedy musical Dr. Rock and Mr. Roll, to have starred Basil Rathbone and Huntz Hall.   Jekyll/ Hyde did appear the next year in Mad Monster Party?, going on a window-breaking spree when he receives Baron Frankenstein's invitation.   (Naturally they returned for the 1972 television followup "Mad, Mad, Mad Monsters.")

A new Mexican version of Stevenson's story surfaced in 1968: Pacto diabólico ("Diabolical Pact") showed Fredric March's Hyde countenance on the advertising posters, but this cheap production bore no resemblance to the Paramount classic.   John Carradine played an aged scientist who, inspired by Dr. Jekyll, prepares a drug from fluids extracted from living female victims.   Somehow this concoction transforms him into a young killer with dark complexion and sharp fangs.   This color epic was directed by Jaime Salvador for the Vergara company; Pact With the Devil, an English-dubbed version, has been set for release by Columbia Pictures.

Dick Van Dyke demonstrated his versatility as a comedian and simultaneously contributed an hilarious black-and-white spoof of the John Barrymore version of the story in The Comic (Columbia, 1968), directed by Carl Reiner.   Van Dyke played silent screen comedian Billy Bright, who stars in a send-up production of Dr. Jerk and Mr. Hyde.   He is shown taking the drug and changing to Hyde by contorting his features à la Barrymore, letting his hair flop over his brow, crooking his fingers and hobbling about with a hunched-over posture.   Immediately he snaps back to Jerk as his fiancée visits him.   Hyde follows her about, tongue wagging like some lecherous canine, instantly becoming the respectable doctor whenever she turns around.   The 1969 picture Dracula (The Dirty Old Man) included a servant named Irving Jekyllman, whose name is somewhat significant in that the character appeared in a horror film.

In 1971 the screen realized a veritable flood of Jekyll and Hyde films, no less than five of which purported to be based directly on Stevenson's novel (though a few of them took outrageous liberties).

The Adult Version of Jekyll and Hide, a color "soft core" sex film, was directed by B. Ron Elliott for Entertainment Ventures. A Doctor Hide in modern-day Los Angeles kills to acquire Jekyll's notebook. As he reads it a flashback is shown of the original Hyde committing sado-sexual acts. The doctor tries Jekyll's experiment on himself, but, instead of becoming a repulsive Hyde, changes into a beautiful blonde woman! In female form, the doctor makes love to his nurse (certainly a bizarre situation if one considers the implications). When Hide is accosted in an alley by a sailor, "she" cuts off his penis. The police, investigating the original murder committed by the doctor, pursue him/her making it impossible for Hide to return to her male identity. They finally stalk her to an upstairs window through which she falls to her death, undergoing a final sex change.

A sex film made in color, Dr. Sexual and Mr. Hyde, produced, written and directed by Anthony Brzezinski, has an old scientist become a young stud. Three British movies, all filmed in color in 1971, went back to the original source material: The Man with Two Heads (which was shot under the title Dr. Jekyll and Mr. Blood) was directed by Andy Milligan and starred Denis DeMarne. The picture received an American release the following year. More prestigious, however, were the British I, Monster and Dr. Jekyll and Sister Hyde.

I, Monster was an Amicus Production directed by Stephen Weeks. Oddly enough the picture was originally intended as a modern-day telling of Stevenson's story, complete with teenagers holding transistor radios to their ears as they walked down London's streets. That was all changed, though, as the story was set back to its proper time period.

Producer Milton Subotsky wrote the screenplay, basing it very closely upon the Stevenson novel after the latter's course of events had been rearranged into the standard linear order. "It is the closest ever to the Robert Louis Stevenson story of any version ever made," said Subotsky. "Absolutely, exactly the Stevenson story in fact, with only one exception at the very end. Stevenson had Dr. Jekyll hole up in his laboratory at the end, destroying it, where he is found

Though the name was changed to Mr. Blake, Christopher
Lee's "Hyde" was his typically evil self in I, Monster (Amicus, 1971).

dead. I thought that was a rather tame ending, so I had
him realize that Utterson was getting wise to him, and he
dies in the attempt to kill his once good friend. Otherwise
I didn't change anything in the Stevenson story and the trouble
with the picture is that in sticking so close to the original
we wound up with a film that was very respectable and rather
boring, whereas the people who made versions not as close
to the original story wound up with more exciting films.
The story, the dialogue, the structure and the incidents we

used were right out of the book.   We didn't falsify anything,
but that turned out to be our problem.   I tried deliberately
not to add anything to it or to sensationalize it, but I see
that that was wrong" [Knight, Chris, "The Amicus Empire,"
Cinefantastique vol. 2, no. 4 (summer 1973), p. 10].

Subotsky also admits to changing the names of Jekyll
and Hyde to Dr. Marlowe and Mr. Blake, ostensibly to take
the stigma off the familiar characters and to reinstate some
of the mystery offered by Stevenson.   But what worked in
the novel did not work in I, Monster.   For while Stevenson
kept the true identity of Mr. Hyde mysteriously shrouded
until the end, we are shown Marlowe becoming the dissipated-
looking, toothy Mr. Blake early into the picture, hardly vali-
dating the rechristening.   Furthermore the names of Utterson, Lanyon, Enfield and Poole have remained intact and it
seems as if the hapless Dr. Jekyll might have been permitted to keep his own name without detriment to the overall production.

Actually, Subotsky did take other liberties with the
original plotline.   Dr. Marlowe (played by Christopher Lee,
who had a supporting role in Hammer's Two Faces of Dr.
Jekyll) is a follower of Freud and tries to explain his dual
identity theories to Utterson (Peter Cushing), Lanyon (Richard Hurndall) and Enfield (now a doctor, which he was not
in the novel, played by Mike Raven).   Before testing upon
himself the serum he believes will separate man's two identities, Marlow experiments on a cat, changing it into a vicious creature, a girl, who becomes a prostitute, and a
megalomaniacal businessman who reverts to a childlike
coward.   Finally Marlowe injects (another deviation from
Stevenson) himself with the serum, unleashing Edward Blake
(who becomes uglier with each successive transformation);
the rest of the film does follow the plot of the novel.

I, Monster was filmed in 3-D but because of the director's unfamiliarity with the stereo process, was released
flat.

Given American distribution the following year by
AIP, was Hammer Films' Dr. Jekyll and Sister Hyde, their
third attempt at shooting the Stevenson story, directed by
Roy Ward Baker.   As if to ensure that the film would be
more successful than either The Ugly Duckling or The Two
Faces of Dr. Jekyll, writer Brian Clemens not only gave
Stevenson's plot a quite exploitable twist, but also included

such familiar historical (early 19th century, actually) horror
personages as graverobbers Burke and Hare and the infamous
Jack the Ripper, all brought together in a cleverly constructed
story.   The gimmick of the film was that Dr. Jekyll would
not become the traditional Mr. Hyde but rather a beautiful
woman.   Jekyll was portrayed by Ralph Bates, a rising horror films performer at Hammer, while his evil counterpart
Sister Hyde was played by exotically beautiful Martine Beswick.   The choice of both performers was logical enough,
each of them bearing an uncanny resemblance to the other.

     In his pursuit of a drug to prolong human life, Dr.
Jekyll inadvertently changes the sex of a fly upon which he
has been experimenting.   Female hormones, he deduces, are
the secret ingredients for the elixir, which he procures from
a local morgue.   When Jekyll finally tries the elixir on himself he undergoes an unexpected sex change and names his
female incarnation Sister Hyde.

     The transformation from man to woman was under-
standably a touchy subject.   Perhaps wisely the change-over
was never actually shown on screen.   Advertisements for
Dr. Jekyll and Sister Hyde boasted: "WARNING! The Sexual
Transformation of a Man into a Woman will actually take
place before your very eyes!" and "PARENTS: Be sure
your children are sufficiently mature to witness the intimate
details of this frank and revealing film." But the picture
did not live up to its lurid advertising, as one might have
suspected from its PG rating.   Certainly it must have disappointed viewers who had drooled over The Adult Version
of Jekyll and Hide.

     When the morgue is no longer able to supply Jekyll
with the cadavers he needs to secure the female hormones,
he turns to the graverobbers Burke (Ivor Dean) and Hare
(Tony Calvin) for help.   But after Burke is lynched and Hare
blinded by an irate mob, Jekyll makes a decision.   Stalking
the Whitechapel section of London, Jekyll utilizes his surgical skills in killing prostitutes and cutting out the required
ingredients, thereby becoming the character known as Jack
the Ripper.   Jekyll the Ripper is forced to take refuge in
the body of Sister Hyde to avoid capture but discovers that
she is possessed of murderous tendencies.   To complicate
matters further she is growing continually stronger and
fights to dominate their shared existence.   Sister Hyde falls
in love with Howard (Lewis Fiander) a man living in the upstairs apartment who believes her to be Dr. Jekyll's sister.

Hammer Films contributed an unusual variation on the RLS
theme with Dr. Jekyll and Sister Hyde (1971), with Ralph
Bates and Martine Beswick playing opposite sides of the
same character.

Jekyll, however, is fond of Howard's sister Susan (Susan
Brodrick) in perhaps the weirdest triangle in horror films
history.   There is nothing more for Jekyll to do than rid
himself of his female counterpart; but to do this necessitates
another murder.   It is the blind Hare that finally betrays
Jekyll to the police, who pursue the doctor to the rooftops.
Hanging from the roof, a horrified Jekyll suddenly finds his
hands transforming into the weaker hands of Sister Hyde.
Unable to maintain his hold, Jekyll plunges to the pavement,
his face now a grotesque mixture of both the male and female.

     As if crossing Dr. Jekyll with the Ripper and Burke
and Hare were not enough, Stevenson was intermixed with
the werewolf legend in the 1971 production Dr. Jekyll and
the Werewolf (discussed in the previous chapter).   The

British 200 Motels, made from a color videotape and directed by Frank Zappa and Tony Palmer, included a spoof
scene of Dr. Jekyll taking his transformation drug.   The
year also brought announcements of a Dr. Jekyll and Mr.
Hyde to be filmed by Dan Curtis, who had already brought
the story to television in two different versions, and the
Italian 12 Plus 1, including a Jekyll and Hyde scene.   Curtis'
film was never made nor, apparently, was the Italian project.

A number of unfilmed titles were announced in 1972,
including Dr. Jekyll and Miss Hyde, Dr. Jekyll and Mrs.
Hyde (to be directed by Bob Mansfield) and Dr. Jekyll and
Mistress Hyde, all of which were probably influenced by
Hammer's essaying of the theme.   A more original project
was A Study in Identity, written by Bill Warren, in which
Sherlock Holmes must expose a killer who has discovered
and put to use Dr. Jekyll's formula.   The Niece of Dr.
Jekyll and The Jekyll and Hyde Portfolio also never went
into actual production.   Naughty Dr. Jekyll (also known as
Dirty Dr. Jekyll) was apparently released in 1973.

In 1974 Horror High (Crown-International), later released to television as Twisted Brain, was made in color
and directed by Larry N. Stouffe.   The picture was a throwback to the teenage monster quickies of the 1950s.   The
opening shot depicts a high-school English class watching a
movie of Dr. Jekyll and Mr. Hyde.   Though we are never
permitted a look at what they see, we hear Stevenson's own
narrative as Jekyll first becomes Hyde.   A friendless biology student and lab assistant named Vernon (Pat Cardi), dis-
paragingly called the Creeper by his classmates, discovers
a formula similar to Jekyll's which bubbles and steams suspiciously like dry ice in water.   The drug changes Vernon
into a hairy-faced, pigeon-toed teenage Hyde who uses his
newly acquired superhuman strength to brutally dispose of
his enemies before taking in the chest a shotgun blast fired
by a policeman.

As early as 1972, Christopher Lee mentioned that a
film company had wanted Sammy Davis, Jr., and himself to
star in a black exploitation picture to be called Dr. Black
and Mr. White.   Not until 1975, though, was such a project
undertaken, when Dimension went into production on a film
of that title.   By the time it was released in color in 1976
the picture was titled Dr. Black Mr. Hyde.   It was directed
by William Crain and starred Bernie Casey as Dr. Henry
Pride, a physician working in a Watts free clinic.   Pride's

research develops a drug that transforms him into a Hyde
with distorted features, opaque eyes and a strange shade of
white skin.   As Hyde he then proceeds to go about the seam-
ier parts of Los Angeles murdering prostitutes (Pride's mother
having been a whorehouse maid who suffered an unpleasant
death).   Eventually, following one of his murder sprees, Hyde
is chased by police to the top of the famous Watts Towers from
which he is shot down after the fashion of King Kong.

Another color exploitation film based on the theme
The Erotic Dr. Jekyll (also known as The Incredible Dr.
Jekyll) provided enough sexually explicit action in 1976 to
please the patrons of the adult movie circuit.   Dr. Jekyll and
Mrs. Hyde, to be written and directed by Peter Cook, was
announced by Memorial Films in 1976.

Jekyll and Hyde's first animated cartoon appearance
known to this writer was in the black and white Three's a
Crowd (1933); Bob Clampett drew the sequence in which
Fredric March's Dr. Jekyll leaps from the cover of Stevenson's novel and becomes Mr. Hyde.   Hugh Harmon and Rudolf Ising directed.   In Impatient Patient, directed by Norman McCabe in 1942, Daffy Duck visits "Dr. Jerkyl" to
deliver a telegram from "Frank N. Stein" and also obtain a
cure for the hiccups.   Jerkyl becomes a hulking dumb brute
until Daffy sprays him with a chemical that transforms him
into a baby.   The characters continued appearing in color
Warner cartoons over the years.   Frank Tashlin directed
Hare Remover (1954), in which Elmer Fudd drinks a chemical concoction and goes through a number of weird color
changes, while Bugs comments that Spencer Tracy did the
scene much better.   When a bear wanders into the laboratory Elmer believes it to be a transformed Bugs.   In Prize
Pest (1951), directed by Robert McKimson, Porky Pig wins
Daffy Duck in a contest.   In order to remain an unwanted
house guest Daffy dons fangs and tries to convince Porky
that he is actually a Hyde character.   The real Dr. Jekyll
brings Bugs Bunny into his home in Hyde and Hare (1954),
directed by Friz Freleng.   Unable to resist his drug, Jekyll
changes into a green, hunched-over Mr. Hyde and pursues
Bugs, periodically returning back to Jekyll.   At the end
Bugs drinks the potion and undergoes the transformation
himself.   Warner Brothers made Dr. Jerkyll's Hide the following year.   In 1969 Tweety the canary grew to gigantic
proportions in Freleng's Hyde and Go Tweety.   And Bugs
Bunny tangled with the Tasmanian Devil in Dr. Devil and
Mr. Hare (1964), directed by McKimson.

Other studios also found the Jekyll and Hyde characters viable for cartoons. A black and white cartoon, Betty
Boop, M.D. (1933), produced by Max Fleischer and directed
by his brother Dave, included an impressively life-like transformation scene of the Fredric March version of the characters. In The Bookworm (MGM, 1939), another of the color
cartoons which for the next three decades would feature Dr.
Jekyll and Mr. Hyde, the characters again spring from the
cover of Stevenson's novel. A sequel, The Bookworm Turns
(1940), brought them back for an encore performance, switch-
ing identities whenever the drug makes one of them hiccup.
The Hyde identity works a fantastic machine to exchange the
minds of the brilliant Bookworm and a stupid raven, with the
worm finally growing to giant size.

A Terrytoon directed by Mannie Davis and released
by 20th Century-Fox in 1944, Jekyll and Hyde Cat (also
known as Mighty Mouse Meets Jekyll and Hyde Cat), had Dr.
Jekyll's cat, now living in the old house once inhabited by
that scientist, mixing the chemicals and becoming the terror
of the mice also living there. Mighty Mouse flies down from
the moon and beats the feline Hyde senseless, after which
some chemicals catch fire and blow up the building. Another
cat and mouse, Tom and Jerry, starred in Dr. Jekyll and
Mr. Mouse (MGM, 1947), directed by William Hanna and
Joseph Barbera. In trying to poison Jerry, Tom succeeds
only in creating a mouse with super-rodent strength. When
Tom swallows the same drink in hopes of becoming super-
powerful he only succeeds in reducing himself to miniature
proportions. Walter Lantz Productions' Hyde and Sneak (Universal, 1962) directed by Paul J. Smith, pitted Inspector
Willoughby against Vampira Hyde, a jewel thief and a quick-
change artist.

Like the Wolf Man, the Jekyll and Hyde characters
provided a challenge to a number of amateur movie makers
who could attempt their own make-ups and transformation
effects. As early as 1932, William Vance directed and starred
in his own Dr. Jekyll and Mr. Hyde short; Pixilated Pictures
filmed another amateur Dr. Jekyll and Mr. Hyde in 1939. Anthony Brzezinski, who directed Dr. Sexual and Mr. Hyde (1971),
made an amateur film entitled The Mysterious Dr. Jekyll in the
early 1960s under the banner of Adventure Film Productions;
Snow Fire, made in 1963 by Steve B. Kaplan's Jayhawk Productions, was about a teenage Jekyll and Hyde; and Teenage Jekyll
and Hyde (Delta SF Film) was made in England the same year.

JEKYLL AND HYDE RETURN

A variety of adaptations of Stevenson's Strange Case
of Dr. Jekyll and Mr. Hyde have materialized over the
years, with radio contributing at least five dramatized versions. Spencer Tracy recreated his role from the 1941
MGM motion picture in 'Dr. Jekyll and Mr. Hyde" as presented that year on "Lux Radio Theatre." 'Weird Circle,"
about 1945, presented its own 'Dr. Jekyll and Mr. Hyde"
radio drama, with some changes from the original story.
Now, a young boy is trampled in the street by Hyde, and
Sir Carew's first name has been changed to Andrew. When
Utterson and Poole break into Jekyll's laboratory, Hyde attacks them, only to be shot down by the lawyer. In death
Hyde becomes Henry Jekyll.

Fredric March recreated his Jekyll and Hyde role
about 1950 when "The Theatre Guild on the Air" (CBS) presented "The Strange Case of Dr. Jekyll and Mr. Hyde."
The story is told by John Utterson (Hugh Williams) who
opens his narrative at the funeral of Dr. Henry Jekyll.
The funeral is a closed-coffin affair because, in an attempt
to remain faithful to Stevenson, the play has Jekyll entering
the grave as Hyde. The rest of the drama is told in flashback, borrowing from both the Stevenson novel and the Paramount film classic.

In employing the medium of radio, the "Theatre
Guild" play presented both Jekyll and Hyde as personalities
existing simultaneously, one alive and in the physical world,
the other a kind of disembodied spirit (with March's voice
spoken through a filter). This permitted both characters to
engage in verbal battles that intensified the conflicts between
good and evil. Even before first consuming the drug Dr.
Jekyll is taunted by the sinister presence that exists within
him.

> JEKYLL: Here, alone in my laboratory, the drugs
>   are ready. Dare I make the experiment?
> HYDE: You said you would. You said you would.
> JEKYLL: My own thoughts answer me. My other
>   self. The other side of my being.
> HYDE: Your other self whom you can set free. You
>   know the secret, Jekyll.
> JEKYLL: Dare I mix the drug? Dare I call forth
>   the unknown?
> HYDE: Courage, Jekyll. A whole new world is

within your grasp.   A whole new life that no man
has ever lived before.
JEKYLL: A new life.   Freedom from all my suppressed longings for nameless pleasures.   The
power for rich experience of all kinds.   Freedom
to my other self ... my self without a name.
HYDE: Give me a name then.   Give me a shape, a
body.   Bring me into the world.
JEKYLL: You are only a thought ... hiding in my
mind.
HYDE: Hyde?   How appropriate.   Call me that.
When you are Mr. Hyde you shall be free of all
your binds.

Jekyll's fiancée is now called Elizabeth Carey.   In a
scene directly inspired by the Paramount film, Jekyll, after
having determined never to become Hyde again, changes involuntarily on a park bench, then proceeds to Elizabeth's
house and attacks her.   Before his eventual suicide by poison, Jekyll hears the spectral voice of Hyde pleading with
him for a mercy which is not given.

Sir Laurence Olivier starred in "The Strange Case of
Dr. Jekyll and Mr. Hyde" as presented about 1952 on the
British radio series "Theatre Royale" (which also dramatized
Stevenson's "Markheim" and "The Suicide Club").   Of all the
radio adaptations of the story, this has been closest to
Stevenson's novel, though Hyde's death is caused by a self-
inflicted bullet wound rather than poison (probably because a
gun shot is more dramatically effective in an auditory medium).

Announcer E. G. Marshall proclaimed that the drama-
tization of "Dr. Jekyll and Mr. Hyde" on the CBS "Radio
Mystery Theater" in 1974 "comes closer to Stevenson's original than any other I know."   In fact, however, the story,
as adapted by George Lowther and directed by Himan Brown,
contained its own digressions from the novel.   Utterson's
friend Lanyon is now the victim struck down in the street
and Lanyon's daughter Beatrice is the young woman engaged
to Dr. Henry Jekyll (Kevin McCarthy).   Soon afterwards,
when Jekyll visits Beatrice, she sees the beginning of his
change to Hyde, though he leaves before the transformation
is complete.   Later, when Utterson refuses to change Jekyll's
will (as per Stevenson's novel) and decides to have Jekyll declared mentally incompetent, the doctor murders him, becoming Hyde in the process.   When Hyde finally attacks

Jekyll's beloved Beatrice she shoots him. Once more Hyde
returns to the form of Jekyll after he dies.

Television discovered The Strange Case of Dr. Jekyll
and Mr. Hyde during the 1950s. Basil Rathbone starred in
a teleplay of "Dr. Jekyll and Mr. Hyde" on the CBS series
"Suspense" on March 5, 1951. Four years later Michael
Rennie played the dual role in "Dr. Jekyll and Mr. Hyde"
on the "Climax" series. "Matinee Theatre" on NBC presented its own live television drama of "Dr. Jekyll and Mr.
Hyde" about 1957, the Hyde make-up a simple affair accomplished by stuffing the actor's cheeks to give them a puffed-
out effect and mussing his hair.

French television contributed an unusual movie version of the story in 1959. Le Testament du Dr. Cordelier
("The Testament of Dr. Cordelier") was written, produced
and directed by Jean Renoir for RFT and Sofirad. This television movie was set in present-day France and starred Jean-
Louis Barrault as the benevolent, white-haired Dr. Cordelier
who becomes the dark M. Opale. While Cordelier resists
his temptation to respond to a seductive patient, Opale has
no such qualms. The crude Opale walks down the street
with a comical, nervous twitch that is almost incongruous
with the murders he commits. What is most astounding in
the film is the differentiae between Cordelier and Opale
which makes it difficult to believe that both characters were
indeed portrayed by the same actor. This adaptation of the
Stevenson classic was titled The Doctor's Horrible Experiment in America and Experiment in Evil in Great Britain.

Producer Dan Curtis adapted the Stevenson novel (with
the obvious influence of the Spencer Tracy MGM film) to his
daytime soap opera "Dark Shadows" in the late 1960s.
Christopher Pennock portrayed blonde, curly-haired Dr. Cy-
rus Layton, a scientist conducting Jekyll-type experiments
in his basement laboratory on a parallel Earth. His version of Hyde is a sadist named John Yaeger, with slicked-
back black hair and a mustache. Pennock's Yaeger, like
Tracy's Hyde, was more of a psychological villain than an
ugly monster.

Curtis took his videotape cameras to Toronto, Canada, in 1967 to produce a two-and-a-half-hour "special" entitled The Strange Case of Dr. Jekyll and Mr. Hyde, which
Charles Jarrott directed for the Canadian Broadcasting Company. This fine adaptation was aired in the United States

Actor Jack Palance and make-up artist Dick Smith combined talents to create one of the most evil Hydes of all for a television production of The Strange Case of Dr. Jekyll and Mr. Hyde (ABC-TV, 1967).

the following year over the ABC Television network. Movie
villain Jack Palance played the timid Dr. Jekyll who becomes
the evil Hyde.

Dick Smith, whose later screen credits would include
The Godfather and The Exorcist, created Palance's Hyde
make-up. The make-up was based on a small ivory carving
of a satyr, with a broad hooked nose, sensual mouth and a
primitive brow. Smith decided that the satyr's features
would perfectly suit the actor's face. For his role of Dr.
Jekyll, Smith gave Palance a more attractive nose. But
once Palance changed into Edward Hyde his face was augmented with a nose, chin, eye bags, brow, upper and lower
lips, ear lobes and other additions, all made from foam
rubber. To these were added a wig and a set of false eyebrows.

Palance portrayed his satyr-like Hyde to perfection,
even after he cracked his left arm falling some twelve feet
from a platform during one scene. Despite the sinister appearance of Hyde, women find him strangely attractive though
he uses them to satisfy his sexual and sadistic lusts. In
one grisly scene Hyde uses his swordcane (he had taken
fencing lessons) to cut off the nose of one of his pursuers.
The storyline was strongly influenced by the 1941 MGM production and climaxes with the police pursuing Hyde to his
laboratory and killing him.

Television's most unusual legitimate adaptation of the
Stevenson classic was the NBC presentation of "Dr. Jekyll
and Mr. Hyde," aired on March 7, 1973. Produced in London, the show starred Kirk Douglas as Jekyll and Hyde, with
Susan Hampshire as his fiancée Isabel, Michael Redgrave as
General Danvers, John J. Moore as Utterson, and Stanley
Holloway as Poole. Lanyon was absent from the cast of
characters. Douglas in the roles was unusual enough, yet
even odder was the fact that this production was a musical,
scored by Lionel Bart (a Tony winner for Oliver!), Mel Mandell and Norman Sachs. But the 90-minute show worked
somehow (even scenes like Jekyll and Isabell singing together
in a cemetery), the music not intruding upon the dramatics.

Kirk Douglas, who had long been wanting to do a
musical, lost the famous cleft of his chin and acquired some
false teeth when he became Hyde. "It's a part any actor
finds intriguing," said Douglas. "The easy way to do it is
get into the makeup room and create a monster. I think

that's a violation of the Stevenson story, which says Hyde is
the monster who dwells within each of us. I twisted my
face and body into a monster without makeup, only adding a
couple of things, like a contact lens to give Hyde a cloudy
eye ... " [quoted in Smith, Cecil, TV Times (March 4-10,
1973), p. 2].

    Other television shows have included Jekyll and Hyde
appearances of less quality. In the middle 1950s, the "Jack
Benny Show" spoofed the concept with Benny's Dr. Jekyll
suspected of being Mr. Hyde. When Hyde is finally appre-
hended and his false teeth yanked from his mouth, he is exposed as singer Dennis Day. "Night Gallery" (NBC) featured Adam West in a comedy vignette in the early 1970s.
As Jekyll drinks his concoction, West essays the famous
transformation scene only to pause and complain that it needs
more vermouth. Jekyll and Hyde also appeared in some
form on the "Bob Cummings Show" (Dr. Jekyll and Mr.
Cummings"), "The Munsters" (both Fred Gwynne and Al
Lewis spoofing the transformation), "The Ghost Busters"
(Joe E. Ross as a caveman-style Hyde), "Sonny and Cher"
(Sonny Bono as Jekyll serving his potion to guests), "Sinis-
ter Cinema," "The Monkees," "Space: 1999," the "Tonight
Show" (Johnny Carson as Jekyll, Tiny Tim as Hyde) and Los
Angeles' "Panorama Pacific" (Bob Burns changing into Hyde
by the colored filter method); on the animated cartoon series
"Abbott and Costello" ("Monster Muddled"), "Laurel and
Hardy," "The Flintstones" ("Dr. Jekyll's Hyde"), the
"Groovie Goolies" and "Sabrina, the Teenage Witch" (a two-
headed character, one Jekyll, the other Hyde) and the "Scoo-
by Doo/Dynomutt Hour"; on specials like "What Are the
Loch Ness and Other Monsters All About?" and "Halleluja,
Horrorwood" (Roy Stuart as Jekyll); and even for a commer-
cial entitled, "The Strange Case of Dr. Jekyll and Mr. Hyde,"
in which Hyde, chased by a London bobby, drinks Alka-
Seltzer and changes to Jekyll to get rid of the "uglies."

    Other editions of Stevenson's original tale include The
Strange Case of Dr. Jekyll and Mr. Hyde and Other Stories
--one from Pocket Books in 1941 and another from Lancer
Books in 1968. Stevenson's story has been reworked into
new forms in more recent years. "The Strange Case of Dr.
Jekyll and Mr. Hyde" was one of the stories in Monsters
(Wonder Books, 1965), in which Walter Gibson rewrote the

Opposite: Kirk Douglas both snarled and sang in this musical "Dr. Jekyll and Mr. Hyde" (NBC-TV, 1973).

Stevenson classic for a young audience.   Terry Stacy focused
on another audience altogether in The Adult Version of Dr.
Jekyll and Mr. Hyde (Calga Publishers, 1970), basically the
Stevenson story rewritten to include sexually explicit scenes.
Jekyll is now tormented by sexual frustration while Hyde
freely indulges in the most grisly orgies, incorporating
blood-drinking, cannibalism and murder to his bestial style.
After Jekyll has sworn never to become Hyde again, the
monster is unleashed while the doctor takes part in an orgy.
Stevenson's plotline is there, albeit oftentimes difficult to
find, buried as it is among Stacy's additions.   A modernized
scene from Stevenson's Dr. Jekyll and Mr. Hyde was part
of the "I Want a Ghoul ..." parody by Jack Sharkey in Playboy (September 1971).   Jekyll drinks his potion and transforms into Spiro T. Agnew at a political gathering.   Another
parody, with sex scenes added, appeared in the July 1977
National Lampoon.

"The Secret Horror of Dr. Jekyll," by Sandor Szabo,
was an undistinguished story in the first issue (February
1962) of Thriller.   Dr. David Rheiner invents a drug which
makes him black out and later find a note admitting to a
brutal murder and signed "Mr. Hyde."   When Rheiner's amorous assistant agrees to stay with him to see if any physical
transformation follows his taking the drug, she becomes
Hyde's next victim.

A juvenile novel, The Munsters and the Great Camera
Caper (Whitman Publishing Company, 1965), by William
Johnston, had the vampiric Grandpa creating a monster using the contents of a bottle labeled "Mr. Hyde."   Another of
Jekyll's family appeared in the "Dark Shadows"-related novel
Barnabas, Quentin and Dr. Jekyll's Son (Paperback Library,
1971), by Marilyn Ross: in 1908, vampire Barnabas Collins
brings Dr. Henry Jekyll to the Collinwood estate in New England.   Jekyll wants to begin a new life where people are unaware of his father's reputation.   When a man is brutally
murdered Jekyll naturally becomes the prime suspect.   But
Barnabas literally unmasks the real killer as a woman who
had set out to destroy the Collins family.   Ironically, in attempting to escape, the woman is attacked and killed by another of Collinwood's resident horrors, werewolf Quentin
Collins.   The Beast with the Red Hands (1973) opens with
a quotation from Spencer Tracy's Dr. Jekyll and Mr. Hyde
while the film itself played as off-screen murders were
committed by the Hydelike Redhead Killer.

Superbestie Dr. Jeckyll ("Superbeast ... "), by Dan Shocker, is a German novel published in 1976 by Zauber-kreis-Verlag. The story paired the "Jeckyll" and Franken-stein families. Frankenstein and the Curse of Dr. Jekyll, a novel by Donald F. Glut soon to be published in Europe, brings a descendant of Dr. Jekyll in search of Dr. Frankenstein, hoping to secure the chemicals required to prevent his becoming Hyde, who revives and befriends the Frankenstein Monster. Both horrors are destroyed in a flooded cave.

Universe Books pleased fans of the Fredric March motion picture in 1975 by publishing Rouben Mamoulian's Dr. Jekyll & Mr. Hyde as part of its Film Classics Library series. The book, edited by Richard J. Anobile, consists of many frame enlargements and the complete dialogue.

The thirteenth entry into the Classic Comics series of illustrated adaptations of famous stories was "Dr. Jekyll and Mr. Hyde" (August 1943). As scripted by Evelyn Good-man and drawn by Arnold L. Hicks, the story bore little resemblance to the Stevenson classic. A quite monstrous Hyde, after becoming a kind of bogeyman, kidnaps Jekyll's fiancée, now called Lorraine. When Jekyll is unable to pro-cure the drugs he needs he seeks help from a fortune-teller, who gives him herbs to mix with his own concoction. Jekyll becomes Hyde again, kills an express driver, then discovers that the witch's brew will not return him to normal. After a frantic chase, the police confront Hyde at the docks and shoot him, a transformation back to Jekyll promptly follow-ing as he dies. In November 1953, the same series, now called Classics Illustrated, issued a new "Dr. Jekyll and Mr. Hyde" which was very close to the Stevenson novel. The story was drawn by Lou Cameron.

The Strange Case of Dr. Jekyll and Mr. Hyde became a serialized newspaper comic strip by a cartoonist named Chad in 1945. A Star Presentation, published by Hero Books, featured a lurid "Dr. Jekyll and Mr. Hyde" in its third issue (May 1950). Stevenson's plot was embellished by a werewolf-style Hyde who takes up with a streetwalker and thief named Flor, eventually murdering both her and Jekyll's fiancée Annabella. The eighth issue of Major Maga-zines' For Monsters Only (July 1969) updated the Stevenson tale with "Jekyll and Hyde '69," drawn by Jerry Grandenetti. It is now Henry Hyde who is wanted for committing some brutal murders. Hyde is really Professor Jekyll who er-roneously lectures to his college students that schizophrenia

can change a man into a hideous monster. The spirits of
both Jekyll and Hyde emerge from their shared body to
battle one another. But after Hyde wins over his weaker
alter ego he is finally captured by the police. Hyde goes to
the electric chair and it is Jekyll's corpse that is unmasked
after the execution. "The Strange Case of Dr. Jekyll and
Mr. Hyde," scripted by Alan Hewetson and drawn by Xirinius,
appeared in the black-and-white comic magazine Nightmare
Annual no. 1 (1972). This time Hyde tramples a Soho child
to death. Pendulum Press' series of Now Age Books presented a graphic story adaptation of Dr. Jekyll and Mr.
Hyde in 1973. This excellent black-and-white version was
scripted by Kin Platt with art by Nestor Redondo. Still another 'Dr. Jekyll and Mr. Hyde" was published in the British
magazine Legend Horror Classics in 1975.

The Marvel Comics Group's Supernatural Thrillers
no. 4 (June 1973) featured 'Dr. Jekyll and Mr. Hyde!" with
script by Ron Goulart and art by Win Mortimer. Liberties
were taken with Stevenson's story, as in the climax where
Hyde, fleeing from the police, falls from a rooftop and becomes Jekyll after fatally striking the pavement. Oddly,
Marvel reprinted an abridgment in full color of the Pendulum Press Dr. Jekyll and Mr. Hyde in the debut issue of
Marvel Classic Comics just three years later.

But Marvel actually borrowed from Robert Louis
Stevenson long before the adaptations of the 1970s. A spoof,
'Dr. Jackal and Mr. Hide," was published in Wild no. 1
(February 1954). Bill Everett supplied the art. Using a
potion spiced with garlic, Jackal tries to become a monster.
But his green-faced Hide proves irresistible to the woman
he hoped to frighten and he is soon the head of a large
family of little Hides.

Marvel writer/editor Stan Lee and artist Jack Kirby
amalgamated qualities of two major horror characters to
create the monstrous star of The Incredible Hulk. The Hulk
was first unleashed in the first issue (May, 1962) of that
magazine in a story titled "The Coming of the Hulk." Over
a decade later Lee wrote: "And--since I was willing to
borrow from Frankenstein, I decided I might as well borrow
from Dr. Jekyll and Mr. Hyde as well--our protagonist would
constantly change from his normal identity to his superhuman
alter ego and back again" [Lee, Stan, Origins of Marvel
Comics (New York, 1974), p. 75]. The Hulk is actually Dr.
Robert Bruce Banner, a scientist who, after being caught in

the blast of a gamma-bomb, becomes a savage monster with
superhuman strength. The popularity of the Hulk resulted
in appearances in most of Marvel's superhero magazines and
a surfeit of licensed merchandise and other extensions of the
character.

Marvel introduced its own continuing Mr. Hyde character to "The Mighty Thor" series in Journey into Mystery
no. 99 (December 1963). "The Mysterious Mr. Hyde!" was
written by Stan Lee and drawn by Don Heck. Hyde was
originally a sinister character called Calvin Zabo who, having been denied employment by lame Dr. Donald Blake (alter
ego of Thor, God of Thunder), determines to enjoy his revenge. Believing the Jekyll and Hyde story to be more than
fiction, Zabo had concocted his own potion to become a mis-
anthropic super-villain with the strength of a dozen men.
Blake becomes the villain's captive in the next issue's (January 1964) story, "The Master Plan of Mr. Hyde!" But
Blake becomes Thor and escapes. Hyde returned numerous
times and in Journey into Mystery no. 105 (June 1964) he
teamed up with a slippery villain known as the Cobra. "The
Cobra and Mr. Hyde!" was written by Lee and drawn by
Jack Kirby; it established the team which has endured to
this day. Hyde's "alliegance" eventually switched from Thor
to the blind superhero Daredevil. "The Concrete Jungle!"
was written by Marv Wolfman and drawn by Bob Brown for
Daredevil no. 142 (February 1977). In this tale Hyde takes
a new drug which makes him more hideous, powerful and
ferocious than ever.

National Periodical Publications, Marvel's greatest
rival in the comic book business, also used the Jekyll and
Hyde theme. The original Two-Face, one of the upper echelon adversaries of the popular Batman, was created by writer and artist Bob Kane as a simultaneous Jekyll and Hyde.
The character first appeared in "The Crimes of Two-Face!"
in Detective Comics no. 66 (August 1942). Assistant District Attorney Harvey Kent (known as Dent in later stories
to avoid confusion with Superman's alter ego Clark Kent) is
scarred when a criminal hurls acid in his face. Half of his
face remains unscathed while the other side becomes a leering, scowling mass of burned tissue. Two-face's countenance seems to have been directly inspired by the posters
advertising Spencer Tracy's Dr. Jekyll and Mr. Hyde. His
two personalities are always at war with each other and the
flip of a coin (scarred on one side) determines whether his
Jekyll or Hyde self will govern his subsequent actions.

A number of other National comic books used the
Stevenson theme.   In "The Madame Jekyll of Metropolis!,"
in Superman's Girlfriend Lois Lane no. 36 (October 1962),
the woman reporter becomes a violent and destructive Hyde
creature after being struck by a neutron beam filtered
through a chunk of Red Kryptonite.   After creating considerable damage and attempting to murder Superman, Lois returns to normal via neutron beam and a different form of
Red Kryptonite.   Kurt Schaffenburger drew the story.   'Dr.
Jerk-ll and Mr. Hyde," written by Arnold Drake and drawn
by Bob Oksner, appeared in The Adventures of Bob Hope no.
92 (April-May 1965).   The cartoon Hope inadvertently sits
on a hypodermic needle containing a Hyde serum and changes
into Mr. Hideous, a monster that becomes a rock music sensation and is irresistible to women.   A similar accident
changes his dog into a canine Hyde.   "The Jekyll-Hyde
Heroes," drawn by Curt Swan for World's Finest Comics
no. 173 (February 1968), had heroes Superman and Batman
periodically becoming two of their most deadly foes.   Not
surprisingly, the Batman becomes "that modern Jekyll-Hyde"
Two-Face.   More in the traditional horror story genre,
"Hyde--And Go Seek!" was published in The House of Secrets
no. 94 (October-November 1971).   Len Wein wrote the script
which was then illustrated by Tony DeZuniga.   Police Lieu-
tenant Homer Plumm, who has been experimenting with
strange chemicals and suffers from recurring headaches, believes that he might be the Hyde murderer that is terrorizing present-day San Francisco.   But when Plumm shoots the
real Hyde, he changes back to his best friend, who had discovered the potion while searching for an alternative to drug
addiction, and murdered women in the streets because his
wife had left him.   When Plumm returns to his own harridan
wife, rather than destroy the drug he anxiously swallows it.

Mr. Hyde's bestial face appeared in a brief series of
Gold Key (Western Publishing Company) comic books written
by Don Glut.   In 'No Place for Hyde," drawn by Dan Spiegle
and published in Mystery Comics Digest no. 6 (August 1972),
Scotland Yard Inspector Klug pursues a new Mr. Hyde during the late 1880s.   When Hyde is shot during an attempt to
steal the chemicals he so desperately needs, Klug learns
that the ugly identity was his true form and that the formula
actually made him appear handsome.   Spiegle also illustrated
Glut's story, "Things of Wax," in Mystery Comics Digest
no. 8 (October 1972), a story in which a wax dummy of
Hyde is brought to life to commit robbery for a museum
proprietor.   In Glut's 'Dr. Spektor and Mr. Hyde," illustrated by Jesse Santos for The Occult Files of Dr. Spektor

no. 5 (December 1973), psychic investigator Adam Spektor
finds the transformation formula in Dr. Jekyll's coffin and
tests it, briefly becoming his own Mr. Hyde. The grandson
of the afore-mentioned Inspector Klug investigates the new
rash of Hyde crimes with Spektor the main suspect. Actually, Howard Jekyll, the doctor's last surviving descendant,
has used the formula to gain courage and power. It is Dr.
Jekyll's ghost that leads the rampaging Hyde head-first into
the stone statue of a dinosaur, killing him instantly. Mr.
Hyde returned twice in this series, once as a conjured-up
illusion and later as a statue briefly possessed by his spirit.

Gold Key's animated cartoon character books also
featured variations of Jekyll and Hyde. 'Dr. Elmer and Mr.
Fudd,'' written by Mark Evanier and drawn by John Carey,
had scientist Elmer Fudd experimenting on animals, changing into the monster ''Mr. Fudd'' and finally being chased by
a Hyde-type mouse. 'Dr. Jerkyll and Mr. Bugs,'' by myself in Bugs Bunny no. 155 (March 1974), had the evil Dr.
Jerkyll forcing his drug down the famous rabbit's mouth, resulting in a monster that menaces Porky Pig.

Archie Comics Publications also used the theme in
their stories. Bats no. 3 (March, 1962) featured 'Dr. Grisley's Experiment,'' a tale in which the head of a scientific
research foundation destroys the laboratory of Dr. Grisley,
only to learn that his monstrous appearance was the way he
really looked. ''The Son of Dr. Jerkyll'' appeared in
Archie's Madhouse no. 21 (September 1962). Jerkyll's offspring transforms into an Elvis Presley type character, then
an Elliott Ness imitation and finally, after forgetting to add
water to his antidote drug, acquires a ''face'' that is totally
blank.

Warren Publishing Company, which established the
black-and-white illustrated horror magazine in the mid-1960s,
tapped the Robert Louis Stevenson theme. In 'Dr. Jekyll's
Jest,'' by R. Michael Rosen and artist Mike Royer for
Creepy no. 30 (November 1969), Henry Jekyll's nephew
James becomes a sadistic surgeon called ''Sikh,'' who ampu-
tates the limbs of his patients to carry on his own grisly
transplant experiments. 'Dr. Jekyll Was Right,'' by Bill
Warren and artist Tony Williamsune (Talarico), appeared
in Creepy no. 33 (June 1970). Jekyll's grandson attempts
to exonerate Henry by releasing the good ''Mr. Seak'' instead
of the evil Hyde. He offers a million dollars to the scientist
who can bring his grandfather's experiment to a successful

conclusion. When one of the scientists develops the coveted
serum, Jekyll drinks it with positive results. But before
the transformed Jekyll can give his serum to other people,
another scientist shoots him dead, Seak being as much of a
threat as the evil Hyde himself.

"Enter: Mr. Hyde," an installment of the And the
Mummy Walks series in Eerie no. 53 (January 1974), was
written by Steve Skeates and drawn by Jaime Brocal. A
scientist, after injecting himself with a longevity serum, becomes a murdering Hyde monster who eventually attacks,
fights and is slain by the series' living mummy. "Storm
Before the Calm!," in Eerie no. 63 (February 1975), initiated the magazine's Night of the Jackass series. Written
by Bruce Bezaire and drawn by Jose Ortiz, the series was
set in late 1890s England. London is ravaged by a horde
of once-human monsters who have taken the suicide drug
Hyde 25, which grants the user twenty-four hours of unbridled power and bestial pleasure after which he dies. The
series lasted for three issues of Eerie.

There have been at least three excellent dramatic
readings of The Strange Case of Dr. Jekyll and Mr. Hyde
on phonograph records. The first was issued by Audio
Books and featured the voice of Gene Lockhart. Another
album from Caedmon Records in 1969 featured Anthony
Quayle and included everything from Dr. Lanyon's narrative
to the end of the Stevenson novel. A reading of the entire
novel by Patrick Horgan was issued on a Listening Library
album in 1977.

Two radio dramas of the story were also issued on
records. Dr. Jekyll and Mr. Hyde (Triple Cross) was a
1970s album featuring a slightly edited "Theatre Guild on the
Air" version with Fredric March. The "Weird Circle" drama
was issued on Murray Hill's 1974 album set, The Great
Radio Horror Shows.

Music from the film Dr. Jekyll and Sister Hyde was
made available on the British album Hammer Presents
Dracula with Christopher Lee (EMI Records, 1974). Jekyll
and Hyde, the Mummy, Invisible Man and Black Lagoon
Creature were all featured in "Monster Movie Ball" on the
album Spike Jones in Stereo (also issued as Spike Jones in
Hi-Fi), on the Warner Brothers label. The album was
based on a Halloween "spooktacular" of the 1958 Spike Jones
Show on television. Sounds of Terror (Pickwick International,

1974) included a brief dramatic cut "Dr. Jekyll and Mr.
Hyde," basically the transformation scene.   Miles Davis re-
corded "Dr. Jekyll" on the Milestones (Columbia) album; and
The Who based two songs on Stevenson's characters, "Dr.
Jekyll and Mr. Hyde" on the album Magic Bus, and "Doctor
Jimmy" on Quadrophenia (both MCA).

The theme of The Strange Case of Dr. Jekyll and Mr.
Hyde has proven its durability in all the media.   Robert
Louis Stevenson wrote his classic tale of dual personality as
an extension of his own longings and beliefs.   But he also
intended it to be an allegory with which his readers could
readily identify.   In reading his story we discover that a
Hyde might be lurking within each of us.   Perhaps, as long
as these latent Hydes exist, the story of Dr. Jekyll will
continue to intrigue and thrill us.

III

THE INVISIBLE MAN AND CO.

Not every laboratory-spawned monster required the grotesque countenance of a Mr. Hyde to be terrifying. This was proven by Herbert George Wells (1866-1946), the author of over a hundred fiction and non-fiction books. In 1897, H. G. Wells saw the publication in England of The Invisible Man, a novel of romantic science fiction. The title character required, in fact, no face at all, ugly or otherwise, yet his egregious crimes have elevated him to the status of a classic fiend.

Wells had hoped to teach biology. But after suffering a siege of tuberculosis, Wells turned to the less taxing profession of writing. His novels were often the sounding boards for his own scientific speculations. All of us must have, at least once, fantasized about being invisible; and in The Invisible Man, the author explored the possibilities and consequences of an unseen human being.

The story of The Invisible Man is basically simple. A mysterious figure wearing a heavy overcoat, his face swathed in bandages and his eyes shielded by dark glasses, arrives during a snowstorm at the Coach and Horses Inn. His arrogance and strange behavior arouse the curiosity of the other people in the establishment. Adding to the mystery are the numerous bottles and chemistry apparatus that the stranger has set up in his room. At last there is a confrontation between the stranger and the curiosity seekers, during which the mystery man removes his coverings to reveal nothing.

> ... Then he put his open palm over his face and withdrew it. The centre of his face became a black cavity. 'Here, ' he said. He stepped

forward and handed Mrs. Hall something which she,
staring at his metamorphosed face, accepted auto-
matically. Then, when she saw what it was, she
screamed loudly, dropped it, and staggered back.
The nose--it was the stranger's nose! pink and
shining--rolled on the floor.
    Then he removed his spectacles, and every one
in the bar gasped. He took off his hat, and with
a violent gesture tore at his whiskers and bandages.
For a moment they resisted him. A flash of horrible anticipation passed through the bar. 'Oh,
my Gard!' said some one. Then off they came.

    On the roadside the Invisible Man harasses a hobo
named Thomas Marvel, forcing him to become his servant.
But Marvel steals his money and notebooks, then flees to an
inn at Port Stowe. The Invisible Man chases and nearly kills
Marvel before becoming wounded by a bullet. Seeking shelter in the home of a Dr. Kemp, the Invisible Man identifies
himself as Griffin of University College. "A younger student
than you were," says the Invisible Man, "almost an albino,
six feet high, and broad--with a pink and white face and
red eyes, who won the medal for chemistry."

    Griffin's revelations to Dr. Kemp reflected Well's
own exploration of the feasibility of becoming invisible. The
unseen visitor tells Kemp how he had become fascinated by
light and optical density; "... the whole fabric of a man, except the red of his blood and the dark pigment of hair, are
all made up of transparent, colourless tissue--so little suf-
fices to make us visible to one another. For the most part,
the fibres of a living creature are no more opaque than
water." Learning how to remove the color from blood,
Griffin, after three years of assiduous labor, developed a
drug and a ray from two small dynamos which rendered him
invisible.

    Once Wells expounded his theories as to the creation
of the Invisible Man, he proceeded to set down the consequences of going about unseen. Certainly it was possible
to do as one pleased; yet being invisible had its drawbacks.
Through the words of Griffin we learn that an invisible man
might freeze due to the effects of the elements on his naked
body. Dogs can detect his scent, his unseen feet leave
quite visible footprints, and snow, rain and fog can create an
outline against his invisible skin. Even eating can betray
his existence for the food remains visible inside his body until digestion has taken place.

Yet even with such drawbacks, the Invisible Man can enjoy great power. In his megalomaniac state, Griffin wishes to enlist Kemp as a confederate in establishing a reign of terror through murder and mayhem. When Kemp betrays Griffin to the authorities, the Invisible Man nearly chokes him to death before receiving a fatal blow to the head by a villager's spade. Dying, Griffin's bones, nerves and blood vessels gradually become visible beneath the transparent skin.

> When at last the crowd made way for Kemp to stand erect, there lay, naked and pitiful on the ground, the bruised and broken body of a young man about thirty. His hair and beard were white, --not grey with age, but white with the whiteness of albinism, and his eyes were like garnets. His hands were clenched, his eyes wide open, and his expression was one of anger and dismay.

(Most editions of The Invisible Man also include "The Epilogue" in which the landlord of the inn at Port Stowe ponders over the notebooks stolen by Mr. Marvel which contain the secret of invisibility.)

The Invisible Man combined science fiction and horror with a humor that endeared the insane Griffin to Wells' readers. Quite appealing was this character who had the potential to rule the world yet could find time to perpetrate such childish tricks as the tweaking of a nose. In two centuries readers have thrilled to the adventures of the invisible Griffin. With all the novel's opportunities for special visual tricks, The Invisible Man was an ideal property to adapt to the motion picture screen.

Apparently a French film entitled The Invisible Man was made as early as 1910. But this picture is most likely just a retitling of Les Invisibles (seen in the United States as Invisible Thief), directed by Gaston Velle and Gabriel Moreau in 1905 for the French company Pathé and released in 1909. Charles Lépire starred in this silent comedy about a thief with a sense of humor not unlike that of Griffin. The criminal goes about unabashedly undressing his victims.

Not until 1931 was an authorized version of The Invisible Man announced for filming. Universal Pictures, which had launched a new cycle of horror films with the successful Dracula, had scheduled three more screen adaptations of famous horror stories--Frankenstein, The Murders in the Rue Morgue and The Invisible Man. All three films were to be adapted and directed by Robert Florey. But Florey was replaced on Frankenstein by the British director James Whale and by the following year the latter had brought in his friend R. C. Sherriff to adapt H. G. Wells' novel to the screen.

Universal had already purchased a novel similar to The Invisible Man, the Philip Wylie story The Murderer Invisible (1931). It was the studio's intention to merge the two stories into one and they brought in a number of staff writers to perform this task. By the time Sherriff was given the assignment of writing The Invisible Man, Universal had already amassed a stack of rejected scripts, from which he was supposed to extract the best elements and create the final screenplay. When Sherriff asked for a copy of the original Wells novel upon which to base his screenplay, he was informed that none existed on the lot and that he was to base his version on the other adaptations on file at Universal. Finally, Sherriff was able to locate a copy of the novel at a market in Chinatown and purchased it for 15 cents.

In his autobiography No Leading Lady (London: Victor Gallancz, 1968), Sherriff describes some of the rejected adaptations of The Invisible Man: "The man who had turned it out no doubt had the original H. G. Wells book beside him, but to justify his employment he had to improve on it. If he had stuck to the original story and made a faithful adaptation the studio would probably have said he hadn't got any initiative or imagination of his own; that they weren't paying good money merely to copy out what Wells had written. So he had set aside the original story and given the invisible man adventures from his own imagination. The studio had no doubt felt there were good ideas in it but not enough, and passed it on to another writer. The second writer had got to go one better and invent a lot more new ideas. The third writer had to trump the one before, and so it went on, each new effort becoming more extravagant and fantastic and ridiculous. One writer took the scene to Tsarist Russia at the time of the Revolution and turned the hero into a sort of invisible Scarlet Pimpernel. Another made him into a man from Mars who threatened to flood the world with invisible Martians, and all of them envisaged him as a figure of indescribable peril to the world, threatening to use his unique invisibility to reform it or destroy it, as

he felt inclined. One thing stood out clearly in every page
I read.   The charm and the humor and the fascination that
had established the original Wells story as a classic had
been utterly destroyed. "

Sherriff ignored what had been written before his being assigned to the project, ignored the Wylie novel altogether, and based his screenplay as closely as possible upon
the Wells novel.   He eliminated the character of Mr. Marvel
and flashback scenes from Wells' story and added two new
characters, Griffin's past colleague Dr. Cranely and Cranley's daughter Flora.   He also introduced the drug monocaine,
which produces a distinct psychological effect upon Griffin's
sanity.

Even as far back as 1931, The Invisible Man was to
star Boris Karloff.   Universal Pictures went so far as to
issue announcements in the form of advertisements, with
Karloff's name heralded as the picture's unseen protagonist.
James Whale had already worked with Karloff in Frankenstein and, the following year, the Universal horror comedy
The Old Dark House.   But in 1933, the year that The Invisible Man finally went into production, when Karloff returned from England after appearing in The Ghoul, the actor
was denied the raise promised in his contract with Universal.
Consequently, Karloff stepped out of the project and Whale
was forced to seek another leading man, this time Colin
Clive whom he had directed as the scientist Henry Frankenstein in the movie Frankenstein.   When Clive suddenly returned to his wife in England, Whale turned to yet another
actor, Claude Rains.

Whale had already seen Rains perform on the British
stage.   But it was his performance in a screen test for the
RKO film A Bill of Divorcement that brought him to Whale's
attention.   Rains (1890-1967) was an unknown to American
audiences, but his anonymity actually proved to be an asset
in his portrayal of the Invisible Man.   Since most of his
scenes would be played while "invisible," audiences would
not be able to identify him in their imaginations (as they
would had Karloff or Clive accepted the part) and his magnificent voice delivering Sherriff's stiring lines would create
one of the screen's classic fiends.

Also slated for The Invisible Man cast was American
actor Chester Morris.   But when the unknown actor Claude
Rains insisted that he be given star billing in the film,

Morris left the production rather than be reduced to the status of co-star. The signing of Rains was to both his and the
studio's advantage. Though his face was seen only in the
final shot of the film, The Invisible Man launched his prestigious screen career, while Universal had to their credit
another classic horror film.

The film opens as does the book, with the appearance
of a stranger at an English inn. Taking a room at the inn,
the stranger insults Mrs. Hall (Una O'Connor, another English friend of Whale, who would later go on to a featured
role in the director's Bride of Frankenstein), the innkeeper's
wife, sends her away confused and offended, then proceeds
to search desperately for a mysterious chemical among his
scientific apparatus. Eventually the police are summoned to
investigate this man behind the bandages, at which point the
stranger rises with the regality of some future despot and
snarls through the gauze covering his mouth: "You're crazy
to know who I am, aren't you? All right--I'll show you!"

What followed seemed impossible to the viewing audience of 1933. The stranger reaches for the nose protruding
from the bandages, yanks it off and hurls it at the townspeople. "There's a souvenir for you!" Next, a gloved hand
removes the dark glasses, revealing what appears to be two
holes. Finally off come the windings of bandages as they
lose the general shape of the human head they had been
covering and reveal nothing but empty space. A country
constable reacts, "Look, he's all eaten away!" Finally the
now apparent Invisible Man slips off his trousers and chases
his intruders about the room, wearing only a seemingly
floating white shirt.

Soon pandemonium breaks out in the village as the
Invisible Man runs rampant, cackling prankishly as he pa-
rades about in a pair of borrowed pants, stealing a bicycle
which he boldly rides through the town to the incredulity of
the residents, knocking off a few hats. Invisibility tricks
had been seen on the motion picture screen before 1933,
but nothing like those in The Invisible Man.

What appeared to be visual miracles were actually
the work of John P. Fulton, Universal's special effects genius who more than two decades later would create the spectacular opening of the Red Sea sequence for the 1956 version
of The Ten Commandments. The scenes in which the Invisible Man was entirely unseen were simple enough for

Claude Rains as Griffin in The Invisible Man (Universal, 1933), the picture that made him a star though his face was seen only in the final scene.

Fulton, who manipulated the "floating" objects handled by the character via "invisible" piano wire. The difficulty was in such scenes as Griffin's removal of his bandages or clothing or in which he appeared only partially clothed. Clothing hanging on wires was unsuitable since, for the effect to be convincing, a solid human body had to give the clothing form from underneath.

Fulton solved his problem by use of the traveling matte process. He clothed Rains' stuntman double entirely in black velvet (which was almost totally nonreflective) tights and helmet, over which he placed the attire of the Invisible

Man. The stuntman then took his place on a set also cloaked in black velvet and proceeded to enact the disrobing or other trick scenes dictated by the script. "This gave us a picture of the unsupported clothes moving around on a dead field," said Fulton (in the September 1934 issue of The American Cinematographer). "From this negative, we made a print, and a duplicate negative, which we intensified to serve as mattes for printing. Then, with an ordinary printer, we proceeded to make our composite: first we printed from the positive of the background and normal action, using the intensified, negative matte to mask off the area where our invisible man's clothing was to move. Then we printed again, using the positive matte to shield the already printed area, and printing in the moving clothes from our 'trick' negative. This printing operation made our duplicate, composite negative to be used in printing the final masterprints of the picture."

But Fulton's biggest headaches seemed not to have come from devising the effects themselves, but rather in the use of the stunt double, "... getting the player to move naturally, yet in a manner which did not present, for example, an open sleeve-end to the camera. This required endless rehearsal, endless patience--and many 'takes.' In many scenes, too, we had to figure out ways of getting natural-looking movement without having our 'invisible' actor pass his hands in front of himself.

"... In some of these scenes, it was possible to leave small eye-holes in the helmet, through which the player could see; but in others--especially the close shots of the unwrapping action--this was impossible, and the player had to work 'blind.' Air had to be supplied through tubes, as in a diving-suit--but the tubes were concealed, usually running up a trouser-leg. On at least one occasion, either the air-supply failed, or the mid-summer heat (aided, of course, by the heat of the lamps) overcame the player and he fainted in the middle of the scene....

"In nearly all of these scenes, though they were made silent, it was difficult--sometimes impossible--to direct the actor, for the helmet muffled the sound from outside, and the air-tubes made a roaring rumble in his ears, which drowned out any sounds which might filter through the padding. When I used a large megaphone, and shouted at the top of my voice, he could just barely hear a faint murmur. Accordingly we had to rehearse and rehearse--and then make many 'takes'; as a rule, by 'Take 20' of any such scene, we felt ourselves merely well started toward getting our shot!"

In a few scenes, neither Rains nor his double were used in unmasking the Invisible Man. When the glasses or artificial nose were removed from the bandaged head, empti- ness had to be revealed, with the gauze in back showing through the holes. For this effect Fulton devised a dummy, complete with a chest that simulated breathing.

The Invisible Man, as per the original novel, is forced to take refuge in the home of Dr. Kemp (William Har- rigan). He reveals his true identity to be Jack Griffin (Sher- riff gave him a first name), a former colleague who had been experimenting with monocaine, an Indian drug capable of making solid objects transparent. Unknown to Griffin, however, is the fact that the use of this drug can eventually drive a person insane. Unable to find a cure for his invisi- bility, Griffin instead succumbs to his growing megalomania. "It came to me suddenly. The drugs I took seemed to light up my brain. Suddenly I realized the power I held--the power to rule, to make the world grovel at my feet. Ha, ha! We'll soon put the world right now, Kemp.... We'll begin with a Reign of Terror. A few murders, here and there. Murders of great men, murders of little men, just to show we make no distinction. We might even wreck a train or two. Just these fingers, 'round a signalman's throat."

Kemp informs Griffin's former friend Dr. Cranley (Henry Travers) and his daughter Flora (Gloria Stuart), whom the Invisible Man loves. The police are alerted, but the insane Griffin escapes to wreck a train, rob a bank and continue his killings (acts denied him in the Wells novel). When a snowstorm forces him to take shelter in a barn, his breathing gives him away. "There's breathing in my barn," the startled farmer tells the police. The barn is set ablaze by the police and the Invisible Man is forced out into the snow. As the police observe a trail of footprints magically appearing in the snow, they fire their guns, hit- ting their unseen target.

Fulton accomplished the scene of the appearing foot- prints by digging a trench and covering it with a board. The footprints had been cut into the board. Then the cut- out prints were put back into the board and covered with the artificial snow. A rope was attached to the pegs beneath

the footprint cut-outs; and when the rope was pulled the footprints appeared as if by the impression of an unseen foot,
while the camera was able to move and the bystanders could
watch with disbelief.

The face of Claude Rains is seen only once, in the
final shot of the picture in which the invisible Griffin reappears in a hospital bed, the antidote to his strange condition
being death.   At first there is only the impression of something indenting the pillow.   Then a skull appears, followed
by the facial muscles and finally the visage of the lifeless
Jack Griffin.   "This was done directly in the camera," said
Fulton in The American Cinematographer.   "First, we
showed the bed, occupied by its invisible patient: the pillow,
indentation and all, was made of plaster, and the blankets
and sheets of papier-mache.   A long, slow lap-dissolve revealed the skeleton (a real one, by the way); another lap-
dissolve replaced the skeleton with a roughly-sculptured
dummy of the actor; and a further series of such dissolves,
each time using a slightly more finished dummy, brought us
to the real actor, himself."

The success of The Invisible Man was due mainly to
three persons and their respective talents: the acting of
Claude Rains, the artful visual effects created by John P.
Fulton, and the direction of James Whale.   The director,
whose earlier films Frankenstein and The Old Dark House
and the later Bride of Frankenstein would include much of
Whale's unique sense of humor, retained the humor of the
H. G. Wells book.   When Griffin is totally invisible, Whale
usually portrays him as a mischievous poltergeist, performing trivial acts of mayhem and delighting, as does the audience, in his every minor deviltry.   The 1973 short film
Rendezvous included scenes from The Invisible Man.

Like Frankenstein and The Mummy, The Invisible
Man is one of the true classic horror films to emerge from
the 1930s.   And like these other two films, it inspired a
number of other films based upon the concept of scientifically-
induced invisibility.   Universal Pictures tapped the invisibility theme in three of their serials following The Invisible
Man's release: The Vanishing Shadow (1934), Flash Gordon
(1936) and The Phantom Creeps (1939).   In The Vanishing
Shadow, directed by Louis Friedlander, a scientist invents
a vest which gives the wearer invisibility.   The great scientist Dr. Zarkov (Frank Shannon) invents an invisibility
machine on the planet Mongo in Flash Gordon, directed by

Frederick Stephani. As Flash Gordon is about to be executed, Zarkov flicks a switch which renders the hero unseen.
Bela Lugosi portrayed the mad Dr. Zorka in The Phantom
Creeps, a chapterplay directed by Ford Beebe and Saul A.
Goodkind. Zorka has invented an invisibility belt which he
uses in his villainous schemes. Despite the fact that all
three serials were made by Universal, none of them were
considered prestigious enough (or were allotted ample budgets) to warrant the use of Fulton's special invisibility effects. In their place were rather obvious scenes of objects
hanging from wires or men grasping their throats as if being strangled by invisible hands.

The official Universal Pictures' Invisible Man series
commenced in 1939 with the filming of The Invisible Man Returns, which was released the following year. With the
original Invisible Man unquestionably dead, it became the
task of writers Joe May and Curt Siodmak (the future creator of the Wolf Man) to revive the character. The problem
was solved credibly enough: The Invisible Man Returns
would feature, not Jack Griffin, but his brother Dr. Frank
Griffin. (Jack's picture, in the person of Claude Rains,
would, however, appear on the wall of Frank's laboratory).
The actual Invisible Man would not be a member of the Griffin family but someone else altogether.

The Invisible Man Returns, which was directed by Joe
May and released in 1940, starred a newcomer to the field
of horror. Vincent Price, who would not be considered an
actual horror films star until the 1960s (primarily in the
series of Edgar Allan Poe films he would do for American
International), was cast as the new Invisible Man. This was
Price's second horror film, the previous one being Universal's Tower of London (1939). But The Invisible Man Returns marked the actor's first performance as a fantastic
character. Like Rains, Price's richly distinctive voice
suited him perfectly to the role of a character who remained
unseen throughout most of the picture.

Geoffrey Radcliffe (Price) has been convicted of the
murder of his brother Michael and is scheduled to be hanged
at dawn for the crime. But Geoffrey's salvation is in the
power of Frank Griffin, who visits his jail cell and gives
him the drug which had made his own brother the Invisible
Man. Escaping to the woods, the new Invisible Man finds
the suitcase full of clothes left him by Frank.

Now the invisibility drug is called duocaine and it is known unquestionably that use of the drug will eventually cause insanity. It thus becomes Geoffrey's task to prove his innocence before the duocaine madness can take hold of him. Wearing the bandages and dark glasses already familiar to movie audiences, Geoffrey, the Invisible Man, takes shelter in the home of a hermit friend of Frank Griffin. Meanwhile, Frank works to find an antidote to Geoffrey's invisibility before he does in fact go mad.

Learning that his cousin Richard Cobb (Sir Cedric Hardwicke) had already given his job at a nearby mine to a drunk named Spears, Geoffrey harasses the man, much in the way that the original Invisible Man tormented Mr. Marvel in the H. G. Wells novel. From Spears, whose testimony was instrumental in convicting Geoffrey, the Invisible Man learns that Cobb had forced him to lie in court.

Geoffrey visits his cousin and tries to force him to confess to Michael's murder. But Cobb is saved by the appearance of the police who detect his presence in a puff of cigar smoke. For The Invisible Man Returns, Fulton perfected two effects only hinted at in the original film. The unseen character's outline can be seen in the smoke and later appears in the rain.

At Frank's house, Geoffrey, wearing his goggles and bandages, begins to exhibit signs of the megalomania that destroyed his predecessor. Laughing insanely, the Invisible Man leaves the room. The next morning Geoffrey, in the presence of Cobb, terrifies Spears into admitting that he saw his employer kill Michael. After a scuffle between Cobb and the invisible avenger, the two of them are soon fighting atop the rails on which the ore cars travel to and from the mine. A shot from the police inspector brings down the Invisible Man, while Cobb, as the side of the car opens, plunges to the pile of ore below. Before he dies Cobb confesses to Michael's murder.

Staggering into the woods, the wounded Geoffrey Radcliffe comes upon a scarecrow in a beautiful scene reminiscent of James Whale. Geoffrey talks to the scarecrow as he "borrows" its tattered clothing. It is a bizarre sight as the Invisible Man, wearing the scarecrow's attire, shambles into town. Frank gives Geoffrey a blood transfusion and the Invisible Man's body materializes, as did Griffin's in the earlier film, the antidote to his condition being blood itself.

Vincent Price (shown here with Nan Grey) was not yet a
horror films star when he played the lead role in The Invisible Man Returns (Universal, 1940).

        The Invisible Man Returns was not as "classic" as
the original Invisible Man.   Yet it did retain the flavor of
the Whale film, with its quaint villagers and policemen and
the special effects of John Fulton.   The "Invisible" films
that would follow from Universal during the 1940s, though
still enhanced by Fulton's wizardry, would be more in the
line of "B" films or "programmers."   Continuity from one
film to the next would not be as rigid as that existing between The Invisible Man and The Invisible Man Returns and
none of the performers who vanished into their roles would
be another Claude Rains.   Nevertheless the later Invisible
Man films were all entertaining thrillers, the highlights of
which were provided by Fulton.

        Writers Siodmak and May diverted only slightly from
the concept in 1940, with a film that was not really a sequel to the first two: The Invisible Woman was a comedy,

directed by A. Edward Sutherland, which starred Virginia
Bruce as the title character.   Any references to the Griffin
family were avoided.   An aging John Barrymore broadly enacted the role of Professor Gibbs, an eccentric scientist who
has invented a serum and a machine (created by Ken Strickfaden, Universal's electrical wizard who created the laboratory apparatus for the Frankenstein doctors and other mad
scientists) capable of rendering a person invisible.   Gibbs
had been sponsored by playboy Richard Russell (John Howard),
who is suddenly broke after paying off his latest romantic es-
capade.   Without financial backing, Professor Gibbs is forced
to run a newspaper advertisement for a willing human guinea
pig for his invisibility experiment.

Kitty Carroll (Virginia Bruce) is an attractive fashion
model who has grown weary of dealing with her overly strict
boss Mr. Growley (Charles Lane) and also with her pompous
customers at the department store.   After submitting to the
professor's weird invention, the Invisible Woman leaves the
laboratory to teach the people she despises a lesson.   For
The Invisible Woman, Fulton created some special effects
that were pleasantly new to fans of the Universal "invisible"
series.   Kitty appears in a department store fashion show in
the latest 1940 dress--sans head and arms, frightening off
the high-nosed society women.   Then she visits Growley,
disrobing before his staring eyes, slapping him with a pair
of white gloves and then upsetting his office.   In another
scene viewers were treated to the sight of Kitty's stockings
taking on shape as she slipped them over her invisible legs.

Eventually a romance develops between Kitty and
Richard.   But when Kitty catches cold from going about naked
and drinks some brandy, the alcohol prolongs the effect of
invisibility.   When the alarmed professor returns to his laboratory, he finds that his equipment is gone.   The machinery
has been stolen by henchmen of Blackie Cole (Oscar Homolka), an American gangster hiding in Mexico with hopes of
creating an invisible gang.   Unfortunately the machinery does
not work without the added injection of the professor's serum.

Professor Gibbs does find another means to bring
Kitty back to visibility.   Yet every time Kitty takes another
alcoholic drink she reverts to her identity of the Invisible
Woman.   After a number of comedy encounters, the criminals are finally captured in Mexico.   Kitty and Richard get
married and have a child which, to their astonishment, fades
away, having inherited her power of invisibility.

The Invisible Woman was a pleasant departure from the more serious Invisible Man films. But the picture was not successful enough to warrant any further adventures of the character. Writer Curt Siodmak returned to the original male concept for the 1942 production of Invisible Agent, directed by Edwin L. Martin and "suggested by 'The Invisible Man' by H. G. Wells." Siodmak, however, reformed the character. We were in the Second World War; surely the Allies could use an agent that could battle the Germans unseen in their native land and be more valuable than a dozen John Waynes.

The story revived the old Griffin family name, centering around Frank Griffin (Jon Hall), not the same Frank of The Invisible Man Returns but rather the grandson of the original Invisible Man. Incognito as Frank Raymond, Griffin runs a print shop in New York just prior to America's entry into World War II. Griffin is visited by two foreign spies, the Nazi Stauffer (Sir Cedric Hardwicke) and the Japanese Ikito (Peter Lorre) who demand that he give them his grandfather's invisibility formula. (Audiences might have thought that the celebrated Oriental detective Mr. Moto had turned bad. Peter Lorre had played the sleuth in a series of films made at Twentieth Century-Fox in the 1930s. The series was discontinued before the Pearl Harbor bombing.) All Griffin possesses, however, is a small dose of the drug which he refuses to give to these enemies of his country. After a fight with the spies Griffin escapes with the precious fluid.

Frank refuses to give the drug to his own government until he learns of the bombing of Pearl Harbor. Then the former printer volunteers to participate in American espionage. Parachuting over Berlin, Frank injects himself with the drug and, thanks to Fulton's expertise, vanishes during his descent. Escaping the German ground troops by shedding his clothing, the Invisible Agent, following his instructions, reaches the coffin shop of Schmidt (Albert Basserman) and then the apartment of the beautiful counterspy Maria Goodrich (Ilona Massey). During one elaborate special effects sequence set in Maria's apartment Fulton's art came under the scrutiny of the censor.

"I had a scene in that picture which was a wonder, if I do say so myself," reported Fulton (in the Hollywood Citizen News of January 17, 1944). "The Invisible Man went to his bath, turned on the water and got under the

shower.   The drops of water sticking to his skin were visible, but the skin wasn't.   So what happened?

"The censors said the bathroom door was open and
there was a woman in the other room.   They said you can't
have naked men, even invisible naked men, in the same
scene with females, and my scene went out.   If the door'd
only been closed we'd have been all right."

Fulton also created a satisfying effect when Maria
asks to see the Invisible Agent: Frank takes some of her
cold cream and smears it across his unseen face, causing
Jon Hall's visage to appear as if floating in the air.

When Stauffer suspects that the Invisible Agent will
rifle his office, the Nazi traps him there in the act of stealing a list of names and addresses of Nazi and Japanese spies
operating in America.   Despite being outnumbered by German
soldiers, Frank gets out with the list.   Soon he intimidates
an imprisoned Nazi officer named Heiser (J. Edward Bromberg) into revealing that Hitler plans to attack the United
States that night.   Knocking out two storm troopers, Frank
dons one of their uniforms, then, careful not to reveal his
invisible face and hands, escapes with Heiser in hopes of
securing a plane to England.

Ikito finally snares the Invisible Agent in a fish net
enhanced by hundreds of fish hooks and takes him to the
Japanese Embassy along with Maria.   When a fight begins
as Stauffer and his Storm Troopers barge into the embassy,
Frank escapes with Maria, leaving Ikito to kill the Nazi officer and then himself in an act of hara-kiri for their disgrace.   Soon Maria is flying a purloined German bomber
over England with the wounded Frank falling into a coma.
As British anti-aircraft guns cripple the plane, Maria heroically parachutes with Frank onto English soil.   Frank re-
covers, to learn not only that the Nazi invasion has been
averted but that the effects of his invisibility are finally
wearing off.   In a simple fade-in (as opposed to the elaborate materializations in The Invisible Man and The Invisible
Man Returns), Frank Griffin becomes visible again, enjoying
the cure denied his murderous grandfather.

Invisible Agent was unique in the "Invisible" series
at Universal, an entertaining propaganda piece that reflected
the American people's attitudes during the War.   Two years
later Universal, without the talent of Siodmak, filmed its

final serious entry into the series. The Invisible Man's Revenge, directed by veteran Ford Beebe, differed from its predecessors in that the humorous aspects of the Invisible Man character were obviated in favor of an outright horror movie.

Jon Hall returned in the role of the invisible protagonist. Now, though, he was Robert (and not Frank) Griffin, an Englishman with apparently no association whatsoever with the secret of invisibility. In fact, save for the name Griffin and the very concept of invisibility, there is no connection between The Invisible Man's Revenge and the earlier entries in this series. Bertram Millhauser's screenplay, apart from being "Suggested by 'The Invisible Man' by H. G. Wells," presented a new storyline altogether, unless by sheer coincidence Robert was never aware of his family's achievements while at the same time the secret of invisibility was discovered by someone else. The purists among us might get some enjoyment out of trying to rationalize Universal's too frequent disregard for continuity.

Robert Griffin returns to England after supposedly being killed during a search for diamonds in the African jungle. (Jon Hall was entirely in character here, considering his many jungle films made during the 1940s.) Calling upon his former partners Sir Jasper Travers (Leland Hodgson) and Lady Irene Herrick (Gale Sondergaard), whom he believes abandoned him to die, Griffin demands his share of the diamonds under threat of exposing them to scandal. The pair drug Griffin, remove from him any evidence implicating themselves, and turn him out. Wandering through the woods, Griffin happens upon the instrument of his revenge.

Griffin comes to the home of eccentric scientist Dr. Drury (John Carradine), who has discovered an invisibility formula. His proof is Brutus, a great dane invisible except for the collar and leash attached to his neck. Agreeing to be the doctor's human subject, Griffin fades to nothingness, then proceeds to utilize his new abilities to enjoy his revenge by killing his enemies while at the same time claiming the love of the evil Lady Irene's daughter, Julie Herrick (Evelyn Ankers, Universal's most popular horror films heroine). John P. Fulton was still devising new special effects, even with four "Invisible" movies behind him. In one fascinating scene Griffin proves his existence by dipping his hand into a fish tank, the displaced water revealing his outline. But Fulton's most unusual effect was saved for the final reel.

Barney (Leon Errol) reacts to the emptiness beneath the head wrappings of Griffin (Jon Hall) in The Invisible Man's Revenge (Universal, 1944).

Learning that only a blood transfusion fatal to the doner can restore him to visibility, Griffin first drains off the blood of Dr. Drury, then proceeds to do the same to hero Mark Foster (Alan Curtis). Before Griffin can take enough of Foster's blood, the police make their entrance with a transparent Griffin fighting them off. The effect is especially impressive in that Griffin's clothes are as solid looking as ever. Before the Invisible Man can completely return to visibility and kill Foster, he is destroyed by an angry Brutus.

The Invisible Man character did not return until 1948 for a cameo "appearance" in the comedy Abbott and Costello Meet Frankenstein. The film ends after the elimination of Frankenstein's Monster, Dracula and the Wolf Man, with the Invisible Man making his presence known to Abbott and Costello. An unbilled Vincent Price provided the voice as a cigarette is lit and puffed by the Invisible Man--which Invisible Man being left to the viewers to decide.

Two years after Abbott and Costello's brief encounter with the Invisible Man, the comedy team shared an expanded adventure with the character. Abbott and Costello Meet the Invisible Man was directed by Charles Lamont, who would in the coming years direct the team's meetings with Dr. Jekyll and Mr. Hyde, the Mummy and, in 1953, their extraterrestrial adventure Abbott and Costello Go to Mars. The Invisible Man spoof was released by Universal-International in 1951. (In France the picture became Deux Nigauds et l'homme invisible--"Two Simpletons and the Invisible Man.")

A surprising amount of continuity existed between Abbott and Costello Meet the Invisible Man and the original Invisible Man, the basic premise being not unlike that of The Invisible Man Returns. The invisibility serum in the Abbott and Costello movie is the same that John Griffin had discovered and his photograph (of Claude Rains) graces the laboratory wall of Dr. Philip Gray (Gavin Muir). In a serious scene that might have come from one of the earlier Universal Invisible Man entries, Gray explains that he has inherited Griffin's serum but has vowed not to use it until he has removed the madness-inducing property that destroyed its discoverer. He demonstrates the serum on a guinea pig (in a scene lifted from The Invisible Man Returns).

Helen Gray, the doctor's daughter, is the fiancée of prizefighter Tommy Nelson (Arthur Franz), who has been accused of murdering his manager. To prove his innocence he hires private eyes Bud Alexander (Abbott) and Lou Francis (Costello). To avoid arrest Tommy disregards Gray's warning about the drug's side effects and injects himself, vanishing in Lou's presence, the last things to disappear being his teeth. The new Invisible Man must now clear himself before the drug makes him a homicidal maniac.

The invisible Tommy explains that he was ordered to throw a fight with boxer Rocky Hanlon (John Day). When Tommy kayoed Hanlon instead, his manager was beaten to death. Tommy believes that he was framed for the crime by crooked fight promoter Morgan (Sheldon Leonard), whose hireling actually committed the murder.

In only one scene does Tommy wear the familiar Invisible Man bandages and dark glasses, and then only briefly. Lou brings Tommy, who is hiding in the woods, the clothes and gauze only moments before the police arrive, alerted by Bud. Immediately, Tommy unwinds himself and

Bud Abbott (far left), Lou Costello (left, pointing), Nancy
Guild, Gavin Muir (kneeling), and William Frawley attend to
the wounded Invisible Man (whose outline was added to this
photo by the publicity department), in Abbott and Costello
Meet the Invisible Man (Universal-International, 1951).

disappears to manifest himself in a series of less complicated (and less expensive) invisibility effects.

Some of the better comedy sequences in Abbott and
Costello Meet The Invisible Man included a poker game
played with the unseen character and a scene in a restaurant
wherein the Invisible Man becomes drunk and rowdy and poor
Bud must cover for him. During this latter scene Tommy
begins to exhibit the beginnings of the encroaching insanity,
raving about his power and how he might rule the world.
The funniest sequence was staged in the boxing ring with
Lou posing as a prizefighter and Bud his manager. The Invisible Man is at Lou's side, slugging Rocky while Lou's

fists never seem to make contact with his opponent. Since
Lou had refused to lose the fight, Morgan orders him killed,
only to meet the invisible Tommy in Lou's dressing room.
In saving Lou's life, the Invisible Man, made visible by a
blast of steam, is stabbed by Morgan's henchman. But as
in The Invisible Man Returns and The Invisible Man's Revenge, human blood acts with the doctor's reagent. Tommy
returns to visibility after receiving a transfusion by Lou. A
twist, however, has the serum backing into Lou's bloodstream,
creating an invisible Costello who causes havoc in the hospital.

Not for more than twenty years would the Invisible
Man be reunited with Universal Pictures.

NOW YOU SEE THEM ...

The Invisible Man inspired a plethora of films which,
if not based directly upon the H. G. Wells novel, at least
capitalized on its title. In 1933, the same year that Universal released its first Invisible Man feature, the German company Ariel Film made Ein Unsichtbar geht durch die Stadt
("The Invisible Man Goes Through the City") [also known as
Master of the World and Die Welt ist mein! ("The World Is
Mine!")], directed by Harry Piel and featuring Fritz Odemar,
Ernst Rothemuend and Walter Steinbeck. The comedy focused
on a helmut found in a taxicab that gives the driver invisibility.

The Invisible Man proved to be an international culprit. He was loose in Turkey in Görünmiyen Adam Istanbulda ("The Invisible Man in Istanbul"), a 1956 picture made
by Kemal. It was directed by Lüftü Akad and starred Atif
Kaptan, who portrayed the famous vampire Count in Dracula
Istanbulda, a Turkish film of 1953. Mexico turned to the
H. G. Wells story in 1957 with El hombre que logro ser
invisible ("The Man Who Benefits from Being Invisible"), a
Calderón production released in the United States during the
mid-1960s as The New Invisible Man. (The movie has also
been titled The Invisible Man in Mexico; in England the title
is the more impressive H. G. Wells' New Invisible Man.)
Directed by Alfredo B. Cravenna and featuring Arturo de
Cordova, Ana Luisa Peluffo and Augusto Benedico, the film
was somewhat of a remake of The Invisible Man Returns,
with a man falsely accused of murder becoming invisible to
trap a killer while going mad in the process. The poor

attempts at imitating Fulton's visual tricks did not enhance
the dull direction.   Japan had its Tômei Kaijin ("Invisible
Man") in 1958, a Toei film directed by Tsuneo Kobayashi
and starring Susumu Namishima and Yunosuke Ito.   Frankenstein contre l'homme invisible ("Frankenstein vs. the Invisible Man") disappointed numerous French viewers when it
played in their country in 1959:   there was no Invisible Man
in this retitling of the American Frankenstein 1970 (Allied
Artists, 1958).   Perhaps the advertised "Invisible Man" was
actually the Frankenstein Monster (Mike Lane) who lumbered
through some scenes wrapped in mummy-like bandages.
About this time surfaced the enigmatic title The Invisible
Man from Space which was apparently never made.   (The
title might actually refer to Phantom from Space, a United
Artists release of 1953, directed by W. Lee Wilder, about
an invisible alien who causes havoc in an observatory by
performing the same kinds of stunts made famous by various invisible men before him.)

A new movie of The Invisible Man was announced in
1959 but remained simply an unfilmed title.   Comedy mixed
with the invisibility theme in another Mexican picture, Los
Invisibles ("The Invisible Men"), also known simply as The
Invisible Man, in 1961.   Jaime Salvador directed this Chap-
ultepec film featuring Viruta, Capulina and Eduardo Fajardo.
Der Unsichtbare ("The Invisible Man"), known in America
as The Invisible Terror, came from the West German company Aero in 1963.   Directed by Raphael Nussbaum and featuring Hanaes Hauser, Ellen Schwiers and Herbert Stass,
the picture was about a criminal who steals an invisibility
drug from its scientist inventor.   About 1966 Daiei announced
a film entitled Tokyo Ninja Butai ("Invisible Men in Tokyo"),
to be directed in color by Tarou Yuge.

Back on American soil, the Invisible Man had not
relinquished his career entirely to foreign movie companies.
Actor John Carradine appeared on a television talk show in
1966 and announced with a raised eyebrow that his next film
would be something called The Invisible Man on Bikini Beach.
While that travesty never went into actual production, a
number of Invisible Man pictures did make it into theatres
in 1967.   Mad Monster Party? featured an animated puppet
of the character, a fez floating above a filled smoking jacket
with the voice of Alan Swift imitating Claude Rains.   (The
Invisible Man became a cartoon figure in the television
followup "Mad, Mad, Mad Monsters" in 1972.)   Argentina had
its own Invisible Man film that year; El hombre invisible

ataca ("The Invisible Man Attacks") was made in color by
Argentina Sono Films, directed by Martín Mentasti and featuring Martín Karadagian, Gilda Lousek and Tristan.

The Italians and French combined their resources
that year to produce Flashman contre les hommes invisibles
("Flashman vs. the Invisible Men"), known in the United
States simply as Flashman.   The hero Flashman masquerades
as a comic-book superhero to fight a criminal who has been
made invisible by a serum.   Mino Loy (J. Lee Donan) di-
rected the picture for Zenith.   It featured Paolo Gozlino
(Paul Stevens), Claudia Lange, Isarco Ravaioli (John Heston)
and Jacques Ary.   El invencible hombre invisible ("The In-
vincible Invisible Man") was the Spanish, Monegasque, West
German, Italian cooperative contribution to the theme in 1969.
The color production, directed by Antonio Margheriti (Anthony
M. Dawson) and featuring Dean Jones, Gastone Moschin and
Ingeborg Schöner, was about a young scientist who takes an
Indian serum which makes him unseen and able to rescue
his kidnapped girlfriend.   Germany knows this picture as
Mister Unsichtbar ("Mr. Invisible"), Italy as L'inafferrabile
Mr. Invisible ("The Unseizable Mr. Invisible"), and South-
east Asia as Mr. Super Invisible.   Other titles for the same
film are Invincible Mr. Invisible and simply Mr. Invisible.
In 1971 Spain contributed Dr. Orloff and the Invisible Man,
another in their series of Orloff movies.

Even animated color cartoons utilized the Invisible
Man theme, but surprisingly few, considering the ease with
which that medium could duplicate the Fulton effects.
Porky's Movie Mystery (Warner Brothers, 1939), directed
by Bob Clampett, featured Porky Pig as an Oriental sleuth
trying to solve the mystery of the Invisible Man, who is
terrorizing the film studio.   In the end the character becomes visible to reveal the caricatured image of comedian
Hugh Herbert.

Amateur Invisible Man movies have provided their
makers with the opportunity of trying to duplicate the Fulton
tricks.   Hollywood movie director Bert I. Gordon, who created some of his own invisibility effects for a ghost story
entitled Tormented (Allied Artists, 1960), made an Invisible
Man film Vanishing Cream while still a youngster.   Don
Glut made a color short The Day I Vanished (1959) and
played the son of the Invisible Man, who goes on a killing
spree before being stabbed to an apparent death.   In the
sequel The Invisible Teenager (1962) the juvenile Griffin

returned, escaping from a mental institution to torment the
person whose court testimony convicted him of murder, only
to be eventually shot to death.

The concept of scientific invisibility has always been
popular in the motion picture medium because of the numerous technical possibilities involved.   An early film The Invisible Fluid (Biograph, 1908) bestowed temporary invisibility
upon men and inanimate objects.   The Unseen (Eclair, 1914)
featured an invisible scientist.   Another silent invisibility
picture was The Unknown Purple (Truart, 1923), featuring
Henry B. Walthal, Johnny Arthur and Dorothy Phillips.
Based on the play by Roland West (who directed the film)
and Carlyle Moore, The Unknown Purple concerned a scientist released from prison after being convicted of a crime
of which he was innocent.   Utilizing his purple light invention to become invisible, he hunts down the real criminals,
his former wife and his unscrupulous partner.

The talkies had their share of science-spawned invisible men.   The Body Disappears (Warner Brothers, 1941),
directed by D. Ross Lederman, was a comedy in which a
formula intended to resuscitate the dead makes them invisible instead.   A Republic Pictures serial of 1941 entitled
Dick Tracy vs. Crime, Inc. (later rereleased as the misleading Dick Tracy vs. Phantom Empire) presented a villain
called the Ghost for the duration of fifteen episodes directed
by William Witney and John English.   The Ghost (Ralph
Morgan) wore a leathery head mask and a belt which made
him invisible.   In the final chapter "Retribution" Dick Tracy
(Ralph Byrd) discovers a ray to conflict with the Ghost's
invisibility device which causes the scene to appear in the
negative as hero and supercop engage each other in a furious
fistfight with the expected outcome.   Republic again delved
into screen invisibility in the 1950 serial The Invisible
Monster, which apparently went into production under the
name of the villain The Phantom Ruler.   Directed by Fred
C. Brannon with a total of twelve chapters, the serial featured an archfiend (played by Stanley Price) who could remain invisible as long as he stayed in a special beam of
light and wore his chemically-treated clothing.   A feature-
length version of this chapterplay was released to television
in 1966 with the new title Slaves of the Invisible Monster.
Columbia Pictures introduced an invisible villain known as
the wizard in Batman and Robin, a fifteen-chapter serial of
1950 directed by Spencer G. Bennet.

Japan entered the vanishing business in 1949 with Daiei's Tomei Ningen Arawaru ("The Transparent Man"), directed by Shinsei Adachi and starring Chizuri Kitagawa and Takiko Mizunoe.   The same studio released a film about a transparent scientist helping the police to hunt down a villain who is only a few inches tall in the 1957 Tomei-Ningen to Hai-Otoko ("The Transparent Man vs. the Fly Man"), also known as The Murdering Mite.   It featured Ryuji Shinagawa and Yoshiro Kitahara; Mitsuo Murayama directed.   Toho International, the studio that unleashed Godzilla in 1953, issued its own Tomei Ningen in 1954 with Motoyoshi Oda directing.

With so many invisible characters creating their mayhem upon the screen, it was inevitable that The Invisible Boy would come along.   Produced in 1957, it was an MGM picture directed by Herman Hoffman.   Richard Eyer played the title character in this tale about a super-computer bent on dominating all mankind.   Though Eyer enjoyed a brief period of invisibility, the real star of the film was Robby the Robot, last seen in the futuristic science-fiction epic Forbidden Planet (MGM, 1956).   In 1958 another invisible man performed his antics in Ramadal, made in the Philippines by Premiere.   The picture featured Effren Reyes (who also directed), Cynthia Zamora and Melita de Leon.   The Amazing Transparent Man, which went into production in 1959 and was released by American International the next year, was yet another variation on the invisible man theme, directed by Edgar G. Ulmer.   Douglas Kennedy portrayed a convict who is snatched from his prison cell in order to become a guniea pig for a scientist hoping to create an invisible crook.   Kennedy is bombarded with weird rays and (in an interesting visual effect) vanishes in segments.   In one amusing sequence the Transparent Man's head reappears during a bank robbery.   During the last minutes of this low-budget, yet entertaining film, the Transparent Man, visible again, tries to kill his scientist boss and become head of their operation, but succeeds only in causing the laboratory to explode like an atomic bomb.

The West German Die unsichtbaren Krallen des Dr. Mabuse ("The Invisible Claws of Dr. Mabuse"), seen in the United States as The Invisible Dr. Mabuse and also known as The Invisible Horror, was directed in 1961 by Harald Reinl for CCC.   Former screen Tarzan Lex Barker portrayed a secret agent out to stop the infamous Dr. Mabuse (first introduced to the screen in Dr. Mabuse der Spieler,

a silent film of 1922 directed by Fritz Lang) now using an
invisibility machine.   More invisible villainy manifested itself
in El asesino invisible ("The Invisible Assassin"), a Mexican
production of 1964 released the following year by Filmadora
Panamericana.   René Cardona directed this picture starring
Ana Bertha Lepe, Guillermo Murray and the "Man in the
Golden Mask," El Enmascarado de Oro.   Another title for
this film is El Enmascarado de Oro contra el asesino invisible ("The Man in the Golden Mask vs. the Invisible Assassin").   Another invisible man "appeared" in the color sex
comedy Henry's Night Inn (1969), coming into view only when
he sneezes.   An Italian picture, Matchless, made in 1966
and released in color by Dino DeLaurentiis in 1967, starred
Patrick O'Neal as a superspy who fights off a master villain's
robots with the aid of an invisibility ring; Alberto Lattuada
directed the picture.   Now You See Him, Now You Don't was
Walt Disney Productions' contribution to the genre, filmed in
color in 1971 and released by Buena Vista the next year.
Robert Butler directed this sequel to The Computer Wore
Tennis Shoes (1969).   Kurt Russell portrayed Dexter Riley,
a student who invents a spray-on invisibility fluid.   The invisible Dexter then foils the plans of a crook A. J. Arno
(Cesar Romero) to turn the former's high school into a
gambling casino.   Arno steals the spray to use in committing crimes until his invisible getaway car crashes into a
swimming pool, the water bringing him and his henchman
back into view.   (A story based on the film was presented
in Western Publishing Company's Walt Disney Comics Digest
no. 37 [October 1972].)

        More invisible shenanigans have occurred in the color
cartoons.   Both The Invisible Mouse and Operation Meatball
(later retitled The Invisible Woody for home movie distribution) used invisible ink as the disappearing catalyst.   The
Invisible Mouse (MGM, 1947), directed by William Hanna
and Joseph Barbera, was a Tom and Jerry cartoon with
Jerry finally getting the upper paw on his perennial rival.
Walter Lantz' Operation Meatball (Universal, 1951) showed
Woody Woodpecker doing his vanishing act in a supermarket.

AGAIN, THE INVISIBLE MAN RETURNS

        The Invisible Man has proven to be a lasting title.
In the years following the premier publication of H. G.
Wells' novel, it has appealed to other writers whether or
not their work had any basis in Wells' novel.   Perhaps if

not for the Wells tale these later writings would have been published under different titles altogether.

"The Invisible Man" was the title of one of the Father Brown mystery stories by G. K. Chesterton, first published in the book The Innocence of Father Brown in 1911. The "invisible man" of the title was actually a killer who goes about disguised (hence, unseen). "The Invisible Man Murder Case," by Henry Slesar, published in 1958, was a legitimate scientific invisibility story and even mentioned the writings of H. G. Wells. The "invisible man" of the title is actually a mystery writer named Kirk Evander whose brother has invented a literally named "vanishing cream." Evander smears the cream over his head, fakes his own decapitation, then proceeds to taunt and kill his enemies in order to prove that the plots of his classic murder mysteries are not only in vogue but are also quite probable. Yet another story "The Half-Invisible Man," by Bill Pronzini and Jeffrey Wallmann, was issued in Ellery Queen's Mystery Magazine no. 366 (May 1974). The "half-invisible man" was in reality a usually unnoticed policeman who displays brilliant detective instincts by solving a locked room murder case.

Ballantine Books published a collection of stories exploring the possibilities and consequences of invisibility in 1960 under the title Invisible Men, edited by Basil Davenport. The collection contained "The Weissenbroch Spectacles," by L. Sprague de Camp and Fletcher Pratt; "The Shadow and the Flash," by Jack London; "The New Accelerator," about moving so fast that one is virtually invisible, by H. G. Wells; "Invisible Boy" (no connection with the film The Invisible Boy), by Ray Bradbury; "The Invisible Prisoner," by Maurice LeBlanc; "Love in the Dark," by H. L. Gold; "What Was It?" by Fitz-James O'Brien; "The Invisible Dove Dancer of Strathpheen Island," by John Collier; "The Vanishing American," by Charles Beaumont; "Shottle Bop," by Theodore Sturgeon; and "The Invisible Man Murder Case," by Henry Slesar.

Cliff's Notes issued a volume on H. G. Wells' Invisible Man in 1969, including a detailed plot synopsis of the original novel. Two books entitled The Invisible Man, one written by Ralph Ellison and published in 1951, the other by Dennis Littrell and issued in 1973, had nothing to do with the Wells classic or theme. Signet Books capitalized on the Wells tale in 1967 with a collection of illustrated satire entitled The Invisible Mad, the cover depicting an invisible Alfred E. Neuman unwinding his wrappings.

A type of invisible man story, "The Man Without a
Body," was presented on the CBS radio series "Suspense" on
June 22, 1943.   But since the Wells novel was in copyright,
the announcer made it clear to his audience that this tale,
though sharing certain similarities with The Invisible Man,
was not based on that book.   The apparently invisible criminal of the radio play was finally exposed as a quite visible
Nazi spy.

He fared better on television.   During the 1950s a
live presentation of the "The Invisible Man" was presented
on "Matinee Theatre" with some excellent special effects.
Another invisible killer was exposed as a fraud on "New Invisible Man," an episode of the Boris Karloff series "Col.
March of Scotland Yard" (1957).

In 1958 a television series called "The Invisible Man"
was filmed in England.   Though it purported to be based on
the Wells novel, the dull series was about Peter Brady, a
man who (along with his clothing) becomes invisible during a
laboratory experiment and then goes on to use his powers to
fight crime while also attempting to find himself an antidote.
Brady was often seen bandaged à la Claude Rains but was
rarely shown actually removing them.   The special effects
were crude and often unconvincing; Brady was usually entirely invisible, his heroics performed by piano wires.   The
actor who played Brady was never identified.   Producer
Ralph Smart explained it in the publicity.   " To give a name
to the star would be an impossibility.   There are so many
who could receive the credit--the man inside the clothes,
the trick-work specialists, the cameraman, the property men
who work so much of the magic. "

Universal Pictures brought the Invisible Man, or at
least a character calling himself by that name, to television
in May 1975.   The Invisible Man was a feature-length television movie made in color and, according to the credits,
"from the novel by H. G. Wells. "   It was directed by Robert
Michael Lewis.

David McCallum played research scientist Dr. Daniel
Weston who, in attempting to teleport objects with his fantastic laser apparatus, discovers the secret of invisibility.
As the apparatus works on animals, Weston, despite the ob-
jections of his wife Kate (Melinda Fee), experiments on himself with lasting success.   Unlike Griffin and the other Universal invisible men, Weston never dons the traditional head

bandages and wrap-around glasses. Instead he devises a
realistic rubber mask and wig which he slips over his head
to change (as Superman donned street clothes to become
Clark Kent) from Invisible Man to blond-haired Dr. Weston.
The Invisible Man wants to use his secret for the benefit of
mankind. The Pentagon and a band of foreign spies, however, want the secret for their own respective invisible
armies. The benevolent Weston becomes an invisible fugi-
tive, finally destroying his invention rather than use it for
aggression. As The Invisible Man ends, Weston has still
not solved his more personal problem--returning to visibility.

The special effects on the television The Invisible
Man were stunning. Tricks that would have been impossible
during Fulton's day were now performed with ease and in
color. According to the official publicity released by Universal, "For the special effect sequences, the producers
used video tape cameras. One camera would focus on the
set; another camera would film the actors working against a
blue cyclorama. David McCallum was dressed in a blue
body stocking and blue hood. Against this background, a
blue-clad person can be made to appear "Invisible" by utilizing an electronic process. The images recorded by both
cameras were then transposed into one image."

A novel of The Invisible Man, by Michael Jahn, based
on the film, was issued as a Fawcett Gold Medal Book in
1975. The movie itself was a pilot film for an hour-long
series intended to be NBC-TV's prime-time superhero star.
McCallum and Fee continued their roles, investigating (as
did Peter Brady) illegal operations and fighting criminals
week after week. In one amusing episode Weston donned a
rubber Frankenstein Monster mask to infiltrate a gang of
identically disguised bank robbers, surprising them all when
he yanks his mask off to reveal a "headless" man. The
scripts were usually entertaining, especially during the verbal exchanges between the amiable McCallum and Fee. Unfortunately "The Invisible Man" series was scheduled opposite some stiff competition, ABC's extremely popular superhero series "The Six Million Dollar Man." The ratings remained low and, after a very short run interrupted with
numerous preemptions, "The Invisible Man" was canceled.

Undaunted by the show's failure, Universal tried yet
another television movie based on the concept, at first announced as The New Invisible Man but finally reaching the
color video screen on May 10, 1976, as The Gemini Man.

Ben Murphy played Sam Casey, a more macho character than McCallum's cerebral Dr. Weston. Casey, an agent for a secret government security organization called Intersect, is trapped in an underwater explosion. Exposure to radiation during the blast gives him the ability to become invisible at will. The only problem is that he can only remain invisible for fifteen minutes per day; any longer and Casey stays unseen forever. To ensure against this eventuality, computer expert Abby Lawrence (Katherine Crawford) monitors his periods of invisibility while the Gemini Man pops in and out of view at will to thwart a group of foreign agents' attempts to take over America's leading industrial complexes. Unfortunately, despite the technology available to Universal, the special effects were minimal, with none of the imagination of its earlier "Invisible Man" series going into "The Gemini Man."

Again "The Gemini Man" was a pilot film which became an hour-long weekly series for the 1976-77 series. Viewers were apparently not enchanted by either the character or the modicum of visual trickery and "The Gemini Man" was canceled before the first of the new year. Among the merchandised items based on this television series was The Gemini Man (Power Records), an album of dramatized stories.

The Invisible Man also appeared (or disappeared) on such television shows as "The Colgate Comedy Hour," "The Steve Allen Show" (a spoof of the novel and Claude Rains movie), "Shock Theater" (Chicago), "Sinister Cinema," "The Sonny and Cher Comedy Hour," "Happy Days" and "Monster Squad." He also manifested himself in commercials for Scotch Brand Magic Tape, and Hanes underwear (pursued by police, an invisible perpetrator forgets to remove his underwear, they're so comfortable), and in an unreleased commercial for a zipper company with Henry ("Happy Days") Winkler as the Invisible Man.

The 1974 play Frankenstein Slept Here included the Invisible Man in its cast of characters, with the various monsters reacting to his unseen presence. The Invisible Man loses a comedic battle with the Werewolf.

Various comic book companies have published adaptations of H. G. Wells' The Invisible Man. The first such was presented in Superior Stories no. 1 (May-June 1955). It was followed in the 153rd issue of Classics Illustrated

(1959), drawn by Norman Nodel. A Mexican version of the story was published as El hombre invisible in 1968. Writer Ron Goulart and artist Val Mayerik adapted the Wells story to the second issue (February 1973) of Marvel Comics' Supernatural Thrillers. Marvel again tackled The Invisible Man, scripted by Doug Moench and drawn by Dino Castrillo and Rudy Mesina, in Marvel Classics Comics no. 25 (1977). A black-and-white adaptation of The Invisible Man appeared as part of Pendulum Press' Now Age Illustrated paperbacks series, adapted by Otto Binder and drawn by Alex Nino.

"The Invisible Mr. Mann," a spoof by Mike Esposito and Ross Andru, appeared in Marvel's Arrgh! no. 5 (September 1975). A police inspector relentlessly pursues the unseen Mr. Mann. Not even the army can stop the criminal and soon it appears as if he will dominate the world. But he surrenders to escape the nagging of his invisible wife. A variation on The Invisible Man was "The Man Who Lost Face," by this writer, in Charlton's Ghost Manor no. 29 (June 1976). This time, however, the bandaged man who arrives at an inn during a snowstorm is actually trying to conceal the fact that his face is a fleshy blank. "The Invisible Man ... or ... What Ever Did His Wife See in Him?" was a spoof published in Quasimodo's Monster Magazine vol. 2, no. 8 (May 1976), with script by Joe Kiernan and art by Norman Nodel. The Invisible Man becomes such in order to go on a robbing spree so that he and his family can live in luxury. He gets shot by the police while robbing a bank and carrying away a huge (and unfortunately visible) sack of money.

A dramatic adaptation of The Invisible Man was issued on an album of the same name by Adventure Records in the early 1960s. Listening Library released its own album of The Invisible Man in 1977 which was a reading by Patrick Horgan of an abridgment of the actual H. G. Wells story. The unseen character was also present in a number of recorded songs, such as "Poisen to Poisen" and "Monster Movie Ball" on the Spike Jones in Hi-Fi (... in Stereo) album. "(I'm in Love with) The Invisible Man" was a song recorded by Hans Conried and Alice Pearce on the album Monster Rally (RCA Victor). The Invisible Man was also incorporated into the lyrics of "Science Fiction/Double Feature" from the musical The Rocky Horror Show (1974; made into a 1975 Twentieth Century-Fox film, The Rocky Horror Picture Show) issued on two albums--the British performance on UK Records and the American on A&M Records.

While the Invisible Man was a fiend created in the laboratory, other horrors were born in the dankness of the tomb. One of these, like Griffin, began as a normal human being. But it required premature burial and the curse of Egyptian gods to produce the Mummy.

IV

THE CURSE OF THE MUMMY

The year is 1921 and a phenomenal discovery is made
within the Egyptian sands. Sir Joseph Whemple (Arthur Byron), an Egyptologist named Dr. Muller (Edward Van Sloan),
and a young assistant named Norton (Bramwell Fletcher)
stand within a heretofore unknown tomb, dominated by a
3700-year-old mummy case. Near the mummy case is an
ancient golden box.

Within the casket is the tall, withered figure of a
mummy, its head lying to one side (an intimation that it had
moved within the confines of the case). The absence of the
tell-tale scar of the embalmer indicates that this man, Im-
ho-tep, was condemned to suffer not only in this life but in
the afterlife as well. For some unknown but grievous crime
Im-ho-tep had been buried alive.

Dr. Muller warns his colleagues not to open the mysterious golden box. The box bears the curse of Pharoah
Amenophis: 'Death! Eternal punishment for anyone who
opens this casket. In the name of Amon Ra, King of the
Gods. " Muller believes in the ancient gods and curses of
Egypt. He fears that the box contains the legendary Scroll
of Thoth which allegedly bears the arcane spell by which
Isis, goddess of fertility, raised Osiris, king of the netherworld, from the dead.

Later, Norton is alone in the chamber with the mummy and scroll. Unable to accept the superstitious beliefs of
his superior, he opens the box and indeed finds that it contains the Scroll of Thoth (named after the ibis-headed scribe
of the gods). Almost silently, Norton pronounces the forbidden words: "Oh! Amon-Ra--Oh! God of Gods--Death is
but the doorway to new life--We live today--We shall live
again--In many forms shall we return--Oh, mighty one. "

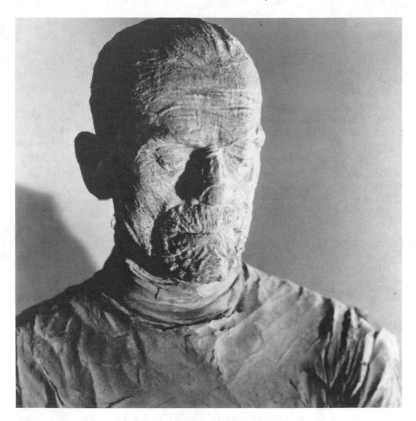

Im-ho-tep (Boris Karloff) before returning to life through the
power of the Scroll of Thoth, in The Mummy (Universal,
1932).

    One glassy eye of the mummy of Im-ho-tep slowly
opens.   Then the bandaged hands begin to move, freed by
the mystic words of their bonds of centuries.

    Norton continues to read the hieroglyphics on the
Scroll as a mummified hand wearing an ornate Egyptian ring
soundlessly touches the parchment.   The scientist's head
snaps around, his eyes suddenly registering horror followed
by madness.   Then Norton begins to laugh maniacally, watching as two strips of gray gauze trail out the door.

    When Whemple and Muller finally come upon Norton
he is babbling, "He went for a little walk!   You should have

seen the look on his face!"   Both the mummy and the Scroll
of Thoth are gone.

   This opening scene from The Mummy, a classic made
by Universal Pictures in 1932, remains one of the finest moments of screen terror in the history of motion pictures.
Boris Karloff, now imposingly billed by Universal as simply
"Karloff," enacted the role of the mummified Im-ho-tep with
no movement other than the almost imperceptible raising of
an eyelid and the stiff lowering and reaching of mold-encrusted
hands.   Most of the horror which Norton beholds is created
offscreen and within the audience's imagination.   What director Karl Freund did not show on the screen triumphs over
the graphically horrific scenes of mummies returning to life
which would flood the screen in later years.

   Karl Freund was primarily a cinematographer; his
work with the camera was manifested in such German masterpieces as Metropolis and The Last Laugh.   One year before The Mummy, Freund created the atmospheric visuals of
Universal's Dracula.   In The Mummy the German made his
directorial debut, maintaining full control of the camera and
creating a fluidity unfortunately absent in the static Dracula.

   The Mummy is, in fact, a veritable remake of Dracula as we shall see.   But its origins lay a full decade before
Freund or any of the Universal executives thought of trying
to repeat the success of the classic vampire melodrama
which had starred Bela Lugosi.   Actually The Mummy was
originally intended to capitalize upon the story that had dominated the newspapers in the latter part of 1922--the discovery of the tomb of the 18-year-old Pharaoh, Tutankhamen,
or, as he is more commonly known, King Tut.

   Tutankhamen (who flourished about 1360 B.C.) was a
king of Egypt's Eighteenth Dynasty.   His queen was named
Ankhesenamon.   Howard Carter and Lord Carnarvon discovered the tomb with its priceless collection of Egyptian
artifacts and, lying inside a coffin of gold, the mummy of
Tutankhamen.   Soon after the opening of the tomb, a series
of mysterious deaths befell some twenty persons associated
with the opening of the tomb or the subsequent examination
of the mummy.   Archaeologists attributed these deaths to
sheer coincidence but the press fed a gullible public stories
that these were the victims of an Egyptian curse.   As most
of these deaths occurred during the 1930s, the atmosphere
was conducive to a film entitled The Mummy.

In 1931, Boris Karloff assumed the position of top
horror star at Universal with his portrayal of the Monster
in Frankenstein. He was the logical choice to play the
centuries-old horror in The Mummy. The first conception
of the story was quite unlike that which finally was enacted
before the camera. Karloff was to play an Egyptian magician, the title character of "Cagliostro," a story by Nina
Wilcox Putnam and later expanded into a screen treatment
by Richard Schayer.

Cagliostro was to have been about an Egyptian who
survives the passing of centuries by injecting himself with
nitrates. The magician destroys everyone who resembles
the woman who betrayed him, finally using such modern
methods as radio and television rays. Yet this was not
really in accordance with the Tutankhamen case. After going through a number of title changes, including The King
of the Dead and Im-Ho-Tep, the script became a strictly
supernatural tale entitled The Mummy, written by John L.
Balderston who had adapted the play Dracula to the screen.

Balderston renamed the seemingly eternal Egyptian
"Im-ho-tep" (after the historical figure Imhotep, who served
under the Pharaoh Zoser as high priest, proverb writer,
architect and physician). He also borrowed the name of
Ankh-es-en-amon from King Tut's queen and transformed
her into Im-ho-tep's lover. But the basic story was a veritable remake of Dracula. Stripped of the pseudo-science of
Cagliostro, the story, like Dracula, pits a seemingly immortal fiend with supernatural powers against a group of
mortals as he attempts to claim a young woman as his own.
Only the efforts of an occult specialist (along with the forces
of Good) eventually bring about the monster's demise. Director Freund even imitated Dracula in casting The Mummy,
bringing back David Manners to assume the role of the young
and ineffectual leading man and Edward Van Sloan, as Dr.
Muller, to recreate his role of vampire hunter Dr. Van
Helsing.

Karloff's metamorphosis from kindly Englishman to a
bandage-swarthed, 3700-year-old mummy required eight
hours of sitting in the make-up chair of Jack Pierce, Universal's resident master of disguise. Pierce based his
mummy make-up upon photographs of the remains of Prince
Seti I of Egypt, which he secured from the museum in Cairo.
The make-up genius perfected a method for "aging" an act-
or's skin, which was certainly necessary for Karloff as

Im-ho-tep.   Pierce stretched his subject's skin and applied
a strip of cotton dipped in collodion, which simulated a
wrinkle after the skin relaxed.   He then brushed a layer of
Fuller's earth over the face, which gave a dry appearance
to the make-up.   Pierce considered this make-up to be his
finest creation.

After the opening sequence of The Mummy, the story
skips ahead in time ten years.   Frank Whemple (David Manners), son of Sir Joseph, has failed in his attempt to uncover an ancient Egyptian tomb.   Then, a mysterious character named Ardath Bey (Karloff) reveals the tomb of Ankh-
es-en-amon, vestal virgin to the goddess Isis.   Ardath Bey
is a gaunt figure with a dry, lined face not unlike that of a
mummy.   He wears a simple tunic and his head is topped
by a fez.   Mysteriously, he will not shake hands.   "I dislike to be touched--an Eastern prejudice."

The remains of the Princess are placed on exhibit at
the Cairo museum, where Joseph Whemple is now curator.
Ardath Bey secretly remains in the museum after closing
time and, using the Scroll of Thoth, attempts to restore
Ankh-es-en-amon to life.   At a dance elsewhere, Helen
Grosvenor (Zita Johann), an attractive woman of Egyptian
descent who is being treated by Dr. Muller for her strange
attraction to the past, leaves and tries to gain entrance to
the museum.   Sir Joseph hears her uttering the name of
Im-ho-tep and speaking a language unheard for over two
thousand years.   A museum guard who interrupts Ardath
Bey's ritual is in the morning discovered to be dead from
shock with the Scroll clutched in one hand.

Helen and Frank become romantically attracted to one
another while Dr. Muller and Sir Joseph discuss the events
that have occurred.   It is Muller's belief that the mummy
of Im-ho-tep was never stolen from its tomb and that he
and Ardath Bey are the same person, brought to life by the
Scroll of Thoth.   Presently Dr. Muller confronts Ardath Bey
with his suspicion, showing him a photograph of Im-ho-tep's
mummy.   They face each other, like Van Helsing and Count
Dracula, enemies to the last.   Ardath Bey raises his ring;
as a light gleams from the ancient jewel, Sir Joseph falls
unconscious.   When Muller threatens to destroy the Scroll if
harm befalls his friends, Ardath Bey grudgingly departs.

Later, as Sir Joseph attempts to burn the Scroll in
his fireplace, Ardath Bey observes the scene in a pool of

The reincarnation of the dead vestal virgin Ankh-es-en-amon (Zita Johann) and Ardath Bey (Boris Karloff) in The Mummy (Universal, 1932).

bubbling, mystic waters.   Uttering an arcane curse, reaching toward the liquid with a clutching, emaciated hand, the revived mummy kills Sir Joseph from a distance, after which his Nubian slave (played by Noble Johnson) retrieves the ancient parchment.

These scenes of Ardath Bey performing his magic before the pool are still chilling even to today's more jaded audiences.   Karl Freund repeated something he had pioneered in Dracula, but with considerable improvement.   Two baby spotlights were focused to illuminate Karloff's eyes while the rest of his face remained in more subdued illumination.   The effect is stunningly terrifying as Ardath Bey's eyes open with unholy light.

Again Ardath Bey summons the entranced Helen, this time to his own quarters where he reveals a scene of 3700 years ago within the heated waters of the pool. Helen observes as a mortal priest named Im-ho-tep grieves over the death of Ankh-es-en-amon. In order to revive the corpse of the beautiful daughter of the Pharaoh, Im-ho-tep dares the wrath of the gods and steals the forbidden Scroll of Thoth. The priest is discovered performing the unholy act of attempting to raise the dead and is condemned by Pharaoh to a most egregious death--burial alive. The slaves that bury his coffin are slain, and then the soldiers that killed those slaves are put to death, so that no one will know the location of Im-ho-tep's tomb. (These scenes from The Mummy, with new shots of Tom Tyler spliced into the Karloff footage, were incorporated into Universal's later films The Mummy's Hand and The Mummy's Ghost.)

Helen is now aware of the truth. She is the living reincarnation of Ankh-es-en-amon whose spirit has transcended death and time and inhabited numerous bodies for nearly four thousand years. Originally scenes were filmed actually depicting Zita Johann in her subsequent incarnations, which included an early Christian, a princess of medieval times, a Viking and a French noblewoman. In each instance her previous lives ended through violence.

Despite Dr. Muller's giving Frank an amulet with the likeness of the goddess Isis, which has powers to ward off Im-ho-tep (as the crucifix has power over the vampire), Helen is entranced a final time and lured to the museum. There, dressed in the garb she wore in her first existence, Helen gazes at the mummy of Ankh-es-en-amon--their faces are identical. Now she learns what is to be her grisly fate. Helen will become the immortal bride of Im-ho-tep/Ardath Bey. But to do so she must suffer a final violent death. The Nubian is already preparing the materials for her mummification!

Im-ho-tep raises the sacrificial knife. There is a brief interruption when Dr. Muller and Frank arrive. But they are powerless in the light of the living mummy's ring. Finally Helen/Ankh-es-en-amon herself pleads to the statue of Isis for life. Yes, she is Ankh-es-en-amon, but she is also the living Helen. Isis hears the pleas of the woman who was once her vestal virgin. Stiffly the stone hand of Isis rises, clutching an ankh which suddenly flares with supernatural brilliance. The Scroll of Thoth bursts afire and Im-ho-tep decomposes to a pile of scattered bones.

The Mummy is one of the few masterpieces of the
horror film. While other films of the genre relied on grotesque faces and shock elements, Freund's excursion into
terror is a mood piece, with Karloff's performance dominating throughout. Karloff underplayed his role of the living
mummy, moving slowly, stiffly, even speaking as if his lips
and tongue were restricted by centuries of entombment.

Karloff's next film, his first to be made in his native
England, was also of an Egyptian/living corpse motif. The
Ghoul was made by Guam in 1933 and released the next year.
Based on The Ghoul, a novel by Frank King and Leonard
Hines, the film was directed with brooding atmosphere by
T. Hayes Hunter. Karloff played Professor Morlant, an
antiquarian who believes he can achieve immortality via
"The Eternal Light," a jewel stolen from an Egyptian tomb.
Morlant must follow a prescribed ritual, being buried in a
reproduction of an Egyptian tomb with the jewel in his hand.
When his servant Laing (Ernest Thesiger) steals the jewel
instead, Morlant, his face not unlike that of Ardath Bey,
returns from the tomb to seek revenge. (The Ghoul was
remade in 1961 as a black comedy by New World and released a year later in England as What a Carve-Up! and in
the United States as No Place Like Homicide.)

A bit of the soundtrack from The Mummy was in-
cluded on the record album An Evening with Boris Karloff
and His Friends. Earlier, Universal authorized Dell Publishing Company to issue a comic book titled The Mummy
(September-November 1962). Very loosely based on the
Karloff film, the story features an Egyptian sorcerer named
Ahmed who gains his powers from the evil god Seth. When
Ahmed levitates an entire pyramid and consequently dese-
crates a royal tomb, he is buried alive for punishment.
Freed centuries later, Ahmed uses his hypnotic eyes to entrance his victims and to blast through the handcuffs that
eventually bind him. Finally the mummy falls from the
summit of a pyramid, leaving only wrappings and a chilling
laugh, along with the promise of a sequel. But Dell's only
followup was a reprint issue including another of their authorized editions, Universal Pictures Presents Dracula, The
Mummy plus Other Stories.

A concise, faithful comic strip adaptation of The
Mummy by Russ Jones and Wallace Wood was published in
the first issue of Warren Publishing Company's Monster
World (November 1964) magazine. A comic strip recreation

of Im-ho-tep's return from the dead was presented with little accuracy (e.g., wall hieroglyphics were substituted for the Scroll of Thoth, and on-screen violence for off-stage mood) as "Scream Screen Scene: The Mummy" in the thirteenth issue of Skywald Publishing Corporation's Psycho (July 1973).

Im-ho-tep had been reborn in The Mummy only to suffer a second and final death. But Universal Pictures would not let the character rest in eternal peace. Almost a decade later he would be, in a fashion, reborn once again. Yet the mummy's presentation, as well as his name, would be different.

KHARIS AND THE TANA LEAVES

Another cycle of horror films dawned in the early 1940s. Unlike the often slowly-paced movies of the previous decade, the new crop consisted of thrillers, emphasizing action and stalking, mute or brainless monstrosities rather than such quietly terrifying fiends as Ardath Bey. Frankenstein's Monster and Count Dracula were no longer scaring adult audiences but were prompting hordes of younger viewers to devour box upon box of popcorn. It was an era of blaring musical scores, chases and monsters carrying off girls in white gowns. In just such an atmosphere, Prince Kharis lumbered from his dank Egyptian sarcophagus to haunt the sound stages of Universal Pictures.

Unlike Im-ho-tep, Kharis was merely a bandaged, shambling monster, never once shedding his moldy wrappings or uttering a single word (having no tongue). He was Universal's latest addition to the studio's pantheon of horrors dominated by Frankenstein's Monster, Dracula and the Wolf Man. It was the Kharis image that materialized in people's imaginations whenever the "Mummy" was mentioned during the Forties, an image which persists to this day. The Kharis films are not classics like the original Mummy but provided more than enough entertainment considering their "B" movie budgets.

Kharis first appeared in a 1940 Universal film entitled The Mummy's Hand, directed by Christy Cabanne. He was portrayed in this film by Tom Tyler, an actor primarily known for his performances in Westerns and serials. Selected because of his resemblance to Karloff, Tyler could somewhat match the shots from The Mummy which would be

incorporated into The Mummy's Hand. Make-up artist Jack
Pierce designed a special rubber mask which sufficed in the
long shots. In order to save time and money, Pierce only
made-up Tyler's face once so that all the close-ups could be
photographed in a single day.

The Mummy's Hand brings an expedition consisting of
Steve Banning (played by another Western star, Dick Foran),
his partner Babe Jenson (Wallace Ford), a pretty young lady
named Marta (Peggy Moran) and her father, a stage magician called Solvani (Cecil Kellaway) in search of an Egyptian
princess named Ananka.

Throughout the centuries a fanatical group called the
High Priests of Karnak have kept alive the Mummy Kharis
to protect the tomb of Princess Ananka against violators.
In a secret tomb the ancient high priest (played by Eduardo
Cianelli) reveals the story of Kharis to his disciple and suc-
cessor Andoheb (George Zucco).

Once again we observe a tale of forbidden love.
Kharis can only watch as his beloved Princess Ananka
perishes. In order to restore her to life, Prince Kharis
stole, not the Scroll of Thoth, but rather a new device invented by the film's writers. Now the power to resuscitate
the dead existed in the forbidden tana leaves. For his
grave sin, Kharis' tongue was cut out so that "the ears of
the gods would not be assailed by his unholy curses" (and
also to establish the Mummy as a silent menace similar to
the 1940s image of the Frankenstein Monster). Kharis was
then buried alive, with the slaves and soldiers suffering the
same fate as those who had entombed Im-ho-tep.

Andoheb is informed that Kharis never really died
and that he has a mission involving The Mummy and the tana
leaves. "Three of the leaves will make enough fluid to keep
Kharis' heart beating," the High Priest tells him. "Once
each night, during the cycle of the full moon, you will dissolve three tana leaves and give the fluid to Kharis....
Should unbelievers seek to desecrate the tomb of Ananka,
you will use nine tana leaves each night, to give life and
movement to Kharis. Thus, you will enable him to bring
vengeance on the heads of those who try to enter.... But
never, for any reason, must you brew more than nine leaves
at one time. Should Kharis obtain a large amount of the
fluid, he would become an uncontrollable monster--a soulless
demon with the desire to kill ... and kill!"

Western movie star Tom Tyler, here carrying Peggy Moran, introduced Prince Kharis to the screen in The Mummy's Hand (Universal, 1940).

There is, unfortunately, an overabundance of comic relief footage in The Mummy's Hand, particularly scenes involving Solvani and Babe Jenson. But once the actual horror of the story begins the film is rather satisfying. Again recalling the rumored curse of King Tutankhamen, the motion picture further establishes the basic theme of virtually all mummy films to follow--that all who desecrate the tombs of the Egyptian dead must perish.

Instead of finding Ananka, the Banning expedition discovers the remains of Kharis. Andoheb reveals to another scientist named Petrie (played by Charles Trowbridge) that Kharis is still alive. Then, feeding him the tana leaf fluid, he has the Mummy strangle the scientist.

Powered by the fluid of nine tana leaves, Kharis performs the murderous tasks commanded by Andoheb. It is Andoheb's intention to destroy every member of the Banning expedition with the exception of Marta. Even a man like Andoheb is capable of love. Now he intends to make both himself and Marta immortal via the mystic fluid.

Kharis stalks through the night, kidnapping Marta from her tent and bringing her to Ananka's hidden tomb at a temple in the Hills of the Seven Jackals. (The temple was built for an earlier Universal film Green Hell.) Before Andoheb can feed Marta the tana leaf fluid, he is shot by Babe outside the temple and falls down the stone steps apparently to his death. Steve enters the temple by a secret tunnel and discovers Kharis stalking toward the bound Marta. Heroically, Steve breaks the cup of tana fluid on the floor, then futiley tries to stop the Mummy with bullets. Kharis is unaffected, casting the scientist aside effortlessly. When Kharis drops to the floor and attempts to scoop up the fluid he needs to remain alive, Babe enters and sets him ablaze with a fiery urn. Kharis, the living Mummy, becomes an inhuman torch to apparently die forever.

By 1940, Universal Pictures was well known for its horror films sequels. Surely the Mummy's spectacular death was no more permanent than the various destructions suffered by Dracula and the Frankenstein Monster. A sequel was inevitable and in 1942 The Mummy's Tomb, directed by Harold Young, was in theatrical release.

Tom Tyler did not return in the yellow-gray wrappings of Kharis. The previous year Lon Chaney, Jr., had

become a star at Universal with his portrayal of Lawrence Talbot the werewolf in The Wolf Man. Universal was grooming the actor as an upper echelon horror films star and as a successor to his father, the celebrated "Man of a Thousand Faces. " The role of Kharis would add yet another character face to Chaney's credits. Also, like Tyler, his tall, husky physique fit well into the Mummy costume.

The Mummy's Tomb opens in Mapleton, Massachusetts, with an aged Steve Banning and Babe Jenson (again played respectively by Foran and Ford) relating to Steve's sister Jane, his son John (John Hubbard) and John's girlfriend Isobel (Elyse Knox) their experiences with Kharis (stock shots from The Mummy and The Mummy's Hand).

In Egypt, the tale is also being related by an old yet still living Andoheb to his new high priest, Mehemet Bey (Turhan Bey). Sheltered within this arcane temple is the body of Kharis. "The bullets fired into me only crushed my arm, " explains the white-haired Andoheb. "And the fire merely crippled and maimed Kharis. Kharis still lives!" Andoheb passes on the tradition to his young successor who swears to use Kharis to kill the desecrators of Ananka's tomb. Shortly afterwards, Andoheb (apparently) dies.

Though alive, Kharis suffers from his ordeal with the fire. One eye is now permanently shut. Except during scenes where he is required to carry off actress Elyse Knox (aided by a brace concealed under his bandages) he has but one good arm. When he walks Kharis must drag behind him a damaged leg. If emoting in the Mummy role was difficult enough for Tyler, Chaney found himself even more severely restricted, his face hidden behind a Pierce mask.

"I didn't like that part at all, " Chaney told writer Ron Haydock during the mid-1960s. "There wasn't anything you could do with the Mummy. You just got into the make-up and bandages and walked around dragging your leg. I liked playing the Wolf Man a lot better, and making those Inner Sanctum films. You had a chance to do some acting, and you had dialogue. All they ever wanted the Mummy to do was put his hand way out in front of him and then grab somebody, and start strangling him. " Of the Karloff Mummy,

Opposite: Lon Chaney, Jr. , assumed the Kharis role in The Mummy's Tomb (Universal, 1942), shown here with Turhan Bey and Elyse Knox.

Chaney told Haydock, "That was a real fine picture. He
wasn't a Mummy all the time either. He played an old
Egyptian too. But when they gave me the role, it was all
changed around. I didn't want to do the part, but I was
under contract, so I did what they gave me" ["The Mummy
Chronicles," Monsters of the Movies no. 6 (April 1975),
pp. 9-10].

Fortunately for Chaney, most of his long shots and
scenes requiring more strenuous feats were performed by
stuntman Eddie Parker. Wearing the mask created by Jack
Pierce, he is almost indistinguishable from Chaney. Parker
continued to double for Chaney as Kharis through the duration of the Mummy series.

In Mapleton, Mehemet Bey assumes the position of
cemetery caretaker and secretly harbors the living Kharis.
Soon the obedient Mummy climbs the arbor to the second
story of the Banning home, choking Steve in his unbreakable
grip. Next Kharis survives the blasts of a caretaker's shotgun as he proceeds to kill Jane Banning. Babe realizes
that the murders were caused by Kharis but, naturally, no
one believes him. Babe's only reward for his knowledge is
being pursued down an alley by the very creature he knows
to exist and being strangled with the monster's good hand.

Mehemet Bey, like his predecessor Andoheb, becomes
smitten by beauty. His next mission for Kharis is sacri-
legious. The Mummy is to bring him the lovely Isobel alive
to become his bride. Kharis grudgingly obeys, bringing Isobel back to the graveyard. John Banning arrives there after
being alerted by an elderly man who had spoken with the
suave Egyptian. Defensively, Banning shoots Mehemet Bey
to death as the Mummy, still carrying Isobel, is pursued by
torch-bearing townspeople (some of which came courtesy of
stock scenes from Universal's Frankenstein, European costumes included) toward the Banning home.

The climax of The Mummy's Tomb was the most
spectacular of all the Kharis films. Kharis flees into the
Banning home as John charges inside to meet him, armed
only with a crackling torch. The Mummy sets Isobel down
to confront the young Banning, but is soon trapped on the
porch of a blazing inferno. John and Isobel watch along
with the satisfied townspeople as Kharis succumbs to the
flames and the crumbling mansion.

The Mummy's Tomb was more of an action film than its predecessor and avoided the unnecessary comedic sequences. Unfortunately differences in the Tyler and Chaney Mummies were obvious with the inclusion of the flashback scenes. Except for the exciting ending of Tomb the film offered nothing that had not already been presented in Hand. Not until the third film in the series The Mummy's Ghost, directed by Reginald Le Borg in 1943 and released in 1944, would Kharis enjoy a story all his own with a climax displaying some originality on the part of writer Griffin Jay (who also wrote the screenplays to both Hand and Tomb). For these reasons, including the fact that some scenes in Ghost are beautifully atmospheric, this third Kharis offering remains, in this writer's opinion, the best of the series.

The Mummy's Ghost opens in Egypt where we learn, once again, that old durable Andoheb (Zucco) has more stamina than most men his age. Having already "died" twice, he is now about to die again. First, however, he must pass on the legend and legacy of Kharis (via the familiar stock footage) to his latest successor, the gaunt Youssef Bey (John Carradine). Inconsistent with the previous entries of the series, The Mummy's Ghost labels the secret Kharis sect as the Priests of Arkhon. After Youssef swears the familiar oath, Andoheb once again submits to a well-timed death.

In Mapleton, Professor Norman, a college teacher of Egyptology, has been experimenting with the tana leaves associated with the living Mummy Kharis who once terrorized the area. Deciphering the meaning of some ancient hieroglyphics, Norman brews nine tana leaves. Attracted by the brew, Kharis (with no explanation as to how he survived the earlier fire unscathed) lumbers out of the forest, chokes the professor and consumes the magical fluid. The following day Norman's corpse is discovered with mold on the throat. By this time there are few skeptics, for the newspaper headline bleats: "Mummy believed to be back in New England!"

Kharis is summoned by Youssef Bey who is performing an Egyptian spell. En route to his newest master, the Mummy passes Tom Herbie (Robert Lowery), one of Norman's students, and his beautiful Egyptian fiancée Amina Mansori (Ramsay Ames) who are kissing in a parked car. Amina has strange longings for Egypt (as did the heroine of The Mummy over a decade earlier) and when the Mummy's shadow crosses her in the car she experiences a weird sensation.

Youssef Bey (John Carradine) gives the Mummy (Lon Chaney, Jr.) the fluid made from life-sustaining tana leaves in The Mummy's Ghost (Universal, 1944).

The mummy of Princess Ananka, Kharis' lost and forbidden love, now reposes on exhibit at the Scripps Museum. After midnight, Youssef Bey reveals Ananka's bandaged remains to a love-struck Kharis. But as the Mummy bends over to touch the lifeless woman, her preserved body crumbles to dust and a pile of tattered bandages. Simultaneously, Amina awakens from her sleep screaming. Ananka's spirit has fled her original body to seek a new and living host.

The possessed Amina begins to change. Her luxurious black hair is now marred by a shock of silver. And

she refuses to marry Tom. Presently, in a beautifully atmospheric sequence, Kharis silently stalks from the woods
to pause outside Amina's house. Rising from her bed like
a zombie, Amina, clad in a form-fitting evening gown of
white satin, walks outside to meet her unaging lover only to
collapse before his hideous presence. Then Kharis bears
her to the shack where Youssef waits to perform the sacred
rites.

Youssef Bey prepares the hypodermic needle of tana
fluid which will mummify Amina, the reincarnation of Ananka,
and make her the bride of Kharis. Already her hair has
completely turned to silver. But, like his predecessors,
Youssef Bey commits the cardinal sin and decides to make
the woman his bride instead. Realizing his master's perfidy,
Kharis stalks Youssef Bey and dashes him to his death.

The ending of The Mummy's Ghost diverges from the
other myriad horror films made at Universal, wherein the
monster is subjected to a spectacular form of destruction
while the hero and heroine survive to enjoy a life of nuptial
bliss. In Ghost, quite contrarily, it is Kharis and his bride
who enact that role. Pursued by the obligatory townspeople,
Kharis carries his reincarnated lover into the swamp. With
his every step her skin continues to age, the centuries of
death affecting her host body within minutes. Finally Kharis
sinks beneath the murky waters of the swamp. The last
view we have of Amina/Ananka is the withered face (a remarkable make-up by Pierce) of a mummified corpse which
promptly vanishes below the water's surface.

The last film of the Kharis series The Mummy's
Curse was the least distinguished of them all. It was also
the shortest (a fast-paced 62 minutes). Directed by Leslie
Goodwins, Curse went into production the same year that
Ghost was in its initial release and was booked into theatres
in 1945. Either writers Bernard Schubert, Dwight V. Babcock and Leon Abrams had not seen the earlier Kharis films
or else they felt that continuity was not important. But
audiences familiar with the Kharis legend noted significant
discrepancies between The Mummy's Ghost and The Mummy's
Curse.

The location of the swamp into which Kharis and his
bride had disappeared was suddenly and inexplicably the
Louisiana bayou! Furthermore, it is explained in the movie
that it was twenty-five years ago that the Mummy vanished

Kharis (Lon Chaney, Jr.), seizes a victim (Kurt Katch) in his superhuman grip in the last official film of the series, The Mummy's Curse (Universal, 1945).

---

into the swamp. (Considering all the Kharis films were made within a span of four years, beginning with The Mummy's Hand, we might wonder as to the fate of more than four decades. While obviously set about the same time as Hand, The Mummy's Tomb presents the members of the Banning expedition as more than twenty years older. Now we learn that The Mummy's Ghost events actually occurred a quarter century before those of Curse. By all logic, then, The Mummy's Curse should have been set in the future world of the middle or late 1980s!)

    In Curse an excavation of the dried-up swamp is underway. Dr. James Halsey (Dennis Moore) of the Scripps

Museum hopes that the digging will uncover the mummies of
both Kharis and Ananka. But Kharis rises from the ground
under his own power, leaving behind only the imprint of a
sizable human body and a bit torn off the centuries-old ban-
dage. Soon the Mummy lies in an Egyptian sarcophagus in
an abandoned monastery near the swamp. Tending to Kharis
is an Egyptian associate of Halsey, Ilzor Zandaab (Peter
Coe) and one of the project workmen, Ragheb (Martin Kosleck). Both Zandaab and Ragheb are priests of Arkhon whose
assignment it is to return the mummies to Egypt.

There is no longer any distinction between Ananka and
her modern-day counterpart. As the earth is being moved,
the withered form of Ananka (Virginia Christine) is revived
by the sun's rays which also restore all of her former
beauty. Soon, dressed in white, the striking beauty is
roaming the swamp, calling out the name of Kharis.

Zandaab deduces that the strange woman is really
Ananka and sends Kharis after her. The Mummy enters the
back room of the cafe where Ananka has been sheltered.
Seeing the horrible form of Kharis standing by her bed, she
flees from the building. The princess is discovered by Halsey and his assistant Betty Walsh (Kay Harding) who take
her to their camp in the swamp. That night Kharis enters
the camp and carries off Ananka who has fainted from the
sight of him. Back at the monastery, the Mummy places
the unconscious Ananka in a waiting sarcophagus.

Meanwhile, Ragheb, who is secretly in love with
Betty, lures her to the monastery. High Priest Zandaab
curses him for bringing the nonbeliever here but Ragheb
shoves a knife into his back. Halsey makes a timely entrance after which Ragheb knocks him to the floor. Suddenly Kharis is in the room and stalking the traitorous priest
into a cell room of the monastery. Ragheb locks the cell
door and threatens that if he perishes the secret of the tana
leaves will also die. Unaffected, the Mummy smashes
through the door, at the same time bringing the monastery
down upon both of them. Presently the shriveled corpse of
Ananka is found inside her coffin.

Chaney disliked The Mummy's Curse more than any
other film in the series. "... I was completely covered
from head to foot with a suit and rubber mask; the only
thing that was exposed was my right [sic] eye! In the last of
that series, the temperature was in the upper nineties! It

was so hot that I went to my dressing room between scenes,
opened a refrigerator and lay down next to it.   It was my
only relief from the heat" ["An Interview with Lon Chaney,
Jr. , " Castle of Frankenstein no. 10 (February 1966), p. 26].

Indeed Ragheb's words at the end of Thc Mummy's
Curse were prophetic.   No one ever again brewed the sacred
tana leaves to bring Kharis stalking through the night to slay
the violators of his beloved's tomb.   By the second film of
the series Kharis' adventures had become repetitious.   It
was miraculous that the Mummy managed to survive the
same plot situations and character motivations through a
total of four movies.

The character of Kharis was simply too limited to
cast him in fresh or original stories.   Unlike Dracula and
the Wolf Man, he was neither cunning nor tragically heroic.
He simply lumbered about the countryside dragging his bad
leg, moving at a cripple's pace.   Somehow he always managed to overtake and strangle his victims, who either blun-
dered into some cul-de-sac or stood in one spot shivering
with fear as the Mummy casually reached out and strangled
them.   The Mummy's Curse terminated the cycle rather
than rehash his story through yet another mundane adventure.   Kharis and the woman he sought through a quartet of
thrillers had finally been reunited in the afterlife.   (Scenes
from The Mummy, The Mummy's Tomb and The Mummy's
Curse later appeared in Rendezvous (1973); and a clip from
The Mummy also appeared in Revenge of Rendezvous (1975).)

Though the Kharis series was no longer in production, the career of the famed Egyptian Mummy was just beginning.   In Kharis, Universal Pictures had created an original character (albeit based upon the earlier Im-ho-tep of
The Mummy), one not rooted in folklore like the Wolf Man
or spawned from literature as was the Frankenstein Monster.
The Mummy Kharis, like the later Creature of Black Lagoon
fame, would transcend its position of utility film monster to
become a popular culture myth.   His image established the
standard; most film mummies to follow would be indebted to
Prince Kharis.

Like the Wolf Man and other Universal horrors,
Kharis would appear for decades in wax museum exhibits,
live horror shows, personal appearances and in the usual
flood of merchandise.

An actor portraying Kharis (wearing a Don Post custom mask) was hunted along with Dracula and the Frankenstein Monster in the 1968 Italian film Isabell, A Dream,
made by Luigi Cozzi. These scenes were later incorporated
into the same filmmaker's 1970 production Tunnel Under the
World. (And scenes from Tunnel Under the World later appeared in Il vicino di casa [released in the United States as
The Man Upstairs], a Cozzi film of the early 1970s.) Another Kharis shuffled through Chabelo y Pepito contra los
monstruos (1973). We might suppose that all living mummies
that appeared in films alongside such Universal stalwarts as
Frankenstein's Monster and Dracula were intended to represent Kharis. Such pictures include the Egyptian comedy
Haram Alek (1953); Kiss Me Quick (also known as Dr. Breedlove), a 1966 nudie made by Russ Meyer's Fantasy Films,
in which a mad doctor creates the Mummy, Frankenstein's
Monster and Dracula; Mad Monster Party? (1966) and its
television sequel "Mad, Mad, Mad Monsters" (1972); and Son
of Dracula (1973).

The Mummy has also stalked through some of the
movies made by amateur filmmakers. Frankenstein Meets
the Mummy was a 1961 production by Steve B. Kaplan. An
ambitious amateur movie entitled I Was a Teenage Mummy
was made in 1963 by Ralph C. Bluemke. The film featured
Michael Harris as the Mummy, Allen Skinner as Professor
Pietri and Scott Mullin ("8 yrs. and 52 lbs. of sheer terror")
as a diminutive Youssef Bey. Based on characters in the
Universal Kharis films, the story brought Youssef Bey and
the Mummy to the United States courtesy of TWA.

The play I'm Sorry, The Bridge Is Out, You'll Have
to Spend the Night (1970) included the Mummy (Peter Soul)
and High Priest Dr. Nasser (Greg Aveco) who intend to sacrifice the innocent heroine to the deity Amon-Ra. In one of
the play's funnier scenes the Mummy and Frankenstein Monster try to communicate with each other by grunts and stiff
gyrations, bridging the centuries-old generation gap by slipping into a rock dance. Learning that Dr. Frankenstein intends to use the girl in an experiment instead of the sacrifice, the Mummy eliminates the other classic monsters in
the play until they all return to life during the finale.

In 1974 the Mummy appeared as a little girl's best
friend in the play Thursday Meets the Wolfman; the next
year "Kharis" enacted the role of a butler in Frankenstein
Slept Here.

During the 1960s the Mummy, played by Gene McCarty, appeared in magician Philip Morris' traveling horror show, Terrors of the Unknown. The Mummy would lumber into the audience, snatch a young woman from her seat and return her to the stage. There Morris would seemingly amputate her arm with a gigantic buzz saw. In Mexico "La Momia" appeared in Morris' (as Dr. Satan) Macabro expectáculo show.

On television Lon Chaney, Jr., submitted to the uncomfortable Kharis make-up and arose from a coffin in the monster episode of "Route 66" (1962). Mummies also apparently representing Kharis have appeared on such television programs as "The Monkees" (Bruce Barbour as the Mummy), "Spike Jones," "The Sonny and Cher Comedy Hour," "Rowan and Martin's Laugh-In," "Nightmare" (St. Petersburg-Tampa, Fla., with John Burke), "Horror Theater" (Charlotte, N.C., with Philip Morris as Dr. Evil, in the garb of an Egyptian priest), "Sinister Cinema," "The Mess America Contest" (North Carolina, with Slim Stokes), "The Mouse Factory," "Get Smart," "Lights! Camera! Marty!," "The Ghost Busters," "Hallelujah, Horrorwood," and the animated "Abbott and Costello," "Laurel and Hardy," "Milton the Monster," "The Groovie Goolies" and its spin-offs, and commercials for Aurora model kits, Colorforms, Post Sugar Crisp and Honeycombs cereals.

The second issue of Monster World (January 1965), from Warren Publishing Company, presented a comic strip retelling of The Mummy's Hand by Russ Jones and Joe Orlando. Life-size model kits of the Mummy, Creature (from The Beast From 1,279 1/2 Fathoms), the Phantom (of Loew's Bijou) and the vampiric Vultura were all brought to life with comedic results by aliens from space in "The Kid Who Made Monsters," published in the 87th issue of The Adventures of Jerry Lewis (March-April 1965), written by Arnold Drake and drawn by Bob Oksner and published by National Periodical Publications. Many comic book stories and series obviously inspired by Kharis have appeared throughout the years but because of Universal's copyright none has been an actual adaptation of the character.

The Mummy was featured in a number of songs on the record album Songs Our Mummy Told Us (Chadwick, 1961), by Bob McFadden and Dor (Rod McKuen). His image has also been used to sell such products as Nestlé's Quick and the newspaper Grit.

Eddie Parker, Chaney's double in the Kharis films, here collaring the popular comedy team, played "Klaris, Prince of Evil," in the spoof Abbott and Costello Meet the Mummy (Universal-International, 1955).

Kharis never arose to star in another film made by Universal. In 1948 the studio considered adding Kharis to the list of monsters which would appear in the classic horror spoof Abbott and Costello Meet Frankenstein. But although the Mummy did not meet the famous comedy team in 1948, a bastardization of the character did encounter Bud Abbott and Lou Costello seven years later.

Abbott and Costello Meet the Mummy was directed by Charles Lamont during the waning period in the comedians' career. Perhaps by now Universal-International realized the dearth of quality in the later Abbott and Costello entries and felt it best not to degrade the Kharis legend. Perhaps--but studio moguls have not been traditionally known to have such regard for fans of their properties. Whatever the reason, the "mummy" of the Abbott and Costello film would suggest Kharis while actually being a new character altogether.

"Klaris, Prince of Evil," was portrayed by reliable Eddie (now billed more formally as Edwin Parker), who had played without credit for so many years beneath the bandages of Kharis.

A three-way search is underway in Egypt for the treasure-filled tomb of Princess Ara. One team is headed by the greedy Madame Rontru (Marie Windsor) and another by Semu (Richard Deacon), leader of a religious cult called the Followers of Klaris. Bud Abbott and Lou Costello (playing themselves) constitute the third team.

After discovering the tomb, Semu finds the mummy Klaris and brings him to life. Klaris proved to be a disappointment to viewers maintaining a fondness for Kharis in their hearts. Parker's mummy outfit, as designed by Bud Westmore and his make-up crew, was ludicrous. The withered face, bandaged except for the mouth and eyes, was adequate; but the body was covered with a one-piece rubber suit, complete with zipper, and it looked like what it was. (The body of the Klaris costume was also worn by the actor playing the obedient mummy in the 1966 Astra film, Orgy of the Dead.) Unlike his predecessor, Klaris stomped about with four good limbs and was never shy to give his impression of a growling, roaring idiot.

Abbott and Costello go through their familiar shtick as everyone continues to seek the treasure. At one point not only one of Madame Rontru's henchmen but also Bud Abbott himself masquerade as Klaris, with poor Costello pulling the real mummy around by the hand. Klaris reveals his true identity when bullets fired by Rontru bounce off his bandaged hide. (This effect, setting off explosive charges called "squibs" beneath the actor's clothing, would become a film convention in the 1960s and 1970s.) After Klaris becomes the last person to catch a sizzling dynamite stick during a deadly game of "hot potato," the resulting explosion buries him beneath tons of rubble and also exposes Ara's treasure. In no way did Abbott and Costello Meet the Mummy approach the quality of the team's earlier encounters with Universal's monsters. It would be their last such meeting (The film was titled Il misterio della piramide ["The

Mystery of the Pyramid"] for Italian distribution and scenes
from the film later appeared in the 1965 film The World of Abbott and Costello and the 1976 TV movie The Kleegars.)

KHARIS IN COLOUR

Hammer Films of London reopened the musty crypt
of Kharis in 1959 with the production of The Mummy, a remake of virtually all the Universal mummy films including
the original starring Karloff.

In 1957 the British film company revived the sub-
genre of old-style horror films with The Curse of Frankenstein, a new version of the Mary Shelley classic.   The film
introduced Christopher Lee, a fine actor impressively six
feet four inches tall, to horror film aficionados in the heavily made-up role of Frankenstein's Creature.   The following
year Lee's acting talents were realized (and his features
revealed) when the same studio released Horror of Dracula,
its motion picture adaptation of the Bram Stoker novel.
Both The Curse of Frankenstein and Horror of Dracula were
written by Jimmy Sangster and directed by Terence Fisher.

The Mummy again reunited Sangster and Fisher, with
Christopher Lee assuming the role of Kharis, his third fantasy characterization.   It also utilized the talents of the distinguished actor Peter Cushing (who played Baron Frankenstein and Dr. Van Helsing respectively in the earlier Curse
of Frankenstein and Horror of Dracula) as archaeologist
John Banning.   Although based on the atmospheric Universal
product of the thirties and forties, the 1959 version of The
Mummy would be distinctly Hammer--abundant in bulging
female cleavage and in graphic gore, all presented in brilliant color.

Christopher Lee was the logical choice to play Kharis.
Not only did his height contribute to a formidable mummy,
but the public was intrigued with his enactments of the
Frankenstein Creature and Dracula.   He submitted to the
uncomfortable make-up applied by Hammer's Roy Ashton
and said after the completion of this role, "I don't want to
go through all that misery...."   The actor later revealed
that the rigors of the part, the carrying off of victims,
caused him to pull most of his neck and back muscles.
Like Karloff before him, Lee saw his career already beginning to soar.   A superb actor, he no longer needed to seek

employment lumbering about in such restricting guises. Appropriately, Kharis would be the last role of this nature for Lee.

Unlike the characters from Hammer's Frankenstein and Dracula films, Kharis was not adapted from the pages of literature. The Mummy was a character born within the studio gates of Universal Pictures. Consequently he was not in the public domain but still under Universal's copyright. In order to film The Mummy (which, though more based on the Kharis films, used the Karloff title), Hammer had to negotiate with the American studio so that Universal would release the film in the United States. Even with the differences cemented between Hammer and Universal, one of the original writers of the 1940s productions claimed damages which, after a while, were settled.

Again, The Mummy is the story of Prince Kharis who, four thousand years ago, loved the beautiful Princess Ananka (Yvonne Furneaux). As in his Universal incarnation, Kharis suffers when his lover dies. There is but one chance to save her, the forbidden Scroll of Life (which replaced both the Scroll of Thoth and the tana leaves in the Hammer film). Kharis steals the Scroll and attempts to speak the magical words inscribed thereon, only to be discovered and sentenced to the same living death as his Universal predecessor. First his tongue is sliced out (in a graphically unpleasant scene excised from the British and American release prints of the film), then he is swathed in wrappings and marched into his coffin to guard forever the tomb of Ananka.

John Banning (Cushing) and his archaeological expedition open the tomb of Ananka forty centuries later. A sinister Egyptian named Mehemet (George Pastell) admonishes Banning not to desecrate the sacred burial place. When Mehemet's warnings are not heeded, the vengeful priest uses the Scroll of Life to revive the guarding Mummy, Kharis, in order to have the members of Banning's party slain.

In England, Kharis crashes through a door and stalks Banning across the living room of his home. Moving quickly, Banning grabs an ancient spear and impales the Mummy on it. The poster advertising The Mummy depicted a followup

Opposite: Hammer Films starred Christopher Lee as the ancient Kharis and Peter Cushing as John Banning in The Mummy (1959).

to this scene, with a policeman shining a light through the
large hole created by the spear in the gauze-wrapped body.
The poster certainly impressed viewers as they entered the
theatre.   The effect was quite startling; audiences were psy-
chologically prepared for the actual scene of impalement and
many viewers actually "remember" seeing daylight through
the Mummy's body and marveling at that special effects
achievement.

Actually, the only daylight seen through Kharis' mid-
section was that superimposed there by suggestible viewers.
Nevertheless the scene was an impressive one.   Christopher
Lee explained the mechanics behind the scene.   "The spear
sequence in The Mummy was done with split-cutting photography.   In one shot Banning thrust the spear in from the
front and kept it there (as this was a telescopic weapon).
The Mummy then moved so that his back was seen by the
camera, showing the head of the spear sticking out of his
back.   This was already there but unseen at the beginning
of the shot.   The total effect was, of course, the spear
going right through" ["The Monster Speaks," Famous Monsters of Filmland no. 42 (January 1966), p. 17].

Before Kharis can administer a painful death to John
Banning, he is stopped by the appearance of the scientist's
wife Isobel (Ms. Furneaux again).   She is the reincarnation
of Ananka and the Princess' physical double.   The Mummy
seizes Isobel and, bearing her in his powerful arms, heads
into the murky waters of the swamp.   She is saved when a
posse of English policemen spray Kharis with a volley of
bullets, driving him to disappear beneath the slime of the
swamp.   "The final shooting sequence," said Lee, "was
done by giving the Mummy two special make-ups in which
his face was first intact and then almost blown away--in between there was inserted a shot of a head & shoulders dummy which was exploded by remote control" [Ibid, p. 18].

The Mummy was handsomely produced and proved
that well-mounted horror films could be made on a low-
budget scale.*   American audiences were hungry for more
of the Hammer product with their new approach to the old

*The film was inadvertently plugged in another British mon-
ster film made in 1959, Gorgo (MGM/King Bros.), in which
a captive prehistoric reptile is driven by truck through London streets past a huge advertisement for the Hammer Mummy.

subject matter. When The Mummy opened in its first Chicago run, "Kharis" himself was booked to make an appearance at selected theatres. I recall seeing a convincing facsimile of the Hammer Mummy standing in the lobby, cordoned
off from the crowd of theatre patrons by ropes. This "Kharis" was shorter than the one impersonated by Lee but his
face did resemble that created by Roy Ashton. After the
intermission was over and the audience returned to its seats,
I asked "Kharis" to explain his association with the motion
picture. Mumbling through the restricting Mummy mask,
the unidentified celebrity claimed to have been Lee's stunt
double in the film--an assertion which has not been con-
firmed.

The Hammer Mummy (in Belgium, known as Le
Malédiction des pharaons ("The Curse of the Pharaohs"),
and in England also as Terror of the Mummy) proved that
the bandaged horror so popular in the 1940s was a viable
product in 1959. Like Dracula, the mummy character would
become a part of a series at Hammer that would eventually
total four filmed adventures. But Hammer had learned a
lesson in having to share their profits with Universal with
their Kharis film. There would surely be a Hammer mummy series--but none of the succeeding entries would borrow
their characters or storylines from Universal. Every new
mummy would be the sole property of Hammer Films alone.
And each film would, like The Mummy, be made in color
with generous helpings of Hammer cleavage and gore.

The Curse of the Mummy's Tomb was Hammer's second mummy film, released in 1964 by Columbia Pictures,
produced and directed by Michael Carreras. Hammer had
meanwhile realized the waste of stuffing a name actor inside
the mummy wrappings. Thus, an unfamiliar Dickie Owen
donned the guise of Ra-Antef, a slightly pot-bellied mummy
who was once an Egyptian pharoah.

Ra-Antef is murdered by his brother during the
pharoah's reign in ancient Egypt. The pharoah is then
mummified and burried with a medallion which supposedly
contains the secret of immortality. Centuries later the
tomb of Ra-Antef is violated despite the warnings of a loyal
follower Hashim Bey (again played by George Pastell, virtually recreating his role from The Mummy). Naturally all
those involved with the opening of the mummy's tomb must
die as Ra-Antef prowls the misty streets of London.

American actor Fred Clark played the obnoxious,
wisecracking showman Alexander King, who acquires possession of the mummy in hopes of showing it for great profits
in Europe and the United States.   Clark's participation
seemed chiefly to add some unnecessary (and mirthless)
comedy sequences to the film.   King unveils his mummy
case, referring to the curse that Ra-Antef will return to
life if his tomb is desecrated, only to find the coffin already
empty.   The welcomed scene in which the mummy meets
King at the top of a flight of stairs and strikes him to his
death terminated the film's attempts at humor, but was also
one of the more atmospheric moments.

Presently the mummy kills Sir Giles Dalrymple, one
of the members of the expedition which uncovered his tomb.
Ra-Antef presses the man against the top of his desk.   The
camera focuses on the mummy as he brings down a heavy
statuette, out of frame, cracking Sir Giles' skull.   The horror of the scene lies in the next several seconds as Ra-Antef
continues to look dispassionately at his victim.

Finally realizing that a living mummy is at large,
the authorities set a trap for him.   Ra-Antef is caught in a
net until he tears himself free with superhuman strength.
Hashim Bey places his head before the mummy's feet and
begs to be punished for his sin of betrayal.   What follows
is a scene of unsettling horror.   The mummy places his
foot atop his servant's head.   The next shot is of the mummy's head and shoulders as he obviously presses down on
something.   At last the camera records the disgust on an
onlooker's face as he turns away quickly and we hear the
ghastly sound of a head being crushed.

The climax of The Curse of the Mummy's Tomb revealed at least some originality by writer Henry Younger
(actually Carreras again).   Adam Beauchamp proudly displays his collection of Egyptian treasure to attractive Annette
Dubois (Jeanne Roland) then places the amulet of eternal life
about her neck.   Beauchamp, we discover, is really the
murderous Be, brother of Ra-Antef, and can only lose his
immortality if slain by the mummy himself.   Offering Annette to Ra-Antef in the sewers beneath his home, Beauchamp is seized by the mummy and drowned in the scummy
waters.   Next the mummy removes the amulet from Annette's
neck and destroys himself by pulling down the ceiling.

The Curse of the Mummy's Tomb was paired on a
double bill with another Hammer film, The Gorgon.

Releasing two such movies on a single program became a
practice of the studio and continued in 1967 when Hammer
released through Twentieth Century-Fox Frankenstein Created
Woman and the second feature The Mummy's Shroud, a film
made the previous year.

The Mummy's Shroud, written and directed by John
Gilling, offered a new premise.   The mummy, now neither
prince nor pharoah, was a tutor named Prem.   (Dickie Owen,
the Ra-Antef of The Curse of the Mummy's Tomb, played
the living Prem while his mummified counterpart was portrayed by Eddie Powell, a six-foot, three-inch stuntman.)
It was Prem's assignment to protect young King Kah-to-bey
from all harm in the Egypt of four thousand years ago.   But
Prem is unsuccessful in protecting the boy, as both of them
are murdered by assassins.   Peter Cushing, the John Banning of the original Hammer Mummy, narrated these scenes
of past history.

Forty centuries later, an archaeological expedition
opens the tomb and the two mummies are discovered.   The
prop mummy representing the dead Kah-to-bey was disturbingly realistic, verisimilar to an actual exhibit at Chicago's
Field Museum of Natural History labeled "Body of a Boy."
The mummy of Prem was also more authentic in appearance
than most film mummies, with its shroud covering the layers
of wrappings.

After Prem is taken to a museum, an Egyptian named
Hasmid (Roger Delgado) uses an incantation to bring him to
life.   (At this point in history, archaeologists should have
known better than to defile Egyptian tombs--especially in the
movies.)   Prem disposes of the desecrators in typical film
mummy style until a buxom archaeologist named Claire
(Maggie Kimberley) speaks a second incantation which decomposes him to a pile of dust.

The Jewel of the Seven Stars, a novel by Bram Stoker, was the basis of Hammer's Blood from the Mummy's
Tomb, which was made in 1971 and released the following
year by American-International Pictures.   Directed by Seth
Holt and Michael Carreras, the film was a diversion from
the usual mummy fare.   There was no actual lumbering
mummy in this entry but the curse against violators of
Egyptian tombs was present all the same.

Tera (played by voluptuous Valerie Leon), an evil
queen, is sealed away in her tomb after one of her hands is

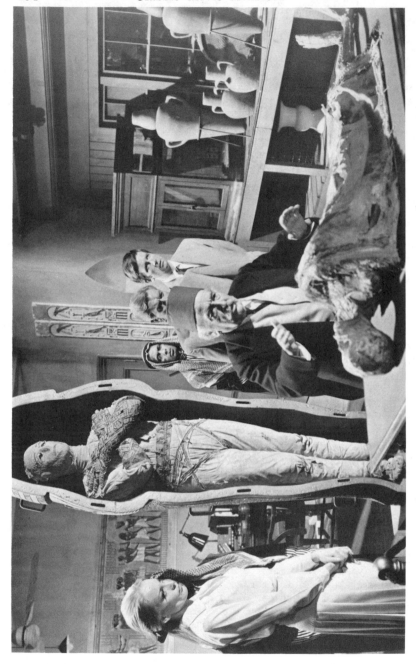

severed at the wrist.   The hand brandishes a ruby ring that
had given the queen mystic powers.   The tomb is opened
thousands of years later and the ring is entrusted to the
daughter of one of the archaeologists, Margaret (also Ms.
Leon).   Instead of leaving her grave in physical form, the
dead Tera possesses Margaret, her spirit infusing the woman with the powers necessary to destroy the desecrators
and recover the treasures removed from the tomb.   Finally
Margaret attempts to physically resuscitate Tera's remains
with the Scroll of Life (not mentioned since The Mummy in
1959).   When the mummy is mutilated a number of demons
are conjured up from Egypt's past.   Whether it is Margaret
or the evil Tera who survives the ordeal is for the audience
to decide.

      Just like the Universal mummies, those which were
given life at the Hammer studios found themselves in media
other than motion pictures.   In 1966 a novel, The Curse of
the Mummy's Tomb, written by John Burke, was published
by Pan Books in London as part of the anthology, The Hammer Horror Omnibus.   A comic book ostensibly based on
the Universal Kharis movies but actually following the storyline and mood of the Hammer films was published during the
latter 1960s in Brazil by Gráfica Editôra Penteado.   The
first issue of Múmia was somewhat based on the 1959 The
Mummy, with succeeding adventures following Kharis as he
pursues his beloved Ananka.   Kharis (resembling the Chaney
version was portrayed as an anti-hero, performing such di-
verse acts as sacrificing human hearts at Stonehenge in turn-
of-the-century England and heroically battling a gang of tomb
plunderers.   In 1970 the publisher Gráfica Editôra Penteado
issued a special edition Almanaque Múmia and gave Kharis
a new origin.   Now Kharis is buried alive by the immortal
priest, Set.   Centuries later Kharis revives (resembling
Prem from The Mummy's Shroud) and battles Set in the sewers (reminiscent of The Curse of the Mummy's Tomb).   This
same Penteado work featured an unusual story in which Kharis
is temporarily given back his youth.

      The Hammer mummy films infused color and vitality

Opposite: Roger Delgado, descendant of a pharaoh's person-
al guard, speaks an incantation over the mummy of boy King
Kah-to-bey as archaeologists Maggie Kimberley, Andre
Morell (partly hidden), and David Buck watch; the mummi-
fied Prem (Eddie Powell) is watching too. ...   The Mummy's
Shroud (Hammer, 1967).

into the subject matter that had been mined at Universal.
There were yet other motion pictures about living mummies.
Some of these were made as early as the first decade of the
twentieth century.

THE OTHER MUMMIES

Egyptian mummies coming back to life is a recurring
theme in motion pictures. The concept is, however, quite
contrary to the actual beliefs of the ancient Egyptians who
preserved their dead as mummies. It is a fact that the
Egyptians of thousands of years ago believed in a life after
death. But this life was not to be enjoyed spent among the
living. The deceased would, so the Egyptians contended,
live on within the confines of the tomb. Simultaneously the
dead person's ka, an invisible corporeal twin, waited in the
afterworld until it and its body would be joined throughout
eternity.

Preparation of a mummy required seventy days.
During this time the inner organs were painstakingly removed
from the body, the brain being taken out through the nostrils bit by bit with hooks and metal probes. If this were
not unpleasant enough, these organs (save for the brain which
was too fragmentary to preserve) were each placed in their
own container (called a canopic jar) and placed under the
care of a prescribed god.

Preservation of the body involved the use of natron,
common salt and sodium bicarbonate. The body cavities
were stuffed with small packets of linen-wrapped natron.
Loose natron or more natron packets were placed on the
outside of the corpse; Egypt's dry air speeded up the desicca-
tion. After the natron absorbed the moisture, the parcels
were removed and the body was bathed with sponges. Anoint-
ing with coniferous resins followed after which the corpse
was stuffed with packets of resin-soaked linen. To give the
corpse the appearance that we recognize as a mummy, the
embalmers wrapped it in several hundred square yards of
linen. Over twenty layers of shrouds and bandages were
then wrapped about the corpse. After the woodworkers and
artisans had finished the coffin (or series of coffins) the
mummy was ready for burial. The mummy was then placed
in its tomb with all the food and luxuries the deceased would
require for his life after death, the canopic jars, often
the mummies of animals and always a copy of the funerary

text, "The Book of the Dead," which the deceased followed
in obtaining entrance to the afterworld.

In the afterworld, after braving the many dangers of
that god and demon-inhabited realm, the deceased had to
convince a group of 42 assessors that his life had been a
virtuous one.   In audience before the god king Osiris, the
jackal-headed deity Anubis would weigh the dead person's
heart against the feather symbol of truth upon the Great
Scales, while Thoth wrote down the result.   To gain entrance into the afterworld the deceased's heart could not
outweigh the feather; if it did, the soul of the hapless person was condemned to haunt the Earth for all eternity.   For
a succinct description of Egyptian mummification and the
afterlife, refer to Richard A. Martin's booklet Mummies,
first published in 1945 by the Field Museum of Natural History Press in Chicago as part of its Popular Series, Anthro-
pology, Number 36 (and still available).

Egyptians were not concerned with reviving their
mummies and having them lumber about in their burial garb.
They were thinking of a more idealized form of life after
death.   The damnation of a spirit to be trapped forever in
our world was certainly undesirable and to be avoided.   The
actual physical resuscitation of a mummified corpse would
have been a ludicrous idea to the Egyptians.   Nevertheless
there is a certain fascination in the latter romantic notion
and it became a popular theme in the movies over a decade
before the furor caused in the 1920s by Tutankhamen's alleged curse.

As early as 1909 scientists were bringing mummies
back to life on film.   The French film La Momie du roi
("The Mummy of the King") was made by Lux, directed by
Gerard Burgeois and released in the United States as The
Mummy of the King Ramsees.   There were three films entitled simply The Mummy in 1911.   The first of these was
made by Britain's Urban films and featured a professor who
dreams that a mummy comes to life.   The Pathé version
had a Professor Darnett invent a life-restorative formula
while his laboratory assistant masquerades as a living mummy and inevitably marries the professor's daughter.   The
final 1911 film under this title was produced by Thanhouser.
This time a mummy is really restored to life.   A charge of
electricity performs the miracle and at the same time transforms the bandaged horror into a lovely Egyptian girl.

"The Mummy" was a popular title during the silent days of motion pictures and refers to an additional five films: two French movies, The Mummy (Gaumont, 1900) and La Momie (1913), and an American film called The Mummy (Fox, 1923) may or may not, according to film historian Walt Lee, have fantastic or horror content. Lee discounts two other French films titled The Mummy, both made by Pathé, in 1908 and 1912, as not meeting those two requirements. El Mumia was the title of yet another film in this latter category. It was made in Egypt in 1969.

Mummies restored to life remained popular during the silent days of motion pictures. In 1913 and 1914 two films were made, both entitled The Egyptian Mummy and both featuring actors masquerading as mummies. The former production was made by Kalem and the latter by the Vitagraph Company of America. Vitagraph's Egyptian Mummy was directed by Lee Beggs and starred comedian Billy Quirk as a young man who tries to collect a professor's reward for a mummy upon which to test his life restorative fluid. Hoping to use the money to marry the professor's daughter, Quirk disguises a bum as a mummy, who then comes to "life" and creates havoc in the laboratory.

Die Augen der Mumie (The Eyes of the Mummy), a UFA film directed in Germany by Ernst Lubitsch and released in 1918, featured a cult of mummy worshippers. But the mummy in this film (starring Pola Negri and Emil Jannings) never came to life. The fantasy of the film was presented in the power of hypnotism and in a woman's death caused by the fright of seeing the apparition of an Egyptian religious fanatic.

The last silent mummy film, Mummy Love, was released by Standard Cinema Corporation in 1926. It was directed by Joe Rock and featured comedy routines in a mummy's tomb. Except for the characters in the film dressing themselves as mummies, there is no living mummy in the film. Most of the mummy films made prior to the beginning of the Hammer series were, with the exception of the Universal productions, comedies. Mummy's Boys (RKO, 1936), directed by Fred Guiol, brought comics Bert Wheeler and Robert Woolsey into a tomb haunted by a villain in a mummy costume. The Three Stooges were similarly menaced by a disguised crook in the Columbia short subject We Want Our Mummy, directed by Del Lord in 1938 and released the following year. The boys played three detectives sent to

Egypt to find a missing archaeologist and the mummy of King
Rootentootin.   In 1948 the Stooges starred in the short
Mummies' Dummies but encountered no bandaged horrors in
this comedy set in ancient Egypt.

Republic Pictures, the action studio, capitalized on
the horror film's popularity by including a variation on the
living mummy motif in G-Men vs. the Black Dragon, a 1949
serial directed by William Witney.   Haruchi (Nino Pipitone),
a Japanese criminal mastermind and head of the Black
Dragon Society, is smuggled into the United States in the
guise of an Egyptian mummy, swathed in bandages and wearing an ugly mask, in a state of suspended animation.   He
returns to "life" in Episode One, "The Yellow Peril."   (A
feature-length film version of this serial was released to
television in 1966 as Black Dragon of Manzanar.)

A more serious treatment was finally given the mummy theme in 1949 with The Mummy's Foot, directed by Sobey
Martin for Marshall Grant and Realm TV Productions.   Based
on a story by Theophile Gautier, the television film brought
an ancient Egyptian princess to a writer who has acquired
her mummified foot.   A variance on the living mummy theme
was Pharaoh's Curse, a film directed by Lee Sholem for
Bel-Air in 1956 and released the next year by United Artists.
Now it is not the mummy itself that rises to destroy those
who have defiled his tomb but his ghost.   The spirit of Ra-
Ha-Teb, a worshiper of the Egyptian Cat God 4000 years
ago, possesses a man and gradually ages his body to the appearance of a mummy.   The possessed man kills a number
of the members of the unauthorized archaeological expedition
before the tomb is sealed once again.   Before the film actually went into production it was known under the title, Curse
of the Pharaoh.   A living mummy joined a cast of monsters
and fiends in a 1966 entry to the British "Carry On" comedy
series, Carry On Screaming, directed by Gerald Thomas for
Anglo-Amalgamated.   Dennis Blake portrayed the mummy
Rubbatiti.   (The film is available for 16mm rental under the
abbreviated title Screaming.)

Another series of living mummy films commenced in
Mexico in 1957.   Yet unlike Im-ho-tep and Kharis, this hideous ambulatory corpse was not Egyptian but a native of the
North American continent.   His motivations, methods of slay-
ing and general appearance, however, were similar enough
to his Egyptian counterparts for one to mistake them for
relatives.   La momia ("The Mummy"), directed by Rafael

Lopez Portillo for Cinematográfica Calderón and released by
Azteca, introduced the character of the Aztec Mummy. An
archaeological expedition discovers an Aztec pyramid where
a mummy has been buried to guard an ancient ceremonial
mask. There are the obligatory flashback scenes showing
the ancient Aztecs entombing their mummy guard along with
the mask. Not surprisingly, the Aztec Mummy returns
centuries later to perform his expected murders as a super
villain known as the Bat (Ramon Gay) attempts to steal the
mask. The monster suffers an ignoble defeat when he is
run down by a speeding car. La momia is also known under
the titles La momia azteca, The Aztec Mummy, The Mummy
Strikes and simply The Mummy. In 1963, Jerry Warren
lifted extensive footage from La momia and added boring
scenes of American actors explaining the plot for Medallion's
Attack of the Mayan Mummy. The next year Warren incorporated much of the footage from La momia into Face of the
Screaming Werewolf, his version of the Mexican mummy/
werewolf film La casa del terror starring Lon Chaney, Jr.,
as the dual monster.

La momia was a crude, dull imitation of the American mummy films. Yet despite its mediocrity, the picture
was followed by three sequels. The 1957 Momia contra el
robot humano ("The Mummy vs. the Human Robot"), again
directed by Portillo, was released in the United States as
The Robot vs. the Aztec Mummy. This second entry to the
series featured considerable flashback footage from La momia
and introduced a Frankenstein theme, as the Bat, aided by
his gangsters, attempts to secure the mask and defeat the
Aztec Mummy by means of an artificially created slave.
The Bat's robot consists of a composite man built from the
organs of several corpses enclosed by a robot body. The
two monsters inevitably do battle until the Aztec Mummy
tears the human robot to pieces of junk, then apparently
slays the Bat. (The film is also known as La momia azteka
contra el robot humano, The Aztec Mummy vs. the Human
Robot and simply El robot humano.)

If the inane plot of the second Aztec Mummy film
was not enough to sate the appetites of his fans, they might
have been glutted with the third in the series, La maldición
de la momia ("The Curse of the Mummy"), which was made
in 1959, again directed by Portillo and released in the United
States in 1961 as The Curse of the Aztec Mummy.* Most

*Excerpts from the soundtrack of The Curse of the Aztec

of the horror of the concept was not replaced by action imitating the old American movie serials, with a superhero
called the Angel battling in white tights and cape against the
Bat, his minions and the reliable Aztec Mummy. Before
the Bat is unmasked as a supposedly slow-witted handyman,
he destroys the Aztec Mummy--but not forever. The creature's most unbelievable adventure (with its most ludicrous
title) was yet to come.

Las luchadoras contra la momia (1964), which was
directed by René Calderón, translates as "The Wrestling
Women vs. the Mummy" (American title: The Wrestling Women vs. the Aztec Mummy). Alfredo Salazar, who also wrote
the screenplays to the other Aztec Mummy films, outdid
himself in preposterousness this time. While pursued by
sinister Oriental members of the "Black Dragon" organization, a team of beautiful women wrestlers pursue the Aztec
Mummy. By this film, the Mummy, which attacks them in
his tomb, has apparently suffered some decomposition. But
he has also gained new powers (and only the Aztec gods know
how). As he fights the courageous wrestling women, the
Aztec Mummy periodically transforms into a vampire bat
and even into a spider. During these crude cuts from mummy to bat and back again, the "Luchadoras" exclaim such
priceless dialogue (which could not have been significantly
less insipid before translation and dubbing) as, "Look! He's
a vampire! No, now he's a mummy again!" The Wrestling
Women did to the Aztec Mummy what even the Human Robot
and the Angel could not accomplish--end his series forever.

The Americans contributed an only slightly less absurd mummy film in 1967. The Mummy and the Curse of
the Jackals (which went into production as The Mummy vs.
the Were-Jackal) has a title reminiscent of a Mexican horror
movie. Whether it meets the same quality standards as the
Aztec Mummy productions will not be known until the film
is someday released.

Non-American mummies were turned out as if by an
assembly line of movie embalmers in the 1970s. A living
mummy joined a horde of monsters in two 1970s productions,
El hombre que vino del Ummo and the Mexican Santo y Blue
Demon contra los monstruos. Mexico, though its Aztec
Mummy had apparently crumbled to dust, had hardly exhausted

(continued) Mummy were included in the student film Glut,
made in 1967 by Basil Polidouris at the University of
Southern California.

its supply of walking, gauze-wrapped corpses.   Santo, Mexico's most popular masked wrestler (male) and superhero,
battled and exposed a fake mummy in Calderón's Santo en la
venganza de la momia ("Santo in the Mummy's Revenge"),
which was made in 1971 and released by Azteca the following year.   René Cardona directed.

Perhaps it was inevitable that a new Mexican mummy
series would surface in 1972, this time in color: Las
momias de Guanajuato was based on an actual tourist site
in Guanajuato, Mexico, where at least one graveyard has a
bizarre tradition.   Graves are rented and unless the rent be
paid ad infinitum the unfortunate deceased defaulter is dis-
interred and displayed before admission-paying tourists.
Santo and two other wrestling masked men, Blue Demon and
Mils Mascaras ("A Thousand Masks," some of which he
wears in his films), battle the mummies which are returned
to life.   Three other super-wrestlers, Blue Angel, Tinieblas
("Darkness") and Superzan (whose name is apparently a port-
manteau for Superman and Tarzan) fight the mummies, now
under the control of a satanist mad doctor who performs a
black mass and transplants an artificial heart, in the second
film, El castillo de las momias de Guanajuato ("The Castle
of the Mummies of Guanajuato").   The superheroes' efforts
were only temporary, though, for the mad scientist and the
nefarious Count Cagliostro resurrect the mummies and control them with electronic gadgets in a plot to conquer the
world in El robo de las momias de Guanajuato ("The Theft
of ... ").   Mils Mascaras, the Blue Angel and a newcomer
calling himself El Ravo de Jalisco ("The Lightning of Jalisco") pit their superb strength and masked identities to (perhaps finally) defeat the Guanajuato mummies and their evil
masters.

Spanish horror actor Paul Naschy, the star of the
Waldemar Daninsky "Wolfman" films, added an undistinguished
living mummy to his growing repertoire of monster characterizations in 1973.   La venganza de la momia (seen in the
United States as The Mummy's Revenge) was a Lotus production directed by Carlos Aured.   Naschy portrayed Amen-ho-
tep, an Egyptian king who is killed for his torturing of women in this cheaply made (and poorly executed) production.
Predictably the mummy returns to life centuries later and,
after resuming his murderous career, perishes by fire.

Mention should also be made of yet one more "series"
character, the Mad Mummy portrayed by Bob Burns.   The

Mad Mummy was originally Burns' own version of Kharis.
Wearing the thoroughly convincing outfit which he made himself, Burns made a number of live personal appearances
and, in 1959, played the character on "Shock Theatre" in
San Antonio, Texas.   In 1961 the costume won first place at
Hollywood's Artists and Models Ball.   During the early
1960s, Burns enacted his mummy role on Hollywood's "Jeepers' Creepers" and "Panorama Pacific" television programs.
The character was officially christened the Mad Mummy for
a series of articles supposedly written by the creature (actually ghost written by Jim Harmon) and published in the
magazine Fantastic Monsters of the Films (1962-63).   After
appearing in person, on television and on the printed page,
the Mad Mummy soon stalked into the movies.   He nearly
killed the title character of the 1963 amateur serial The Adventures of the Spirit (in which the shot of the unwrapped
mummy utilizes the mask made by Jack Pierce for The
Mummy's Tomb) before getting unraveled by the Shadow
(Harmon) of radio and pulp magazine fame.   He returned as
one of a crew of amateur film-makers in a short subject
called The Lemon Grove Kids Meet the Monsters, a color
film of 1966 directed by Ray Dennis Steckler for Morgan-
Steckler Productions.   The movie included a break where the
Mad Mummy (a hired performer wearing a new mummy costume and a Don Post mask since the original suit was de-
teriorating) went into the audience.   Steckler intended to make
a horror film starring the Mad Mummy in 1966 entitled Land
of the Living Mummy but, except for a few test scenes, the
movie never went into production.

     The ancient Egyptians might never have conceived of
a living mummy stalking from its tomb to haunt the desert
sands or the banks of the Nile.   But there is something romantic in that notion and in the rumors of pharaohs' curses.
The lure of such themes have attracted motion picture audiences since the earliest days of the art form and, like the
sands of Egypt, will probably remain with us for quite some
time.

V

QUASIMODO OF NOTRE DAME

"Quasimodo was born one-eyed, humpbacked, lame."
Such an unfortunate character as Quasimodo, of Victor Hugo's
historical novel Notre-Dame de Paris (which is known in
America under the more famous title The Hunchback of Notre
Dame) might have qualified as a monster in the medical
sense. Actually, despite his misshapen exterior, Quasimodo,
the bell-ringer of Notre Dame Cathedral in Paris, was a
kindly, loving sort. It was via the medium of the motion
picture, especially through the performances of Lon Chaney
and Charles Laughton, that the hapless Quasimodo would join
the screen's pantheon of immortal horrors. Today the name
of the Hunchback of Notre Dame is spoken within the same
context as the Mummy, the Phantom of the Opera and the
Creature from the Black Lagoon.

Notre-Dame de Paris was written in 1831. Victor
Hugo (1802-1885) claimed to have been inspired to write the
massive novel by the strange word anangke, which he had
seen scratched on one of the cathedral's walls. The translation of anangke is "fate" and Hugo's character Claude
Frollo, archdeacon of Notre Dame, writes this very word
upon the cathedral wall in the novel. Fate determines the
directions of the lives of Hugo's characters. Yet before
Hugo had ever seen the word anangke, if in fact he actually
did, he had chosen the symbol of Notre Dame to tell his
story. This is the Notre Dame of 1482, before cleanings
and restorations destroyed much of the cathedral's architecture and sculpture. Hugo maintained a serious interest in
architecture and its preservation and in the study of Gothic
and Romanesque monuments. The publication of Notre-Dame
de Paris brought the preservation of architecture to the attention of the authorities and secured him a position to a
new government committee for just that purpose.

Quasimodo was an orphaned infant found in the cathedral by a priest, Claude Frollo, on Low Sunday, 1463. On that day, while returning from saying mass, Frollo observed a group of old women cackling about the child. When Frollo removed the child's coverings, he saw that the babe was deformed, with "a prodigious wart over his left eye, his head was close to his shoulders, his back arched, his breast-bone protruded, and his legs were twisted...." Frollo baptized his adopted son, naming him Quasimodo, "either to commemorate the day on which he had found him, or to express the incomplete and scarcely finished state of the poor little creature. In truth, Quasimodo, with one eye, hunchback, and crooked legs, was but an apology for a human being." The name comes from the beginning words of the Latin Introit for Low Sunday, quasi modo geniti infantes ("as newborn babes").

Quasimodo grows up, an outcast of the Paris populace, amid the spires and gargoyles of Notre Dame. He and the cathedral share a harmony, each reflecting the physical deformities of the other. The Hunchback hops, twists and scampers along the "dark, damp pavement, among the grotesque shadows thrown down upon it by the capitals of the Roman pillars." The cathedral is Quasimodo's only home, its boundaries defining his restricted world. By the year 1482, the Hunchback has become the bell-ringer of Notre Dame, mechanically grasping the rope in the tower, to set the bells clanging by hanging to it, though by the time Quasimodo is 14 the volume of Notre Dame's bells have broken his ear drums and rendered him deaf.

Hugo provides his most vivid description of Quasimodo as the people of the city seek their Pope of Fools, the winner having the dubious distinction of possessing the most horrible countenance. It is, naturally, Quasimodo who beats all the competition:

> ... we shall not attempt to give the reader any idea of that tetrahedron nose, of that horse-shoe mouth, of that little left eye stubbled up with an eyebrow of carroty bristles, while the right was completely overwhelmed and buried by an enormous wen; of those irregular teeth, jagged here and there like the battlements of a fortress; of that horny lip, over which one of those teeth protruded, like the tusk of an elephant; of that forked chin; and above all of the expression, that mixture

of spite, wonder, and melancholy, spread over
these exquisite features. Imagine such an object,
if you can.... [H]is prodigious head was covered
with red bristles; between his shoulders rose an
enormous hump, which was counterbalanced by a
protuberance in front; his thighs and legs were so
strangely put together that they touched at no one
point but the knees, and seen in front, resembled
two sickles joined at the handles; his feet were
immense, his hands monstrous; but, with all this
deformity there was a formidable air of strength,
agility and courage.... [H]e looked like a giant
who had been broken to pieces and ill soldered together.

The novel's plot concerns Claude Frollo's infatuation
with Esmeralda, a Gypsy dancer. Frollo orders Quasimodo
to kidnap Esmeralda, but she is rescued by the handsome
philanderer Phoebus de Châteaupers, Captain of the Royal
Archers. Frollo stabs the soldier to death, leaving the witness Esmeralda to be convicted of his crime. Esmeralda
is saved from the scaffold by Quasimodo, grateful for a
previous act of kindness on her part, and brought to the
sanctuary of Notre Dame. The Hunchback repels the Gypsies,
thieves and beggars who try to "rescue" her from the cathedral. After Frollo is discovered in an attempt to disguise
himself and flee with Esmeralda, the crafty archdeacon
leaves her with a half-crazed woman whose daughter had
been stolen years ago by Gypsies. An amulet worn by Esmeralda proves that she is the woman's daughter but that
knowledge is too late in coming. The officers of the guard
tear Esmeralda away from her mother--who lies dying on
the pavement--to be executed upon the gallows. Seeing the
woman he loves swinging from the noose, Quasimodo discovers Frollo gloating over the crime he engineered. The
Hunchback seizes his former master and dashes him from
the balustrade of Notre Dame to die on the cobblestones below.

About a year and a half or two years after the
events this history concludes, when search was
made in the vault of Montfaucon for the body of
Olivier le Daim ... among these hideous carcasses
were found two skeletons in a singular posture.
One of these skeletons, which was that of a female,
had still upon it some fragments of a dress that
had once been white; and about the neck was a

necklace of the seeds of adrezarach, and a little
silk bag braided with green beads, which was open
and empty. These things were of so little value
that the hangman no doubt had not thought it worth
his while to take them. The other, by which this
first was closely embraced, was the skeleton of a
male. It was remarked that the spine was crooked,
the head depressed between the shoulders, and one
leg shorter than the other. There was, however,
no rupture of the vertebrae of the neck, and it
was evident that the person to whom it belonged
had not been hanged. He must have come hither
and died in the place. When those who found this
skeleton attempted to disengage it from that which
it held in its grasp, it crumbled to dust.

Notre-Dame de Paris brought both wealth and new
fame to Victor Hugo. His novel was well received by all
classes of people and it was inevitable that the story would
be adapted to the stage.

NOTRE-DAME DE PARIS DRAMATIZED

In 1831, the year of the novel's first publication,
German author Charlotte Birch-Pfeiffer adapted Notre-Dame
de Paris to the stage. A play entitled The Duke's Daughter;
or The Hunchback of Paris, a three-act play by Anicet
Bourgoise and Paul Feval, opened in London in 1863. But
though the title intimated the play was an adaptation of the
Hugo story, and though the play featured such familiar elements as Gypsies and a hunchback (named Aesop), the drama
was actually taken from Feval's story "Le Petit Parisien."
The play was also presented that same year under such
titles as The Duke's Bequest, Blanche of Nevers; or, I Am
Here, The Duke's Device, The Duke's Signal and The Duke's
Daughter; or, The Hunchback and the Swordsman.

The Hugo story was adapted to the English stage and
premiered on April 18, 1870 with a pun in its title, Quasimodo, the Deformed; or, The Man with the Hump and the
Belle of Notre Dame, by Burl H. Spry. The next year the
Hunchback's story became a three-act farce by Andrew J.
Halliday, entitled Notre Dame; or, The Gipsy Girl of Paris.
The play opened at England's Adelphi Theatre on April 10,
1871. Two years later, on September 11, the play was presented in New York. Esmeralda was portrayed by Jeffrey

Lewis, a slender, attractive brunette, "possessing several
physical qualifications for the part...," said the Herald on
September 12, 1873. "It requires but little stretch of the
imagination to attribute to her the Andalusian foot, upon
which the novelist dwells, while Esmeralda is executing her
Provençal saraband.... Threading the dance to the mingled
music of the balatoes, the tambourines, the goats' horns
and Gothic rebecs, she was the picturesque embodiment, so
far as physique and motion were concerned, of a delicate
and poetic ideal." In the role of Quasimodo was Thomas C.
King, an actor renowned for his work in tragedies and melo-
dramas presented at England's lesser noted theatres. An
existing photograph of King as Quasimodo shows his version
of the Hunchback to have been rugged and mustachioed but
hardly grotesque. The Herald described his talents: "Mr.
King will not rank here as a great actor, but he will be
respected as an intelligent and earnest one." Notre Dame
was quite successful during its first American run. In
1923 a play of The Hunchback of Notre Dame was presented
at London's Empire Theatre.

Victor Hugo's story proved to be more durable on the
operatic stage. In 1836, Louise (Angélique) Bertin, who also wrote operas of Le Loup-garou and Faust, adapted the
novel to an opera entitled La Esméralda. This was the authorized operatic version of Notre-Dame de Paris, in four
acts, with text by Hugo himself and vocal score by Franz
Liszt. Yet even with such fine collaborators, the opera,
which opened on November 14 at Paris' Académie Royale de
Musique, was a failure. Giacomo Meyerbeer unsuccessfully
tried securing a German production of the opera in 1838.
Excerpts from the Bertin opera were presented in concert
form in Paris on July 6, 1865.

Bertin's opera was but the first of many based upon
Victor Hugo's novel. The most successful of all the Notre-
Dame de Paris operatic adaptations was the four-act Esmeralda, by Alberto Mazzucato, with text by F. de' Boni.
Esmeralda proved to be Mazzucato's most successful operatic venture. It premiered at Lisbon on January 1, 1840,
and at Barcelona on November 14.

And there were other operas based on the story:
Esmeralda, in four acts, by Aleksandre Dargomyshsky with
text by the author, translated from the 1836 version, which
played in Russia from 1847 to about 1876; Ermelinda (also
known as Esmeralda), by Vincenzo Battista with text by D.

Bolognese, which premiered on February 15, 1851 in Naples and was quite successful in Italy; Notre-Dame of Paris, by William Henry Fry with text by his brother J. R. Fry, which opened on May 4, 1864, at the American Academy of Music in Philadelphia; the four-act Esmeralda, written by Fabio Campana with text by G. T. Cimino especially for Adelina Patti, and which debuted at St. Petersburg on December 30, 1869; Esmeralda, a four-act opera by Arthur Goring Thomas with text by T. J. H. Marzials and A. Randegger, which premiered in London on March 26, 1883; and Notre Dame, a two-act opera by Franz Schmidt with text by the composer and L. Wilk, which opened on April 1, 1914. Notre Dame is considered to be Schmidt's finest opera; it was also his first. Even today the Hunchback of Notre Dame has been associated with the stage and music. About 1972, Lionel Bart of Oliver! fame wrote a musical version of the Hugo story--with the perhaps inevitable title of Quasimodo!

The Hunchback of Notre Dame joined the Gill Man from the Black Lagoon for a horror comedy skit performed at Universal Pictures on Friday the 13th of February, 1976, during which "Baby Frankenstein" was brought to life for delighted tour patrons.

Today the plays and operas based on Victor Hugo's novel are relegated mainly to history while Notre-Dame de Paris is not widely read. Quasimodo, however, continues to be a popular character, mainly because of his appearances on the motion picture screen. As a film "monster" the Hunchback of Notre Dame ranks as a classic.

THE HUNCHBACK OF THE SCREEN

Generally it is believed that the classic movie of The Hunchback of Notre Dame starring Lon Chaney was the first screen adaptation of Victor Hugo's novel. Actually, there were a number of silent films based on the story before the Chaney motion picture. The first was a ten-minute short called Esmeralda and was released by the French film company Gaumont in 1905. Esmeralda was directed by Alice Guy-Blanché and starred Denise Becker and Henry Vorins, presumably as Esmeralda and Quasimodo. According to Denis Gifford, "The plot was pirated around the world, in America by Vitagraph, The Hunchback (1909), and Selig, Hugo the Hunchback (1910), while the first production of that long-lived British emporium, Butcher's Films, was

The Loves of a Hunchback (1910). As with his transatlantic
cousins, this humped hero followed in Quasimodo's pathetic
footsteps by saving his unrequited love and dying with what
passed for a brave smile on his face" [Denis Gifford, A
Pictorial History of Horror Films (London, 1973), p. 24].

Another French version was released by Pathé in
1911. Entitled Notre-Dame de Paris, the film introduced a
new supernatural element to the storyline. Now the ugly
Quasimodo (Henri Krauss) becomes handsome when kissed
by Esmeralda (played by dancer Stacia Napierkovska). An
extant poster from the film depicts a suitably hideous Quasimodo being given water by Esmeralda while bound to the
whipping wheel, as crowds watch from the streets of fifteenth-
century Paris. We can only guess at whether or not the
movie boasted such spectacle. Albert Capellani directed.

An English version, Notre Dame (also known as
Notre Dame de Paris), was made in 1913 and released by
Pathéplay with tinted scenes. Fox made its American version of the story, The Darling of Paris, in 1916 and released it the following year. J. Gordon Edwards directed
this film with one important ingredient conspicuously missing.
Quasimodo (Glen White) was not ugly! Silent film vamp
Theda Bara played Esmeralda; at the film's climax she is
won by her loving Quasimodo. In 1919 the film was reissued with a new ending, wherein Esmeralda is executed
while Quasimodo slays the perfidious clergyman.

Yet another Esmeralda film was directed by Edwin J.
Collins for the British company Master in 1922 and featured
Booth Conway as Quasimodo, Sybil Thorndike as the Gypsy
girl of the title, Arthur Kingsley as Phoebus and Annesley
Healy as the priest.

German director F. W. Murnau made Der Bucklige
und die Tänzerin ("The Hunchback and the Dancer") for
Helios in 1923. But, like the play The Duke's Daughter; or,
The Hunchback of Paris, the film seems to have been so
titled in order to capitalize on Hugo's story. Der Bucklige
und die Tänzerin was apparently based on Reinhardt's
Sumurun.

Not until 1923 did any filmed version of Notre-Dame
de Paris achieve classic status. That was the year that
Universal Pictures made The Hunchback of Notre Dame on
a grand scale, directed by Wallace Worsley. Universal's

President, Carl Laemmle, had been searching for a spectacle
which would win distinction as "The Crowning Achievement of
the Screen. "

"I have been repeatedly asked why I selected The
Hunchback of Notre Dame for such a massive production, "
said Laemmle later, "but I do not think that anyone coming
fresh from its showing will ask the question.   He will have
the answer in his own emotions.   Hugo's eternal classic
was selected because it was the creation of a giant among
authors; because it is established in the appreciation of the
wide world and as a work of creative art, has the perma-
nence of the ancient cathedral itself.

"A romance established in the hearts of millions that
will endure for centuries, the book will pass its spell from
generation to generation--never old, but always with the
freshness and fire of the author's flesh and blood expression.
Such a book should make a picture with the same time-de-
fying quality.   With the aid of a staff of skilled editorial
minds, all the world's literature was debated to select the
ideal story--the story of human conflict, absorbing action
and with the spectacular element that furnishes high pictorial
value.

"All along I had in mind Victor Hugo's romance and
I was gratified when the majority, reporting individually,
named The Hunchback of Notre Dame as the ideal story.
To tell the truth, I was so carried away with the large possibilities of it that I would have produced it whatever the
verdict of the others.

"I feel that there has been put into the production all
the beauty, color and charm of the book--all of its massive
character and as it stands, it is not a production only for
today.   It is, like the storied cathedral, for all days to
come. "

Universal's Hunchback of Notre Dame was certainly
an epic.   A year of planning ensured that the film would be
the most spectacular version of the story yet to go before
the motion picture cameras.   A detailed replica of Paris
during the Middle Ages was built on the Universal backlot.
A reproduction of Notre Dame Cathedral 225 feet tall and
150 feet wide was built, so sturdy that it was used in later
films and exists in part to this day to the delight of visitors
to Universal Studios.   Thousands of costumes were made to

clothe the nearly four thousand actors and extras who would appear in the film (the latter being mobilized military style by former officer Charles Stallings and directed via microphone and loudspeakers by Worsley). The film required four months of shooting and cost Universal an unprecedented $1,250,000.

The role of Quasimodo was played, in one of the greatest triumphs of screen portrayal, by Lon Chaney. He was born Alonzo Chaney to deaf mute parents on April 1, 1883, at Colorado Springs, Colorado. At the age of three, Chaney was already in show business, performing the pantomime sketches and charades staged by his mother. The young Chaney learned to communicate with his mother through sign language and mime. As he grew older, he haunted the theatres to observe the performers, learning the acting trade. By 1901, when the 18-year-old Lon Chaney joined his older brother John's stock company, he was already skilled in communicating with audiences.

Lon Chaney focused his talents in the still new medium of motion pictures in 1913. The following year he joined Universal Pictures. When he was asked by a youthful production chief named Irving Thalberg to portray Quasimodo in The Hunchback of Notre Dame, Chaney, now an actor with star status, gave his price for the role as $1,500 per week. Chaney was refused, but when Universal was unable to secure another actor capable of creating the role, Chaney upped his price to $2,000 a week. The back-and-forth bickering continued until Universal, unable to find another actor, grudgingly settled for Chaney's latest demand, a weekly salary of $2,500.

Chaney's ability to communicate to audiences without the benefit of sound was not Thalberg's only reason for wanting him to play Quasimodo. The actor was a master of character make-up, creating magic from his box of primitive cosmetics materials. Only through the make-up genius of Chaney and the actor's ability to bring the tragic character to life through pantomime would Quasimodo's unfortunate lot be understood and felt by the movie audience.

As with his other character roles, Chaney determined to become Quasimodo, experiencing as best he could the anguish of the Notre Dame bell-ringer. First he read the description of the Hunchback given by Hugo, then he proceeded to recreate the hapless character with astounding

The immortal Lon Chaney as Quasimodo and Patsy Ruth
Miller as Esmeralda in the Universal classic, The Hunchback of Notre Dame (1923).

accuracy.   He built up his nose and cheeks and covered one
eye with mortician's wax.   Heavily applied greasepaint
covered his face.   An uncomfortable set of oversized false
teeth were fitted over his own teeth while a wire kept his
mouth open.   Chaney completed the make-up with a bushy
wig and shaggy eyebrows.

But the face was only the beginning of Chaney's Quasimodo.   The actor donned shoulder pads and a harness-like
device which prevented him from standing erect even if he
so desired and simulated the hunchback.   The whole affair
weighed a pressing seventy pounds!   Over this appliance
Chaney added an artificial skin, made of rubber, onto which
was affixed more unsightly hair.   This Quasimodo was unlike
any ever seen on the screen before, truly--along with the
later Phantom of the Opera--one of the greatest triumphs of
this actor, already known as the Man of a Thousand Faces.

It required four hours every morning for Chaney to
transform himself into Quasimodo and all of his moments
before the cameras were spent hobbling and crouching to
maintain the characterization.   Since liberties were taken
with Hugo in filming The Hunchback of Notre Dame, allotting
more of the story to Quasimodo (who had a smaller role in
the novel), it is indeed fortunate that Universal met Chaney's
weekly pay rate.

Apparently Chaney enjoyed his work on Hunchback.
Motion picture film exists, and has been shown on television,
taken on the set of the movie wherein Chaney is seen joking
with crew members and clowning about the cathedral set.
(Some scenes of Chaney sans Quasimodo make-up clowning
about the Hunchback set were included in the third installment of the series Life in Hollywood in 1927.   The film
brought viewers to Universal Pictures in a type of precursor
to the studio tour so popular today.)   Except for a few of the
more dangerous scenes, Chaney did his own stuntwork and
was consequently uninsurable.   Strongman Joe Bonomo donned
the Hunchback outfit to perform some of the more hazardous
long shots.

In The Hunchback of Notre Dame the Gypsy girl Esmeralda (Patsy Ruth Miller) lives in the Court of Miracles,
the meeting place of beggars and thieves, where the blind
can see and the lame walk.   Quasimodo's domain is the
great cathedral of Notre Dame from which he scoffs at the
populace below and taunts them like some hump-backed

gargoyle.   A major change from the Hugo story was that
the archdeacon Dom Claude (Nigel De Brulier) is a saintly
man, clad in symbolic white.   Dom Claude's black-attired
brother Jehan (Brandon Hurst) performs the villainies and
leads the obedient Quasimodo about like a trained dog.

It is the Festival of Fools, the one day of the year
during which the oppressed Parisians indulge in unbridled
pleasure.   Quasimodo goads them from his cathedral perch
but soon it is he, wearing a mock crown and robe, who becomes their "king."   Esmeralda dances in his presence but
is repulsed by his ugliness.   Watching Esmeralda licentious-
ly is the plotting Jehan, who later commands the Hunchback
to kidnap the Gypsy girl.   Esmeralda is rescued by her
Prince Charming, Phoebus (Norman Kerry), the Captain of
the Royal Guard, while Quasimodo is captured by his men.

The Hunchback of Notre Dame is chained to a wheel
the following day and whipped for the pleasure of the uncar-
ing crowd.   When the misshapen being cries out, "I thirst!"
(in an allusion to the crucified Jesus Christ), he is given
water by a compassionate Esmeralda.   Later, Jehan stabs
Phoebus and Esmeralda is tortured into confessing to the
crime.   When, disguised as a priest, Jehan declares his
love and attempts to rescue Esmeralda from her prison cell,
she says she would rather die.

Thus, the next morning, it is Quasimodo who sounds
the knell for the Gypsy dancer's execution on the gallows,
the bells of Notre Dame being the only sounds his deaf ears
can perceive.   But the Hunchback has remembered Esmeralda's kindness.   Heroically he slides down a 150-foot-long
rope and knocks aside the guards, tossing Esmeralda over
one shoulder and carrying her into Dom Claude's cathedral,
claiming "Sanctuary!"

At first Joe Bonomo refused to perform the rope-slide
stunt because his leather gloves did not offer suitable protection.   A second stunt double was then brought in who did
enact the feat, only to suffer a broken leg and severe rope
burns.   Bonomo was not about to let another stuntman injure
himself while substituting for him.   He lined his gloves with
metal foil and sewed foil strips to his pants and completed
the spectacular job without hurting himself.

In the bell tower of Notre Dame, Quasimodo rings
his music for the woman he now hopelessly loves.   Yet while

the Hunchback protects the woman, Clopin (Ernest Torrance),
the king of thieves who had brought the infant Esmeralda
from Gypsies and raised her among his people, plans to
rescue her from the monster Hunchback.   In the most exciting scenes of the film, Clopin's people storm Notre Dame,
while Quasimodo fights them off, hurling down timbers and
huge blocks of stone and finally scalds them with molten
metal intended for making new bells.   Even during Quasimodo's triumph the evil Jehan attempts to claim Esmeralda
as his own.   No longer the obedient slave, Quasimodo turns
upon his former master.   Before the bell-ringer can complete his assault on him, though, the dying Jehan stabs him
fatally.   Esmeralda learns that her Phoebus still lives in a
happier ending than given the readers of Notre-Dame de
Paris.   Then, after ringing his own death-knell with his beloved bells, Quasimodo, the Hunchback of Notre Dame, dies.

The Hunchback of Notre Dame was hailed as a masterpiece and soon made back its cost at the box office.   The
film, along with The Phantom of the Opera two years later,
bestowed prestige upon Universal Pictures, a studio whose
usual fare was action pictures and Westerns.   When seen today, however, the film is quite slow, even considering the
grand spectacle of the production.   Chaney's performance
remains so masterful and enduring that viewers often tend to
await impatiently his next appearance while plodding through
scene upon scene in the Court of Miracles or the Grand Ball
of King Louis XI.   The picture is overly long (103 minutes)
and might have been edited down to a shorter, tighter version had not Universal been so intent on creating an epic
masterpiece.

Scenes from Chaney's Hunchback of Notre Dame appeared in Highlights of Horror, an early 1960s home movie
issued by Entertainment Films, and in the short film Rendezvous (1973).   An edited version of the picture was given a
comedy soundtrack and retitled Dinky Dunsen, Boy Cheer-
leader in 1962 for the Jay Ward television series "Fractured
Flickers."   The actor's son Lon Chaney, Jr., sued for defa-
mation of his father's creation.   "The Hunchback of Notre
Dame" was a fiction piece adapted from the Universal picture by Janey Reid in the December 1923 issue of Motion
Picture Monthly.

Lon Chaney's star status transcended to that of superstar (some half century before the coining of the term) with
The Hunchback of Notre Dame, followed by a more lucrative

career at MGM.   He had just made the crucial transition
from silent films to talkies, finishing The Unholy Three in
1930, a remake of his silent version of 1925.   While working on a railroad film titled Thunder, Chaney got a piece of
artificial snow, made from mica, lodged in his throat.   The
irritation soon developed into cancer of the lumbar region.
On the morning of August 26, 1930 the hospitalized actor
suffered a final hemorrhage.   Within thirty minutes, the
screen's Man of a Thousand Faces was dead.

Even with the Chaney Hunchback of Notre Dame only
a few years old, other film companies were again making
their own versions of the story.   Enmei-in no Semushi ("The
Hunchback of Enmei-in") was a Japanese version made about
1925.   A remarkable adaptation of the story was made in
1926 by First National Pictures--remarkable, in that even
with the Chaney film yet in the minds of movie audiences,
this version, The Dancer of Paris, eliminated the Hunchback!
(There is also the elusive title Esmeralda--Dancer of Paris,
but nothing else seems to be known about the film.   The
title could very well be an alternate one for some other
movie.)   Mack Sennett ignored the Hugo story altogether but
did lampoon the title for his 1920s comedy short The Halfback of Notre Dame.

The Hunchback joined other Chaney characters in the
filmed variety show Hollywood Review of 1929, directed by
Charles Reisner for MGM, where Chaney was then under
contract.   Gus Edwards sang the number "Lon Chaney's
Gonna Get You If You Don't Watch Out," while the actor's
creations cavorted about the stage.   Strangely, Chaney himself was not in the film.

In 1932, Universal Pictures announced a remake of
The Hunchback of Notre Dame to star Boris Karloff, fresh
out of his starring role in Frankenstein, as Quasimodo.
But the picture was never made.   It took an animated cartoon Mickey's Gala Premiere (United Artists, 1933) to revive the character courtesy of the Walt Disney studios ani-
mators for a cameo appearance with Dracula and the Frankenstein Monster.   This cartoon short was issued in a home
movie edition titled Movie Star Mickey by Hollywood Film
Enterprises.   The Quasimodo scene also appeared in the
satirical independent cartoon Uncle Walt.   Two Indian versions of the Hugo story were filmed in 1937:   the first, entitled Dhanwan, was "inspired" by Notre-Dame de Paris.   It
was directed by P. Atorthy and starred Ratanbai and

Hafeesjee.   The second film, Nav Jawan, starred Harishchandra with Aspi directing for the Wadia company.

The greatest of all cinema versions of Hugo's novel
was made in 1939 by RKO Radio Pictures.   Under the superb
direction of William Dieterle, The Hunchback of Notre Dame,
as this version was also called, was less of an historical
drama and more of a horror film than was the Universal
film.   Esmeralda was played by red-haired beauty Maureen
O'Hara, High Justice Frollo (who never quite made priest)
was played by Sir Cedric Hardwicke and, though Lon Chaney,
Jr., tried to secure his father's old role for himself, Quasimodo was portrayed by corpulent Charles Laughton.

The RKO publicity department was cautious not to release advance photographs of Laughton's Quasimodo make-up
and shots of his face existing today (with the exception of
blow-ups from the actual motion picture film) are exceeding-
ly rare.   The studio thought it best to let audiences be
thoroughly shocked by the first, sudden, full-face close-up
of Laughton in the film, which they certainly were.

Fortunately for Laughton, make-up techniques had advanced since the days of Lon Chaney and, though a wire ar-
rangement forced him to shamble about in a hunched over
posture, he essayed the characterization with little discom-
fort.   Latex covered two thirds of his face, requiring three
hours of application and thirty minutes to remove.   While
not as grotesque as Chaney's make-up, Laughton's Quasimodo visage was in its subtle way even more horrifying.
His nose was upturned like that of a human pig and one eye
stared blankly from its socket, located noticeably lower than
the other.   After the application of the facial make-up, a
two-pound hump of papier-mâché was attached to his back.
A reddish wig and a coarse sack cloth shirt worn over tights
completed the bizarre guise.

Laughton, less acrobatic than Chaney, shuffled through
the gothic magnificence of Notre Dame, lending bits of humor to his characterization which only made his Hunchback
the more pathetic.   The plotline follows Frollo's treachery
in trying to steal the love of Esmeralda, with the scene of
Quasimodo swinging down upon a rope to carry her off Tarzan style absolutely thrilling.   The ending, however, di-
verged even farther from that devised by Victor Hugo and
both Esmeralda and Quasimodo survive.   In a memorable
and poignant final shot, Quasimodo speaks to one of the

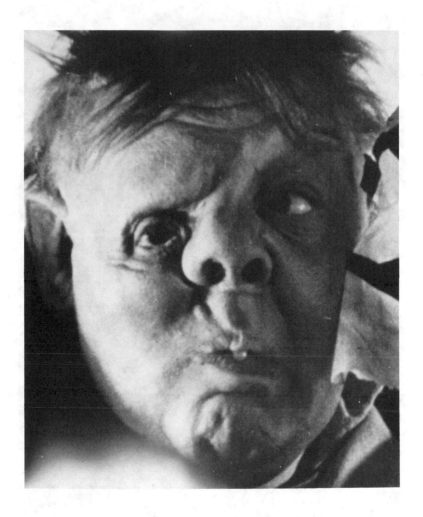

A rare photograph of Charles Laughton as Quasimodo in the
RKO masterpiece, The Hunchback of Notre Dame (1939).
Courtesy of Forrest J Ackerman.

stone gargoyles, wondering, "Why was I not made of stone?" Then the camera smoothly pulls back until Quasimodo is but a moving speck, perhaps another gargoyle as seen from this distance, upon a high edifice of Notre Dame.

Yet another Indian version, Badshah Dampati (also known under the more popular title The Hunchback of Notre Dame), was made in 1953. Amiya Chakrabarty produced and directed this movie starring K. N. Singh, Usha Kiron, Pradeep, Agha and Ulhas as the Hunchback.

The story was filmed again under its original title Notre-Dame de Paris in 1956 by Paris Film Productions and released by Allied Artists the following year. (In America the film was given the more commercial title The Hunchback of Notre Dame.) This French/Italian co-production was made in color and wide screen and was directed by Jean Delannoy.

The strikingly beautiful Italian actress Gina Lollobrigida portrayed an earthy Esmeralda in this 1956 production while the latest Quasimodo was enacted by Anthony Quinn. Given a larger nose, oversized ears, a Neanderthal brow and one bad eye, all with latex appliances, Quinn's interpretation of the role was neither as frightening nor as physically powerful as Chaney's or Laughton's. His Quasimodo is now the servant of archdeacon and alchemist Claude Frollo (Alain Cuny).

As per the original story, Esmeralda is arrested for Frollo's stabbing of Phoebus (Jean Danet). Charged with the crime of witchcraft, Esmeralda confesses under intense torture. The King's troops storm Notre Dame cathedral, where Esmeralda, rescued from hanging by Quasimodo, has been given sanctuary. During the final battle between soldiers and Esmeralda's friends, the Gypsy girl is killed. Realizing that Frollo is really the one responsible for Esmeralda's death, the Hunchback hurls him down from an upper gallery of the cathedral, then enters the burial vault where he embraces the woman that he loved. As in Hugo's novel, years later their skeletons are discovered in a close embrace.

Opposite: Gina Lollobrigida as Esmeralda and a less frightening Anthony Quinn as Quasimodo in the 1956 Paris Film Productions' Notre-Dame de Paris (released in the United States by United Artists as The Hunchback of Notre Dame.

Notre-Dame de Paris lacked the sense of spectacle that had marked its two major predecessors, but it did bring back to the story elements of the occult which had been in the novel.

There were two other films released in 1957 presenting the Quasimodo character. Daiei, a Japanese production company, lampooned the Hugo story with Nanbanji no Semushi-Otoko, which is also known as Return to Manhood. Torajiro Sato directed this story of a drunken warrior who is transformed by sake into a hunchbacked bell-ringer, certainly a good case for temperance groups. Only after the hunchback slays his enemy does he resume his normal appearance. Nanbanji no Semushi-Otoko featured Achako Hanabishi, Shunji Sakai, Naritoshi Hayashi, Tamao Nakamura and Kyu Sazanka.

Man of a Thousand Faces was Universal-International's biographical tribute to Lon Chaney, with James Cagney portraying the master of make-up and pantomime. The film depicted Chaney's summons by Irving Thalberg (Robert J. Evans) to play the role of Quasimodo in The Hunchback of Notre Dame in a way that audiences could know the pain of being born in such a grotesque form. Cagney, through the painless make-up artistry of Bud Westmore and his crew, recreated many of Chaney's characterizations, including (through the use of latex) the Hunchback. Director Joseph Pevney recreated the whipping wheel sequence in front of the original Notre Dame set.

(A comic strip spoof of the film, "The Man of 1000 Faces 500 Bodies and 348 Voices Growls and Shrieks," appeared in the sixth issue (January 1958) of Humbug (Humbug Publishing Company). The Hunchback is revealed to be, not a Chaney creation, but a real creature.)

Quasimodo appeared as one of numerous wax exhibits in Santo en el museo de cera (1963) and also joined the festivities of Mad Monster Party? (1967) and its television followup "Mad, Mad, Mad Monsters" (1972). For a while in the early 1970s, during the height of the black exploitation film, there was talk about a possible film to be entitled The Hunchblack of Notre Dame. Mercifully this take-off was never made.

Since Quasimodo first loped froglike across the motion picture screen, numerous sinister and pathetic hunchbacks,

James Cagney as Lon Chaney's Hunchback, one of many
characterizations recreated for the biography, Man of a
Thousand Faces (Universal-International, 1957).

obviously inspired by their Notre Dame predecessor, have
made their appearance.   To list all of them would be a fu-
tile venture, especially when considering how many of the
screen's mad or otherwise unorthodox scientists seem to
have a proclivity towards obedient hump-backed assistants
(such as Henry Frankenstein who made use of the sadistic
hunchbacked dwarf Fritz, played by Dwight Frye, in the
1931 version of Frankenstein).   A modicum of "hunchback"
films do deserve a brief mention, though, since their titles
or presentation might have been different if not for the existence of the Notre Dame bell-ringer.

     The Hunchback of Cedar Lodge, a 1914 Balboa pro-
duction, was a ghost story set in a library.   Universal's
House of Frankenstein (1944) featured J.   Carrol Naish as
the hunchback Daniel who was unabashedly intended to suggest the earlier Chaney creation.   Daniel was shown in a
menacing close-up on the film's advertising posters and
listed as the "Hunchback" amid a line of other famous monsters, obviously intended to bring Quasimodo to the minds
of movie-goers before entering the theatre.   In the film poor
Daniel falls in love with a pretty Gypsy dancer named Ilonka
(Elena Verdugo) and heroically rescues her from a whipping.
When his love is unrequited there is little doubt as to
Daniel's inspiration.   Der Bucklige von Soho (The Hunchback of Soho), a 1966 German film made in color by Rialto,
was based on several Edgar Wallace mysteries and featured
a hunchbacked killer who stalks the foggy streets in search
of victims.   El jorobado de la morgue ("The Hunchback of
the Morgue"), a Spanish coproduction of the Eva and Janus
film companies, starred Paul Naschy as an insane hunchback
who not only keeps the corpse of the woman he loves in a
morgue but also indulges in the questionable (but typical for
horror film hunchbacks) profession of supplying cadavers to
feed a mad doctor's carnivorous monster.   Javier Aguirre
directed this atrocious color film of 1972.

MORE QUASIMODOS

     Quasimodo hobbled his way across the radio airwaves
in 1932.   George Edwards starred as the character in The
Hunchback of Notre Dame, an unbearably long serialized version of the tale.   In this primitive radio melodrama Edwards
emoted archaic dialogue taken directly from the Hugo novel.

     Television has not ignored Quasimodo.   On November
8 and 15, 1954, "The Hunchback of Notre Dame" was

performed in two hour-long installments before the live
cameras of "Robert Montgomery Presents" on the NBC network. Robert Ellenstein played Quasimodo in a make-up apparently patterned after that of Charles Laughton in the 1939
motion picture.

In 1961, Roald Dahl's television series "Way Out"
brought viewers two fantastic Quasimodo faces in the episode
titled "Face in the Mirror." Alfred Ryder played an actor
who is about to portray Quasimodo on the legitimate stage.
Happening upon a skid row derelict with a face resembling
the famous Hunchback, the actor pays him for permission to
copy his face. After some treachery by the actor (along
with a sprinkling of supernatural intervention), he discovers
that his own face has now really become that of Quasimodo.
For this show, two Quasimodos were created by make-up
artist Dick Smith. After reading the script, Smith submitted
sketches of his proposed make-ups to the producer, who rejected them because the nearly normal eyes did not appear
gruesome enough. After studying some medical books,
Smith created a make-up with a leprous face, thick lips and
puffy cheeks and jowls. A scar and a hideous bulging eye
completed the guise which, because of its ugliness, had to
be modified for television. The final version, even with the
smaller eye, was still thoroughly horrifying.

Lon Chaney, Jr., who failed to win the Quasimodo
role in the 1939 feature-length film, was able to ape his
father's characterization on "Route 66" (1962), wherein he
was given the obligatory bad eye and oversized false teeth
for a brief scene as the Hunchback of Notre Dame.

In 1977 television returned to the original Victor Hugo
classic with a faithful BBC-produced version of The Hunchback of Notre Dame, which played in the United States over
the NBC network. The videotaped presentation starred Warren Clarke as Quasimodo and Michelle Newell as Esmeralda.

Quasimodo's other television appearances include "Get
Smart," "The Mouse Factory," "Sinister Cinema," "House
of Horror" (Portland, Ore.), "The Sonny and Cher Comedy
Hour," the "Horror Hall of Fame" special, "The Beatles"
(cartoon), and even a commercial for Post Sugar Crisp.

Calga Publishers issued a novel in 1970 called The
Adult Version of the Hunchback of Notre Dame, Hugo's story
rewritten for the pornography market. Mayfair Publications

Lon Chaney, Jr., essayed his father's Quasimodo role on
television's "Route 66" (1962).

---

changed the title of its Monster World magazine to Quasimodo's Monster Magazine with the third issue (July 1975).
But it was the illustrative pages of the comic books that
proved most conducive to the Hunchback's adventures.

A number of comic books have retold the Victor Hugo
story. Classic Comics no. 18 (1944) had an adaptation,
"The Hunchback of Notre Dame," drawn by Allen Simon,

with the ending rewritten to somewhat follow the 1923 Universal film. Quasimodo is pursued by soldiers to the cathedral's bell tower. A hurled dagger pierces his hand and, as he drops toward the pavement, the bells begin to clang by themselves. Esmeralda survives to find her beloved Phoebus still alive. In 1960 (the magazine's title changed to Classics Illustrated) the story was presented in a new edition with new art. Prior to the American release of the Anthony Quinn Notre-Dame de Paris, Dell Publishing Company issued a comic book of The Hunchback of Notre Dame based on the movie. The altered ending left Quasimodo alive and ringing the bells to mourn the dead Esmeralda. Another version of the Hugo story was published in the late 1960s in the Brazilian comic book Almanaque ostorias de terror from Gráfica Editôra Penteado. A comic strip based on the Lon Chaney Hunchback of Notre Dame was drawn by Bill Nelson and published in The Monster Times no. 28 (November 1973). The Hunchback of Notre Dame, by Naunerle Farr and artist Jon Lo Famia, in 1974, was part of the black and white Now Age Illustrated series. (An edited reprint of this version appeared in color as the third issue of Marvel Classic Comics.) A spoof "The Hunchback of Notre Doom," drawn by Joe Maneely, appeared in an early 1950s issue of one of the Marvel Comics Group's satire magazines. It exposed the hunchback "Quasimudpuddle" as a handsome police spy in disguise.

A story inspired by Quasimodo was "The Hunchback of Hollywood and the Movie Murder," drawn by Jack Kirby for the third issue of Timely Comics' (Marvel) Captain America (May 1941). When a film company moves into an old castle to shoot an anti-Nazi movie set during medieval times, a Quasimodo lookalike goes on a murder spree. Under the creature's heavy make-up is a bund member trying to sabotage the production.

The Quasimodo theme has also overlapped into the legend of the Frankenstein Monster. "Death O'Clock," written and drawn by Dick Briefer, appeared in the 33rd and final issue of Frankenstein (October-November 1954), from Feature Publications. Like Quasimodo, Koro is a deformed bell-ringer (a dwarf) in an old European town. One day Koro discovers that the hideous Frankenstein Monster is using the bell tower to hide from his enemies. The two tragic characters become commiserating friends. When a half-wit named Pol tries to kill Koro for his job, the Monster intervenes, harpooning the villain to the clock outside with one of its giant hands.

The Notre Dame bell-ringer made an anachronistic appearance in the Frankenstein comic strip running in Sky-wald's Psycho magazine. "Freaks of Fear!" was written and drawn by Sean Todd (Tom Sutton) and published in Psycho no. 4 (September 1971). As the chained Franken-stein Monster is exhibited before Notrc Dame cathedral, Quasimodo appears, swinging down on a rope to abduct a woman dear to the creation of Frankenstein. After a chase into the bell tower, the Hunchback sends the Monster falling to an apparent doom by deafening him with his clanging bells.

The most unusual version of the Hunchback of Notre Dame to appear in comic books was the character of Quasi-modo which debuted in the fourth "king-size special" of Fantastic Four, published in November 1966 by the Marvel Comics group. Quasimodo, the creation of writer Stan Lee and artist Jack Kirby, was a super-computer whose metallic form suggested the slumped posture of the famed bell-ringer and whose electrons shaped themselves into a familiar face. The computer's name stands for Quasi-Motivational Destruct Organ and its human personality pleads with its creator, the Mad Thinker, as many motion picture hunchbacks have begged their mad scientist masters. Quasimodo wants to be repaid for his loyalty by being put into human form. The story ends with Quasimodo alone, bemoaning his entrapment.

Quasimodo finally does acquire this boon in the next Fantastic Four special (November 1967) in "The Peerless Power of the Silver Surfer," again by Lee and Kirby. Sym-pathizing with the suffering machine, the Silver Surfer wields his cosmic power to reshape Quasimodo into anthropomorphic form. Now more than ever resembling his namesake, the hunchbacked humanoid turns upon his superhero benefactor, only to be reduced to an unmoving statue high atop a tower clock.

Although the Hunchback of Notre Dame has not lent himself to as much merchandise as his more popular com-rades like Frankenstein's Monster, Count Dracula and the Wolf Man, he has managed to reap some impressive profits for companies using his image for their products. There have been Quasimodo masks by Don Post (based on James Cagney's version), Aurora model kits, trading cards and calenders bearing his image, and toy figures, for which Victor Hugo would be collecting some handsome royalty checks if he lived today. The Hunchback has served as a popular exhibit in wax museums throughout the world, made

personal appearances in live horror shows and been used to
advertise S. D. Stern Communications.

There is great empathy for the unfortunate Quasimodo.
For readers of the original novel he represented more than
merely a loving person trapped within the form of a living
gargoyle.   Quasimodo represented a part of the Church, a
part of the city itself and every person living there.   All of
us have been unable to express ourselves, to speak our
deepest feelings, to possess that which we love most.   His
is the stuff of immortal characters, a kind of grotesque
Everyman.

Still, it is the 1923 movie of The Hunchback of Notre
Dame which is the most popular presentation of Victor Hugo's
story.   But for Lon Chaney, his greatest triumph, in the
opinion of many film buffs, was yet to come.   In 1925 his
frightening image would again be haunting Paris.   This time,
however, it would not be the cathedral of Notre Dame, but
the Opera House.

VI

THE PHANTOMS OF THE OPERA

The single most frightening moment in all the era of silent motion pictures was the famed unmasking scene in The Phantom of the Opera, a Universal Pictures classic of 1925. Reportedly people in the audience fainted as the hideous visage of Erik, the Opera Phantom, was laid naked before their incredulous eyes. Whether or not such faintings were only part of Universal's publicity campaign, the screams aroused by the Phantom's unmasking were certainly real.

The film was based on the novel The Phantom of the Opera, a romantic horror story by Gaston Leroux, published in 1908. Leroux's prologue unabashedly states:

> The Opera ghost really existed. He was not, as was long believed, a creature of the imagination of the artists, the superstition of the managers, or a product of the absurd and impressionable brains of the young ladies of the ballet, their mothers, the box-keepers, the cloak-room attendants or the concierge. Yes, he existed in flesh and blood, although he assumed the complete appearance of a real phantom; that is to say, of a spectral shade.

The Opera ghost, or Phantom, was, according to Leroux, an unfortunate man named Erik, born with such ugliness that even his parents were repulsed and terrified by him. Naturally the youthful Erik could not live in a house where his mother and father regarded him as a monster. He ran away to join a fair where an exhibitor put him to work. Erik became the fair's "living corpse."

Following his brief show business career, Erik fell
in with Gypsies where he acquired an education as an artist
and magician. Soon the young man became an accomplished
singer, ventriloquist and conjurer; these skills eventually
made him a favorite entertainer at the court of the Shah of
Persia. While in Persia, Erik pleased the Shah by proving
that he could not differentiate between good and evil. Erik's
talents contributed to a number of political assassinations.

Displaying an aptitude for architecture, Erik designed
an edifice for the Shah so that His Majesty could skulk
around his palace unseen. Of course, Erik could not be allowed to live since he was the only person other than the
Shah to know of the secret places. The hideous Erik was
only saved when a friend substituted in his place a corpse
already half-eaten by scavenger birds.

Later elsewhere in Asia Minor, Erik pleased a Sultan
by constructing all the trap-doors, strong-boxes and auto-
mata "which were found at Yildiz-Kiosk after the last Turkish revolution." But eventually Erik grew weary of such adventures and longed to enjoy a life "like everybody else."
His first mundane work was as a building contractor; he was
responsible for the construction of the Paris Opera House's
foundation. Erik utilized his knowledge and talents to mold
the lower haunts of the building to suit his own needs, creating "a dwelling unknown to the rest of the earth, where he
could hide from men's eyes for all time."

Leroux described the ghastly appearance of the Opera
ghost through the lips of Joseph Buquet, the chief scene-
shifter and a man who had actually beheld the creature's
face:

'He is extraordinarily thin and his dress-coat
hangs on a skeleton frame. His eyes are so deep
that you can hardly see the fixed pupils. You just
see two big black holes, as in a dead man's skull.
His skin, which is stretched across his bones like
a drumhead, is not white, but a nasty yellow.
His nose is so little worth talking about that you
can't see it side-face; and the absence of that nose
is a horrible thing to look at. All the hair he has
is three or four long dark locks on his forehead
and behind his ears. '

According to Leroux, Erik died a peaceful and private death. His skeleton was later discovered in the cellar of the Opera House. The author offered his own opinion as to how the bones might have been disposed. "I say that the place of the skeleton of the Opera ghost is in the archives of the National Academy of Music. It is no ordinary skeleton. "

Universal Pictures acquired the rights to film Gaston Leroux's novel and commenced production in 1924. The studio's president Carl Laemmle, Sr. , realized that films were in stiff competition with a medium that provided sound without pictures as opposed to the movies' pictures without sound. To compete with the growing popularity of radio, The Phantom of the Opera would be an expensive, spectacular production. In bringing Leroux's story to the screen Laemmle spent the then incredible sum of one million dollars.

A good portion of that million was allotted to the construction of a convincing facsimile of the Paris Opera House. The vast interior set reproduced the stages, balconies, dungeons and other rooms of the original, including a great subterranean lake. The grim, gothic labyrinths beneath the Opera House perfectly reflected the appearance and personality of the malformed being who lived there. The main stage with its balconies and five tiers was of such detail and permanent construction that it was not torn down after the completion of The Phantom of the Opera but, like the "Frankenstein streets" and the colonial mansion in which Kharis perished in The Mummy's Tomb, were preserved and retained for use in a myriad of films that came afterward, a few of them being The Raven (1935), The Mad Ghoul (1943), The Black Castle (1952) and The Perils of Pauline (1967). *

In 1924 there was but one actor capable of interpreting the role of Leroux's Opera ghost on the screen. Lon Chaney, one year before, had triumphed at Universal in his role of Quasimodo in The Hunchback of Notre Dame. Only

---

*Lon Chaney, Jr. , attended a ceremony on the opera set stage on December 11, 1940, in which a plaque was put up with the inscription: "Dedicated to the memory of Lon Chaney, for whose picture 'The Phantom of the Opera' this stage was erected in 1924. " The stage can now be seen by visitors to the Universal Pictures studio tour along with an actor who impersonates the Phantom.

Chaney had the skill to alter his appearance in accordance with the description of the Phantom in Leroux's novel. And Chaney's masterful uses of pantomime assured that Erik the Phantom would emerge on the silent screen as a real, in-depth character.

The Phantom of the Opera was directed by Rupert Julian, but he never completed the project. Julian was a difficult man to get along with and fashioned himself to be another Erich von Stroheim (whom he replaced as director of the 1923 film Merry Go Round). Like von Stroheim, Julian enforced his directorial commands rigidly and consequently alienated himself from not only a number of cast and crew members but also Chaney himself. Chaney insisted that the direction of the Phantom be handled according to his own interpretation, with Erik being an awesomely impressive figure who would never be dwarfed by the grandeur of the opera or the Opera House. Consequently, Chaney directed many of his own scenes. Julian delivered a finished print of the film ten weeks after production began.

Carl Laemmle was not pleased with Julian's version. Universal's chief executive decided that new footage would be added, especially a lengthening of the movie's climax. Julian was not to be associated with the new scenes. He either walked off the production voluntarily or was given his notice by Laemmle.

In Julian's place was Edward Sedgwick, a director especially known for his action films and comedies. But Laemmle was still dissatisfied, even with Sedgwick's contribution to the picture. Again scenes were added by Sedgwick including a new romantic subplot. The Phantom of the Opera was previewed in this latest version on April 26, 1925, to an unfavorable reception. Again Laemmle set to work on the film, hoping that the elimination of all the new footage with the exception of the climax and the addition of some comedy sequences provided by funnyman Chester Conklin would salvage the production. This latest tinkering succeeded only in making The Phantom of the Opera more of a hodgepodge than ever and it required the efforts of new editors to snip out Conklin's footage and create the motion picture classic that premiered on September 6 of that same year.

The Phantom of the Opera is the story of a man born with the appearance of a living skeleton who haunts the lower

One of the most frightening faces ever beheld on the screen,
Lon Chaney's Erik in The Phantom of the Opera (Universal,
1925).

regions of the Paris Opera House. The Phantom has a permanently reserved private box from which he observes the
Opera House performances. The elusive, ghostlike figure is
rarely seen, and then usually in shadow, and his voice is
sometimes heard issuing through the building as if from nowhere. Only one other mysterious character, known simply
as the Persian, has ever been inside the Medieval torture
chambers and dungeons over which the Opera House was
built and which now serve as the Phantom's domain.

The Phantom's voice, identifying itself as the Spirit
of Music, has been coaching an attractive young singer
named Christine Daaé (Mary Philbin). The voice has ad-
vised her to think only of her art and then, someday, the
Spirit will take form and claim her love.

The Phantom sends a threatening letter to Carlotta
(Mary Fabian), the famous prima donna of the opera, warning her not to appear in the new production of Marguerite.
Christine must sing the lead or else the Opera House will
suffer disaster. The opera star becomes mysteriously ill
and Christine does make her starring debut upon the Paris
stage. The following night, however, Carlotta ignores the
Phantom's second warning note and replaces Christine. As
the plump singer performs, she and the audience see a flickering in the overhead lights. Unseen, the Phantom whispers,
"Beware! She is singing to bring down the chandelier!"
From offstage the Phantom manipulates the huge chandelier
suspended high above the audience; shortly afterwards the
huge chandelier breaks loose and crashes down upon the
terrified opera patrons.

Julian's uninspired direction shows in this sequence,
which might have been one of the more suspenseful moments
in The Phantom of the Opera. Unfortunately there is little
suspense as we briefly view the Phantom's shadow while he
tampers with the chains and pullies which maintain the chandelier at its zenith in the Opera House. There are the expected reaction shots of Carlotta and the members of the
audience. The chandelier begins to plummet from the ceiling. But the scene cuts so abruptly to the chandelier already pinning its victims to the floor that the viewer is left
with the feeling that some footage has been deleted. More
suspense was generated from similarly staged "cliffhanger"
scenes in the less prestigious motion picture serials being
made at the time.

During the confusion caused by the chandelier, Christine returns to her dressing room.   There the unseen Spirit informs her that it is finally the time for him to receive her love.   Her mirror slowly opens, revealing a secret passageway.   Christine enters to find her secret mentor, a cloaked, strangely tragic figure whose face is concealed by a mask.   The Phantom takes her on a journey, first on horseback and then via gondola on a black lake reminiscent of the River Styx, five levels beneath the Opera House.   In his private chambers the formidable masked man reveals a pathetic, human side to his enigmatic personality: He is what he is because of the misunderstanding and torments of other men.

As the Phantom sits at the organ, playing his own composition, "Don Juan Triumphant," Christine, overwhelmed by curiosity, inches toward him, mustering the courage to touch his mask.   At last the fearful woman tears away the mask, revealing the face of the Opera Phantom, a living skull with deathly pale skin hanging against the bone underneath, the glaring eyes, the peg of a nose and misshapen teeth, the sparse hair hanging from a domelike cranium. Surely this was the most horrible countenance ever seen on the motion picture screen, all the more effective when beheld by incredulous audiences in 1925.   The Phantom's face was such a triumph of Chaney's make-up artistry, so unsettlingly realistic, that Universal wisely forbade the release of any photographs of the character unmasked prior to the film's premiere.   Audiences were expecting to be frightened, but the shock of seeing that living human skull surpassed anything they might have conjured up in their imaginations beforehand.

The Phantom was Lon Chaney's supreme motion picture characterization, surpassing even his Quasimodo of The Hunchback of Notre Dame.   Chaney played the role of the Phantom with broad mime bordering on overacting, yet the theatrical style was perfectly suited to the grand gothic setting and mood of the Opera House.   When asked how he accomplished his remarkable Phantom make-up, Chaney humbly replied:

"There are tricks in my peculiar trade that I don't care to divulge any more than a magician will give away his art.   In The Phantom of the Opera people exclaimed at my weird makeup.   I achieved the death's head of that role without wearing a mask.   It was the use of paints in the

The Phantom (Lon Chaney), masquerading as Edgar Allan
Poe's "Red Death," makes a public appearance, in The
Phantom of the Opera (Universal, 1925).

right places--not the obvious parts of the face--which gave
the complete illusion of horror.   My experiments as a stage
manager, which were wide and varied before I jumped into
films, taught me much about lighting effects on the actor's
face and the minor tricks of deception.   These I have been
able to use in achieving weird results on the screen."

        Actually, Chaney's explanation was overly modest.
According to most film scholars, his Phantom make-up required not only more technical effects than mere lighting
and shading but also a considerable amount of physical dis-
comfort.   Chaney's face was elongated by means of a false
head piece with matted wig and by taping back his ears.
Putty was molded over the cheeks to give them a more

prominent and skull-like appearance.   Painful hooks expanded
the nostrils.   A set of uncomfortable false teeth made from
gutta percha simulated the leer of the Death's Head visage.
Celluloid disks were placed inside the mouth to further accen-
tuate the cheekbones while his lips were pulled down by
means of small metal clamps.   Once again, Chaney had
sacrificed his own personal comfort for his art in the creation of an immortal character.

After unmasking the Phantom, Christine quite naturally refuses his love and begs to be released from his cavern-
ous lair.   In another display of emotion, the Phantom agrees
to free her but in return she must not resume her love affair with the handsome Comte Raoul de Chagny (Norman
Kerry).

Later, Christine reveals her experience to Raoul during the Opera House's annual masked ball and admits that
she will never comply with the Phantom's wishes.   Unknown
to Christine, her words are heard by the Phantom who
strides regally into the midst of the revellers, elegantly disguised as the scarlet-cloaked Grim Reaper figure from Edgar Allan Poe's "Masque of the Red Death."   This "Red
Death" sequence (as with sequences from the opera Faust)
were shot in the old two-color Technicolor process.   In a
subsequent black-and-white scene, with the Phantom perched
atop a stone Apollo on the roof of the Opera House to over-
hear more of Christine's infidelity, his cloak, majestically
billowing in the nighttime wind, was hand-tinted a brilliant
red.

Once again the Phantom brings Christine to his subterranean lair.   Raoul is now told by the Persian, actually
an agent of the French police named Ledoux (Arthur Edmund
Carew), that the Phantom is a maniac named Erik, a self-
educated master of the Black Arts and musician who has
escaped from his exile on Devil's Island.   The two new
allies descend into the Opera House catacombs in pursuit
of Christine but become the victims of the Phanton's heat
trap and are almost burned alive.

It is for Christine to decide the fate of her pursuers.
If she chooses to marry the Opera ghost, Raoul and Ledoux
will live; otherwise she can set off explosives that will
destroy the Opera House and everyone within or beneath it.
Christine chooses marriage but the Phantom, instead of releasing them, attempts to drown his two captives.   Finally

Erik relents, then finds himself the quarry of a Parisian
mob. The chase continues outside where the Phantom flees
past the imposing cathedral of Notre Dame (a set still standing from Chaney's Hunchback of Notre Dame film) and to the
brink of the River Seine. There he halts the mob under
pretext of holding a hand grenade. When the Phantom opens
his hand to reveal nothing, the mob descends upon him violently and tosses him into the dark waters.

The Phantom of the Opera opened officially on September 6, 1925, and was to become an unqualified success for
Universal Pictures. It was awarded the distinction of being
among the Ten Best Films of the Year, much of which was
due to the impressive Opera House settings, the gothic atmosphere and the extraordinary make-up and performance of
Lon Chaney. The motion picture certainly ranks among the
most memorable films of any genre made during the sound-
less days of the medium and brought not only huge profits to
Universal but also a certain amount of prestige.

In 1929, to capitalize on the sound craze initiated by
The Jazz Singer (1927), Ernst Laemmle directed new footage to be incorporated into the silent Phantom of the Opera.
Mary Philbin and Norman Kerry were recalled to speak
their lines before the cameras while the old footage was
augmented with music, sound effects and poorly dubbed dialogue. The voice of the Phantom was provided, curiously,
by an actor other than Chaney. Some footage from the silent version was deleted altogether. This "Talking, Singing,
Dancing, Sound Effects, Music, Color!" version, released
in 1930, was unsuccessful and it is the original silent version of The Phantom of the Opera that is still revived for
present day audiences; even over a half century after the
Phantom's premiere unmasking, viewers are still impressed.

Entertainment Films incorporated scenes from The
Phantom of the Opera into the home movie Highlights of
Horror and Blackhawk Films issued an abridged home movie
version of the Chaney film as Great Moments from the
Phantom of the Opera.

OTHER PHANTOMS, OTHER OPERAS

Erik the Opera Phantom may have sunk lifeless beneath the Seine, but his legend was only in its infancy. Universal attempted to recapture some of the glory (and profits)

from The Phantom of the Opera with the 1927 film The Last
Performance, which went into production under the title
Erik the Great.   Not only did the studio resurrect the name
Erik for the entirely new character in The Last Performance,
it also dusted off the grand Paris Opera House set and used
it to stage another tale of gothic horror.

The Last Performance, released in both silent and
sound versions, was directed by Paul Fejos and starred
Conrad Veidt, who was known for his macabre characterizations in silent films, as Erik, a stage magician who boasts
authentic hypnotic powers.   Erik is in love with his beautiful assistant (played by Mary Philbin again) and gains an
hypnotic control over her actions.   The magician is, however,
like the legendary Svengali, unable to win the woman's love
in this fashion and eventually becomes the victim of one of
his own stage illusions.

A "prettified" version of the Phantom of the Opera
(resembling the later cartoon spook Casper the Friendly
Ghost) appeared in MGM's Hollywood Review of 1929.   The
same studio apparently attempted to capitalize on the success of The Phantom in 1931 by filming another Gaston Leroux novel, Ceri-Bibi.   With Leroux's name associated with
the film it was a natural move to change the title to The
Phantom of Paris.   Little imagination was required by potential viewers in linking the name of Leroux with the Phantom of the title.   John S. Robertson directed this story of
a man altering his facial features to that of a murder victim
to trick the killer into admitting his guilt.   Warner Bros.
had the Phantom, along with Mr. Hyde, the Frankenstein
Monster, and Dr. Fu Manchu, all emerge from books in the
1938 color cartoon, Have You Got Any Castles?, directed
by Frank Tashlin.

Not until 1943 did Universal return to the actual Phantom character with a lavish remake in Technicolor and sound.
The Phantom of the Opera was directed by Arthur Lubin and
starred Claude Rains, who had acquired some stature as a
horror films star in such earlier Universal films as The Invisible Man (1933), The Mystery of Edwin Drood (1933) and
The Wolf Man (1941), as the Phantom, Erique Claudin.
Again the original Phantom sets were utilized.   But director
Lubin concentrated more on lavish production numbers than
upon the gothic mood of the Chaney version and detracted
from the aura of mystery surrounding the Phantom by hu-
manizing the character and bestowing upon him a specific

origin. Nonetheless, despite the complaints of horror buffs
that the film boasted too much Opera and not enough Phantom, this Phantom of the Opera remains a classic in its
own right and is in many ways more fluid and entertaining
than the original.

The motion picture, Universal's most expensive en-
deavor up to that time, costing a total of $1,750,000, was
well received by the public and garnered the studio a pair
of Academy Awards, one for best use of color.

Erique Claudin, a violinist in the Paris Opera orchestra, suffers from arthritis and hopes to compensate for his
loss of employment by selling his lifetime work, a piano
concerto. With his anticipated profits, Erique wishes to
continue paying for the voice-training of lovely Christine
(played by popular opera star Suzanna Foster). When
Erique goes to his potential publisher and is told that the
manuscript has been rejected, and then hears it being played
from another room (by maestro Franz Liszt, played by
Fritz Lieber, Sr.), he assumes that his work has been
stolen. Erique attacks and strangles the publisher, after
which the latter's secretary throws acid in the composer's
face and callously watches his agony. Clutching his seared
flesh, Erique flees to the sewers and the sanctum beneath
the Opera House. Now he is hopelessly insane.

Erique wants Christine to become the star of the
Opera. The operatic numbers of The Phantom of the Opera
were created especially for the film with lyrics added to
the music of Tschaikovsky, Chopin and Flotow. During
these musical performances, the Phantom, face hidden by a
prop room mask, strikes. He sneaks a drugged goblet to
the prima donna Madame Biancarolli while she performs on
stage, in order that her understudy Christine can replace
her. After Madame Biancarolli denies Christine the fame
she deserves, the Phantom secretly enters the prima donna's
room and strangles both her and her maid.

Later, after a brief period during which the Opera
House is closed, French police inspector Daubert (Edgar
Barrier) enacts a plan to lure him out into the open. He
insists that Christine does not appear, substituting another
soprano in her place. He dresses his men in prop masks
like the Phantom's (in a sequence replacing the "Red Death"
masque of the 1925 version) and publicizes the fact that
Liszt will play Erique's concerto following the last curtain
of the opera.

But Erique has plans of his own. He murders one of
Daubert's men and dons his hooded cloak. Then he appears
at the chandelier which hangs majestically above the audience. This sequence is surely the prime moment of the
1943 Phantom, a supreme exercise in suspense utilizing both
sound and visuals, as Erique saws away at the chandelier's
chain in tandem with the music below, both reaching for a
climax.

The chandelier sequence is perfectly described by
writer Chris Steinbrunner: "A rapt audience concentrates on
a stage ringing with passionate music ... while the camera
slowly moves upward, far above the pit and stage, far above
the horseshoe tiers, slowly ascending to the very dome of
the opera house, where Erique Claudin hangs above a vast
chandelier, maniacally loosening its roots! Cut to the stage
once more--and voices lifted in song. Cut to the audience:
the orderly rows upon rows, hushed in the semi-darkness,
unaware of the second drama taking place high above them.
The camera cuts back to the Phantom, his saw inexorably
cutting through the chain which holds the massive ironwork
fixture. Then back to the opera-in-progress. Lubin cross-
cuts for what seems like an endless amount of time, in an
unbearable little masterpiece of cinematic suspense. Then,
the chain is cut through, and the chandelier breaks away.
Quick closeup of the soprano, screaming. For one breathless second there is absolute silence, as the great circular
frame hurtles straight down upon the audience. Then, a
sickening crash, and pandemonium" ["The Incredible Mr.
Lubin," Castle of Frankenstein no. 5 (1964), p. 47].

During the commotion, Erique, claiming to be one of
the policemen, manages to kidnap Christine and bring her to
his sinister underground realm. There, the Phantom proudly plays her his concerto on the piano. Christine tears away
his mask as the camera quickly dollies in for an extreme
close-up and the music blares to a crescendo. Again, as
in 1925, audiences screamed--yet not as loudly as they had
at Lon Chaney.

Rains was no Lon Chaney and was certainly not expected to suffer the pains of the original Phantom make-up.
His make-up, created by Jack Pierce, consisted only of scar

Opposite: Claude Rains (the Phantom) and opera star Suzanna Foster (Christine) in the Universal color and music remake of The Phantom of the Opera (1943).

tissue marring one side of his otherwise handsome face.
This visage was horrifying when seen for the first time via
the quick "shock cut" which climaxed the unmasking. Nevertheless the studio has never released still photographs of the
make-up and the only existing close-up pictures are enlargements from the actual movie frames.

Christine's horror of the Phantom changes to grief
and pity when her two suitors, Daubert and opera star Ana-
tole (the extremely popular actor and singer Nelson Eddy),
enter his lair. During their attempt to save the woman
from this scar-faced fiend, Daubert fires his pistol which
precipitates a cave-in. Christine has been saved while all
that remains of Erique Claudin is a discarded violin.

The Phantom of the Opera of 1943 was such a tremendous success that Universal, as they had with the 1925
version, followed it with another horror movie with the same
sets and atmosphere. The Climax (1944) again featured
Suzanna Foster as the female lead and starred Boris Karloff
in his first color film as the mad menace. The film was
directed by George Waggner. Based on The Climax, a play
by Edward Locke, the film introduced a more mild-mannered
fiend than the Phantom. Karloff, who had been starring in
a series of "Mad Doctor" films at Columbia (The Man They
Could Not Hang in 1939, The Man With Nine Lives, The
Devil Commands and Before I Hang in 1940, and The Boogie
Man Will Get You in 1942), played another mad doctor in
The Climax. As Dr. Hohner, the physician of the opera
house, Karloff loves Marcellina, a beautiful opera star.
Jealous of her career, Hohner strangles the singer. A decade passes and Angela (Suzanna Foster), a new singing
sensation, displays a voice identical to that of Marcellina.
Determined that Angela's voice will also be kept from the
public, Hohner hypnotizes her into not wishing to sing.
When his treatments inevitably fail, Dr. Hohner returns to
an underground chamber where the preserved corpse of his
past love lies within a glass coffin. Both Hohner and
corpse are destroyed when the draperies catch fire and develop into an inferno. The Climax proved to be an incredible bore, saved only by the usual fine performance of Karloff.

Not for nearly two decades would there be another
serious remake of The Phantom of the Opera. (Scenes from
both the Chaney and Rains versions of The Phantom of the
Opera appeared in Rendezvous (1973) and Revenge of

Rendezvous (1975).) Variations on the character were not,
however, absent during the intervening years. El fantasma
de la opereta ("The Phantom of the Operetta") was a spoof
of horror movies made in Argentina by Gral. Belgrano and
released in 1955. Enrique Carreras directed this production, which included Argentinian versions of Frankenstein's
Monster and Count Dracula in its storyline. A Mexican
film entitled El fantasma de la opereta was made in 1959 by
Brooks & Enrique and directed by Fernando Ruanova. Mexican comedian Tin Tan encountered an entire horde of masked,
cloaked Phantoms in this spoof of the original story. Actor
James Cagney in Universal-International's Man of a Thousand
Faces (1957) recreated the famed unmasking sequence from the
Chaney classic, wearing a quite comfortable make-up designed
by Bud Westmore. The distortions in Cagney's face were
achieved through the use of latex appliances. The Italian film
Il vampiro dell'opera ("The Vampire of the Opera"), also known
as Monster of the Opera, was directed by Renato Polselli in
1961 for NIF. In this hybrid Dracula and The Phantom of the
Opera, a vampire (played by Giuseppe Addobati) inhabits the
lower regions of the Paris Opera House. The vampire's
slave, a ghost, tries to warn a theatrical troupe of the
cloaked bloodsucker. Like the Phantom, the vampire lures
the troupe's star down into his lair but is eventually destroyed by fire on the Opera House stage. That same year
Universal-International made The Phantom of the Horse
Opera, a Woody Woodpecker color cartoon directed by Paul
J. Smith.

    Hammer Films, the British company which had been
successful at remaking the Universal classics like Frankenstein, Dracula and The Mummy, turned to the Leroux property in 1962. The Phantom of the Opera, Hammer style,
was directed by Terence Fisher and released by the studio
which still retained the film rights to the novel, Universal.
Fisher once stated in an interview, "I did see three reels of
the Claude Rains Phantom, which I loathed" ["Horror Is My
Business," Monster Mania no. 2 (January 1967), p. 9].
Perhaps Fisher should have sat through more of it, for his
version of The Phantom of the Opera proved to be a travesty
of both the Rains and Chaney versions.

    The fine British actor Herbert Lom portrayed the new
Phantom. (The role had originally been offered to Christopher Lee.) Despite Lom's acting abilities, his Phantom was
directed by Fisher mainly for pathos and subsequently lost
the menace inherent in the earlier Universal versions. ("The

new Phantom is about as dangerous as dear old grandad
dressed up for Halloween," mocked Time magazine.)

Now it is the London Opera House which is reputedly
haunted by a Phantom who sits in his private box. The
prima donna Maric (Liane Aukin) is discouraged from singing
again when she is interrupted during her aria by the appearance of a hanging corpse. Stage producer Harry Hunter
(Edward de Souza) later replaces Marie with Christine
(Heather Sears), a singer from the chorus. After the pompous Lord Ambrose D'Arcy (Michael Gough), who had supposedly written the new opera, makes advances toward
Christine, she is warned against the lecher by the Phantom.
Rejecting Lord Ambrose, Christine soon finds herself replaced by another singer Yvonne (Sonya Cordeau).

Harry later discovers some old manuscripts by a
Professor Petrie whose face had been seared with acid during a fire at a publishing plant. The Professor had taken
refuge in the Thames and was presumed dead, though his
body was never found. There is little doubt as to the identity of the Phantom or the fate of the Professor.

Christine is caputured by a dwarf (Ian Wilson), who
originally rescued the Professor from the Thames and actually commits the most grisly murder in the film, gouging a
man's eye out in brilliant color. In the underground chambers beneath the opera house, Christine meets the elderly
Phantom, his face hidden behind a crude, one-eyed mask.
The Phantom then proceeds to train Christine to become a
star of the opera.

In the ludicrous finale, the Phantom watches as
Christine sings the opera written by him and stolen by Lord
Ambrose, the very music the Professor was trying to destroy when the fire started at the publishing plant. During
the performance the dwarf is discovered and breaks loose
the chandelier. The Phantom then rips off his own mask,
exposing the hardly frightening "burnt face" make-up created
by Roy Ashton, and leaps onto the stage in the style of John
Wilkes Booth, sacrificing himself beneath the crushing chandelier before it can hit Christine.

"We only showed Lom's face very briefly," said Ashton, "which had been severely burned by acid, but it was
entirely different from Chaney's. As for the mask that Lom
wore--it was a real last-minute job. We were three weeks

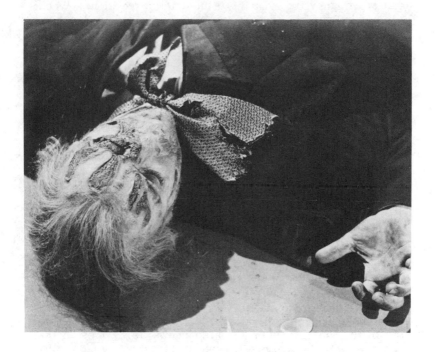

The Phantom (Herbert Lom) lies dead and unmasked at the climax of Hammer Films' version of The Phantom of the Opera (1962).

---

into the film and the producers still hadn't decided what they wanted him to look like.

"They wanted a mask, but they couldn't make up their minds about the design. Then came the first sequence where they were going to show the Phantom and no one knew what to do. So I said hang on, and I got a piece of rag, some tape, bits of string and rubber and in about five minutes I had a mask. And the producers said, Ah yes, that's just what we want ... and that's what we used" [John Brosnan, "Roy Ashton, Hammer's Master of Macabre Make-Up," The House of Hammer no. 2 (December 1976), p. 41].

The public scoffed at this pale pretender to the Phantom's subterranean throne, especially those viewers who had seen the Chaney or even the diluted Rains version. When Hammer's Phantom of the Opera was released to American television, scenes were added involving a pair of detectives trying to solve the case, which only made the overall product seem even more pedestrian.

In 1963 the Phantom was again on screen, appearing as a wax museum exhibit in Santo en el museo de cera. The next year an actor in a commercially sold Ellis Burman mask cavorted at a party in the Atlantic Cosnat movie The Candidate, directed by Robert Angus.   Santo, the silver-masked wrestler, punched and grunted through his own version of the Leroux story in Mexico's Santo contra el Estrangulador ("Santo vs. the Strangler"), which was directed in 1964 by René Cardona for Class-Mohme.   The superhero finally captures the theatre-haunting masked strangler, but the fiend returned in a sequel also directed by Cardona, El espectro del Estrangulador ("The Ghost of the Strangler") which is also known as Santo contra el espectro ("Santo vs. the Ghost").   The Phantom was impersonated by a man in a Burman mask in the color musical Double Trouble (MGM, 1967), directed by Norman Taurog.   A mad killer used a Don Post Phantom mask to terrify a victim in Crown-International's 1969 color Nightmare in Wax (shot as The Monster of the Wax Museum and also known as Crimes in the Wax Museum), which Bud Townsend directed.   And in 1974 European horror star Paul Naschy announced that he was to make his own version of The Phantom of the Opera.   The Opera Ghost also proved to be the masked Phantom Avenger who bossed a gang of monsters in the amateur serial The Adventures of the Spirit (1963).

A fantastic reworking of the old Phantom theme was Phantom of the Paradise, a horror musical written and directed by Brian De Palma and released in vivid color by Twentieth Century-Fox in 1974.   The film was originally announced as Phantom of the Fillmore (when the setting was to be that great rock music emporium of the 1960s) and later simply Phantom.   The former title was abandoned when De Palma was unable to secure the Fillmore rights while the latter was suppressed by King Features, which claimed that the abbreviated title infringed upon their copyrighted newspaper comic strip, The Phantom.   Further complications were heaped upon De Palma when Universal Pictures threatened him with a lawsuit, insisting that his film was an unauthorized remake of The Phantom of the Opera.

"I never had any intention of simply remaking Phantom of the Opera," said De Palma when interviewed. "I took its idea of a composer having his music ripped off, endeavoring to kill the people who are massacring his music and putting on the girl he loves to sing it the way he wants it to be sung. That was the basic concept. I like the idea of a phantom haunting a rock palace as opposed to an opera house, but it isn't simply a matter of up-dating" ["De Palma of the Paradise," Cinefantastique vol. 4, no. 2 (summer 1975), pp. 8-10].

Phantom of the Paradise is not only reminiscent of the various versions of The Phantom of the Opera. De Palma, a movie buff, enriched his production with visual references to such earlier films as The Picture of Dorian Gray, Psycho, Frankenstein, Touch of Evil and Das Kabinett des Dr. Caligari; and the film itself is as much a version of Faust as it is a rock adaptation of the Gaston Leroux classic. Paul Williams not only starred as the Faustian antagonist of the film, he also wrote the music and sang much of it, creating what is in reality a concise history of rock music from the naiveté and simplicity of the 1950s to the bizarre imagery of the 1970s.

The Phantom figure this time is really Winslow Leach (William Finley), a young composer and singer whose rock opera based on Faust is stolen by the mysterious Swan (Paul Williams), an ageless driving force behind rock 'n' roll music. Leach ventures to Swan's mansion to retrieve his music. There he meets a pretty singer named Phoenix (Jessica Harper) and is, shortly afterwards, thrown out of the building. After another attempt at reaching Swan, Leach is framed on a drug charge and jailed. In prison, Leach suffers the extraction of all his teeth and their replacement with steel dentures in a sadistic experiment. Finally he goes berserk, escapes and rushes to Swan's record plant to destroy the stolen music. A guard wounds him; he staggers into a record pressing machine where his face is grotesquely disfigured, after which he plunges into the river presumably dead.

As Swan prepares his own version of the stolen Faust, a cloaked figure wearing a silvery birdlike helmet begins to sabotage the production. This Phantom, alias Winslow Leach, is tricked into a blood contract with Swan in order that Phoenix will be made the star of the production. When Swan substitutes a glitter rock singer named Beef (Gerrit Graham)

in her place, the Phantom impales him with a neon sign.
Later the diabolical Swan intends to wed Phoenix on the
Paradise stage and then to have her assassinated before the
screaming fans.

The climax of Phantom of the Paradise is unfortunately rather choppy. Swan appears at the wedding wearing a
mask apparently for but one purpose--to become unmasked
after the Phantom destroys the videotapes of the rock promoter which, like Dorian Gray's portrait, contain the essence of his youth. Then, swinging from a rope like a
silver-masked Batman, the Phantom saves Phoenix at the
cost of his own life. Before perishing, his mask is torn
off to reveal his scarred face. Unlike the Herbert Lom
Phantom of the Opera, Finley's role as a sympathetic Phantom worked.

Phantom of the Paradise failed at the box office despite its being one of the best horror films of the 1970s.
Nevertheless there were plans for a possible sequel while
fans of the movie were able to purchase a number of related
items. There was a novelization, Phantom of the Paradise,
by Bjarne Rostaing, issued by Dell Publishing Company in
1975; a soundtrack album from A&M Records; a planned
comic strip adaptation from the Marvel Comics Group which
never materialized; and such merchandise as posters and T-
shirts.

Shortly after the original release of the film Phantom
of the Paradise, Part II, a sequel was announced but never
went into production. In 1976 the picture was rereleased
with a new advertising campaign, which played up its horror
rather than musical merits in the hopes that the film would
finally earn the profits it so richly deserved.

THE PHANTOM OF THE MEDIA

The Opera Ghost's career was not limited to Leroux's
novel and the movies. There is something intriguing about
the character whose face is concealed behind the featureless
mask and a catharsis when that mask is torn aside to reveal
a ghastly countenance, perhaps even more hideous than we
fearfully imagined. The popular Phantom would return.

The Phantom of the Opera became a play for the
first time in 1975, adapted from the Leroux novel and

directed by David Giles, and performed by the Actors' Company at England's Wimbledon Theatre.   Giles employed the
Wimbledon itself as the Paris Opera House, with the audience becoming an unrehearsed part of the production.   In
the role of Erik was Edward Petherbridge, who played his
part for pathos when unmasked by Christine (Sharon Duce).
Petherbridge's Phantom make-up consisted of putty which,
during at least one performance of the play, literally came
apart and fell off his face.   (When the BBC televised Edward
Petherbridge in his Phantom make-up, numerous viewers
wrote in to complain that the horrid countenance was too of-
fensive to be broadcast into the home.   As a result of the
outrage the BBC televised an official apology.)

A less ghastly version of the character appeared in
Sherlock Meets the Phantom (1957), a one-act comedy play
by Tim Kelly.   The Phantom is the mysterious terror of the
Virginia City Opera House.   He climbs walls and swings from
the scenery, creating general mayhem whenever he appears.
It necessitates the talents of Sherlock Holmes to expose the
Phantom as a man who had eaten some peanuts injected with
Serum of Anthropoid and thus assumed simian traits!   The
Opera Phantom also "ghost starred" in the Haunted Mountain
1976 Halloween show at the Magic Mountain amusement park,
Valencia, California.

The appeal of the Opera Phantom was perfect for
radio drama, a medium in which his exposed features could
be as grotesque as the listener's imagination might conceive.
Strangely, Leroux's story has but a minimal radio history.
Basil Rathbone starred as Erique alongside Nelson Eddy and
Suzanna Foster in "The Phantom of the Opera," a 1943 adaptation of the Claude Rains film on "Lux Radio Theatre."
Over three decades later, "The Phantom of the Opera" was
adapted and directed by Himan Brown (the former producer/
director of "Inner Sanctum") for his "CBS Radio Mystery
Theater."   "I remember Phantom of the Opera with Lon
Chaney," said Brown.   "But it's a huge novel.   How do you
do such a novel in fifty minutes?   Well, you can't really do
all in fifty minutes, no more than they could have done it
as a movie in two hours.   But somehow I distilled the horror of the opera ghost, the chandelier falling, the ghost being chased through the flies, backstage and up onto a roof
in my framework. ...   The locale is the Paris Opera House.
An opera was going on in the background.   I can effectively
create that illusion" ["The Master of Radio Horror: Himan
Brown and the CBS Radio Mystery Theater," Quasimodo's
Monster Magazine no. 5 (November 1975), pp. 36-38].

On television the Opera Phantom had a more flourishing career. Versions of the character have appeared on such
programs as "Get Smart," "Midnight Special," "The Funny
Side," "The Ghost Busters" (the Phantom of Broadway, a
spectral ventriloquist), "Don Adams' Screen Test" (Jack Cassidy recreating the unmasking scene from the 1943 Phantom
of the Opera), "Horror Theater," "The Santa Claus Lane
Parade" (in Hollywood, plugging the Universal tour), "Nightmare" (John O. Burke), a production of Olsen and Johnson's
"Hellzapoppin'," Universal's "Night Gallery" (with Kevin McCarthy in a parody of Chaney's unmasking scene), "Holmes and Yo-
Yo" (in which the director of a new Phantom movie is murdered),
the animated "Milton the Monster" (Heebie) and "Porky Pig and
Daffy Duck Meet the Groovie Goolies" (the Phantom terrorizes
a movie studio). He also appeared in commercials for Wurlit-
zer Organs, the Universal tour and Luden's cough drops.

The most ambitious television variation on The Phantom of the Opera theme went into production in 1974 as The
Phantom of Lot 2. This feature-length movie was first
aired on February 5, 1975, over the CBS-TV network as
The Phantom of Hollywood. The Phantom appears in the
garb of the classic executioner. He haunts Lot 2 of Worldwide Studios (actually MGM) where he wreaks destruction and
death against those who would tear down the old backlot sets
which have been his home for some thirty years. The Phantom is unmasked in classic style to expose the hideously disfigured face of a former matinee idol (played by Jack Cassidy) in a make-up created by William Tuttle. In a poignant
scene the Phantom shows scenes from his old movies in
which his face was handsome and unmarred--before the filming accident that drove him into madness and seclusion.
The Phantom of Hollywood utilized actual footage of the
demolition of the old MGM sets intercut with scenes from
the films that had been shot there. Film buffs protested the
destruction of these historically important sets. They em-
pathized with the Phantom as he carried out his vengeance
and grieved at his inevitable death. For once the Phantom
figure, even in the garb of a mace-swinging executioner,
emerged as the hero.

Television's most popular Phantom imitator was John
Zacherle, who appeared as Roland, the "Cool Ghoul," a
gleeful fiend in make-up fashioned after Chaney's Phantom.
Roland first appeared in 1957 as the host of "Shock Theater"
on Philadelphia television station WCAU. The character became so popular that he moved to WOR-TV in New York

where, simply known as Zacherly, he starred in another
version of "Shock Theater." Zacherly was the most successful of all the television horror films hosts.   During the
height of his popularity during the latter 1950s and early
1960s he guest starred on a number of other television and
radio programs, became a recording star and was the editor
and subject of several books.

Outside of the Leroux novel, the Opera Phantom has
made other literary appearances.   He became flesh and blood
in the Bloch story "The Plot Is the Thing" (1966).   "The
Phantom of the Opera's Friend," an outstanding short piece
by Donald Barthelme, was published in The New Yorker
(February 7, 1970).   While writing The Phantom of the
Opera, Leroux himself encounters the Phantom (whose face
had been destroyed by acid), now 65 years old and about to
embark on a new life outside the Opera House.   Leroux
tries to arrange for a plastic surgery operation for the creature.   Another short story, "Letter to an Angel," was included in the book Science Fiction Worlds of Forrest J Ackerman & Friends (Powell Publications, 1969).   Ackerman's
story described in meticulous detail what it was like to behold Chaney's Phantom unmasked on the silent screen.   The
Phantom also haunted the novel As Mascaras do pavor (1974).
An anonymous text story with the misleading title "The Phantom of the Opera" was published in the comic book Chilling
Tales no. 15 (April 1953), from Youthful Magazines.   The
story was actually about a ghostly songstress who leaves her
grave and sings at a Naples opera house.   "The Phantom of
Kensington Theatre," another derivative story, appeared in
Stanley Publications' Horror Stories no. 6 (August 1971),
under the byline of "ghost-hunter" Gabriel Varney.   The
spirit investigator discovers that the extrovert ghost haunting
a theatre and frightening the actors is that of a murdered
chorus girl.   The spirit still craves performing.

The Phantom's spooky appearances were more numer-
ous in the comic books.   "Scream Test," written by John
Benson and Bob (Bhob) Stewart and illustrated by Angelo
Torres, was published in the 13th issue of Warren Publishing Company's Creepy (February 1966).   The organist at an
old, closed-down silent movie theatre is infatuated with Lon
Chaney in such films as The Hunchback of Notre Dame and
The Phantom of the Opera and identifies with him.   As
Phantom plays on the screen, a curious woman recalls the
fire that once hit this theatre and unmasks the burned, Erik-
like face of the organist.

During the late 1960s the Phantom was awarded his
own rather shabby comic book series in Brazil. The premier issue of O fantasma da opera, by Moacir Rodrigues,
has composer Pierre "Leroux" share the same origin as
Claude Rains in the 1943 Phantom of the Opera. Pierre unmasks himself in the apartment of the woman who threw the
acid--and then he strangles her. Taking sanctuary within
the Paris Opera House, he creates the usual Phantom mayhem, unmasked throughout. The crudely written and drawn
book was printed in black and white.

Following his adventure with Quasimodo, the Frankenstein Monster met the next logical French horror in "The
Phantom of the Opera," an installment of the "Frankenstein"
comic strip series running in Skywald's Psycho magazine
and published in the sixth issue (May 1972). The Monster
is saved from a mutant squid which inhabits the sewers of
Paris by Erik, the Phantom, who makes the patchwork creature a prisoner. The mad Phantom hopes to send the indestructible Monster through the centuries via his time-
warping pipe organ in order to bring back treasures of
beauty. The Monster escapes and inadvertently journeys
into the future, while Erik is destroyed by his exploding
time machine. An adaptation of the Leroux story, "The
Phantom of the Opera" was published in the third issue of
Skywald's Scream (December 1973). "Horripilate Host," by
this writer and artist Dick Giordano in Red Circle's (Archie
Music Corporation) Chilling Adventures in Sorcery no. 4
(December 1973), featured a Zacherly style television star
who was a green-faced look-alike to Chaney's Phantom.

National Periodical Publications has not been lacking
in Phantom of the Opera type stories. A classic villain
from the early Batman stories was Clayface, who first appeared in Detective Comics no. 40 (1944), the story untitled.
"Clayface was a take-off on the Phantom of the Opera," admitted Bill Finger, a writer of the early Batman comic book
series [Steranko, Jim, History of Comics, vol. 1 (Reading,
Pa. , 1970), p. 48]. A mysterious cloaked figure in a slouch
hat and green make-up is committing murders to sabotage
the filming of a movie called Dread Castle. Batman and
Robin finally capture the fiend, a former movie villain called
Clayface, and unmask him as Basil Karlo. The insane actor
had resented this remake of one of his old thrillers and determined to again become the real villain of the picture.
Clayface returned in a number of other Batman tales. Batman tangled with another Opera Phantom in "Murder

in Movieland" in <u>Detective Comics</u> no. 314 (April 1963).
The Phantom was really actor Roger Carlyle who, after an
automobile accident, begins to forget his lines and lose his
acting ability.   When the three bosses of his studio Monarch
Pictures suggest he rest in a hospital, he vows to murder
them according to the scripts of three of his earlier films.
On the old Opera House set, the "Phantom" crushes one of
the executives beneath a falling chandelier before Carlyle is
captured by Batman.

    Incarnations of both the Phantom and Quasimodo ap-
peared in "Panic in the Night!" in National's comic magazine <u>The Phantom Stranger</u> no. 23 (January-February 1973),
drawn by Jim Aparo.   A ghostly Quasimodo rings the bells
of Notre Dame, after which a glowing Phantom saws down
the Paris Opera House's giant chandelier.   There is even
an unmasking scene of the Phantom at the organ beneath the
Paris sewers, where both "spectres" are exposed as human
terrorists seeking vast powers to "reshape the world" according to their own designs.   This Phantom joins the Phantom
Stranger and both defeat the Hunchback and his minions
aboard a fantastic airship.

    Jack Kirby wrote, drew and edited a three-issue
Phantom of the Opera variation in <u>The Demon</u>, a comic book
published by National.   "Phantom of the Sewers" in <u>The
Demon</u> no. 8 (April 1973), featured a masked Phantom inhabit-
ing a lair within the city's sewer system.   The second installment "Whatever Happened to Farley Fairfax?!!" appeared in the next issue (June 1973), wherein the Phantom
is revealed as a former stage idol, having been disfigured
by a sorceress' spell.   Not until the tenth issue of <u>The De-
mon</u> (July 1973) does the sorceress Galatea restore Farley's
handsome and youthful features, after which his true age
returns; the shock of his realizing this kills him.   The same
company published "The Real Phantom of the Opera" in the
57th issue of <u>Ghosts</u> (1977).   It was the story of an authenti-
cated spirit manifestation.

    "Phantom of the Soap Opera," published in Gold Key
Comics' Walter Lantz <u>Woody Woodpecker</u> no. 137 (July 1974),
was about a masked, cloaked husband who steals the films
of a television soap opera because his wife's dedication to
the show interfered with her housework.

    The Opera Phantom has been heard on a modicum of
phonograph records issued during the Seventies.   <u>The Phantom</u>

of the Organ (Electric Lemon Record Company, 1973) con-
sisted of the eerie music "Horror of Erik," "Depression,"
"Symphony of Death," "Dementia," "Macabre," "The Devil's
Love," "Sound Trip Through the Catacombs (Including the
Phantom's Love Theme and Unmasking)" and "Echoes of the
Organ," all written and performed by make-up artist Verne
Langdon.   The Phantom's "cathedral" was presented on the
album Ghostly Sounds while the madman was explained as a
former opera star who suffered facial burns on stage in
"Phantom of the Opera," a cut from the album Sounds of
Terror (Pickwick International, 1974).   A life-size mechani-
cal Erik periodically appeared to saw at the chandelier hanging over the bar at The Haunted House, a nightclub in Hollywood, which opened in 1966.

Like such indestructible horrors as the Wolf Man and
the Mummy, the Phantom of the Opera now haunts the world
of merchandise, where he shall continue to endure, maintaining his position of one of the screen's greatest fiends.

VII

THE CREATURE--MONSTER OF THE FIFTIES

The Gill Man or Creature was the successor to the throne vacated by the classic horrors of the thirties and forties. But Frankenstein's Monster and the other fiends that dominated the fright films of Universal Pictures in decades past owed their origins to literature and folklore. The Gill Man, the amphibious star of Universal-International's Creature From the Black Lagoon, was truly a product of the fifties.

The 1950s was an era of a very real monster that posed a threat to the motion picture industry. This "monster" (sometimes referred to as the "one-eyed monster") was more threatening than any shambling mummy or hungry werewolf could ever be. The monster was television and studio executives knew that to compete with a device that brought motion pictures into the living room without cost required more than fiery torches or silver bullets.

One method by which the film studios combated television was to offer audiences motion pictures made in a plethora of new processes. Wide screen and stereo films had existed since the earliest days of the movies, but in the 1950s such processes were suddenly "new" again. Television might have been able to provide free home entertainment. But TV could never offer films in such processes as Cinemascope, Cinerama and 3-D. During the 1950s the public's acceptance of and demand for three-dimensional movies would explode into an actual craze.

What better genre was more suited to the stereo process than the horror or monster film? Incredulous viewers, hiding behind uncomfortable 3-D glasses, screamed as claws lashed out from the screen, seemingly into the darkened audience itself. Grotesque faces leered at us, stopping

257

mere inches away, while mangled corpses dropped into our
shaky laps. People in the theatre audience often ducked
rather than be touched by these horrors of shadow and light.

In 1953 Warner Brothers aroused the shrieks of audiences with House of Wax and went into production of the Poe-
based Phantom of the Rue Morgue, both in 3-D. Allied
Artists' film The Maze and Astor's Robot Monster played to
stereo-goggled viewers. That same year Universal-International contributed its first venture into three-dimensional
horror, It Came From Outer Space.

During the 1930s and 1940s, Universal Pictures was
the unchallenged metropolis of the horror film. Not every
Universal horror entry was a classic and most of them, especially those produced during the forties, were "B" films.
Yet that studio was responsible for a veritable stock company of monsters which appeared in sequel after sequel and
are as popular today on television, theatre revivals and
merchandise as they ever were during their first appearances
on the screen.

Frankenstein's Monster, Count Dracula, the Wolf Man,
the Mummy and the Invisible Man have achieved a kind of
immortality similar to that enjoyed by such classic characters of popular fiction as Sherlock Holmes, Tarzan and
Superman. In their own way the old Universal horrors have
transcended to the stature of popular myth. It was for another such myth that Universal-International was looking.

By 1954 the classic Universal monsters, though still
revered by their fans and yet bringing in returns at the box
office, were merely part of the studio's history. Universal
had long since exhausted the possibilities of presenting fresh
stories involving any of these characters. Abbott and Costello had met them all (destroyed them, in the opinion of the
more serious-minded film buffs) and there was obviously no
returning to the glory of the previous two decades. Besides,
the fifties was a decade not of vampires and werewolves and
stitched-together living corpses, but of monsters spawned by
atomic tests and prehistoric beasts awakened from millenia
of suspended animation.

The days of the human monster, the ill-fated Wolf
Man or Dr. Jekyll, were mostly in the past. Now even bipedal monsters with the general shape of a human being
were hardly more than snarling, brainless beasts whose only

human attribute seemed to be a licentious yearning for the lovely female heroine.

It was in an atmosphere of 1950s monsters and 3-D films that the Gill Man from the Black Lagoon was spawned.

The origin of the Gill Man, or Creature as he is commonly known, is generally attributed to producer William Alland. Supposedly Alland recalled an obscure South American legend about a mysterious prehistoric creature that was reputed to be extant in the swamps and jungles of that continent. This Creature, a throwback to the Devonian Period, the age of fishes of some 500 million years ago, was described as a bizarre combination of turtle, fish, alligator and, which made it all the more intriguing, man. Naturally such a monstrosity violated the precepts of science, but Alland was convinced that, if handled properly, the Gill Man could become a popular horror of 1954.

Alland promised Bud Westmore, head of Universal-International's make-up department, that he could guarantee a finished script about the character once a suitable monster costume was designed. The visual conception of the Creature was still rather vague. But studio director Jack Arnold, who had already brought It Came From Outer Space to the screen and would direct Creature, made a rough sketch showing the basic design of the Gill Man.

"I remember one day I was looking at the certificate I received when I was nominated for an Academy Award," Arnold told writer Bill Kelley. "There was a picture of the Oscar statuette on it. I said, 'If we put a gilled head on it, plus fins and scales, that would look pretty much like the kind of creature we're trying to get'" [Kelley, Bill, "Jack Is Back!", Cinefantastique vol. 4, no. 2 (1975), p. 21].

The creation of the Gill Man was indeed a challenge. In order for the Creature to surpass the level of the standard movie monster the costume had to be thoroughly convincing. Westmore, along with Jack Kevan, Bob Hickman and Chris Nueller, determined to make the Creature a masterpiece in its own right. They took the work seriously and the final results would show it.

The only bust with a neck that existed in the old make-up shop at Universal-International was that of actress

Ann Sheridan.   Mueller began to sculpt the features of the
Gill Man over "Miss Sheridan" with modeling clay.   The features seemed logical to the monster's design.   It was Bud
Westmore's contention that the absence of a nose always
made a monster appear even more monstrous.   Since the
Creature would spend most of his time underwater, he hardly required nostrils.   The area where the nose might have
been now extended to the mouth like the face of a fish.
"Breathing" would be accomplished by three rows of flaring
gills, which could be made to pulsate realistically.

The Creature's mouth and chin were based upon those
of the frog.   At first the Westmore crew added a pair of
crablike claws and a mechanical tail with enough power to
knock a man off his feet.   Both of these ideas would have
restricted the actor wearing the Creature outfit from movement, especially during the underwater scenes, and so were
abandoned.

Following the sculpting of the Creature outfit, the
various segments were cast in molds, then produced in foam
rubber.   The final result was the finest monster creation
since Universal Pictures became Universal-International.
The Creature was entirely green, save for the livid red lips,
and was covered with ichthyoid scales.   Fins graced the
forearms, back and legs.   The hands were great, webbed
claws.   The overall effect was startlingly realistic.   It
should have been, since the overall cost of the outfit totaled
some $12,000, certainly a fortune to be paid out for a mon-
ster in 1954.

Alland was impressed.   As he had promised, a script
was solicited from writers Harry Essex and Arthur Ross.
There was also the matter of casting the role of the Gill
Man.

Glenn Strange was one of Universal-International's first
choices for the part of the Creature.   The six-foot, three-
inch actor, known primarily for his work in Westerns, was
no novice to the horror film genre.   He had done three
monster movies for Universal, among his fright credits,
playing the giant Frankenstein Monster in House of Frankenstein, House of Dracula and Abbott and Costello Meet Frankenstein.   Strange was an athletic type, having performed as
a stuntman, wrestler and professional rodeo rider.   His
swimming abilities were adequate enough for him to be at
least considered for the part finally won by Johnny Weiss-
muller in the MGM Classic Tarzan the Apeman.

Strange told me in an interview conducted in 1965,
"... I just swim. I was supposed to originally play the
Creature from the Black Lagoon too, but that was another
underwater hazard. They told me how much water there
was, and I said, 'No, I don't want it. ' It turned out they
used a swimming double after all, Ricou Browning from
Hawaii. "

Actually, there was no need to find an actor with
name value as a horror star for the part of the Gill Man.
Since the Creature was not of the Wolf Man or Frankenstein
Monster mold, in which the actor is recognizable beneath
the make-up or is required to emote, all that was needed
was someone tall who could fill out the costume. Besides,
the lack of a name horror star could lend an aura of mystery about the Gill Man. This was simply the Creature.
And the costume was realistic enough for some impression-
able viewers to believe that there was nothing beneath the
green scales except internal organs and fish bones.

Actually, a United States Marine, Ben Chapman,
was hired to enact the role of the Gill Man. His
height made him quite formidable in the green costume.
Chapman was to play the Creature on land while the shorter Ricou Browning would handle the water work.

Chapman's most grueling experiences as the Creature
happened not before the cameras but within the privacy of
Westmore's make-up shop. The actor would strip down and
take his place upon a clay slab. Then Westmore and his
monster makers would begin their work. An exact mold of
his body was made. The segments of the Creature costume
had to be constructed so that they fit Chapman and no one
else and fit like a new epidermis. The torso, head, hands
and feet were baked in an oven in the various molds. The
finished segments were later adorned with the characteristic
rubber fins, scales and claws. The Creature costume could
be worn only by the actor for whom it was intended and afforded him the freedom to walk and attack and swim.

Ricou Browning was outfitted in his own Creature
suit, seemingly lighter in color to stand out against the darkness of the Black Lagoon during underwater scenes. Browning could hold his breath underwater for five minutes before
grasping the nearby air hose and thrusting it into his mouth.
He developed a distinctive swimming style for the Creature,
twisting his body from side to side. This style became as

much associated with Browning as with the Gill Man. Browning later performed underwater in such television series as
"Sea Hunt," "Flipper" and "Voyage to the Bottom of the Sea."
In one episode of "Voyage" he played a miniature "gill man"
(obviously inspired by the Creature) which was enlarged by
scientists to the size of a man. In each of these performances the Creature seemed to be swimming again. Only the
exteriors were different.

Creature From the Black Lagoon takes its viewers to
a bank of the Amazon in the vicinity of the murky, almost
prehistoric Black Lagoon (actually the Florida Everglades).
A scientist and his native help discover an amazing fossil
protruding from the rocks — the skeletal talon of a manlike
being with ossified webbing between the fingers. Obviously
this is some kind of missing link between the fish and mammal kingdoms. Even as the scientist marvels over the find
a portentious bubbling occurs in the waters of the Black Lagoon, followed by the unnoticed emergence of a scaly claw.
The scientist entrusts the dig to his native assistants, then
returns to civilization to organize a larger expedition. The
natives believe they are guarding something corresponding to
a local legend about a living monster.

During the scientist's absence the "Creature" proves
to be more than either mere fossil or legend. Something
which walks like a man yet growls like some unearthly beast
raids the camp. An oil lamp is upset during the conflict
between men and monster and the invader's face is set
ablaze. Wild with rage, the Creature wrecks the camp and
returns to the wet safety of the Black Lagoon.

Director Arnold kept his audience in suspense, wondering just what horrid apparition this Creature might be,
until later on in the film. The scientific expedition, including scientist frogmen David Reed and Mark Williams, played
by Richard Carlson and Richard Denning (both familiar stars
of 1950s horror and science fiction movies), journey along a
tributary of the Black Lagoon in hopes of discovering more
fossil remains of the Gill Man. Included in the expedition
is Reed's assistant, Kay, a beautiful young woman played by
Universal-International starlet Julia (later simply Julie)
Adams. When Ms. Adams enjoys a swim in the refreshing

Opposite: The Gill Man, or Creature (Ben Chapman), in the
first of his three films, Creature from the Black Lagoon
(Universal-International, 1954).

Black Lagoon waters we are given our first actual look at
the Creature.

   In his book Science Fiction in the Cinema, John Baxter hails Jack Arnold as an unsung genius and describes in
detail his impressions of this particular scene.   During a
sequence beautifully photographed by James C. Haven, Ms.
Adams swims and frolics sensuously near the water's surface, her white body and swim suit contrasting against the
dark atmosphere.   From below watches the Creature, supreme in his underwater element.   Aroused, as this lovely
invader of his domain engages herself in an underwater
dance, the Gill Man swims after her.   As Baxter states,
"Gliding beneath her, twisting lasciviously in a stylised representation of sexual intercourse, the creature, his movements brutally masculine and powerful, contemplates his
ritual bride, though his passion does not reach its peak until the girl performs some underwater ballet movements,
explicitly erotic poses that excite the Gill Man to reach out
and clutch at her murmuring legs" [John Baxter, Science
Fiction in the Cinema (New York: A. S. Barnes, 1970), p.
121].

   Baxter also sees the Creature as an allegorical Luci-
fer with the Black Lagoon and its depths, suggestive of Doré,
his Hell.   Jack Arnold, appearing in a panel discussion at
the 1972 World Science Fiction Convention in Los Angeles,
did not admit to much of what Baxter had ascribed to him.
Whether or not Arnold consciously or unconsciously intended
Creature From the Black Lagoon to be more than a quality
production is, perhaps, unimportant.   What he succeeded in
doing was to take a monster that could have been just another in the menagerie of giant insects and lumbering reptiles and, with a great deal of care and understanding,
create a character of mythical stature.

   Despite its fishlike and inhuman appearance, the Creature was given a touch of humanity by Arnold; and it is humanity which endears even such behemoths as King Kong
and Godzilla to the public.   Arnold affectionately referred to
the Gill Man as "The Beastie" and presented him in such a
way as to arouse the emotions of the audience.   "I set out
to make the Creature a very sympathetic character," said
Arnold.   "He's violent because he's provoked into violence.
Inherent in the character is the statement that all of us have
violence within, and if provoked, are capable of any bizarre
retaliation.   If left alone, and understood, that's when we

overcome the primeval urges that we all are cursed with"
[Kelley, "Jack Is Back!," p. 20].

Though the Gill Man should be indifferent to a female
of an alien species, he is most definitely attracted on the
physical level to Kay. The implication is that there is a
human being awaiting birth underneath the green scales and
fins, even though he might not surface until the next 500
million years. Not only is the Creature attracted to the
image of female beauty as determined by human standards,
but he is also, as the expedition is soon to learn, quite
cunning.

As the Creature follows his lovely prey, he is snared
in a net cast off the side of the expedition's boat, the Rita.
The boat rocks violently as the Creature tears himself free
of the net. When the net is brought out of the water it contains a single sharp nail like that on the fossil claw discovered earlier. (The fact that the Creature lost its nail
was never again mentioned in the film. Later appearances
showed the Gill Man with all of his nails intact. Perhaps
he grew a replacement between scenes.)

Donning their frogman gear, Reed and Williams tress-
pass upon the Creature's underwater kingdom. The Gill
Man attacks them and, after a physical encounter, is driven
away by their spearguns. Following an unsuccessful attempt
to capture the Creature by dumping a toxic chemical powder
into the water, the scientists discover that their exit from
the lagoon has been prevented by a barricade of wood apparently set up by the Gill Man himself. While Reed removes the barrier the cunning monster stealthily boards the
ship and leaps back into the water with Kay in his viselike
arms.

The climax of the film is set in the Creature's misty
lair, a temple-like grotto accessible by an underground
stream where Kay now lies semiconscious, draped over a
rock like a sacrificial victim awaiting her god. Reed embraces the woman he loves as the scaly deity himself lumbers toward them, growling gutterally. There is a brief
battle between Reed and the monster with the human stabbing
his knife into the Creature's thick shoulder.

Seconds later, the Gill Man staggers across the land,
mouth gasping for oxygen. Unable to survive out of water
for any length of time, the Creature staggers toward the

lagoon as his human pursuers fire rifle bullets into him.
Apparently killed--by the beings his kind might someday be-
come--the Creature gracefully sinks into the serene waters
of the Black Lagoon. (Castle Films' condensed home movie
version of the film became the abbreviated Creature From
the Lagoon. In Spain the feature was released as La Mujer
y el Monstruo ["The Woman and the Monster"]. Scenes
from Creature From the Black Lagoon eventually turned up
in Rendezvous (1973).)

The care taken with the Gill Man's creation and by
Arnold in the direction of the film was appreciated by the
public. By the end of 1954, Creature From the Black Lagoon had grossed an impressive $3,000,000. To promote
even more profits from the picture, a huge theatre display
from the film served as a background for the famous scene
of Marilyn Monroe's skirt being blown over her head in the
1955 Universal-International comedy, The Seven Year Itch.

The Creature proved too viable an investment to lay
mouldering beneath the Black Lagoon's murky waters or
hanging in Universal's make-up workshop. Inevitably there
would have to be a sequel--in which the monster would swim
and stalk again. Revenge of the Creature was the commercial enough title for the second film of the series. It was
made in 1955 and, fortunately, directed again by Jack Arnold. (In Spain, the film is known as El regreso del mon-
struo--"The Return of the Monster. ")

Revenge was also made in the stereo process, though
the public had already tired of wearing the glasses and the
3-D craze was nearly dead. Ben Chapman no longer played
the Gill Man and the role was fully inherited by Ricou Browning. Changes were made in the Creature suit, not for the
better, with the eyes now bulging and the upper lip protruding more in the manner of a fish.

Another expedition ventures to the Black Lagoon, this
time headed by a scientist played by John Agar. Not surprisingly, the Creature is discovered again very much alive,
perhaps rejuvenated by the water itself. After another
battle against his human enemies, the Creature is taken
captive and promptly transported to the Ocean Harbor Seaquarium in Florida.

In the manner of walking sharks, the Gill Man is
"walked" through the water of his tank by his keeper, as

Ricou Browning took over the Gill Man role for the first of the sequels, Revenge of the Creature (Universal-International, 1956).

spectators observe from above.   Suddenly the Creature's
body begins to jerk.   Moments later he lashes at his keeper
and climbs the side of the tank as the crowd of curiosity
seekers and reporters scatter.   A boathook sends the Gill
Man back to the water, a captive of his human foes.

Chained, a living exhibit to satisfy the curiosity of
the public, the Creature becomes infatuated by yet another
beauty, this one played by starlet Lori Nelson.   In a burst
of strength, the Creature breaks his chains and escapes the
seaquarium, but with the woman's image indelible on his
primitive brain.

The Creature returns for his latest love as she and
Agar dine at a seaside nightclub.   Eyes staring, a growl
coming from parted lips, the Gill Man staggers among the
patrons, almost violently takes his "bride" in his arms, and
plunges with her into water as black as that of his own lagoon.   He is soon found near a riverside park.   Since the
Creature can only remain out of the water for short periods,
he is forced to leave his victim while he returns to the
water.   The Creature emerges from the water to face the
glare of his hunters' searchlights, after which he receives a
spray of bullets that sends him back beneath the water's
surface, again apparently dead.

Even with a monster as impressive in appearance as
the Gill Man, the character was limited insofar as story
possibilities were concerned.   The popularity of the Creature
was waning, the 3-D fad already history.   Though Arnold
had infused the Creature with some semblance of humanity,
the monster was still far too limited to continue in anything
other than the "monster is loose" variety of horror film.

The third film of the series, The Creature Walks
Among Us (1956), attempted to elevate the status of the Gill
Man from beast to near-human.   What it actually succeeded
in doing was to destroy the very image that the public had
accepted so readily back in 1954.   Though he had been offered the new Creature entry, it was not directed by Jack
Arnold (who might have saved it in spite of itself) but by
John Sherwood.   Arnold felt he had already explored all the
possibilities of the concept.

I was twelve years old in 1956.   Two years earlier
I had seen Creature From the Black Lagoon in its initial
theatre release and had been so affected by the original Gill

Man image that I eagerly sought out the first sequel.   I recall seeing the coming-attractions trailers to The Creature
Walks Among Us along with some friends of the same age.
The mutual disappointment we experienced at sight of what
had been done to a monster created ostensibly for us was
overwhelming.   Reluctantly we went to see the third Creature film when it opened the following week.

The Creature Walks Among Us brings a party of scientists to the Everglades, where the Gill Man (Browning
again) is believed to be alive and in hiding.   After a furious
battle during which the Creature is set afire with burning
oil, the monster lies apparently dead in the water.   But the
Creature still lives, rendered unconscious after suffering
third-degree burns.

Inadvertently the fire had revealed a startling fact
about the Creature's physiology.   The flames burned away
the scaly epidermis to show a more human skin underneath.
More startling was the X-ray that revealed a heretofore un-
used set of lungs not unlike those of a human being.   One
of the scientists (played by Jeff Morrow) concludes that,
with some careful surgery, the Gill Man might be evolved
to the next step on the scale of life.   It was this bit of mad
science that destroyed the Creature more than any flaming
oil or bullets ever could.

Don Megowan played the "new" Gill Man.   Gone were
the characteristic scales that had contributed to the Creature's appeal.   Somehow the monster managed to gain both
mass and height (mainly due to the size of actor Megowan).
And since this revamped Creature was considered to be more
manlike, he was given a set of clothing that made him appear more to be the Frankenstein Monster in an unfinished
Gill Man mask.

Apparently the fire and surgery had awakened some
human consciousness within the Creature's brain.   Now he
not only gazes longingly at the human females, but is also
capable of some understanding.   No longer able to breathe
water, he complacently allows himself to be caged like a
wild beast.   At one point he even kills a wolf to save a
flock of sheep.

In order to save the third woman that had attracted
him during his film career, the Creature bends the bars of
his electrified fence, goes on a rampage and finally strides

The "humanized" Gill Man (Don Megowan) menaces actress
Leigh Snowden in this publicity still from The Creature
Walks Among Us (Universal-International, 1956).

across a dawn-lit beach.   He pauses, staring longingly at
the ocean in which he can now drown.   As the picture fades
to black the Creature rushes anxiously toward the sea, apparently finding death in his own element better than survival in an alien world.

The Creature Walks Among Us--for some reason, a
Chicago drive-in advertised the film as The Creature Walks
With a Brain--ended the Gill Man series, although rumors
existed at the time that a fourth film was in the planning
and could even have reached the scripting stage.   Perhaps
the waters could have violated the rules of evolution, with
the Creature becoming an atavism of its present incarnation.
But not enough persons, whether at Universal-International
or in the audience, really cared.

The Creature, though his series comprised but a tril-
ogy, was far from dead.   He made a number of appearances
in the various media.   Just one year after the Creature
walked among us in semi-human form, a kin appeared in
the Mexican film El castillo de los monstruos ("The Castle
of the Monsters").   This Creature appeared more human
than ever, as he was played by an actor in a shoddy Gill
Man outfit resembling a pair of leathery pajamas.   A mad
doctor creates him from a tiny fish; the monster enjoys a
brief career as the "Creature From the Dry Lagoon" before
returning to his original form.   A slightly more impressive
version of the Gill Man (with vampire-type fangs and a long
tongue added for effect) swam through another Mexican production, Chabelo y Pepito contra los monstruos (1973).   In
1967 the Gill Man-inspired "Creature" appeared in the children's movie Mad Monster Party? and returned for television's sequel "Mad, Mad, Mad Monsters" (1972).   The claws
of the Universal-International Gill Man (recreated by Don
Post Studios) made an appearance in the 1975 color science
fiction spoof Dark Star, directed by John Carpenter and released by Bryanston.   The claws, added to a beachball, con-
stituted an hilarious alien life form loose aboard a space
ship.

Before Creature From the Black Lagoon was released,
the Gill Man made an appearance on "The Colgate Comedy
Hour" (NBC-TV) in 1953.   "Ricou and I did a live show with
Sonja Hennie and Bud [Abbott] and Lou [Costello]," said
Glenn Strange.   "I did the Monster and he did the Creature."
Abbott and Costello visit a representation of the Universal-
International prop department, which is adorned with dummies

The Creature from the Dry Lagoon, an inferior Mexican imitation of the Universal-International Gill Man, with comic Clavillazo in El castillo de los monstruos (1957).

of the Wolf Man (resembling more a stuffed gorilla), Mr. Hyde (as he appeared in the Abbott and Costello movie), the Invisible Man and Dracula. As Costello reads a story called The Monster and the Miser, the comedian is menaced first by the Frankenstein creation and then, appearing from behind a curtain, the impressive Gill Man. The skit was written by John Grant, one of the script writers of Abbott and Costello Meet Frankenstein. Curiously, Strange was credited at the end of the show as Glenn "Strangle."

During the mid-1960s the Creature appeared on the CBS television series "The Munsters." In the final moments of the episode "Love Comes to Mockingbird Heights," he is revealed to be the mysterious and wealthy Uncle

Gilbert (Richard Hale).   Only the Creature's head and hands
were shown (commercially sold pieces manufactured from
the Universal molds by Don Post Studios), the rest of the
body covered by a long raincoat.   This time the Creature
spoke.

The Gill Man appeared in part when his legs, arms
and claws contributed to the demon of "Pickman's Model,"
an H. P. Lovecraft story adapted to Universal's "Night Gallery" television show in the early 1970s.   Versions of the
Creature also appeared on "Ultra Man" (giant gill-man
vs. giant superhero), "Sinister Cinema," "The Krofft
Supershow," "Halleluja, Horrorwood," "Holmes and
Yoyo," the animated "Abbott and Costello" show and a commercial for Colorforms.

A novel of Creature from the Black Lagoon, written
by Vargo Statten (actually John Russell Fearn), was issued
in England as "A Dragon Publication" in 1954.   Another
novel, entitled The Creature from the Black Lagoon, was
issued by Berkley Medallion Books in 1977 as part of a
series based on Universal horror films.   (Other novels in
this series included The Wolfman, Werewolf of London, The
Mummy, The Bride of Frankenstein and Dracula's Daughter.
All of these novels appeared under the byline of Carl Dreadstone.)

Monsters directly inspired by the Gill Man have long
been appearing in comic books.   In 1954 the amphibious superhero Prince Namor the Sub-Mariner battled a monster
that could have been the Gill Man's brother.   "Vengeance"
was written and illustrated by Bill Everett in Marvel Comics'
Sub-Mariner no. 35 (August 1954).   A mad scientist creates
a Gill Man type amphibian called "Elmer"; but when he discovers that his creation has an aversion to water he tries
to give him Namor's brain.   The resourceful Sub-Mariner
escapes his bonds and blasts Elmer with a water hose, sending him crashing out a window with a box of nitro glycerin
unfortunately held in his claw.

Marvel published another take-off on the Gill Man,
"The Monster from the Lost Lagoon!," in Fantastic Four
no. 97 (April 1970), written by Stan Lee and drawn by Jack
Kirby.   The monster has the power to alter his Gill Man
appearance to resemble a human being, in which guise he
rides dolphins at an oceanarium.   In the end the "monster"
is revealed as an extraterrestrial being, who crash-landed

on Earth and attacked passing ships to protect his mate.
The alien creature made a comeback appearance in Fantastic
Four no. 124 (July 1972), "The Return of the Monster!," by
Lee and artist John Buscema.   The being steals some drugs
and abducts Sue Storm, the Invisible Girl of the Fantastic
Four, from the waiting room of a hospital.   In the followup
issue (August 1972), "The Monster's Secret!," it is explained that the drugs and Sue Storm's aid are needed to
help cure his mate of an Earth virus.

      During the early to middle 1970s, Marvel wanted to
acquire the rights to do an authorized Creature from the
Black Lagoon comic strip.   When the deal with Universal
was never completed, Marv Wolfman created The Manphibian
strip for the first and only issue of the black-and-white
comic magazine The Legion of Monsters (September 1975).
"Vengeance Crude" was plotted by Wolfman, written by Tony
Isabella, with art by Dave Cockrum and Sam Grainger.   The
Manphibian is a Gill Man type monster that emerges from
an oil well and possesses a sophisticated intelligence and
set of human emotions.

      The Gill Man was awarded his own authorized comic
book by Dell Publishing Company in 1963.   The first (and
only) issue of The Creature (December-February) follows
the basic premise of the original motion picture.   The story,
"Creature from the Amazon," follows a paleontologist to
South America after studying a fossil claw discovered in the
Amazon.   Accompanying the scientist on the expedition are
a wealthy playboy in search of treasure and a group of sinister German criminals determined to get the treasure for
themselves.   The Creature goes through a number of action
scenes inspired by scenes from the film before being killed
underwater by the heroes' spearguns.   The final panel shows
a gelatinous mass stuck to the boat containing a number of
unborn "Creatures."

      Don Glut included a take-off of the Creature in the
story "Queen of Horror," which was drawn by Dick Piscopo
for the second issue of Warren Publishing Company's illustrated magazine Vampirella (November 1969).   "Rico Chapman" is shown enacting the part during the filming of a
movie called "The Gill-Monster Strikes Back."   Skywald
Publishing Corporation's Nightmare no. 14 (August 1973) included a story called "The Creature from the Black Lagoon,"
drawn by Ricardo Villamonte.   The story depicted a scene
that was not in the motion picture in which the Gill Man

kills both of his skin diving hunters to protect his domain.
The tale concluded with the explanatory caption, "For copyright reasons, this is not an actual scene from Universal's
'Creature from the Black Lagoon' ... but an example of the
weird story."

Shortly after the release of Creature From the Black
Lagoon, Buchanan and Accles issued a satiric record called
"The Creature" on the Flying Saucer label, backed by "Meet
the Creature." Hans J. Salter's music from Creature From
the Black Lagoon, Herman Stein's from Revenge of the Creature and Henry Mancini's from The Creature Walks Among
Us was re-recorded by Dick Jacobs and his orchestra for
the album Themes from Horror Movies (Coral Records,
1960). A comedy song "(I'm in Love with) The Creature
from the Black Lagoon" was included on the album Monster
Rally.

Like the Wolf Man, Mummy and other movie horrors,
the Gill Man stalked and swam through the gamut of merchandise, including a mechanical Creature fish tank acces-
sory. Moor Fabrics used his likeness in its advertising.
In the middle 1960s a mechanical life-sized Gill Man was a
popular attraction at the Universal Pictures studio tour and
at a Hollywood nightclub called The Haunted House. A decade later his full-sized effigy could be seen luring the customers into various shops in Tijuana, Mexico, proving that
his image was commercially viable even outside the country
that invented him, twenty years after his last official screen
appearance.

OTHER CREATURE FEATURES

With the culmination of the Creature series at Universal-International, other studios began to capitalize on the
Gill Man's image and reputation.

The She Creature (American International Pictures,
1957) was one of numerous monster films that contributed
to the horror cycle of the fifties. Inspired by the Gill
Man's adventures, The She Creature was actually a story
about reincarnation. Marla English played Andrea, a lovely young woman who is actually the future incarnation of a
prehistoric sea monster. Through the dubious efforts of a
hypnotist, Dr. Carlo Lombardi (Chester Morris), the She
Creature is recalled in ghostly form from the churning sea

while Andrea lies in a trance. Then taking on solid form, the monster proceeds to slay the hypnotist's enemies. When Lombardi finally commands the She Creature to kill the man Andrea loves, the monster attacks him instead. Viewing Andrea, its entranced counterpart, the She Creature again assumes spectral form and returns to the sea. Lombardi's dying act is to bring Andrea out of her trance.

The film, directed by Edward L. Cahn, was surprisingly better than most of the horror and science fiction films being made by American International at the time. There was atmosphere, suspense and an impressive monster suit designed and worn by Paul Blaisdell. The actual construction of the suit was a joint effort by Paul and his wife Jackie.

The She Creature (affectionately referred to as "Cuddles") was built from foam rubber and latex. The reptile-like monstrosity stood six and one half feet tall in the "outrigger" boots which Blaisdell had designed. In general appearance, the She Creature resembled a kind of human lizard, with scales and a thick, armored epidermis, lobster-like claws, great pointed ears, fangs, horns and long, combed-back "hair." It was Cahn's request to add the heavy reptilian tail and the grotesque set of scaly "breasts."

Wearing the heavy costume (92 pounds, including the boots) Paul Blaisdell could register facial expressions, slap about the tail, eat, drink and smoke. The suit was designed to give adequate leverage to the actor inside so that the She Creature could easily lift a 140-pound man in one arm. The hide was thick enough for Blaisdell to withstand the close range firing of .22 blanks.

"The She Creature was never designed to go underwater," Paul Blaisdell told me. "It could, however, go into the ocean, to a limited extent, with some degree of safety. Unfortunately, the foam rubber had a habbit of taking on a considerable poundage of water, which slowed you down considerably if you had to make a transition from water to land. On the opposite side of the coin, she did contain a small reserve of air which was never timed, but could probably be rated as one to two minutes. This was

Opposite: Paul Blaisdell both created the outfit, with Jackie Blaisdell, and played the title role in The She Creature (American International, 1957).

handy in dealing with chemical smoke fumes in some of 'her'
pictures. " With his She Creature, Blaisdell proved that an
impressive and functional monster suit could be built without
the $12,000 budget of the Gill Man. *

Like the Gill Man, the She Creature was simply too
good and dependable a monster to be relegated to some obscure storeroom. She returned, in various forms, in a
number of appearances. Make-up artist Harry Thomas made
a new skull-like head for the She Creature body for its appearance in American International Pictures' Voodoo Woman
(1957). The head (without the body this time) adorned the
wall of the mad make-up artist's personal museum in AIP's
How To Make a Monster (1958). A slightly revamped She
Creature unmasked itself at the climax of Ghost of Dragstrip
Hollow (a 1959 film which went into production as The
Haunted Hotrod), revealing an unnamed and unbilled Paul
Blaisdell as the uncredited actor who had been appearing in
so many of these films. Blaisdell himself shot new footage
of the She Creature, showing the facial movements that were
never photographed for the original motion picture, for his
commercially sold film of 1962, Filmland Monsters. This

---

*Paul Blaisdell is truly an unsung star of 1950s monster
films. Before working in motion pictures, he was an illus-
trator for such publications as The Magazine of Fantasy and
Science Fiction and Spaceway. His first movie monster was
the small puppet magnified to life-size proportions in the
1955 film Beast With a Million Eyes. He designed the dinosaur-like monster for the 1956 Phantom From 10,000 Leagues
and the three-eyed mutant for its co-feature, The Day the
World Ended, for which he also enacted the monster's role.
These latter two American International films established
him with that studio and in the following years he built
for them the vegetable creature of It Conquered the World
(1956) the were-cat mask of The Cat Girl, the space ship
and megacephalic aliens of Invasion of the Saucermen, the
rotting corpse from The Undead (all 1957) and another such
carcass in Earth vs. the Spider (1958). He built props for
such American International productions as The Amazing Colossal Man (1957) and Attack of the Puppet People (1958) and
a whole set of his monster heads and props were displayed
in the horror museum of How To Make a Monster. Blaisdell's personal favorite is the costume (worn by former cowboy star Ray "Crash" Corrigan) of the blood-drinking Martian
that stows away on an Earthbound space ship in the United
Artists film It! The Terror From Beyond Space (1958).

was a compilation film from Blaisdell's company Golden
Eagle Films including new and trailer footage from It Conquered the World, The Day the World Ended and Invasion
of the Saucermen.

In 1957 the She Creature (now played by Bob Burns)
appeared on two Los Angeles television shows, "Quinn's
Corner" and "Campus Club," and in 1962 Golden Eagle
Films issued a set of 35mm color slides called "Hollywood
Monsters" which included shots of the female amphibian.

Blaisdell commented on the final remains of the She
Creature.   "The body was put in storage in the Santa Monica
mountains, but it became wallpaper for a den of eight rac-
coons.   The head was put on display, but eventually disinte-
grated due to the sulphuric acid in the smog.   I'm saving
the 'Frankenstein' boots for the next time we have a flood."

Ten years after The She Creature was released, AIP
produced a shoddy remake called Creature of Destruction,
directed by Larry Buchanan.   Even with color the film was
not worthy of theatrical release.   Its premiere showing was
on afternoon television.

Like the She Creature, other movie monsters were
designed to capitalize on the Gill Man's image without tang-
ling with Universal's legal department.   In 1958 Jack Kevan,
one of the creators of the original Creature suit, produced
The Monster of Piedras Blancas for VanWick Productions,
directed by Irvin Berwick.   Kevan designed, built and enacted the part of this hideous sea monster that menaces a
lighthouse and tears the heads from its human victims.   Not
only did the monster vaguely resemble the Gill Man but
roared in a convincing impression of its predecessor.   Unfortunately none of the quality of Creature From the Black
Lagoon found its way into The Monster of Piedras Blancas.
The movie was released in 1959.

In 1961, Roger Corman produced and directed Creature from the Haunted Sea for Filmgroup.   This was a delightful spoof of horror and spy films with a humanoid sea
monster emerging from Caribbean waters to menace a motley group of characters.   The Horror of Party Beach, which
was made by Iselin-Tenney Productions (who first put it into
production as Invasion of the Zombies) and released in 1964
by Twentieth Century-Fox, was a crude conglomeration of
teenagers, rock 'n' roll and blood-drinking monsters created

by radioactivity acting on plankton. Del Tenney directed this
utter fiasco. Jon Hall directed and starred in The Beach
Girls and the Monster which was made in 1964 and released
the next year by American International Television as Monster From the Surf. Between stock scenes of teenagers
surfing, Hall played a killer who masqueraded in a monster
suit consisting of a phony Gill Man type head and a pile of
seaweed in a film of equal quality. (Other titles for this
film are Surf Terror and Invisible Terror.)

Jacques Tourneur directed the 1965 color film War-
Gods of the Deep for American International. Inspired by
two stories by Edgar Allan Poe, "City in the Sea" and "A
Descent into the Maelstrom," the film begins as a Gill Man
type monster kidnaps a young woman and brings her into an
underwater city inhabited by smugglers from an earlier century. This amphibian and others which swam those deep
waters were more impressive than most imitations of the
Creature, but no one expressed remorse when they were
destroyed in the explosion that wrecked the city. The movie
went into production as City in the Sea, was released in
England as City Under the Sea and is also known under the
title War-Lords of the Deep.

Destination Inner Space (United Pictures, 1966), directed by Francis Lyon, brought a colorful amphibious monster to Earth, hatching aboard a submerged spacecraft.
This creature, most definitely inspired by the Gill Man, was
a brightly blue anthropomorphic fish with a shiny red dorsal
fin. During some nicely photographed underwater scenes the
monster swam in the style established by Browning's Gill
Man. Eventually the man-fish was destroyed when its space-
ship exploded underwater. Various cuttings from Destination
Inner Space were made available in home-movie editions under such titles as Terror of the Deep, The Thing and Sea
Monster.

La mujer murcielago ("The Bat Woman"), a Mexican
film directed in color by René Cardona in 1967 and released
the next year, starred Maura Monti as a caped superheroine
investigating the murders of wrestlers. The investigation
leads to a mad doctor who has created a Gill Man type being
called Pisces, a man-fish with which he hopes to conquer
first the sea and then (not too surprisingly) the Earth. Naturally, Bat Woman gains control of the cheap Creature imitation, turns him against his creator and leaves audiences
wishing they were viewing the genuine article.

In 1971, Harry Essex, the writer of Creature From
the Black Lagoon and It Came From Outer Space, produced
and directed Octa-Man with hopes of recapturing the success
of the first Gill-Man feature. Storywise Octa-Man is a
veritable remake of Creature with a prehistoric octopus-man
(perhaps the most ludicrous evolutionary link yet in films)
discovered in rural Mexico. From there on all similarities
end.

Artist George Barr originally designed the Octa-Man
as a creature which would utilize all eight tentacles. Essex
was dissatisfied with the drawings of the monster. When
Barr finally (and jokingly) sketched a man with an octopus
for a head, Essex accepted it. Rick Baker, who within a
few years would emerge as one of Hollywood's top make-up
artists and monster builders, built the Octa-Man suit. It
was his first film.

"The original script was written so that the Octa-Man
itself was never seen head-to-toe except for one establishing
shot," Rick Barker told Al Satian, Heather Johnson and me
during an interview. ["Make-Up Man: From Schlock to The
Exorcist," Monsters of the Movies no. 4 (December 1974),
p. 45-46.] "The whole story built up to that shot. Well,
it was a ten-day shooting schedule, and they lost a couple of
days at the outset due to poor planning.... When the initial
shooting was completed, they wound up with a film that didn't
make any sense at all. There was nothing that held the plot
together. So, they spent some additional money, brought
the costume out of retirement after it had been torn to
shreds, fixed it up a little, and shot about 45 additional
minutes of the monster. For instance, they added a scene
of the Octa-Man wrestling with a stuffed alligator.... A
stiff, fully lacquered, stuffed alligator!"

There have been myriad imitations of the Creature
from the Black Lagoon in films, yet none of them has managed to achieve the enduring appeal of the original.

VIII

HIS MAJESTY, KING KONG

No ikon in the history of monster films has proved as famous or durable as King Kong perched on the summit of the Empire State Building. The monster gorilla, a survivor from prehistoric times, clutches a screaming blonde woman in one massive paw. Then after setting her down, he lashes out at the swarm of biplanes that blast him with barrages of machine-gun fire.

This screen image, since it was first viewed by the public in 1933, has passed into the category of the popular myth. The huge ape's confrontation with the seemingly almost as primitive airplanes has been spoofed more times than any other single sequence from a fantasy motion picture. Immediately a giant gorilla atop any building brings to mind the classic and original King Kong, considered by most aficionados as the greatest single monster film ever made.

Basically, five men were responsible for the creation of King Kong--producer Merian C. Cooper, writer Edgar Wallace, director Ernest B. Schoedsack, sculptor Marcel Delgado, and special effects maestro Willis O'Brien.

Known as the Sphinx of Hollywood (and to his friends as simply "Obie"), Willis O'Brien (1886-1963) had perfected the art of puppet animation or, as he put it, "animation in depth." Simply stated, the process, also known as stop motion, involves the movement of an inanimate object on the screen. A model or puppet is moved a fraction of an inch, after which the camera clicks off a single frame of motion picture film. The procedure is then repeated, with countless movements and single frame exposures. The end result of this process is a strip of film, each frame having

282

recorded another succeeding increment of movement. When
projected, our persistence of vision interprets the footage as
if the inanimate object were moving. This process can be
incredibly time-consuming but the miracles that may be
achieved through skillful puppet animation can certainly be
worth the effort.

O'Brien did not invent the process. It had been utilized in films during the very early part of the century.
But he did perfect the art to the extent that dimensional animation made the transition from the simple trick photography
of the short novelty films to one of the important processes
used in the production of feature-length motion pictures.

He discovered animation after a varied career during
which he worked as a prize-fighter, factory worker, wilder-
ness guide and fur trapper, sports cartoonist (for the San
Francisco Daily World), cowboy, railroad brakeman and sur-
veyor. In 1915, O'Brien was sculpting models in clay for
an exhibit at the San Francisco World's Fair. He and his
brother were modeling miniature clay boxers and soon were
pitting one fighter against the other by bending them into
various positions. When O'Brien saw the possibilities in
applying such manipulations to the still new motion picture
medium, he brought the tiny boxers to the screen in an experimental and crudely executed short. This was the beginning of Willis O'Brien's motion picture career.

O'Brien began to experiment. He had a fondness for
prehistoric life and had even served as a guide for a group
of University of Southern California scientists brought to un-
earth a fossil sabre-tooth cat in the Crater Lake region.
Besides, puppet animation seemed to be designed for bringing to life dinosaurs and other extinct beasts which had few
other opportunities for resuscitation. Animating a clay
model Apatosaurus (commonly known as Brontosaurus) and
caveman, O'Brien produced 75 feet of film comedy--the first
of his many prehistoric animal films.

In 1917, Willis O'Brien made a one-reel comedy
short, The Dinosaur and the Missing Link, which was later
bought for $525 by the Thomas A. Edison Company and
theatrically released. The entire cast for this film consisted of animated models constructed of wooden "skeletons"
over which the likenesses were sculpted in clay. Working
from the basement of San Francisco's Imperial Theatre,

O'Brien manipulated his cave people and prehistoric animals over a period of two months.

The Dinosaur and the Missing Link was indeed prophetic. The picture involved prehistoric human beings in an anachronistic adventure with creatures that should have been extinct for some 70 million years.* The real star of the picture was the Missing Link himself, a mischievous ape who eventually battles and is killed by a brontosaur. O'Brien later referred to the prehistoric simian as "Kong's ancestor." Fortunately this and other early O'Brien efforts are extant and we can make the comparisons between the Missing Link and King Kong ourselves.

Following The Dinosaur and the Missing Link, Willis O'Brien shot a number of animated shorts. Three of these, Morpheus Mike, R. F. D. 10, 000 B. C. (or Rural Delivery, Ten Thousand B. C.) and Prehistoric Poultry were made for Edison in 1917 and featured all-puppet casts of cave people and prehistoric animals. Seen today, the films are crude yet imaginative and enchanting. O'Brien was not striving for realism in these early pictures. That came a scant two years later.

The Ghost of Slumber Mountain was made in 1919 for World Cinema Distributing Company. Major Herbert M. Dawley produced, wrote and directed the picture and later, as we shall see, claimed credit for work he had not even performed. Under the guidance of Dr. Barnum Brown, the famed American Museum of Natural History paleontologist, O'Brien constructed his first realistic prehistoric animals (as opposed to the caricatures of the 1917 productions), fashioned from clay and cloth. Brown also made suggestions as to the behavior of the creatures and O'Brien

---

*The erroneous combination of cavemen and dinosaurs in motion pictures, while ridiculed by the scientists, has become a convention in motion pictures since the silent era. D. W. Griffith made Man's Genesis in 1912 for the Biograph Company and one year later filmed a sequel under the title War of the Primal Tribes, which was copyrighted as The Primitive Man. The film, which was officially released as Brute Force, brought cavemen up against prehistoric reptiles. An alligator and a snake were given horns and other attachments to make them appear to be prehistoric monsters. But the real saurian star of the production was a life-sized moving mock-up of the horned flesh-eating dinosaur Ceratosaurus.

followed them quite closely.

O'Brien's dinosaurs do not appear until the final minutes of The Ghost of Slumber Mountain. Under the provocation of his young nephews, Uncle Jack tells of his adventure
on Slumber Mountain and Dream Valley, where the River of
Peace flows. The mountain is the site of the supposedly
haunted cabin of Mad Dick, a hermit who also happened to
be a paleontology buff. In the cabin the ghost of Mad Dick
(allegedly played by O'Brien himself) appears to Uncle Jack
and points out a strange instrument. When Uncle Jack peers
through the instrument toward the valley, he beholds the region as it existed millions of years ago. Uncle Jack watches
as various prehistoric monsters feed and battle to the death.
A carnivorous Allosaurus vanquishes a three-horned Triceratops, after which the towering predator turns on Uncle Jack.
But before the bipedal dinosaur can feast on human flesh,
Uncle Jack awakens from a dream. This most convenient
of all silent movie denouements suited the storytelling frame
of The Ghost of Slumber Mountain.

Once The Ghost was released, Dawley assumed full
credit for the apparent miracles audiences had seen on the
screen. Dawley went so far as to claim that one of O'Brien's
miniature monsters was actually his own "17-foot high" creation. Since the film was cut down to nearly half its original
length before release, Dawley found himself with a considerable surplus of O'Brien's animation footage. This he edited
into his own 1920 film Along the Moonbeam Trail, but as
O'Brien's talents continued to mature there was little doubt-
ing who accomplished the special effects in The Ghost of
Slumber Mountain. The dinosaur scenes from The Ghost,
along with footage of Carl Hagenbeck's life-sized dinosaur
models in Hamburg, Germany's Zoological Park, were later
incorporated into the documentary film Evolution, produced
by Max Fleischer in 1923 for Red Seal and released in 1925.
All of the Evolution dinosaur scenes were then used in Mystery of Life (Universal Pictures, 1931), a sound documentary
directed by George Cocharne. Later yet, in the early 1960s,
the Allosaurus vs. Triceratops battle from The Ghost of
Slumber Mountain became part of a television commercial
for a candy company.

One of the persons to become suitably impressed by
O'Brien's work in The Ghost of Slumber Mountain was Watterson Rothacker who, with Earl Hudson, had purchased the
motion picture rights to The Lost World, a novel by Sir

Arthur Conan Doyle, published in 1912. Doyle's fantastic
adventure opens with a dying man staggering into an Indian
village in the Amazon jungle, his possessions including drawings of a plateau inhabited by dinosaurs. Professor Challenger, a boisterous explorer (who appeared in other Doyle
novels and later pastiches), organizes an expedition to this
"lost world," discovering living counterparts of such extinct
saurians as the flesh-eating Megalosaurus and the herbivorous
Iquanodon, the latter having been domesticated by primitive
man. After a number of perilous incidents, the explorers
return to civilization. In Challenger's possession is a living pterosaur, a winged reptile which he exhibits to a packed
audience at Queen's Hall in London. The animal flies over
the audience, creating some panic before escaping through
an open window.

The Lost World was scheduled for shooting in 1925
by First National, with Harry O. Hoyt directing. Two years
earlier O'Brien, who was then attending Otis Art Institute
in Los Angeles, was considering the elaborate special effects
required by a project like The Lost World. The cruder
models animated in The Ghost of Slumber Mountain simply
would not suffice and O'Brien realized his need for an assistant.

It was during O'Brien's attendance at art school that
his historic meeting came with Marcel Delgado, a fellow
student who had been earning his tuition by doubling as a
school monitor. Delgado was a sculptor and it was shortly
after the meeting that O'Brien suggested that they join forces
on The Lost World. O'Brien offered his new friend an impressive $75 a week but Delgado declined, afraid that taking
the job would take precious time away from his art studies
and eventually forestall his hopeful art career. Delgado had
come from an impoverished family in Mexico and considered
a career in art to be more secure than a job in the motion
picture industry.

Delgado did, however, accept O'Brien's invitation to
visit the First National studios. O'Brien personally guided
the sculptor's tour of the studio and finally brought him into
a workshop with numerous dinosaur models and reproductions
of Charles R. Knight's famous paintings of prehistoric animals. (Knight's paintings of extinct life have graced such
institutions as Chicago's Field Museum of Natural History,
New York's American Museum of Natural History and the
Los Angeles County Museum of Natural History. Reproductions of his restorations of prehistoric animals have appeared

in countless books and articles on paleontology.) Over four
decades later, Marcel Delgado recalled it this way:

> 'Well, Marcel [said O'Brien], how do you like
> your new studio?' Stupefied as I was, I said,
> 'What studio?' He said, 'The one you are standing
> in. It is all yours. That is, if you want it.' I
> really didn't know what to say. I had been taken
> completely by surprise. 'O'Bie' had finally won.
> So he said, 'Well, when are you going to start?'
> 'Right now,' I replied. He took me to the office
> and signed me up, and I started to work that day.

Basing his models on the Charles R. Knight restorations, Marcel Delgado constructed them roughly 18 inches
in length. Over ball-and-socket-jointed "skeletons" Delgado
built up the musculature from sponge rubber, over which
he added the animals' latex skins and finally all external
protuberances. For added realism Delgado built an air-
bladder apparatus into some of the models which could simulate breathing. O'Brien was pleased with the monster
menagerie created by Delgado; for sheer realism they surpassed any prehistoric animals as yet created especially for
the motion pictures.

Using Delgado's creations, Willis O'Brien finished a
short piece of film showing the dinosaurs in action. Doyle,
who was in New York on a lecture tour, approved of the
footage in which various genera of dinosaurs battled one another. An audience of professional magicians, including the
incomparable Harry Houdini, marveled at what they saw on
the screen and were unable to discover O'Brien's secret.

Herbert M. Dawley, however, did know how the effects were done and used that knowledge to threaten Rothacker and Doyle with a $100,000 law suit. Dawley claimed that
he had invented the puppet animation process, completely ignoring the fact that such effects were pioneered on the
screen long before the making of his Ghost of Slumber
Mountain. Furthermore he stated that his former employee
had stolen the process for use in The Lost World. But
Dawley's case did not halt production on the new First National motion picture.

The Lost World was almost a blueprint for the later
masterpiece King Kong. Not only were both films enhanced
by Willis O'Brien's animated effects, they were also similar in

story structure, so much, in fact, that King Kong is often
regarded by film historians as an unauthorized remake of
The Lost World. The film opens with newspaper reporter
Ed Malone (Lloyd Hughes) unable to marry his fiancée until,
on her insistence, he first accomplishes an act of heroism.
Meanwhile, the boisterous and bearded Professor Challenger
(Wallace Beery) is derided for his theory that explorer
Maple White had discovered a plateau teeming with prehis-
toric life. Challenger detests reporters and fights Malone
from his house and into the street before accepting him as
a member of his expedition to the "Lost World." Soon
Challenger, Malone, Maple White's daughter Paula (Bessie
Love) and Sir John Roxton (Lewis Stone), a big game hunter,
number among the professor's expedition into the unexplored
Amazon jungle.

     From the base of the plateau, the group sees a liv-
ing Pteranodon, a giant winged reptile. Perhaps propheti-
cally the group is watched by a beastlike apeman, or another
Missing Link (played by Bull Montana), and his pet chimpanzee. (This was Montana's second foray into an apeman role.
In the 1920 silent film Go and Get It, directed by M. Neilan
and Henry R. Symonds, he played the monstrous result of
the transplantation of a dead criminal's brain into the skull
of a gorilla.) Scaling the towering walls of the plateau, the
explorers encounter a number of supposedly extinct prehistoric creatures--including a massive, snaky-necked Apatosaurus. After a battle with a carnivorous Allosaurus, the herbivorous giant plunges from the cliffside to land in a mud
pool below.

     In The Lost World live actors and dinosaurs appeared
simultaneously on screen, which was certainly a startling
image to behold in 1925. To achieve this effect O'Brien
animated his dinosaurs on a miniature set with flora made
of sheet metal to insure against unnecessary movement.
The scenes of the live actors were photographed separately.
By masking off portions of the animation and live action
footage, O'Brien was able to combine the two, arriving at
such impressive composites as Challenger and his colleague
Professor Summerlee (Arthur Hoyt) crouching behind a tree
to observe a passing Apatosaurus.

     After the group finds the skeletal remains of Maple
White, a natural phenomenon occurs which, over the follow-
ing years, would become a cliché of the "dinosaur" film.
The volcano, which had apparently been content to merely

Professor Challenger
(Wallace Beery)
observes his beloved
"Brontosaurus" in
The Lost World
(First National,
1925), based on
Sir Arthur Conan
Doyle's novel.

belch smoke for millions of years until the arrival of the
explorers, erupts. In an incredibly spectacular sequence
(tinted red) virtually the entire cast of O'Brien's animated
characters flee the descending fire and lava, often many of
them in a single shot. At last the human band manage to
climb down the cliffside via a rope. The apeman grabs the
rope (another prophesy of King Kong) while Malone is descending but Roxton shoots the monster, saving the life of
his rival for the love of Paula.

The final sequences of The Lost World set down the
rules for the King Kong style film. Professor Challenger,
aided by the Brazilian government, returns the trapped
"brontosaur" to London where he plans to exhibit the animal. But the monster breaks free of its cage and soon the
streets of London are in panic as a frightened and rampaging Apatosaurus charges through the streets. The dinosaur,
seen in more of O'Brien's composites and also thundering
through a miniature representation of London, destroys some
of the city's landmarks. Finally the creature steps onto
London Bridge which, quite literally and perhaps traditionally, starts falling down beneath the monster's thirty-ton
weight. The dinosaur splashes into the Thames River, presumably to return to the Lost World. Paula and Malone go
off to be married, though audiences quickly forgot the film's
romantic sequences; what stayed in people's memories were
the dinosaurs of Delgado and O'Brien.

A sequel to The Lost World, again to be directed by
Hoyt and animated by O'Brien, was planned well into 1928,
but this followup was never filmed. Still there was considerable mileage to be derived from the original film and
the story on which it was based.

Encyclopedia Britannica Films issued a short subject
in 1948 under the title A Lost World, using footage from the
1925 production enhanced by a soundtrack. Magic Memories,
a compilation film of various trick scenes, included a battle
between a Tyrannosaurus and Triceratops purporting to be
from O'Brien's Lost World. But the scene does not appear
to be O'Brien's work. The dinosaur models seem almost
comical, the animation is crude and jerky and there is considerable blood flowing when the flesh-eater bites into the
neck frill of its horned adversary. The origin of this sequence remains a mystery unless it is actually part of the
test reel screened in the presence of Sir Arthur Conan
Doyle. Scenes from the real Lost World (in addition to

scenes from Brute Force and other movies) appeared in
Blackhawk Films' Film Firsts, Chapter II.

Buddy's Lost World was a cartoon spoof of The Lost
World made in 1935 by Warner Brothers (the company which
owned the 1925 movie) and released the next year.   Jack
King directed and Bob Clampett wrote this animated short
in which the character Buddy sails to a prehistoric island
where he mistakes the legs of a huge Apatosaurus for trees.
The brontosaur gives Buddy a wet "slurp kiss."

When a child, Clampett had seen The Lost World in
its original release.   Marveling at the dinosaur effects, he
quickly began work on his own epilogue to the film using a
comical version of Professor Challenger and a sea serpent
counterpart to the movie's Apatosaurus.   Soon, using hand-
puppet versions of the characters and a "Jocko" monkey puppet that reminded him of The Lost World's Missing Link,
Clampett staged his own amateur productions.   His sea serpent character (who frequently made use of the "slurp kiss")
eventually evolved into Cecil the Sea Sick Sea Serpent who
starred in the television puppet serial "Time for Beany"
during the early 1950s.   Among the show's regular cast was
Captain Horatio Huffenpuff who was based directly upon Wallace Beery's Professor Challenger.   In 1962 the characters
from "Time for Beany" became animated cartoon figures in
the "Beany and Cecil" television series.

Every film in which a party of explorers discovers a
land inhabited by prehistoric beasts owes its very existence
to The Lost World, some more so than others in plot or
title.   Two Lost Worlds (United Artists, 1950), directed by
Norman Dawn, was a tale of piracy and kidnaping during
the nineteenth century, concluding on a prehistoric volcanic
island.   But, like seemingly countless other films of this
type, all the monster scenes came from an earlier epic One
Million B.C. (Hal Roach, 1940).   More obvious in story was
Lost Continent (Lippert, 1951), directed by Samuel Newfield.
A group of scientists tracks an atomic rocket to a mountain-
top where prehistoric life yet flourishes.   As in The Lost
World, an Apatosaurus figures prominently and, as in King
Kong, traps one of the explorers in a tree and kills him.
The dinosaurs of Lost Continent appeared in crude model
animation with all the scenes set in that prehistoric world
tinted green.   Dinosaur footage from Lost Continent later
reappeared in the unbelievably cheap Robot Monster (Astor,
1953), a 3-D movie that also used extensive regular footage

from One Million B. C. , and in the television series "The
Adventures of Rin-Tin-Tin. " Both Two Lost Worlds and
Lost Continent climaxed with that convenient plot device introduced in The Lost World, the erupting volcano.   A Japanese film Daitozoku ("Samurai Pirate"), made by Toho International in 1963, was a color fantasy having nothing to do
with The Lost World.   But when it was released two years
later in the United States, American International Pictures
called it The Lost World of Sinbad.

An actual remake of the Doyle story came out of
Twentieth Century-Fox in 1960, produced and directed by
Irwin Allen.   Much excitement was generated among movie
enthusiasts when it was announced that the film would not
only be made in color but also feature special effects by the
great Willis O'Brien.   To everyone's utter disappointment--
most of all O'Brien's--the remake utilized live lizards instead of puppet animation, surely a waste of the master's
abilities.   The new version of The Lost World starred
Claude Rains as a less boisterous Professor Challenger, who
discovers atop the prehistoric plateau man-eating plants, a
giant spider, headhunters and modern-day lizards unconvincingly adorned with shields, horns, spines and nodes to represent dinosaurs.   Even the youngest members of the audience chuckled when Challenger points to an overblown iguana
and stakes his reputation on its being a living "Brontosaurus!"
The Missing Link of the first version was now a beautiful female savage.   Added to the plot were such elements as
Roxton's (Michael Rennie) financing the expedition because he
believes the Lost World to hold a treasure in diamonds.
The ending of the new Lost World was most disappointing to
those who fondly recalled the 1925 picture.   After leading
his crew to safety through a graveyard of dinosaur bones
and following an encounter with a "fire monster" (actually a
tegu lizard decorated with fake horns and other unconvincing
attachments) that lives in a stream of hot lava, Challenger
shows them what he plans to bring back to civilization--the
"fire monster's" egg.   The group watches the egg hatch into
a junior version of its parent.   And when Challenger identifies this mythical creature as "Tyrannosaurus rex!" the audience has even more reason to laugh.   The film ends with
the hint of a sequel, which was announced in 1964 as Return
to the Lost World, but, perhaps fortunately, the picture was
never made.   The movie's "dinosaur" footage, however, was
used again and again in Irwin Allen's various television
series, including "Voyage to the Bottom of the Sea" and "The
Time Tunnel. " Several shots from the picture even made an

unwelcomed appearance in When Dinosaurs Ruled the Earth
(Hammer Films, 1970), which otherwise featured the superb
model animation of Jim Danforth.

     To publicize The Lost World, Twentieth Century-Fox
issued a one-page newspaper comic strip.   In 1960 Dell
Comics (Western Publishing Company) presented a comic book
of The Lost World, based on the remake film.   During the
1940s, Planet Comics (Fiction House) ran a series called
"The Lost World," about Earth's future take-over by con-
querers from another planet.   During the early 1940s there
was also a radio drama of "The Lost World," written by
John Dickson Carr and serialized by the BBC.

     In 1930, Marcel Delgado was telephoned by Willis
O'Brien.   Following the completion of The Lost World, Delgado had lost his prestige at the studio.   "Only the 'top'
stars and officials were allowed to visit our department,"
Delgado wrote.   "Among the 'Greats' was Milton Sills, who
had formerly been a college professor.   He talked to me for
hours about dinosaurs and prehistoric animals, which helped
me a great deal in my work.   I also had the great privilege
of meeting Greta Nisson, Nita Naldi, Colleen Moore, Bessie
Love, Rudolph Valentino, Lewis Stone, Wallace Beery, and
many others.   These people were all very gracious to me,
but I was to find that after The Lost World was finished
and I had to seek employment in the regular miniature department of the studio, I was treated with disrespect and
discriminated against because of my Mexican heritage.   I
realize now that it was a mistake for me to have taken work
in the regular department but I felt it was necessary in or-
dor for me to continue my work along that line."   O'Brien
told Delgado that he and director Harry Hoyt were about to
embark on another dinosaur project, this time for RKO-
Radio Pictures.   The film was to be called Creation with
special effects to make The Lost World appear crude by
comparison.   Naturally, Delgado joined the team.

     Creation was to be an adventuresome story of a group
of people who journey by submarine to an enormous promon-
tory that rises to the surface of the sea during an earthquake.
Stranded on this body of land, the party encounters more
brontosaurs, a pair of battling Triceratops and other prehistoric animals.   Later, one of the crew members (played by
Ralf Harolde) kills a baby Triceratops, after which its
mother pursues and gores him to death (this sequence being
the only extant footage from Creation).   The action continues

as the group is pursued by a plated Stegosaurus to the ruins of an ancient temple, after which the dinosaur fights and is killed by a hungry Tyrannosaurus. It is during another volcanic eruption that the group is finally rescued by two Chilean airplanes.

Delgado, O'Brien and Hoyt worked on Creation in 1930 and 1931. Had the picture been completed it would have exceeded the million-dollar price range. But except for some impressive test scenes, it was never finished, though Harry Hoyt was determined to keep the project alive. Revamping the Creation storyline, Hoyt planned to make Lost Atlantis in 1938, utilizing the talents of Fred Jackman, one of the special effects technicians on The Lost World, who built 25 new dinosaurs for the upcoming production. The picture was halted prematurely but was revised in 1940, with Walter Lantz and Edward Nassour intended to create the dinosaur effects. But Hoyt's Lost Atlantis project, like its namesake, perished, never to resurface again.

Even so, the Creation project was not entirely dead. Elements from it would merely be shifted to a new home, the stunning special effects designed for a film that brought to life the prehistoric denizens of the unmapped Skull Island. This was the domain of Kong.

EIGHTH WONDER OF THE WORLD

Merian C. Cooper and Ernest B. Schoedsack had been prominent military figures during the second decade of the twentieth century. Their exploits in foreign lands were heroic and colorful enough to rival those of their imaginary counterparts, Carl Denham and Jack Driscoll, the two heroes of King Kong. In 1923 the two men formed Cooper-Schoedsack Productions, a company to specialize in documentaries on such subjects as wild animals and savage tribes. But their first movie venture, capturing native Africans on film, ended in disaster, as a ship explosion destroyed all of the team's precious footage.

Grass (1925), a film made by Cooper, Schoedsack and author Marguerite Harrison, followed Mrs. Harrison into Asia in search of a lost tribe. She was shown accompanying the forgotten Baba Ahmedi tribe in search of grasslands in the valleys near Persia's central plateau. Following her filmed adventure, Mrs. Harrison left Cooper and

Schoedsack who went ahead with another motion picture two
years later.

It was with this 1927 production, Chang, that Cooper
and Schoedsack were planting the seed which would eventually
mature into the classic King Kong. Set in a Thailand jungle,
Chang is a man-vs. -beasts story in which a Lao tribe is in
conflict with the predacious cats of the jungle. Yet the
people's most dangerous threat is the dreaded chang, which
is finally caught in a trap and exposed as a baby elephant,
a creature that had ruined the rice patch necessary for their
survival. The high point of the films was an elephant
stampede that destroys the village before the chang monsters
can be rounded up and dominated. Insofar as the film's advertising was concerned, chang was a word enveloped in
mystery and with an obvious similarity to the name Kong.
The animal footage from Chang was later incorporated into
a good number of films including The Last Outpost (1935)
and The Jungle Princess (1937), both made by Paramount.

But Cooper wanted to film "the ultimate in adventure,"
something to thrill not only the demanding public but himself
as well. He was thinking in terms of a fantasy as opposed
to the Chang style of dramatic documentary. In Cooper's
mind was the image of an enormous gorilla battling a fleet
of fighter planes from its perch atop the Empire State Building. (In 1962 French writer Jean Boullet suggested that
King Kong might have been strongly influenced by Jonathan
Swift's 1726 novel of Gulliver's Travels. Illustrations from
various editions of Gulliver's Travels depicting an enormous
monkey or ape tenderly caressing Gulliver, reaching for him
through a window, carrying him across the rooftops and finally holding him while surmounting a tall towerlike building,
though published long before King Kong, bear striking re-
semblances to scenes in Cooper's motion picture.)

Cooper's friend W. Douglas Burden had related his
adventures on the Malaysian island of Komodo, inhabited by
the giant Komodo dragons (Varanus komodoensis), the largest
existing lizards, some weighing 250 pounds and attaining
lengths of ten feet. Knowledge of these formidable reptiles
fed the plot hatching in Cooper's brain. He envisioned a
prehistoric island where a primitive people gave worship to
ancient gods, where saurians from the dinosaur era roamed
and hunted at will, and all under the domination of his original conception of a gigantic gorilla. Then Cooper began
to backtrack, considering the expedition that would discover

the great anthropoid monster and bring him to Man's world.
Gunfire would prove useless against the huge creature, yet
there would be one weapon against which not even he could
survive. Cooper recalled the fairy tale of Beauty and the
Beast.

Cooper's original idea was to feature an actor in a
gorilla suit for the proposed film while the prehistoric reptiles would be played by live Komodo dragon lizards. But
the project would have been a time-consuming and expensive
one which neither Paramount nor Metro-Goldwyn-Mayer
cared to undertake. For a while Cooper abandoned the motion picture medium altogether to pursue a new career in
the aviation industry.

In 1931, Merian C. Cooper was commissioned by
RKO-Radio Pictures producer David O. Selznik to salvage a
number of unfinished movie projects including the scrapped
Creation. Cooper did more than merely salvage the footage.
He felt that Creation was not viable in its present form of
"just a lot of animals walking around" but he recognized
O'Brien's prehistoric world as the perfect setting for his
monster gorilla.

Both Willis O'Brien and Marcel Delgado were soon
working again on what was developing from their aborted
Creation project. After Selznik gave Cooper the go-ahead
to produce a reel of test footage, O'Brien instructed Delgado as to the design of Kong, Cooper's gorilla. Following the animator's description, Delgado created a combination gorilla and human being, which Cooper dismissed as
resembling a "monkey and a man with long hair." When
Delgado's second attempt at creating a suitable ape monster
still retained certain human characteristics, Cooper roared
that he wanted the most brutal and monstrous gorilla that
anyone had ever seen. O'Brien argued that human qualities
were necessary in order for the public to sympathize with
the beast, but General Cooper, accustomed to giving commands, insisted that the amount of sympathy aroused for
the ape was in direct proportion to its degree of brutishness.
For the final word in the monster's design and proportions,
Cooper received the cooperation of Harry C. Raven, curator of zoology at the American Museum of Natural History
in New York.

For the present, Cooper's project was entitled The
Beast and O'Brien commenced to shoot a test reel. Delgado

constructed the 18-inch-tall ape's body from a metal, ball-
and-socket-jointed "skeleton" and padded him with realistic
cotton muscles.   The outer covering was made from rabbit
fur.

    Meanwhile mystery writer Edgar Wallace was assigned
to write the script for The Beast.   Actually, Wallace's work
on the production was minimal insofar as the final product
was concerned.   He prepared a 110-page scenario titled Kong
which he admitted was mostly Cooper's story.   In the Wallace version of the plot, Carl Denham, an explorer, circus
man and once friend of P. T. Barnum, is aboard a tramp
steamer when he rescues the survivor of a shipwreck on an
uncharted island.   Denham laughs at the man's tale of sea
serpents.   Meanwhile, Shirley and John, the heroine and
hero of the story, and crew of ex-convicts are in a lifeboat
which is overturned by an Apatosaurus.   The survivors reach
the island where prehistoric monsters abound.   Shirley becomes the intended rape victim of the crew when Kong appears, rescuing her from one "fate worse than death" and
carrying her through the jungle to one considerably worse.
In his cave Kong displays his affections for Shirley by gently
caressing her cheek and offering her a pterodactyl egg.
Later a drugged Kong is exhibited to the public in Madison
Square Garden.   But when the giant ape sees his beloved
Shirley menaced by Denham's circus tigers, he escapes his
cage and kills them.   His final stand atop the Empire State
Building occurs during a storm.   After being riddled with
bullets fired by airborne policemen, Kong is electrocuted by
a bolt of lightning.

    When RKO disdained the Kong title because of its
Oriental sound and its similarity to Chang, Wallace suggested
that the project be renamed King Ape.   The title was considered; but that change proved to be the end of Wallace's
involvement with the picture.   Early in February of 1932 he
was stricken with pneumonia and on the tenth of that month,
his condition further complicated by diabetes, Edgar Wallace
died.   Schoedsack's wife Ruth Rose (whose daring and loyalty to her husband's adventurous career were the inspirations
for King Kong's heroine Ann Darrow) wrote the final version
of the film which went into production as The Eighth Wonder
of the World.

    Using the woodcut illustrations of Gustave Doré (The
Divine Comedy, Paradise Lost and The Bible) for a basis,
O'Brien's craftsmen created an atmospheric nightmare realm

in miniature, with added detail and depth achieved by painting scenery on sheets of glass. For economy some of the
prehistoric creatures left over from Creation were taken out
of storage. With the Kong model completed, the test reel
for the film was ready to be shot.

The utmost secrecy was maintained as O'Brien shot
his creatures frame by frame. Meanwhile, Cooper and
Schoedsack had joined forces in 1932 for The Most Dangerous
Game, a movie based on Richard Connell's famous short
story about a big game hunter who stalks human beings. A
moody jungle set was erected for the movie, with dense foliage, rocks and even a ravine bridged by a fallen tree.
Starring in The Most Dangerous Game were Robert Armstrong and Fay Wray. Cooper lured Miss Wray to the Kong
project by promising that she would star opposite "the tallest, darkest leading man in Hollywood." While Schoedsack
directed The Most Dangerous Game, Cooper managed to borrow both Armstrong and Wray between takes, using their
talents in the Kong live-action footage. He also utilized the
ravine and its log, shooting scenes to match what O'Brien
was creating on his animation tables. The result was a remarkable ten minutes of action-jammed footage.

The test reel of Kong opened with the Creation scene
of the man being slain by the irate Triceratops. Meanwhile,
Kong is carrying Ann Darrow (Fay Wray) across the log
bridge. Denham (Robert Armstrong) and his crew members
are charged by an Arsinotherium, a fantastic, extinct horned
mammal. When the men are forced onto the log, Kong shakes
them off and into the ravine, where they become food for an
enormous spider, octopus and various lizards seemingly born
in Doré's engravings. The sequence climaxes with Kong's
battling a huge Tyrannosaurus to protect Ann, after which a
monstrous vulture (Teratornis) flies away from its scaly
corpse.

The test reel, most of which would inevitably be used
in the finished production, was received with general enthu-
siasm. Kong, or King Kong as it was later rechristened to
make the title sound less Oriental, was given the official
RKO go-ahead. Delgado promptly constructed an additional
five Kong models. For shots in which human beings and
Kong were shown in close proximity, the RKO propmen built
an enormous paw (that could grasp and release Miss Wray
and whomever else it held), a foot and a full-sized bust of
the King. This latter contrivance had a face six and one

half feet wide, ears 12 inches long and 10-inch fangs.
Eighty-five motors permitted the eyes and face to move realistically, all operated by six men crowded together inside
the chest.   The whole affair was covered with the skins of
thirty bears.   Brow furrowing, eyes rolling, nostrils flaring
and mouth opening to reveal the white teeth, this apparatus
provided some terrifying close-ups of an angry or curious
Kong.

In animating the miniature figure of King Kong, Willis
O'Brien infused much of his own personality into the giant
ape.   Darleen O'Brien, his widow, has been reported as
stating that Kong's mannerisms were her husband's, and that
is yet another reason for the durability of the mighty anthropoid.   Kong, though usually a mere miniature puppet brought
to life by the animation process, had personality, a quality
that is sorely lacking in most film behemoths.   For the
story that Merian C. Cooper had in mind, the film required
a monster for whom his audience would care.

King Kong unreels with a title card quoting a seemingly authentic "Old Arabian Proverb" which states: "And
the Prophet Said--And lo, the beast looked upon the face of
beauty.   And it stayed its hand from killing.   And from that
day, it was as one dead. " In truth the proverb was penned
by Cooper himself, though, like the often quoted poem from
The Wolf Man, it has become assimilated into the canon of
popular mythology.   Cooper's proverb established the Beauty
and the Beast theme right from the outset, though audiences
were about to watch the strangest variation on that theme
ever filmed.

Aboard the Venture, a steamer docked outside New
York, Carl Denham, a disgruntled motion picture producer
specializing in films about animal life, informs a theatrical
agent that his next movie needs a woman to meet the public's demand for a love interest.   The agent has not supplied Denham with an actress because the producer has
planned a voyage to some unknown destination aboard a ship
harboring a large supply of ammunition and several boxes
of gas bombs.   Actually, Denham represented Cooper, who
was often cruising to savage lands to photograph the unknown.   (Denham's stated disdain for cameramen, one of
whom panicked at the sight of a charging rhinoceros even
though Denham was standing nearby with a rifle, paralleled
an actual and quite similar incident experienced years earlier by Cooper.)

Denham is forced to hunt the streets of New York for an actress, finally coming upon an attractive (and hungry) blonde named Ann Darrow who was in the process of stealing an apple from a fruit vender.   After Denham offers her a chance at movie stardom, she agrees to go on his mysterious voyage.   First mate Jack Driscoll (Bruce Cabot) complains about having a woman aboard ship, but the <u>Venture</u> begins its voyage on schedule.

With the <u>Venture</u> somewhere in the Indian Ocean "way west of Sumatra," Denham at last reveals their destination to Captain Englehorn (Frank Reicher), who claims that there is nothing out there for thousands of miles.   But Denham's map was drawn by the captain of a Norwegian barque who had sketched an uncharted island.   "And across the base of that peninsula," says Denham, "cutting it off from the rest of the island, is a wall ... built so long ago that the people who live there now have slipped back, forgotten the higher culture that built it.   But it's as strong today as it was centuries ago.   The natives keep that wall in repair.   They need it.   There's something on the other side ... something they fear. "

When Englehorn suggests a hostile tribe, Denham returns with the name of Kong, which the captain believes refers to a Malay superstition.

"Anyway," Denham replies, "neither beast nor man. Something monstrous, all-powerful ... still living, still holding that island in the grip of deadly fear. "

Driscoll gradually becomes infatuated by Ann and worries for her safety as Denham shoots her screen test. Ann is dressed in a filmy "Beauty" costume (<u>Beauty and the Beast</u> the basis for Denham's film as it is Cooper's).   Denham directs her to scream, which Ann does thereby continuing Fay Wray's reputation of the screen's champion screamer.   (Fay Wray had given out comparable screams in the earlier horror films <u>The Mystery of the Wax Museum</u>, <u>The Most Dangerous Game</u>, <u>Dr. X</u> [all 1932] and <u>The Vampire Bat</u> [1933].)

When the <u>Venture</u> finally hoves to at their destination, Skull Island (so named for a mountain suggesting a human skull), Denham goes ashore, taking Driscoll, Englehorn, some of the crewmen, and of course the star of his intended motion picture, Ann Darrow.   In his direction of

the island scenes, Schoedsack was careful to photograph his
human actors with as few close-ups as possible. Most of
these scenes were taken in full or long shots and often from
a high angle, as if to imply right from the beginning the
presence of something huge dominating the island.

   The rest of Denham's cast is already involved in a
show all their own. Dwarfing the village of Skull Islanders
is an expansive wall with two enormous wooden gates and
surmounted by a tocsin gong. (Actually this magnificent set
was not built for King Kong. The wall was standing on the
lot of the RKO-Pathé Studio in Culver City and was originally constructed for Cecil B. DeMille's 1927 biblical epic,
The King of Kings. After its appearance in King Kong, the
wall with its gong became part of the lost island of Lemuria
in the serial The Return of Chandu (Principal, 1934), starring Bela Lugosi as the famed magician. The serial was
later re-cut into a feature-length movie, Chandu on the Magic Island, in 1935, while scenes from the chapterplay were
included in the compilation feature Dr. Terror's House of
Horrors, released by National Roadshow in 1943. The wall
made its final stand in the Selznik epic Gone With The Wind
(MGM, 1939) during the spectacular burning of Atlanta sequence, staged by special effects expert Lee Zavitz. Few
people in the audience recognized the camouflaged structure
that blazed in the background as the wall from King Kong's
island.)

   There is never any explanation given as to why the
wall would be equipped with the gates. Certainly whoever
built the wall would not have provided an easy entrance for
whatever titanic being lived on the opposite side. A native
ceremony is in progress in front of the wall, with a young
native girl adorned by flowers and several warriors dancing
about clad in the skins of gorillas. The savages are shouting "Kong! Kong!" to the thunderous sound of drums.

   The scene was augmented by the powerful strains of
Max Steiner's music score. Steiner, whose distinguished
career would eventually include scoring more than 300 motion pictures, had watched the King Kong footage sans music
and wrote what he felt, resulting in an impassioned masterpiece that perfectly conveyed the power and raw savagery of
the King and his primitive world. Using a stopwatch, he
timed his music so that it coincided perfectly with the visuals. (When the tribal chieftain, played by Noble Johnson,
notices the presence of the Caucasian intruders, his every

The giant (mechanical) head of Kong created for the original
King Kong (RKO, 1933), perhaps the greatest monster movie
of all time.

step matches a beat of Steiner's music.) King Kong proved
to be one of the earliest fully-orchestrated motion pictures
with an extensive score and its music was later recycled
for a number of films. (Steiner's musical score for King
Kong included the following selections: "King Kong," "Jungle
Dance," "The Forgotten Island," "A Boat in the Fog," "The
Railing," "Aboriginal Sacrifice Dance," "Meeting with the
Black Men," "Sea at Night," "Stolen Love," "The Sailors,"
"The Bronte," "Cryptic Shadows," "The Cave," "The Snake,"
"Humorous Ape," "The Peri," "Furioso," "The Swimmers,"
"The Escape," "Return of Kong," "King Kong March,"

"Fanfare No. 1," "Fanfare No. 2," "Fanfare No. 3," "Agitato," "Elevated Sequence," "The Train," "The Aeroplane" and 'Dance of Kong. ")

The chief and the witch doctor want to replace the native girl with the golden-haired Ann for the "Bride of Kong. " Naturally Denham refuses, quietly ushering his group back to the ship. That night Ann is kidnaped by the natives and forced back to the island. By the time that Denham and Driscoll realize she is missing, Skull Island is already alive with flickering torches and rhythmic drum beats.

The gates of the great wall are opened and Ann, screaming desperately, is dragged through them and up to a raised altar, where she is bound between two pillars. The chief, standing at the top of the wall, invokes the name of Kong while his men sound the ritual gong. Ann writhes as she hears the sounds of ponderous footsteps and bestial grunts (all timed with Steiner's music). Then, as the trees are torn aside, she stares into the leering face of Kong, a monster gorilla about fifty feet high. Kong releases her from bondage and, fascinated by her beauty, carries her into his jungle kingdom. Peering through a window at the bottom of the wall, Driscoll briefly glimpses the hairy abductor of the woman he loves.

Never is it explained just what Kong does with his human 'brides. " Nor is it ever revealed just what his fascination is for the yellow-haired Ann Darrow unless it is her uniqueness on this island. Whatever his attraction to her, it is enough for him to be virtually tame when alone with her and a raging monster when her life is threatened. Biologically there can be no real sexual attraction by a gorilla for a female Homo sapiens--especially when the ape is some fifty feet tall. Surely the relationship between King Kong and his blonde captive remains one of the most bizarre "love affairs" ever photographed by motion picture cameras. Somehow audiences accepted it.

Denham, Driscoll and a rescue party, leaving a number of sailors with the natives, pursue Kong on the other side of the wall, guided by a trail of giant footprints, broken foliage and the sounds made by the giant ape. Yet there are horrors besides Kong in this prehistoric jungle. The party is attacked by the plated dinosaur Stegosaurus, which Denham fells with his gas bombs. (The King Kong Stegosaurus,

showing the dorsal plates paired and with eight deadly spikes
on the tail, was actually in error, apparently based upon restorations of the animal by E. Ray Lankester in 1905 and
Richard Swann Lull in 1910. A more correct restoration of
the animal, with alternating plates, four tail spikes and a
less "squarish" body shape was made by Charles R. Knight
as early as 1903. *)

The chase continues as the rescue group comes upon
a misty swamp. But as they traverse the water in a hastily
constructed raft, their craft is overturned by an angry
Apatosaurus, which snaps some of the men up in its powerful jaws and charges the rest of the group onto the beach.
One crew member is trapped in a treetop by the roaring
saurian and meets a gruesome end in the monster's teeth.

Hearing the approach of his human pursuers, Kong
places Ann in the fork of a gnarled tree, then confronts
them in an edited version of the King Kong test reel. Six
sailors are trapped by Kong on the log bridge (the Arsinotherium footage having been excised) and shaken off to perish
in the pit below. Driscoll, who has managed to climb down
a liana, watches in horror from a shallow cave in the cliffside. Originally Driscoll beheld the devouring of the men
by a giant spider and other nightmarish creatures of the pit,
but that footage never survived into the theatres.

A popular legend insists that the spider sequence was
censored for its being overly gruesome. But actually Merian C. Cooper snipped it out of the work print before the
film's initial release because "It slowed down the action,"
as he said to me in 1966. Following its deleted performance in King Kong, the giant spider enjoyed a brief motion

---

*Details pertaining to the prehistoric animals in King Kong
have often come under criticism by paleontology-minded film
buffs. The Apatosaurus is portrayed as an aggressive, possibly even carnivorous animal, while in real life it was a
passive herbivore. Tyrannosaurus is portrayed with three
claws on each hand while most paleontologists agree that the
animal possessed only two. The flying Pteranodon, while
shown in King Kong as capable of actual flight, was probably
only a glider. In general all of the reptilian monsters of
Skull Island were considerably larger than their fossil remains have proven. But their gigantism seemed appropriate
for coexistence with the mighty Kong, especially when considering Cooper's constant demand to "Make it bigger!"

picture career. In Genius at Work (called Master Minds before its completion), an RKO movie directed by Leslie Goodwins in 1946, the spider model and other creatures from
King Kong and The Son of Kong can be identified on a background shelf of a movie studio set. The spider later returned in full animation in The Black Scorpion (Warner
Brothers, 1957), directed by Edward Ludwig, with special
visual effects by Willis O'Brien and Pete Peterson. In many
ways this film about giant scorpions emerging from underground to menace civilization is similar to King Kong. A
scorpion is shown in its underground domain where it battles
and kills such monstrous enemies as the spider and a number of oversized worms. Later the scorpions attack mankind and are finally destroyed. The last appearance of the
King Kong spider was in the science fiction picture Women
of the Prehistoric Planet, which went into filming as Prehistoric Planet Women in 1965 and was released the next year
by Realart. Arthur C. Pierce both produced and directed
the color low-budget picture. The spider was not animated,
however. It simply "jumped" when a technician manipulated
an unfortunately obvious "invisible" wire.

Having dispatched the sailors, Kong attempts to
snatch up Driscoll in his huge paw. The first mate slashes
Kong's fingers with his knife, then cuts down a weird reptilian creature (with two claws on each hand yet lacking any
hindlimbs) which had been climbing the vine. Driscoll is
saved when Ann's screams and the roars of a Tyrannosaurus
attract the ape's attention. (During the 1960s, Merian C.
Cooper referred to this theropod dinosaur as an Allosaurus.
But the animal was clearly modeled after a painting of Tyrannosaurus in the American Museum of Natural History by
Charles R. Knight. Tyrannosaurus rex translates as "King
Tyrant Lizard" and it is only fitting that "King" Kong should
confront the so-called "king" of the dinosaurs.)

The battle between Kong and the Tyrannosaurus remains one of the most memorable scenes from King Kong.
Kong fights his scaly adversary with near-human cunning,
leaping on the dinosaur's back, punching it with prize-fighter
expertise, using a crude judo throw on it. During the
struggle, the tree in which Ann had been placed crashes to
the jungle floor. But at last Kong manages to tear open the
tyrannosaur's jaws and kill the monster. (This entire sequence was devoid of music, the only sounds being those
made by the two battling creatures.)

Carl Denham returns to the great wall while Jack
Driscoll resumes his trailing of Kong. Within Skull Mountain, Ann is menaced once again, this time by an Elasmosaurus, a reptile with a squat body, serpentine neck and
four paddlelike appendages (and somehow remembered by
most viewers as simply a colossal snake, the flippers being
forgotten). With O'Brien's attention to detail we literally
see the tiny figure of Driscoll swimming through the cavern
lake from which the saurian had emerged. Kong battles the
plesiosaur which coils about him like a prehistoric boa con-
strictor. Using the reptile's neck like a whip, Kong dashes
its head against the rocks until the neck dangles lifelessly
in his paws. The ape roars triumphantly and beats his
chest, then carries Ann to a ledge which overlooks the island and the docked Venture.

Outside the cave, Kong sits with his golden prize,
gently touching her, sniffing her and tearing away her clothing like the petals of a flower. But Kong's idyllic moments
are interrupted once again, this time by a bat-winged
Pteranodon, which swoops down and attempts to fly off with
the woman in its hind claws. While Kong tears the pterodactyl to death (in a battle that required some seven weeks
of animation), Driscoll and Ann attempt an escape on a vine
hanging down from the cliffside. Kong begins to pull up on
the vine when Driscoll and Ann drop down into the lake below.

Breathless, Driscoll and Ann return to the safety of
the wall, when Denham's mind begins to work. "We came
here to make a moving picture," he shouts, "but we've got
something worth more than all the movies in the world!"
From Kong's point of view, that something is Ann and soon
he is at the gates, then breaking through the massive doors
despite the huge bolts. When he does burst through, he unleashes his full wrath against the villagers in an attempt to
retrieve his "bride." Natives flee in terror as their god
grinds them between his jaws and stomps them beneath his
feet. Only the gas bombs hurled by Denham and his men
eventually bring down the mighty Kong so that he lies unconscious on the beach. "We'll give him more than chains,"
promises Denham. "He's always been king of his world.
But we'll teach him fear. Why, the whole world will pay

Opposite: It is King vs. King as, watched by Ann Darrow
(Fay Wray) in a tree, Kong battles the king of dinosaurs,
Tyrannosaurus rex, in King Kong (RKO, 1933).

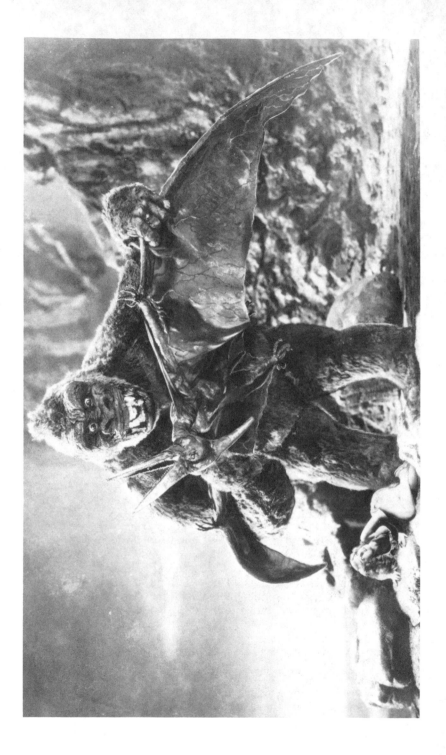

to see this! We're millionaires, boys! I'll share it with all of you! In a few months it'll be up in lights ... 'Kong, the Eighth Wonder of the World!'"

Denham's prediction proves entirely true. Though we are never actually shown just how the bulk of Kong was shipped to the city of New York, his mysterious name is soon luring in the patrons at ten dollars per ticket. The live action for this sequence was shot in Los Angeles, at the Shrine Auditorium. (Originally, Kong was intended to break loose at Yankee Stadium.) Denham, wearing a tuxedo, proudly steps upon the stage to address the crowd: "Ladies and gentlemen, I'm here tonight to tell you a very strange story, a story so strange that no one will believe it. But ladies and gentlemen, seeing is believing. And we--my partners and I--have brought back the living proof of our adventure, an adventure in which twelve of our party met horrible deaths. But first I want you to see the greatest thing your eyes have ever beheld. He was a king and a god in the world he knew. But now he comes to civilization merely a captive, a show to gratify your curiosity. Look at Kong, the Eighth Wonder of the World!"

When the curtain rises the crowd gasps, for upon the stage, strapped to a crosslike structure by chrome steel bands, is the helpless Kong. Denham brings Ann and her fiancé John Driscoll onto the stage, then summons the news photographers to snap the first pictures of Kong in captivity. Kong, however, believes that the flashbulbs are harming Ann. With a mighty burst of strength, the ape frees himself from the steel manacles and shackles. Moments later he is loose in the streets of New York.

As in the village, Kong is on a destructive rampage. Driscoll, meanwhile, has led Ann to the safety of a hotel room. Hearing a scream from an upstairs window, Kong ascends the wall of a building, seizing a woman thinking her to be Ann. Realizing his mistake, Kong lets her drop to the pavement head-first. Continuing his search, Kong peers through another window and perceives Ann. There is a crash of shattering window glass and Ann is again in the hand of Kong. Just as King once confronted the Elasmosaurus on Skull Island, he now becomes intrigued by an

---

Opposite: Again, Ann (Fay Wray) watches in terror as Kong kills the giant winged reptile Pteranodon, in King Kong (RKO, 1933).

approaching snakelike object which glows bright in the darkness. Kong's head emerges through the elevated tracks to
see the train approaching (its cars boasting advertisements
for Cooper and Schoedsack's earlier film Chang). Again the
ape is the victor as he smashes the train with his fists while
the tiny human beings inside drop to the street.

The climax of King Kong is the most famous sequence
of all. Just as Kong once roared his defiance from the
highest point of Skull Island, now he seeks the tallest peak
on his second island home of Manhattan. With the Empire
State Building standing out against the dawning sky, the distant figure of King Kong can be seen scaling the towering
walls.

The long shot in which King Kong scaled the Empire
State Building has long been a source of controversy. The
story has persisted through the years that this scene employed an actor in a gorilla costume. The logic behind it
was sound enough: Why bother to use the time-consuming
animation process for a shot in which the ape could hardly
be seen? The story was reinforced by a feature in the
April 1933 issue of Modern Mechanix and Invention magazine.
The article depicted an actor in an ape suit scaling a replica of one side of the Empire State Building which had been
built along the studio floor. Furthermore the "normal size
actor in ape costume" was shown atop the Empire State
Building's dirigible mooring mast, recreated in miniature,
swatting at a scene of attacking airplanes on a rear projection screen.

The myth was given more credence by a number of
actors who claimed to have essayed the part of King Kong.
Charles Gemora, a Filipino actor who specialized in portraying motion picture apes, was reputed to have played the
title character in King Kong. His New York Times obituary
was headlined, "'King Kong' is Dead at 58" and declared,
most likely wrongly, that he had played that role. (Gemora
did, it is certain, spoof Kong on two occasions.) Ken
Roady was given the same credit in the December 21, 1969,
issue of the Chicago Sun-Times and claimed to have shared
animosities with Robert Armstrong and Fay Wray during
production of King Kong. Later he identified himself

Opposite: One of the most famous movie images of all,
Kong atop the Empire State Building swatting biplanes, in
King Kong (RKO, 1933).

as Carmen Nigro, whose story was published in the
March 4, 1976, edition of the same Chicago newspaper when both Paramount and Universal were battling for the remake rights to King Kong. Nigro
claimed to have stood atop a model of the Empire
State Building while the photograph accompanying the write-
up clearly showed the miniature animation model battling the
planes. His description of the sequence was the same as
that in Modern Mechanix and Invention. "The way it worked,"
he added, "I had this little doll in my hand that was supposed
to be Fay Wray. I put the doll down on the ledge, and then
I had to catch one of them little planes. I was wearing ballet shoes covered with fur, and I had rubber suction cups
on the bottoms so I could stay balanced on top of the building. It took about four hours to shoot it." Nigro also
claimed to have portrayed the gorillas in Tarzan of the Apes,
Tarzan and His Mate and Mighty Joe Young, the third of
these actually featuring another ape animated by O'Brien. A
later newspaper article published a photograph of Nigro in
his gorilla suit which, after being examined by several authorities on motion pictures, make-up and ape costumes,
was said to depict a completely unfamiliar ape; Nigro's
claims are unable to be substantiated.

Cooper denied any performance by an actor in a gorilla costume in King Kong. A good photograph does exist
of animator Buz Gibson manipulating a Kong model up the
side of a miniature Empire State Building. Perhaps a human actor was used in a bit of forgotten test footage before
the film went into production, but thus far the matter remains a mystery.

At the top of the old dirigible mooring mast of the
Empire State Building, King Kong seems impervious to all
harm. It is Driscoll who suggests "There's one thing we
haven't thought of--airplanes! If he puts Ann down and they
can pick him off without hurting her...." Soon four Navy
biplanes are circling the hairy giant like four mechanical
Pteranodons. But these winged attackers are equipped with
machine guns that blast into his hide, confusing as well as
hurting him. Kong grabs one of the planes and sends it
crashing down to the street, but his victory is short-lived.
A final volley of machine gun fire (the two pilots in this
death ship being played by Cooper and Schoedsack in an unbilled cameo) tears into Kong's throat. Dying, a saddened
Kong looks toward Ann then topples off the mooring mast.
(A high angle shot of a superimposed Kong falling to the

street was photographed but never used, as the ape appeared transparent.) As King Kong lay dead in the street, a police officer says to Carl Denham that the airplanes got him. "Oh, no," says Denham shaking his head while speaking the classic lines, "it wasn't the airplanes. It was Beauty killed the Beast."

King Kong cost a total of $430,000 (or $650,000 including the money spent on Creation). What Cooper had was an economically produced epic that ran a total of 14 reels. In his opinion, however, the picture ran too long. Cooper cut the film down to a more commercially viable length, snipping out some of O'Brien's animation footage including scones of the Arsinotherium, Styracosaurus and Triceratops, along with a shot of Kong descending Skull Mountain in pursuit of Driscoll and Ann. The final cut of the picture was ready for public screening by March of 1933. (Scenes from King Kong later appeared in the movie Morgan, A Suitable Case for Treatment (seen in the United States as Morgan!), from Cinema V in 1966, in Rendezvous (1973), and Revenge of Rendezvous (1975). King Kong footage was also incorporated into the television special, "Hollywood: The Selznik Years." A strange piece of film purporting to be from King Kong was included in the "Monsters We've Known and Loved" segment of the "Hollywood and the Stars" television series in 1964. The scene, showing an unconvincing giant gorilla exhibited on an auditorium stage, was obviously not from this movie.

The picture premiered at both the New Roxy and Radio City Music Hall on March 2, 1933, the only film ever to play simultaneously at New York's two largest theatres. Accompanying the film was a spectacular stage musical, "Jungle Rhythms," which helped to pack in the crowds. When the picture opened in Hollywood at Sid Grauman's Chinese Theatre, patrons were greeted by the actual mechanical bust of Kong in the forecourt. Before the film flashed upon Grauman's screen for the first time, Jimmy Savo's chorus line of fifty black dancing girls performed a spectacular number called "The Dance of the Sacred Ape." The picture had been brought to the public with a ballyhoo worthy of a real life Carl Denham. And like the mythical Kong himself, the film proved to be something "the whole world will pay to see." King Kong paid RKO's bills, raising the studio up from debt. It also became one of Hollywood's finest classics.

King Kong is not only one of the best fantasy pictures
of all time but simply one of the greatest movies of any
genre. The story is perfectly paced, the special effects superb. Only the acting and dialogue are dated by today's standards, but those supposed faults actually contribute to the
picture's charm. Intellectuals have attempted to read certain symbolisms into King Kong: Kong represents a Depres-
sion-stricken people lashing out against society; Kong is a
Christ figure crucified on a stage before an audience of spectators; Kong symbolizes the black man and his conflict
against his white oppressors; Kong on the Empire State Building depicts the most spectacular phallic symbol ever captured by film; and so on. Cooper has disavowed these "in-
sights" into his film; he was not the kind of person to consider injecting such messages into his productions. (The
Empire State Building, for example, was simply the tallest
structure in New York and paralleled Kong's own perch on
Skull Mountain.) What Cooper and his associates accomplished was the creation of a masterpiece of cinematic fan-
tasy--a picture made with care, skill and integrity. Whatever messages might lurk beneath the film's surface were
entirely coincidental on Cooper's part or, at best, sublimi-
nal. Merian C. Cooper had endeavored to give his audience
a romantic and improbable adventure, something they had
never before seen. He succeeded admirably.

King Kong has become a perennial success. Reportedly a theatre in Africa has been running the picture on a
daily schedule for years. During the late 1950s a New York
television station soared in the ratings by broadcasting the
picture twice each day for a full week on its "Million Dollar
Movie" series. (When King Kong was re-released in 1938,
a number of scenes were deemed objectionable by the Hays
Office and cut from American prints. The censored scenes
included the Apatosaurus chomping on sailors, Kong tearing
the clothes off Fay Wray, Kong brutally attacking the natives
on a scaffold, Kong flattening a native under his pressing
foot, Kong chewing on various human beings and Kong discovering the wrong girl and dropping her to the pavement in
New York. The scenes reveal a more brutal Kong. These
outtakes have been shown in British prints of King Kong all
along and were reinstated to the American theatrical prints
in 1968 by Janus Films.)

The picture is unique though the giant monster style
of motion picture has become a familiar cliché. Two of the
better motion pictures to imitate King Kong were again the

results of a group effort instigated by Cooper. But not even
Delgado, O'Brien, Schoedsack and Robert Armstrong could
surpass their original.

THE KING'S SUCCESSORS

The same month that King Kong was premiering in
New York and Hollywood, Schoedsack and Cooper were al-
ready at work on a mysterious film project called Jamboree.
The budget for the picture was $250,000, which meant that
whatever the nature of the film it could not be another King
Kong.

But, in a way, it was. Jamboree was actually a sequel to King Kong, a quickly made comedy followup described
by one advertisement (depicting a smiling ape wearing a
sandwich board with the picture's final title) as "A Serio-
Comic Phantasy." The title Jamboree had been used to keep
curiosity-seekers off the set. When the film was released
in 1933 its title The Son of Kong was descriptive enough.

The Son recreated the grandeur of the original, albeit
on a smaller scale. The sequel ran only 70 minutes (as
opposed to the 100 minutes of its predecessor). Cooper and
Schoedsack were producing and directing again, with Robert
Armstrong returning as a more sympathetic Carl Denham.
Marcel Delgado created some new prehistoric creatures for
the second Kong production which Willis O'Brien animated.
Recycled were an Apatosaurus and Styracosaurus left over
from King Kong, scenes of the latter model being one of the
casualties of Cooper's final editing job on the original pic-
ture. The music in The Son of Kong was again Max Stein-
er's (and were titled "Runaway Blues," "King's Theme,"
"Ship at Sea," "In Dakang," "Hootchie-Kootchie," "Fire Mu-
sic," "The Warning," "An Offer of Help," "Chinese Chatter,"
"Love's Awakening," "The Forgotten Island," "Monotony,"
"The Quicksands," "The Old Temple," "The Stegosaurus,"
"The Black Bear," "First Aid," "The Coconuts," "Evening
Quietude," "The Discovery," "Johnny Get Your Gun," "The
Comedian," "The Lizard Fight," "Mazeltof," "The Earth-
quake" and "Calm Sea").

Carl Denham now lives in a sleazy boarding house
room adorned by a theatrical poster depicting King Kong,
the monster who created so much damage in New York that
the former film producer is now haunted by creditors and

reporters. With a grand jury indictment and several lawsuits also threatening him, Denham leaves the country with
Captain Englehorn (Reicher again), operating the Venture in
the China Sea as a cargo vessel. While in the port of Malaya, Denham attends a performance of a cheap tent circus
operated by an old alcoholic named Peterson (Clarence Wilson) and his songstress daughter Hilda (Helen Mack). The
show's main attractions are the girl's songs and, to Denham's amusement, a monkey act. After nightfall the down-
and-out Captain Nils Helstrom (John Marston) argues with
Peterson, strikes him with a bottle and inadvertently sets
fire to the tent. Peterson perishes in the flames.

Helstrom is now afraid that he will be arrested for
murder. Coincidentally he is the same Norwegian captain
that had originally sold Denham the map to Skull Island.
Helstrom tells Denham that the people who had built the
Great Wall had also left behind a vast treasure, thereby in-
spiring Denham and Englehorn to return to the island with
Helstrom accompanying them. As the new voyage of the
Venture gets underway, Denham discovers that Hilda has
stowed away. Helstrom, meanwhile, excites the crew to
mutiny, which they do on the morning of the vessel's arrival at Skull Island. Certainly not a loyal bunch, the crew
then casts Helstrom overboard, leaving him, Denham, Hilda,
Englehorn and Charlie the Chinese cook (Victor Wong, another survivor from the previous film) stranded on Kong's
former home.

Naturally the natives are not too receptive, recalling
the damage to their village the last time Denham and company visited their island. The chief (Noble Johnson, recreating his part from the first Kong film) drives them away,
forcing them to gain access to the island via a narrow inlet.
Once on the island, Denham and Hilda set off on their own,
coming upon a flight of stone steps. But they also encounter something quite unexpected--a huge albino gorilla (about
fifteen feet tall), the apparent Son of Kong, trapped in a
pool of quicksand.

Marcel Delgado constructed his "son" models over
the armatures that once formed the metal skeletons of the
original King Kong. There were three such models of the
little Kong, all capable of registering considerable expressions. (No full-size mock-up of the ape's head and shoulders was built for The Son of Kong; O'Brien animated the
facial expressions on the miniature for the close-up cameras.)

King Kong's successor proved to be more lovable than menacing in The Son of Kong (RKO, 1933).

Since The Son of Kong was essentially a comedy, the white-
furred Kong was often animated in fulfillment of the old
adage "Monkey see, monkey do. " Little Kong rolled and
blinked his eyes inquisitively, scratched his head in puzzle-
ment and reacted with human "takes. " More than a monster,
he was a giant and lovable teddy bear, entirely sympathetic
and perfectly suited to the tongue-in-cheek flavor of the picture.

Denham, feeling a sense of responsibility to Little
Kong because of what happened to his father, pushes over a
tree so that the ape can extricate himself from the quagmire.
Meanwhile, Englehorn and the others barely escape death on
the horns of a spike-frilled Styracosaurus. When Denham
and Hilda are menaced by a huge prehistoric cave bear,
Little Kong engages the beast in a furious battle. After he
kills the animal, the small version of King Kong nurses a
wounded finger, bandaged with a strip of material from
Hilda's slip.

The next morning Denham, Hilda and Little Kong
come upon an ancient temple. Inside, draped across the
stone face of a demonlike idol, are the jewels which Denham
assumes to be the treasure of Skull Island. Unnoticed by
the threesome, a strange long-necked reptile (a creation of
Delgado not found in any paleontology book) enters the cave
which houses the temple. The battle between Little Kong
and the saurian is exciting and at the same time humorous.
Apparently killing the monster, Little Kong dangles its neck
and peers into its open mouth. But as the ape turns away
to join his human friends, the reptile lifts its head to bite
him in the rump. Kong finishes the creature with a well-
placed blow to the head.

When Englehorn and the others arrive on the scene,
Helstrom is astounded by the discovery of the treasure,
admitting that he had invented the legend in order to escape
Malaya. Upon first seeing Little Kong, Helstrom tries to
escape in the lifeboat, only to be devoured by a hideous sea
serpent (another invention by Delgado).

The Son of Kong utilized the deus ex machina climax
so familiar to the "lost world" motion picture or story.
Skull Island has existed since Mesozoic times, but now that
modern Man has journeyed there the island is suddenly attacked by an angered Nature. The traditional volcano was
replaced with an earthquake and flood as Skull Island begins

to sink beneath the sea. Denham again rescues Little Kong,
whose foot is caught in an earth fissure. But Kong's salvation is brief as he returns the favor, holding the former
film producer high above his head as the waters continue to
rise and the final vestiges of the island vanish below the
waves. Denham is pulled into the rowboat occupied by Captain Englehorn, Hilda and Charlie, after which Little Kong's
hand disappears beneath the depths. Soon four persons, all
rich now from the treasure of Skull Island, are picked up by
a ship. At last Carl Denham reveals himself to be more
than a motion picture entrepreneur. He and Hilda are des-
tined for marriage before the fade-out.

The Son of Kong was a fine sequel though it suffered
in comparison to the grandeur of the original King Kong.
(A scene showing animated birds from The Son of Kong later
appeared in a background shot of the celebrated Citizen Kane
(RKO, 1941).) Willis O'Brien would have preferred a more
serious approach to The Son of Kong and, in the years that
followed, spoke little about the film. Part of O'Brien's reti-
cence in this matter was probably due to his own personal
tragedy that occurred during the production of the movie.

O'Brien had been married to a mentally ill woman
Hazel Ruth Collette, whose problems were compounded further by tuberculosis and cancer. Hazel was under narcotic
sedation when, in a state of severe depression on October 7,
1933, she fatally shot both of their sons and then turned the
weapon upon herself. The boys died that day while she survived but a year longer. (In 1934, O'Brien married Darlyne
Prenette and lived a happy life with her until his death in
1063.)

For a while Cooper considered making yet a third
Kong epic, flashing back to before Denham transported the
original ape to New York. King Kong was to escape in the
Malay Archipelago for an untold adventure. It remained unfilmed.

In 1935, O'Brien joined Cooper and Schoedsack again,
this time to create the spectacular destruction sequence (all
executed in miniature) of The Last Days of Pompeii, another
RKO epic. Four years later Cooper, O'Brien and Delgado
began an ambitious project titled War Eagles. The premise
was that natives living in a prehistoric world have tamed
gigantic eagles and ride them on saddles made from the
skulls of the horned dinosaur Triceratops. Astride these

great feathered monsters, the natives battle such adversaries
as Tyrannosaurus. Eventually they invade New York where
they engage in aerial combat with a number of dirigibles.
O'Brien animated Delgado's eagle and Tyrannosaurus models
for some color test scenes. But the project waned, primarily because of Cooper's stint in the armed services.
During the interim dirigibles had already become passé and
War Eagles dropped into oblivion, existing today only in the
form of a script, a few stills and some frames of color ni-
trate motion picture film.

   War Eagles was but one of many such aborted projects; Gwangi, which had been in the planning stages as early
as 1942, was another RKO project about a Delgado-built
Allosaurus, to be animated by O'Brien as it fought against
capture by a group of lariat-casting cowboys. O'Brien's
successor Ray Harryhausen finally brought the project
to the screen more than twenty-five years later. The
new version of the story was called, again, simply
Gwangi during its early stages and went into production in
1968 under two titles The Lost Valley and The Valley Where
Time Stood Still. But it was The Valley of Gwangi that finally reached the theatres in brilliant color in 1969. Gwangi
is an Allosaurus, one of several prehistoric animals inhabi-
ting a lost valley in North America during the early twentieth century. In tribute to O'Brien, Harryhausen had his
Allosaurus pause to scratch its "ear" as had the Tyrannosaurus in King Kong. The Allosaurus is finally captured
and exhibited at a circus, from which it breaks loose to
terrorize a Mexican town. Gwangi finally meets destruction
inside a burning cathedral. The Valley of Gwangi was directed by James O'Connolly and released in color by Warner
Brothers-7 Arts. (Though Gwangi never enjoyed the popularity of King Kong, there was some merchandising in association with the picture, including a record album, a Gold
Key comic book, coloring book and a plastic Allosaurus assembly kit obviously modeled after the Harryhausen creature.)

   Though Delgado's original Allosaurus model apparently never went before O'Brien's stop-motion camera, elements
of the Gwangi project were finally salvaged as Cooper (teamed
with producer John Ford) and Schoedsack enlisted the talents
of the two men for a film that went into production in 1946
at RKO. It was motivated by a desire by the producers and
director to give the public another King Kong, which they almost did.

The picture was originally entitled Mr. Joseph Young
of Africa though it was released in 1949 as the more commercial Mighty Joe Young. (The movie is also known as
The Great Joe Young and, in Germany as the misleading
Panik um King Kong ("Panic Around King Kong").) Structur-
ally the story bore strong similarities to King Kong. Even
the irrepressible Robert Armstrong was hired to reenact his
Carl Denham performance, though now he was almost a
comic figure, a show business entrepreneur named Max
O'Hara. The real star of the film, however, was Mighty
Joe Young himself, another huge gorilla though he was more
the size of the son of Kong than the King himself.

O'Brien actually did only some 15 percent of the animation in Mighty Joe Young. The remaining 85 percent went
to a capable newcomer named Ray Harryhausen, a young
man who had worshipped O'Brien since his first of countless
viewings of the original King Kong. After mustering the
courage to show O'Brien some of his 16mm footage of animated dinosaurs and fairy tale characters, Harryhausen was
made the master's assistant for Mighty Joe Young. (Harryhausen later acquiesced to the position vacated by O'Brien
after the latter's death and created the special visual effects
for some of the finest fantasy pictures ever made.)

The model for Joe Young was the celebrated gorilla
Bushman,* the star attraction at Chicago's Lincoln Park Zoo.
Bushman was photographed so that O'Brien and Harryhausen
could later study his movements, frame by frame, and attribute to Mighty Joe the gait and mannerisms of a real gorilla. It was Harryhausen who designed the metal armature
for the new giant ape, basing it directly upon an authentic
gorilla skeleton.

The animation in Mighty Joe Young proved to be

---

*Born approximately 1928, Bushman was a Cameroon gorilla.
During his early years, the baby Bushman was walked about
the zoo on a leash. By adulthood the ape was six feet, two
inches tall when standing erect and weighed 550 pounds.
Bushman was, perhaps, the finest gorilla specimen ever to
live in captivity. He was known for a rather pleasant disposition though he became rather cantankerous in his later
years. The magnificent ape survived until New Year's Eve,
1951, and all Chicago mourned his passing. Today, thanks
to the art of the taxidermist, Bushman can still be viewed
in Chicago's Field Museum of Natural History.

much smoother than that in King Kong. Willis O'Brien even
won an Academy Award for the special visual effects.   Still,
Mighty Joe Young never garnered the critical acclaim or
popularity of its 1933 inspiration.   Though a more realistic
gorilla than Kong, Joe Young was more lovable than monstrous and his screen adventure lacked the spectacle of its
two predecessors.

Joe Young, unlike Kong, was simply an oversized
African gorilla, thereby lacking the exotic appeal and mystery of the King of Skull Island.   (One criticism of both
King Kong and Mighty Joe Young is that the sizes of the
apes are sometimes inconsistent from one shot to the next.
Joe, for example, ranges from slightly bigger than a real
bull gorilla to approximating the enormity of Kong himself.)
An African native trades the infant gorilla to Jill Young, a
child who had given her father's flashlight in return.   Joe,
as Jill names him, grows up as a relatively gentle pet on
her father's African estate.

When Max O'Hara gets the idea of having American
cowboys roping wild animals in Africa for his new nightclub,
the Golden Safari, the group makes the unexpected acquaint-
ance of Joe.   In a sequence originally planned for O'Brien's
Gwangi, the cowboys attempt to rope the huge gorilla.   (In
reality they were lassoing a jeep, the ape figure being later
inserted into the scene.)   But when the gorilla lashes back,
only the intervention of Jill, now a young lady played by
Terry Moore, saves their lives.

O'Hara, like Denham, has big plans for Joe and soon
the mysterious name of "Mr. Joseph Young of Africa" is
in lights above the Golden Safari in the United States.   The
club has an African setting, with live lions prowling in their
glass cages behind the bar.   Mighty Joe Young makes his
public debut on the stage of the Golden Safari.   The gorilla
holds above his head a platform upon which Jill sits playing
"Beautiful Dreamer," Joe's favorite song, on a grand piano.
After the audience has stopped gasping at the awesome sight,
O'Hara and Jill put Joe through such routines as engaging a
group of strongmen in a tug of war.

Joe's only real opportunity to be monstrous in the
film occurs when several drunks slip backstage and get him
intoxicated.   The drunken simian goes on a rampage that
wrecks the Golden Safari in an incredible display of special
effects and stuntwork.   During the conflict O'Hara's lions

An intoxicated giant gorilla on the rampage in an African-
decor Los Angeles nightclub, in the last great movie of its
type, Mighty Joe Young (RKO, 1949).

---

are freed from their enclosure, only to meet the full violent
fury of Mighty Joe Young. Regarding him now as a dangerous beast, the police order him destroyed, after which
O'Hara, Jill and cowboy Tex (Ben Johnson) smuggle him
away in a truck. On their way to the airport, the group
passes a burning orphanage. Joe Young charges to the rescue, saving the trapped children from death and redeeming
himself before a blazing tree to which he clings splits in
half, sending him falling to the street with two youngsters
hanging onto his hairy back. Joe, unlike Kong and his son,
survives to return to Africa with Jill and Tex, living out
his days peacefully and bringing to a fade-out the last of
the great films about a giant ape.

One of the Mighty Joe Young models was eventually displayed at the special effects exhibit at Hollywood's Lytton Center in 1966. The model was identified as King Kong. Special Effects, an 8mm film of this exhibit, was made available by this author. Mighty Joe Young was also worked into the lyrics of "Ape Call," a song recorded by Nervous Norvis during the 1950s.

THE SECOND BANANA KONGS

Just one year after the release of King Kong and The Son of Kong, parodies of the concept were in production. Hollywood Party (1934) featured a man in an ape costume who is introduced at a party as "Ping Pong, the son of King Kong."

Charles Gemora, who made a career of portraying some of the most realistic gorillas on film, gained some publicity before his death as the actor who had played the original King Kong. He did not, of course, at least in the 1933 motion picture. Yet Gemora's confusion might well have been the result of the passage of years since his participation in two spoofs of King Kong.

The Lost Island was an ambitious project, a planned musical comedy from the Christie Studio, directed by LeRoy Prinz in 1934 and filmed in the old three-strip Technicolor process. Technically the picture was a reverse on King Kong: the giant gorilla was played by a human actor (Gemora) in a gorilla suit while the fanciful dinosaur that inhabits a great cavern was also a costumed performer. All the human characters, however, were now marionettes in the image of famous screen personalities. Wah Ming Chang, Blanding Sloan, Mickey O'Rourke and Charles Cristadoro designed the puppets. A Mae West marionette filled in for Fay Wray and was bound to a pedestal from which Kong abducted her. When The Lost Island proved overly expensive, the project was terminated before completion.

Gemora was also suited up to play a giant legendary ape in the comedy Africa Screams (also known as Abbott and Costello in Africa), directed by Charles Barton for United Artists in 1949. While Mighty Joe Young was appearing at the Golden Safari, Frank Buck and Clyde Beatty were heading an expedition into the jungle in search of a monstrous missing link. Lou Costello inadvertently discovers

Jungle girl (Julie London) and her pet gorilla (played by Ray "Crash" Corrigan) in Nabonga (PRC, 1944).

the creature when he finds himself standing between its shaggy legs.

During the 1930s and 1940s, Gemora's major rival in the portrayals of gorillas was Ray "Crash" Corrigan, a star of Western movies who moonlighted as a screen anthropoid. Corrigan's ape suit was a shaggy, monstrous creation, more a product of the imagination than was Gemora's more authentic costumes. Corrigan's association with King Kong is only peripheral, beginning with his performance in

the PRC programmer Nabonga. The film starred Buster
Crabbe with Julie London as a white jungle woman whose
protector is a bull gorilla. The Belgians must have considered the ape suitably Konglike for they retitled the picture
Fils de King Kong ("Son of King Kong"). (The picture is also known as Gorilla, The Girl and the Gorilla, Nabob, Jungle Witch and The Jungle Woman.) Nabonga was filmed in
1943 and released the following year.

A similar change in title was made by the Italians
for the 1945 PRC movie White Pongo. Corrigan played a
dual role in this film, his standard gorilla plus a highly intelligent white ape believed to be the missing link. Though
neither anthropoid was of gigantic size the film was known
as La sfida de King Kong ("The Challenge of King Kong") in
Italy. (Other titles include Congo Pongo, Blond Gorilla and
England's Adventure Unlimited.) Both films were produced
by Sigmund Neufeld and directed by Sam Newfield.

Corrigan assumed a more authentic Kong-type role in
Unknown Island (Film Classics, 1948), another variation on
the "lost world" theme, directed in color by Jack Bernhard.
Among the denizens of a prehistoric island is a giant ground
sloth, presumably similar to the extinct Megatherium. Yet
ground sloths were passive creatures with thick tails. Corrigan's aggressive, tailless sloth seemed to be merely a
strange looking ape. The snorting and gorilla style lope
added to the simian effect.

In a scene obviously influenced by the battle with the
Tyrannosaurus in King Kong, the shaggy sloth fights a flesh-
eating dinosaur (another costumed actor) and finally shoves
the reptile off a cliffside to its death. The victorious monster then lumbers offscreen to nurse its wounds. Many
viewers of Unknown Island would have preferred instead another screening of O'Brien's ape vs. dinosaur fight.

When Merian C. Cooper became head of production
for the Cinerama organization in the early 1950s, he considered remaking King Kong in the three-screen process and
under the title The Eighth Wonder--but his plan never reached
fruition.

Two strange Kong creatures did reach the screen in
1959. Gekkoh Kamen ("The Moonbeam Man"), a Japanese
picture made by Toei and directed by Satoru Ainuda, was
one in the series of films featuring a superhero known as

Ray "Crash" Corrigan aped King Kong when he played this giant prehistoric sloth in the film Unknown Island (Lippert, 1951).

the Man in the Moonlight Mask.   Also known as The Monster Gorilla, this fourth entry to the adventure series featured Mammoth Kong, a giant ape armed with a horn protruding from its forehead.   To combat Mammoth Kong a scientist creates an equally monstrous Robot Kong, equipped with deadly laser beam vision.

The British Konga, directed by John Lemont and released in color by American International Pictures in 1961, was more traditional, though it hardly validated its advertising.   ("Not since 'King Kong' has the screen exploded with such mighty fury and spectacle!")   Konga was produced by Herman Cohen, the man responsible for I Was a Teenage Werewolf and I Was a Teenage Frankenstein, so it is not

Dr. Decker (Michael Gough) is destroyed by the monster he
created in Konga (American International, 1961).

surprising that his giant ape movie went into production the
year before its release under the inane title I Was a Teenage
Gorilla. (An even more misleading title for Konga was ascribed to the picture for release in Germany, where it became known as Konga--Frankenstein's Gorilla. A Chicago
drive-in theatre advertised the picture as Theory of the Evil
Satan, with "Congorilla Konga. ") Konga, however, did not
even begin his career as a gorilla, teenage or otherwise.

The plot of Konga was standard mad doctor fare. Dr.
Charles Decker (Michael Gough), a botany professor, returns
to London from the African jungle with slips from carnivorous
plants that seem to be a link between the animal and plant

kingdoms.   He also brings back a friendly chimpanzee which
he calls Konga.   Back in his laboratory, Decker tests a
growth serum extracted from the weird plants on the ape
after which Konga grows and evolves into a full-sized gorilla.

While Charles Gemora and Ray Corrigan essayed
most of the gorilla roles in films made during the 1930s and
1940s, George Barrows provided some stiff competition during the next two decades.   Barrows' costume was less the
mythical monster created by Corrigan, but still not as authentic a gorilla as that played by Gemora.   Yet it was his
costume and not Barrows himself that went to England where
Konga was to be filmed.   (In 1963, Barrows and Michael
Gough teamed-up for Dlack Zoo, another horror film produced by Herman Cohen; Barrows played another gorilla that
suspiciously resembled Konga.)   Konga (another actor wearing Barrows' ape suit) carries out the orders of his insane
master, namely murdering his enemies.   When Foster (Austin Trevor), the dean of Decker's college, reproves him for
discussing his growth theories with the press, he becomes
a victim of the hypnotized Konga.   After Decker learns that
an Indian botanist Professor Tagore (George Pastell) might
steal his glory by working on a similar experiment, Konga
claims his second victim.   The third person to be crushed
to death by the ape is Bob Kenton (Jess Conrad), the boyfriend of Sandra (Keire Gordon), a blonde and shapely student on whom Decker has licentious designs.

Posters boasted that the picture was filmed in "Spec-
taMation," though this cinematic "miracle" was nowhere to
be seen during the final minutes of Konga.   Decker has
brought Sandra to his home for dinner and then lures her
into his greenhouse where he declares his love for her.
But his proclamation is overheard by Decker's assistant and
fiancée Margaret (Margo Johns).   Vengefully she injects
Konga with an overdose of the growth serum.   Suddenly
Konga's head reaches the ceiling of the laboratory.   Konga's
disposition has also changed for he destroys the laboratory,
creating a traditional horror-films inferno, then tosses
Margaret into the flames.

The only impressive shot in the film depicts Konga
bursting through the roof of the laboratory, his size still
increasing.   The rest of the picture is hardly memorable,
as he spots Decker through the greenhouse windows forcing
his kiss on Sandra and then snatches him up in his enormous
paw.   Sandra falls victim to a flesh-eating plant while Konga

lumbers off through London's streets still clutching Decker.
The army makes its not unexpected appearance, blasting
Konga with rockets, rifles and machine guns, as the ape is
trapped near Big Ben.   Unlike King Kong, this gorilla does
not climb the towering structure.   Fatally wounded, Konga
dashes his former master to the street, then shrinks to the
size and form of a dead chimpanzee.   The brief sequence
with the Kong-sized Konga was surely not worth the wait.

At least some executives in the publishing industry
considered Konga a commercially viable product.   In 1960,
Monarch Books published a novel Konga, written by Dean
Owen.   The book was based on the storyline of the film
with some mild (by today's standards) sex scenes added.
Monarch Books was a division of the Charlton Publications.

Another branch of the company, the Charlton Comics
Group, issued a Konga comic book based on the movie in
1960.   Steve Ditko provided the artwork.   Some changes were
made in the film's storyline: Margaret is now Decker's wife,
Konga begins his career as a small monkey instead of a
chimpanzee, there is no attempted love affair between Decker and Sandra (hence, no deaths of either Sandra or Bob)
and Konga injects himself with the serum that makes him as
tall as King Kong.

Konga proved to be a popular one-shot comic book
and Charlton soon realized the possibilities in issuing it as
a series.   Konga no. 2 was dated August 1961 and featured
the story "Return of Konga."   Bob and Sandra marry, carry
on Decker's experiments and adopt another monkey called
Konga, which soon follows in the paw prints of his predecessor.   The friendly monster is then taken to an island inhabited by prehistoric animals and, after killing a Tyrannosaurus, presumably dies during a volcanic eruption.

But Konga did not perish.   He returned for a total
of 23 issues of Konga comic books in which he aided people
in distress and battled a long list of monsters, aliens, Communist spies and evil dictators.   A lapse in the series' continuity occurred in "The Lonely One," Konga no. 12 (May
1963), wherein it was explained that the current Konga was
synonymous with the creature spawned by Dr. Decker.   The
original Konga, we are now told, never really died!   The
last story in the Konga comic book series (dated November
1965) was "The Creature of Uang-Ni" and pitted the lovable
giant ape against a Godzilla type, fire-breathing, prehistoric

reptile. What would have been the 24th issue of Konga became Fantastic Giants (September 1966), which reprinted the
first movie-based story.

Charlton also issued special edition comic books featuring their monster star. The Return of Konga (1962) presented "A Mate for Konga." A Russian scientist clones a
female gorilla giant called Torga from a cell scraping of
Konga's hide. Torga becomes a rampaging monster, shot to
death in a city by a Russian gunboat. With the second issue of this series (summer 1963), the magazine's title became Konga's Revenge and featured a tale in which the giant
ape shrinks down to miniature size. Konga's Revenge survived two more issues, the last of which saw publication in
December 1968.

An Indian motion picture entitled King Kong was made
in color for Santosh in 1962. It was directed by Babubhai
Mistri and starred Kum Kum and wrestler Darasingh.
Whether the picture was a fantasy or featured an ape of any
sort is not known. Tarzan and King Kong was another Indian production, made in 1963 by Saegaam Chittra Ltd., and
starring Darasingh, a wrestler, in the role of Edgar Rice
Burroughs' Apeman. Because of difficulties with copyright
the picture has rarely been screened.

Willis O'Brien had been intrigued with the possibilities in animating a Frankenstein movie as early as 1928; in
1961 he expanded the concept to include his beloved Kong.
King Kong vs. Frankenstein was to have been a tongue-in-
cheek conflict between the great ape and a new version of
Frankenstein's creation, shot in full color. O'Brien wrote
a treatment and a sampling of the script and later changed
his title to King Kong vs. the Ginko (the word "Ginko" being
a play on both the words "King" and "Kong"). O'Brien also
prepared some watercolor paintings of Kong and the Ginko.
(Shown here are black-and-white prints of those paintings.)

The story itself was an unusual one. Carl Denham
explains that Kong never really died but was smuggled, after
his plunge from the Empire State Building, back to Skull Island. Denham's idea is to retrieve the mighty gorilla and
stage a boxing match between him and some other monster
in San Francisco. That "other" monster is created by Dr.
Frankenstein's grandson from the organs of rhinoceroses,
elephants and other ponderous African animals. In a San
Francisco auditorium a girl walks a tightrope held high in

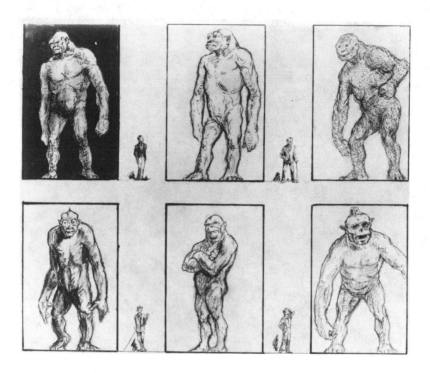

Willis O'Brien's drawings of six potential Frankenstein creatures for an unfilmed project originally titled King Kong vs.
Frankenstein.

---

the hands of the Ginko. When the rope breaks, Kong, believing the Ginko to be harming the girl, breaks free of his
cage and attacks the towering Frankenstein creature. The
battle of the beasts continues through the San Francisco
streets until both King Kong and the Ginko fall from the
Golden Gate Bridge and into the sea.

When O'Brien took his project to producer John Beck,
the latter eliminated the animator altogether and assigned
the property to George Worthing Yates, who wrote a new
version of the story in 1961 known both as Prometheus vs.
King Kong and King Kong vs. Prometheus. The old Ginko
was now called Prometheus while Denham's part in the film
was dropped entirely. "Prometheus V" is the creation of

Kurt Frankenstein who had dreamed of manufacturing an
army of giant workers.   But after the monster demonstrates
his abilities in San Francisco's Candlestick Park, he reveals
himself to be a crafty being who kills the man controlling
him.   King Kong, also in the park, and Prometheus then
battle their way to O'Brien's original climax.

When Beck could not get financing for the project in
the United States, he took Prometheus vs. King Kong to Toho
International in Japan.   Toho was interested in the basic
theme, the staging of a battle between King Kong and some
other gigantic monster.   But national chauvinism dictated the
removal of the Frankenstein characters in favor of Japan's
own King of the Monsters.   Thus the flame breathing prehistoric reptile Godzilla was brought out of retirement for his
first and only bout with America's monster King.   Kingu
Kongu tai Gojira went into production in 1962 (the same year
O'Brien died), directed in color by Inoshiro Honda and
(American scenes) Thomas Montgomery.   The following year
it was issued in the United States by Universal under its
translated title King Kong vs. Godzilla.

Devotees of the original King Kong shuddered at the
thought of it.   First, though a giant gorilla, Kong's fifty-
foot height could in no way even approximate the size of the
400-foot long Japanese sea monster.   There was also the
problem of Kong's survival after his drop from the Empire
State Building.   Most ominous of all, however, was the
knowledge that Toho traditionally used actors in monster
costumes rather than the more satisfactory animation process.

Kingu Kongu tai Gojira proved to be neither a direct
sequel to King Kong (though it was to the previous Godzilla
epic) nor a serious picture at all.   Whether or not the King
Kong who appeared in the Japanese film was the King Kong
of RKO fame was never revealed.   If they were one and the
same, Kong had mysteriously grown, for now his head
reached as high as Godzilla's.   (The publicity was that King
Kong was 148 feet tall and weighed a massive 55 million
pounds.)   Somewhere along the way he also developed the
ability to thrive on electricity.   One thing is certain; the
shabby Kong suit worn in the new picture ranked alongside
some of the worst gorilla outfits ever seen on film, even
those in silent movies.   The Japanese King Kong was so ridiculous in appearance that the film's advertisers wisely
chose to paste-up shots of the original 1933 Kong over
scenes of Tokyo for their display stills and lobby cards.

Thankfully, Kingu Kongu tai Gojira was played tongue-in-cheek. The owner of a pharmaceutical firm wants a live monster to publicize his products. The answer to his dream comes when reports of a giant monster god existing on remote Faro Island reach him. One stormy night the natives (all Orientals wearing blackface make-up and rather unconvincingly) are menaced by a giant octopus. The scenes of the huge cephalopod are very atmospheric and realistic as the tentacled monster slithers about their village. When Kong appears, beating his breast, he battles the octopus to the death.

The victorious King Kong is given some wine made of Faro Island berries which makes him groggy enough to be floated on a raft back to Japan.

Godzilla is discovered in an iceberg (where he had been hibernating since his last Toho adventure) by the crew of a nuclear submarine. After destroying the ship, the prehistoric reptile proceeds to Japan, following a kind of homing instinct. Kong revives as he is being floated near to the coast of Japan. Sniffing the scent of Godzilla, a natural enemy, Kong wades to shore in pursuit of the scaly creature.

Inevitably the two monsters meet, lashing into one another in slapstick style like a pair of monstrous sumo wrestlers. In an imitation of a famous publicity still from the original King Kong's fight with the Tyrannosaurus, the ape rams a treetrunk down Godzilla's throat. But Godzilla retaliates with his radioactive breath, scorching Kong and rendering him unconscious. Then Godzilla goes off on his own spree of devastation.

A bolt of lightning revives King Kong. In Tokyo the ape monster attempts to reclaim past glories by reenacting some of his New York scenes. He destroys an elevated train. Then he snatches a lovely young woman off the street and, while a sentimental melody plays over the soundtrack, promptly falls in love. Since there is no Empire State Building in Japan, he carries her instead to the top of Tokyo Tower where more of the Faro berries render him unconscious.

Opposite: Two of the world's mightiest monsters battle each other in the Japanese fantasy Kingu Kongu tai Gojira [King Kong vs. Godzilla] (Toho, 1963).

When the authorities deduce that the two monsters can be used to dispose of each other, the drugged Kong is floated by balloons to the top of Mount Fugi, where he and Godzilla engage each other in their most spectacular (and ridiculous) fight.   After much kicking, biting and monstrous "laughing," King Kong and Godzilla fall into the sea.   The hairy figure of a giant ape rises to the surface and swims away, probably back toward Faro Island.   The rumor has persisted since the film's release that two endings were filmed, with Oriental countries seeing Godzilla rather than the "foreign" King Kong emerge the victor.   However, according to Saki Hijiri, a fantasy film buff living in Kyoto, the endings of both the Japanese and American versions of the film are the same.   It is understood among Japanese movie fans, said Hijiri, that Godzilla merely went back into hibernation underwater until his next screen appearance.

Kingu Kongu tai Gojira is an unpretentious fantasy comedy.   Making no claims to rival the "real" King Kong, the picture stands on its own merits.   Surely it is an entertaining hour and a half or more and the special effects (the ape suit notwithstanding) of Eiji Tsuburaya are impressive.

The title Frankenstein vs. King Kong surfaced in 1965.   This time the film was to be another Toho spectacle.   But the picture was not made and Kong did not appear in another Japanese epic until 1967.   Kingu Kongu no Gyakushu ("King Kong's Counterattack") went into production at Toho that year, again directed by Honda with Tsuburaya handling the visual effects.   Shot in color, the picture was issued in America by Universal the next year.   The American title became King Kong Escapes.   (Other titles for the picture include Kingukongu no Gyaskushu, Revenge of King Kong and Germany's King-Kong Frankensteins Sohn [son].   Scenes from the film later appeared in the 1968 Godzilla sequel, Kaijû Sôshningeki.)

The American pressbook for the film blatantly pronounced: "The 35th birthday of the most famous monster in films is marked by the Universal release of the Toho Production in Technicolor, 'King Kong Escapes,' now at the ..... Theatre.   It was in the early thirties that 'King Kong' burst upon the scene to become one of the most successful movies of the era.   The all new 'King Kong Escapes' is far superior in its technique showing the tremendous advances made in the cinematic art, and is in beautiful Technicolor."

One thing was certain: the picture was in "beautiful
Technicolor. " But the production did not even approach
Kingu Kongu tai Gojira in either quality or entertainment
value. A new Kong suit was built for this second Toho outing into the giant ape genre. If this new Kong seemed more
of a cartoonlike character, with its sleepy eyes and its absurd face, perhaps Honda and Tsuburaya were attempting to
achieve that effect upon the screen--which certainly has some
validity. The plot itself is like something found in a comic
book, or more accurately, an animated cartoon, the true
origin of this particular King Kong movie. For Kingu Kongu
no Gyakushu is actually based on the animated cartoon "King
Kong" television series which had debuted on American television a couple of years earlier. The new Toho live action
film was a full-blown expansion of one of the television program's individual episodes. Both were aimed directly at the
juvenile market. Unfortunately the point was missed by the
American distributor who packaged King Kong Escapes as
just another monster movie.

The evil Dr. Who (the arch-fiend from the "King
Kong" cartoon show) is out to conquer the world by means
of a huge robot in simian form called, after its hairy inspiration, Mechani-Kong. But Dr. Who's mechanical monster
fails to mine Element X, the radioactive material the mad
doctor needs to carry out his plan. Meanwhile, Captain Nelson (Rhodes Reason playing the same heroic figure from the
television cartoons) and his United Nations nuclear submarine
crew, come upon Mondo Island. There an old hermit warns
them to keep away, shouting the legendary name "Kong!"
The explorers, including a pretty young technician named
Susan (played by Linda Miller) are menaced by a sea serpent and then by a huge green dinosaur (called Gorosaurus
when he returned in the multi-monster picture Kaijû Sôshingeki in 1968). Not surprisingly, King Kong also inhabits
this island and promptly makes his appearance. Kong fights
the flesh-eating reptile and finally kills it, then, as is traditional, seizes and falls in love with Susan.

Dr. Who learns of the great discovery after Nelson's
press conference. The megalomaniac's henchmen subdue
Kong with tranquilizing bombs then utilize a helicopter fleet
to transport the animal to their Arctic secret complex. Hypnotized by Dr. Who, Kong then proceeds to dig out Element
X. But as the mighty gorilla continues to claw at the radioactive material, an explosion occurs which severs Dr. Who's
hypnotic bond. Kong, free of the madman's mental bondage,

jumps into the icy water and swims to Japan. There, in
perhaps the world's most monster-beset city, he encounters
his robot counterpart. Decidedly Mechani-Kong has the advantage; he feels no pain and is equipped with beams of mes-
meric light. Still, the real Kong puts up an impressive
battle which eventually brings both monsters to the top of a
skyscraping television tower (another attempt to at least suggest the famous Empire State Building scene). This time,
however, the real Kong survives as his mechanical double
falls to crash on the street below in a pile of useless junk.
In an amusing epilogue, Kong runs down the waterfront alongside the speeding car with our heroes and then destroys the
evil Dr. Who in his submarine.

Kingu Kongu no Gyakushu was neither as entertaining
nor successful as Kingu Kongu tai Gojira and Toho abandoned
the giant ape for any later productions. Besides, RKO, the
owners of the simian property, demanded payments for use
of the character. Toho found greater profits in continuing
the screen adventures of their own Godzilla and other monstrous behemoths.

But King Kong films were still being made by other
companies. Hor Balevana ("A Hole in the Moon"), an
Israeli film of 1965, included a fantasy sequence featuring
King Kong. Uri Zohar directed it for the Navon company.

Mad Monster Party? (1967) climaxed with a King
Kong-spoof sequence in which a giant brown gorilla rises
from the sea to attack Baron von Frankenstein's castle.
As per custom, he falls in love with the Baron's pretty
daughter. During the final moments of the picture the ape
has all of the monsters held in his gigantic arms and, like
Kong atop the Empire State Building, is perched high on a
mountain peak. The Baron and his fleet of old-fashioned
airplanes attack the creature while von Frankenstein destroys
everyone with his newly developed explosive. The animation of the models was crude in comparison to that in King
Kong, The Son of Kong and Mighty Joe Young. Still, it was
refreshing to see a new film with a stop-motion giant gorilla.
(The ape returned with a giant mate in the television feature
cartoon "Mad, Mad, Mad Monsters" in 1972. This go-round
he fights the Frankenstein Monster for possession of the

Opposite: Japanese Kong against his robot counterpart in
Toho's second adventure of the gigantic ape, Kingu Kongu no
Gyakushu [King Kong Escapes] (1967).

latter's newly-assembled bride.)

The Italian color film Necropolis (Cosmoseion & Q
Productions, 1970), written and directed by Franco Brocani,
was made up of plotless episodes about life starring various
movie and historical villains. The Minotaur appears as
King Kong unwinds a string that marks the way through
a labyrinth to the picture's opening set. The Mighty Gorga
(American General Pictures, 1970) was a less pretentious
offering directed in color on a modest budget by David Hewitt.
A group of treasure hunters discovers a prehistoric plateau,
like that in The Lost World, somewhere in Africa. Ruler
of this dinosaur land is a fifty-ton gorilla called Gorga
(played by an actor in a shoddy ape suit) which one member
of the expedition, a circus owner, decides to capture. (In
1976, with a number of studios vying to remake King Kong,
plans were initiated to reshoot the special effects scenes of The
Mighty Gorga using model animation and to reissue the film.)

Flesh Gordon (Griffiti Productions, 1972), a sex spoof
in color of the old Flash Gordon movie serials, paid tribute
to King Kong as the huge alien "god" Porno (an animated
model) seizes heroine Dale Ardor (Suzanne Fields) and carries her to the summit of a tower. Mike Light directed.
John Landis wrote, directed and starred in the color Schlock
in 1972 released the next year by Jack H. Harris Enterprises.
Schlock spoofed virtually all ape movies and referred to Kong
(and Godzilla) as if he were an historical figure. A prehistoric
Schlockthropus, part man and part ape, is thawed out, goes on
a murderous rampage and falls in love with a teenage girl
named Mindy (Eliza Garrett). In one scene "Schlock" admires
a poster from King Kong vs. Godzilla on a movie theatre wall.
Finally he climbs a building before receiving the fatal gunfire
of the National Guard. Rick Baker, who four years later would
literally become King Kong, created the apeman costume.
Closed Mondays (1974), a color short subject by Will Vinton and
Bob Gardiner, also paid tribute to King Kong. Among its cast
of animated clay characters was a miniature gorilla sculpted
in the image of Kong. In Germany Gojira tai Megaro was
called King-Kong, dä Monen aus dem weltall while Gojira tai
Mechagojira became King Kong Gegen Godzilla.

THE USURPERS OF THE THRONE

No studio had yet been able by the mid-seventies to
secure the rights from RKO General to remake King Kong.

Hammer Films had tried to buy them in 1970 but were refused. Though RKO would license other studios to make sequels or new adventures with the huge anthropoid, the original King Kong story was to remain unique. Surprisingly
RKO reconsidered four years later; and by 1975 it seemed
as if everyone was planning a remake of the classic.

Filmmaker Steve Barkett and model animator Jim
Danforth were perhaps the first persons actively to pursue
the remake rights for King Kong in 1974 after meeting with
RKO's Daniel O'Shea. It was O'Shea's job to negotiate the
sale of RKO's old properties. But their project was drowned
by the publicity amassed by two giant studios, Universal and
Paramount, when in 1975 they both announced their own remakes of King Kong. What followed was gorilla warfare.

The King Kong remake controversy originated in the
spring of 1975 when the American Broadcasting Company's
Michael Eisner saw Bette Midler in a Kong spoof in the musical show, Clams on the Half Shell. Eisner, conceiving
a rock musical version of King Kong with Midler as Ann Darrow, relayed his idea to a seemingly uninterested Sid Sheinberg, head of MCA (which owns Universal). Eisner then
suggested a King Kong remake to Paramount Pictures chair-
man Barry Diller. Diller was seeking the participation of
Italian film mogul Dino De Laurentiis while Sheinberg was
looking for a producer at Universal, each without the other
knowing. The world became King Kong conscious when both
studios announced that they had the rights to remake the famous film.

Already there was consternation among the cult of
devotees that had grown about the original King Kong.
'Don't Rape the Ape!" became a slogan among fans at science fiction and film conventions who did not want their beloved classic tampered with; the memories of the Toho Kong
efforts had left permanent scars. There was no real artis-
tic reason to remake King Kong, the original being perfect
in its own right. The fear existed that neither studio would
make the film utilizing the talents of a model animator like
Ray Harryhausen or Jim Danforth. Many fans hoped that
neither Universal nor Paramount would eventually secure the
coveted rights.

Universal's claim to have bought the rights was based
on an alleged verbal deal made between O'Shea and MCA
lawyer Arnold Shane. But De Laurentiis and RKO had signed

a mutual agreement.   Soon both studios were in a legal
battle to make their respective picture and each was suing
the other.

While the legal battle raged, advertisements began to
appear in January 1976 depicting a new King Kong straddling
the twin towers of New York's World Trade Center, a girl
clutched in one paw, the other hand battling jet planes.
The poster boasted that there was only one new King Kong--
Paramount's--and that it would premiere in theatres by the
following Christmas.   A coupon accompanied the color poster
offering a copy free of charge; Paramount was deluged with
poster requests.

Paramount's King Kong poster aroused new anxiety
for the fans who held so dear the original.   Soon television
news broadcasts showed ape-suited protestors carrying picket
signs across the observation deck of the Empire State Building, insisting that Kong not perish atop the World Trade
Center in the new version but where he had fallen in 1933.
De Laurentiis was setting his version of King Kong in the
1970s and the old Empire State Building simply was not tall
enough to meet his demands.   Universal's remake would be
set during the thirties when the Empire State Building was
still the tallest structure in New York.   There was some
discussion of the two studios' joining their resources and
making King Kong as a combined effort, but Paramount and
Universal were both adamant in keeping their stories within
their selected time periods.   The fight would not end by
amalgamating.

Further complications arose after an investigation into
the copyright of the original King Kong.   A question existed
as to whether or not the copyright on the picture had ever
been properly renewed.   One thing was certain, however:
the original story version of "King Kong," published prior to
the film's release, had lapsed into the public domain.

Universal Pictures announced that its version, entitled The Legend of King Kong, would be based upon the
story rather than the movie.   Other producers also seized
upon this revelation.   Producer Roger Corman of New World
Films announced his own remake; another was rumored to
be originating in Japan; one more King Kong was to be shot
in Korea in a three-dimensional process.   Corman quickly
abandoned his own King Kong project.   Pressure by Paramount necessitated the changing of the Korean film's title to

Ape.   Soon the trade papers announced the forthcoming
Kongorilla, Queen Kong, Queen Kong: The Illegitimate Son
of You Know Who and Italian filmmaker Mario Bava's Baby
Kong.   Both Ape and shorter-titled Queen Kong began shooting during the war between Paramount and Universal.

The final court decision was that Dino De Laurentiis
and Paramount owned the rights to remake the movie King
Kong and could begin immediately.   At first Paramount used
the title King Kong: The Legend Reborn.   Universal agreed
to postpone its story-based version The Legend of King Kong
for 18 months and, meanwhile, settle for 11 percent of
Paramount's profits on their remake.   De Laurentiis already
announced two sequels, The Bionic Kong (capitalizing on the
popularity of "The Six Million Dollar Man" and "The Bionic
Woman," two Universal television successes) and King Kong
in Africa.   Gradually, with Paramount's King Kong before
the cameras, interest in The Legend of King Kong waned at
Universal.

Of the two major remakes, The Legend of King Kong
was the most promising.   The picture was to utilize the
studio's gimmick "Sensurround," which had made its bow in
the spectacular Earthquake (1975).   Peter Falk was intended
to play Carl Denham with Ann Darrow tentatively to be portrayed by Susan Blakley.   (Fay Wray herself was to appear
in a cameo.)   The music was to be the original score written by Max Steiner for the 1933 movie.   At first most of
the gorilla scenes were to be enacted by an actor in a gorilla costume (test footage having been shot of ape-suited
Bob Burns, his gorilla head made by Rick Baker, going
through actions on a miniature jungle set) while the dinosaurs,
and Kong during his battles with the dinosaurs, would be
brought to the screen through stop motion.   Jim Danforth,
perhaps the finest three-dimensional animator in the motion
picture industry and twice an Academy Award nominee (for
his work in The 7 Faces of Dr. Lao, 1964, and When Dinosaurs Ruled the Earth, 1970) was put on salary at Universal.
"I saw no reason to remake King Kong," Danforth told me.
"But I felt the Universal script to be far superior to Paramount's."   Eventually the decision would be made not to use
a gorilla-suited actor and to create all the monster effects
through animation.

Since The Legend of King Kong was to be based on
the King Kong story instead of the 1933 movie, Danforth was
instructed to design a new set of prehistoric creatures for

Universal's picture. Bo Goldman's screenplay also made the legally-required changes though he retained the period setting and flavor of the original King Kong.

Carl Denham is now an unlikable, greedy showman who thinks nothing of risking the life of his motion picture star, Ann Darrow. On Skull Island he and his crew encounter such monsters as a huge lizardlike creature, giant dragonflies and carnivorous beetles that devour the carcasses of animals. Instead of battling a Tyrannosaurus, Kong now saves Ann from a herbivorous ceratopsian dinosaur, a Danforth invention he dubbed "Triclonius," somewhat resembling the familiar Triceratops. Kong then carries Ann to his cave and shares his food with her, after which he kills a huge arthropod and drives away a leathery-winged pterosaur. After Kong is overpowered on Skull Island, the doors of the Great Wall become the raft that brings him to New York. In the city Kong wrecks a steam shovel (replacing the elevated train) and finally meets his demise atop the traditional Empire State Building. Still hoping to get some spectacular footage of Ann in the grip of Kong, the unscrupulous Denham is killed while grinding his camera.

The Korean Ape (also known as A*P*E), which went into production after De Laurentiis began lensing his King Kong, was made on an incredibly low budget, most of which seemingly went into the color film and stereo equipment. The picture was directed by Paul Leder and starred Rod Arrants as a journalist and Joanna DeVarona as a young starlet. The picture was made by the Lee Ming Film Corporation and picked up for American release by Jack H. Harris (who released Schlock) and Worldwide Entertainment Corporation.

The producers of Ape originally sought Rick Baker, already working in the Paramount King Kong, to build the ape suit. Baker deliberately quoted them a low bid, knowing their financial limitations. His price proved too expensive still and Ape utilized instead a standard gorilla outfit sold by the Don Post Studios.

The Ape is another oversized gorilla who stomps through some cheap miniature sets (no optical effects were used because of their interference with the 3-D process), wrecking a boat and a native village, and then fighting a giant shark (an attempt to capitalize on the shark craze instigated by Universal's Jaws in 1975). Of course, the simian

falls in love with the starlet, who is on location shooting a
movie in his turf. The journalist, her boyfriend, tries to
save her with the aid of the Korean and American armies.
The Ape fights off some toy tanks and helicopters before dy -
ing from the countless bullet wounds. "He was too big for
a world as small as ours," says the journalist, comforting
his girlfriend before the final fade -out.

Paramount Pictures felt that Ape infringed on their
King Kong rights. The advertising for Ape flashed in big
letters, "Not to be confused with King Kong." Paramount
won its injunction against the picture and Harris altered his
advertising. The court case had already given Ape a wealth
of free publicity. The picture was completed in time to
beat the release of the De Laurentiis King Kong.

Queen Kong: The Illegitimate Son of You Know Who
was to be a Harlequin Productions spoof, produced and directed by David Winters from a script by Batman creator
Bob Kane. This Queen Kong is, said Winters, "a homosex-
ual gorilla who falls in love with the Bruce Cabot character."

The official story from Paramount Pictures was that
Dino De Laurentiis had been inspired to make his King Kong
after spotting a poster from the original film on his daughter's wall. Schlock's John Landis claims to have suggested
the Kong property to De Laurentiis after the latter expressed
interest in making a movie about a giant space monster.
Whatever the real origin of Paramount's King Kong, the picture remains as one of the true fiascos in the genre, a film
that in the opinion of this writer should never have been
made.

Dino De Laurentiis was determined to make his King
Kong a grand scale epic, far surpassing in quality the 1933
King Kong. "'No one cry when Jaws die,' Dino says, his
voice rising in passion.... 'But when the monkey die,
people gonna cry. Intellectuals gonna love Konk; even film
buffs who love the first Konk gonna love ours. Why? Because I no give them crap. I no spend two, three million
to do quick business. I spend 24 million on my Konk. I
give them quality' " [Schickel, Richard, "Here Comes King
Kong," Time vol. 108, no. 17 (October 25, 1976), p. 70].

But fans of the original King Kong were doubtful that
De Laurentiis would give them the promised quality. The

picture was originally budgeted at an incredible $16 million;
but before the project had reached completion that figure had
escalated to nearly $25 million. Soon the news broke that
the new Kong would be played by an actor in a gorilla suit,
arousing visions in many film buffs of another Konga or
Japanese version of the King. Further disappointment arose
with the leak that the new King Kong would be so "stream-
lined" that all the dinosaurs, so much an integral part of
the original, had been dropped from the remake's cast list.

Lorenzo Semple, Jr. , hastily turned out a screenplay
for King Kong, updated with the obligatory profanities and
minus all giant residents of Skull Island save Kong himself
and a giant snake. The names of the characters had been
changed from the original. Dwan, the Ann Darrow character of the new version, was given such inspired dialogue as,
"You goddamn chauvinist pig ape, what are you waiting for?
If you're gonna eat me, eat me!"

On a televised press conference, De Laurentiis unveiled his stars. Though Barbra Streisand, Cher Bono and
Goldie Hawn had all been considered for the female lead, the
part went to a newcomer, New York fashion model Jessica
Lange. Jeff Bridges was to play Jack Prescott (the Driscoll counterpart), a vertebrate paleontologist, while Charles
Grodin would play the Denham-inspired Fred Wilson.

King Kong himself was not so easily cast. One thing
was certain, however: the animation process for which most
Kong devotees had been praying would not be used. De
Laurentiis wanted to make his Kong big--both on screen and
in front of the cameras. This bigness was originally to be
manifested in an ape-suited actor. But when a notice appeared in Variety asking for "ape-like" black actors to test
for the role of Kong, the production was immediately lam-
basted by civil rights groups. De Laurentiis then countered
with the announcement that his King Kong would be played by
a life-sized mechanical robot, a concept that seemed impossible considering the actions a realistic Kong would have
to perform on screen.

When an aircraft company informed De Laurentiis
that they could build such a robot given two year's time, he
went elsewhere for the artificial beast's construction. King
Kong had already been booked into a thousand theatres across
the United States with a premiere date of Christmas Eve,
1976. Italian special effects expert Carlo Rambaldi told

De Laurentiis that he could build the monster right on the
lot of MGM (where much of King Kong was being lensed) in
time to perform his stunts before the cameras. The robot
would be 42 feet high.

But even as the King Kong mechanical giant was under construction, De Laurentiis was employing 25-year-old
Rick Baker to develop a gorilla costume in the event that
the mechanical version should suffer a mishap. Baker had
designed the apeman outfit for Schlock and two-headed gorilla
suit for The Thing With Two Heads (1972); his hand had already doubled for King Kong in a television commercial. He
had won an Emmy award for aging makeup applied to actress
Cicely Tyson in the television drama "The Autobiography of
Miss Jane Pittman." A long time enthusiast of authentic
and screen gorillas, Baker looked forward to creating the
most realistic movie gorilla of all. "'King Kong' offered
the one chance to do a really perfect gorilla suit," Baker
later said. "With the money and the time it could have
been outstanding. Unfortunately, it wasn't. There were
compromises and enforced deadlines. A once in a lifetime
opportunity was lost" [Kilday, Gregg, "The Making of a
Movie Prop: Kicking the Kong Around," Los Angeles Times
(December 30, 1976), p. 10].

Originally, De Laurentiis had wanted his Kong to be
not a gorilla but a manlike missing link. Baker refused to
build anything other than a gorilla suit with the producer
meeting him halfway, agreeing to a creature with "the body
of a gorilla and the mind of a man." Soon both Baker and
Rambaldi were competing with one another to design the
best Kong suit. Baker's was a simian masterpiece, complete with extension arms and articulated fingers, while
Rambaldi adhered to the concept of an anthropomorphic missing link. When the director of the picture John Guillerman
(who had acquired the King Kong job as a result of directing
another special effects epic, The Towering Inferno, in 1975)
saw both ape suits, he declared Baker's version the winner.

Meanwhile, the giant mechanical Kong was beset by
problems. Somehow the creature acquired two right hands
during the process of its construction. Glen Robinson (who
won Oscars for his special effects in The Towering Inferno
and The Hindenburg), Supervisor of Mechanical Effects, over-
saw the robot's construction. The giant was given "life" by
a hydraulic system, worked by a staff of technicians at a
control panel with almost 70 hydraulic levers. Once completed,

The much publicized 42-foot-tall robot that cost over $2 million but appeared in only a few shots of Paramount's $25-million remake, King Kong (1976).

television news broadcasts were featuring the robot and tan-
talizing viewers without showing them too much. "He is
fully functional," said Rambaldi, "the first such creature
conceived by Hollywood. His arms can move in sixteen different positions. He can walk and turn at the waist. His
eyes and mouth move. He is a very human monster, terrifying when aroused but with the soul of a romantic lover."
The finished mechanical monster cost between two and three
million dollars and proved to be a diamond mine of publicity.
Unfortunately the thing did not perform as its designers had
anticipated. The two functional hands designed by Rambaldi,
also hydraulically powered and equipped with safety devices
to ensure that Jessica Lange would not be crushed in Kong's
grip, were quite impressive. But it was soon obvious that
the forty-two foot-tall robot would not be able to perform in
most of the scenes requiring a full-bodied Kong. It was
time to call upon Rick Baker.

Baker was finally given the job to play King Kong in
most of the scenes (Bill Shepard enacting the scenes wherein
Kong battles the serpent, is trapped in a pit and takes fantastic leaps), wearing a gorilla suit designed by both himself
and Rambaldi. It was Rambaldi who designed the seven
mechanized masks for the suit worn by Baker. Activated at
a distance, the heads could register thirty different expressions. These facial movements were indeed marvelous; yet
none of the masks really matched up with the less realistic
features of the giant King Kong robot. All the more reason,
then, for the ape suit to dominate the screen action. The
robot itself was relegated to a few dark long shots lasting
such a short time that most viewers did not have time to
compare it with the costume. Nevertheless the publicity
proclaimed that King Kong was being portrayed in the remake
by a life-sized mechanical prop. Baker's credit in the
film's end titles was reduced to "... a special contribution,"
all the glory for Kong's creation being heaped upon Rambaldi
and his technicians.

Baker (officially referred to as the "miniature" Kong)
wanted to play the part like a real gorilla, walking on all
fours. But De Laurentiis was still determined to humanize
his ape. Director Guillermin demonstrated the gait and upright posture that he wanted to see in Kong and Baker had
no choice but to comply. Furthermore, De Laurentiis wanted
his Kong to be more of a romantic character than a fierce
monster. Though Baker played the part as best he could
under the circumstances, the new Kong emerged as a rather

Rick Baker's personally-chosen photograph of himself as Kong in Dino De Laurentiis' King Kong (Paramount, 1976).

weary old character--and quite bored, probably from lack of
monsters to fight on Skull Island. (In King Kong's early
stages of production, Paramount came to Jim Danforth to invent a scene wherein Kong fights some kind of prehistoric
beast. Danforth was to select the animal and then animate
the scene. After reading the script of King Kong, however,
Danforth refused to be associated with the Paramount version.) The movie became a love story rather than a fantasy,
adventure or horror film.

The new King Kong follows an oil company expedition
headed by Fred Wilson to an uncharted island perpetually
blanketed by fog. Wilson hopes to make the greatest oil
find in history for his employers, the Potrox Oil Company.
Stowing away aboard Wilson's vessel, the SS Petrox Explorer,
paleontologist Jack Prescott comes forth with reports of a
huge beast associated with the island as early as the year
1605. No one believes him.

Dwan is discovered unconscious in a rubber lifeboat.
Reviving on board the Explorer, she explains that she was a
starlet aboard her future director's yacht. Had she been in
the cabin with him watching a print of Deep Throat, she too
would have been killed when the yacht exploded.

The story progresses as per the 1933 King Kong,
with the discovery of the wall and the interruption of the native ceremony. Later, Dwan is kidnapped from the Explorer,
drugged and dressed in native attire to become the replacement "Bride of Kong." Dwan revives to scream at her first
glimpse of the giant gorilla.

Kong's initial appearance is hardly exciting. At first
we see his face in extreme close-up. When he finally
grasps her (the full-sized mechanical hand) there seems to
be little menace despite his towering height. Kong merely
stands there, holding his blonde bride. Then, after roaring
his approval, Kong disappears into the jungle.

Little happens on the island as Prescott, Wilson and
members of the Explorer crew set off to rescue Dwan.
Most of the footage seems to have been devoted to Kong
holding Dwan, exploring her with his fingers and registering
the gamut of the very impressive mechanized facial expressions. Dwan, during these scenes, supplies such dialogue
as: "I can't stand heights! Honest to God, I can't! When
I was ten years old and taken up the Empire State Building,

I got sick in the elevator!" And, "I'm a Libra. What are
you? Don't tell me. You're an Aries! Of course, you
are! I knew it!"

Only one of these moments actually shone out in the
film. Dwan falls into a mud puddle, after which Kong holds
her under a waterfall, then puffs out his cheeks to blow her
dry (a feat no real gorilla could perform). Amazingly, the
scenes with only human actors are generally more interesting
than those featuring Kong. Scenes that should have been exciting, such as Kong shaking the men off the log and into
the "bottomless" ravine and Kong reaching down to grasp the
hiding Prescott, are slow, dull, as if Guillerman knew how
to handle people but not giant apes. The Skull Island sets
are also dull and unconvincing, obvious studio mock-ups.
(Many of the exteriors for the Skull Island scenes were shot
on Kauai, one of the Hawaiian Islands.)

In his volcano crater lair, Kong battles an enormous
snake (an obvious mechanical prop), apparently the only other
monster on the island, while Prescott absconds with Dwan.
Wilson, meanwhile, learning that the oil on the island requires another 10,000 years to be of any use to Petrox, decides to bring Kong back to the United States instead as a
kind of monstrous living commercial. Kong bursts through
the gates of the Great Wall; but instead of channeling his
wrath against the native village, the ape immediately stumbles
into a pit especially prepared with chloroform.

The romantic implications of the Kong/woman relationship are stronger in the 1976 King Kong. On board ship,
deprived of his miniature bride, Kong nearly bursts free of
the huge tank which contains him. Wilson threatens to have
the beast destroyed rather than lose his ship, but Dwan,
feeling strong affection toward the ape now, manages to quiet
down the monster. (What happened aboard ship in the original King Kong was left to the viewer's imagination.)

There is no build-up to Kong's escape from Shea
Stadium. A quick cut shows Dwan descending via helicopter
to race up the glamorized reproduction of the island's sacrificial pillar, behind which is a red, white and blue mock-up
of the Great Wall. After a few words from Wilson, King
Kong, wearing a silly crown on his head, tears himself free
of his cage, manages to single out Wilson from the crowd
and crush him to death underfoot.

Only during Kong's escape was the full-sized robot used, and then in such distant quick cuts that the average viewer was not aware of the difference between mechanical prop and ape-suited actor. (Less than a minute of actual footage of the ape robot appears in the final cut. *) The differences were obvious, however, to anyone bothering to compare the giant and "miniature" Kongs.

I was an extra during the shooting of the stadium scenes. After hours of retakes, during which the Kong robot remained hidden behind the Petrox Wall and while master of ceremonies Bob Hastings kept reminding everyone that the star of this picture was a mechanical marvel over forty feet tall, the giant Kong finally made his appearance. He did not walk out; he was rolled into view with cables supporting him under the arms. When the crowd demanded that Kong move, Hastings explained that one of the cables had broken down earlier that day but that the monster would definitely move the following night.

Writer Bill Warren, who had been one of the crowd on a subsequent evening, reported: "The thing was holding parts of its cage in its hands, and our first action, after a half-hour wait, was to slowly edge off the bleachers and out of the arena. The robot then went as berserk as it could, waving its feet, turning its head and snarling, and lowering its arms to drop the pieces of cage. Large cranes then ran into the scene, and workmen picked up the parts and handed them back to the robot for a retake while a minor comic hired for the occasion blathered on about the robot, how it cost a million bucks (I've heard three million from people in a position to know), how it was the electronic wonder of the age. I thought for all that wonder they could have taught it to pick up things when it drops them, but that was just a passing idea. Not once did the comic mention that most of the time on the screen, you won't be seeing this electronic marvel, you'll be seeing one of two guys in a monkey suit. . . . The robot broke down frequently, and as the comic muttered on about its supreme wonderfulness, one of the technicians on the film grumbled, 'Wish to hell the thing worked!' " [Warren, Bill, "Model Animation? What'sa dat?," Cinefantastique vol. 5, no. 3 (winter 1977), p. 34.]

---

*A number of out-takes from this sequence and behind-the-scenes shots showing the robot in its slow-moving action appeared in "King Kong: Fact or Fantasy," a 1977 episode of the documentary television series "Wide World of Adventure. "

De Laurentiis' attempt to create a totally sympathetic Kong fully emerges during the last part of the film. Dangerous though he may be, Kong is not a particularly formidable monster. He hides behind miniature buildings rather than lash out at man and his machines. Somehow he does manage to wreck the one elevated train in which Dwan and Prescott are fleeing. Later on, Kong manages to abduct Dwan from the one tiny bar in all of New York where she is having a much-needed drink.

Prescott wants to save Kong and preserve his species by returning him to Skull Island. But once Kong climbs with Dwan to the top of the World Trade Center, the Mayor (played by John Agar) orders his squadron of helicopters to open fire. The final scenes do not duplicate the original poster showing a defiant Kong, one leg atop each of the towers. Kong is literally dwarfed by the structure and must take an enormous leap to reach the safety of the second tower once the helicopters begin to shoot at him. There is no classic image of the raging beast fighting to the end while perched at the city's highest point. The helicopters merely swoop down at him like exterminators come to eliminate a rooftop pest.

Dwan begs Kong not to set her down. 'No, Kong. Pick me up. They'll kill you!" The strange love between them reaches its peak as Kong faces the fire power of the helicopters, which splatter his chest and back with gore. Instead of immediately plunging to the city street, Kong lies atop the tower roof. When Dwan finally reaches out to touch him, he undramatically drops off the side, making his descent off screen.

The original publicity promised that the full-sized robot Kong would perform these scenes on top the actual World Trade Center. The excuse for the scene being done in the studio and in miniature was that the robot was too heavy to be safely lifted above the streets of New York. A full-sized styrofoam mock-up of Kong was assembled at the base of the World Trade Center for the final shots in the picture, however. Crowding around the dummy were 30,000 curious unpaid extras, there to witness the demise of King Kong.

Just prior to the film's release, Dino De Laurentiis sought an Academy Award for his robot. Naturally the Academy of Motion Picture Arts and Sciences was not about

to award an Oscar to a mechanical contrivance.   It was then
that De Laurentiis admitted that most of the scenes were
performed by the very non-mechanical Rick Baker, who certainly would receive an Academy Award.   KNX radio carried
the story on a news broadcast.

Nevertheless, when King Kong opened on schedule in
color, wide screen and stereophonic sound, millions of
people had already been swept up by the publicity over the
robot's alleged performance.   Supposedly knowledgeable
critics were still writing extensively about the robot's incredible abilities and participation in the film.   Regardless
of what might have been said later about Rick Baker and the
gorilla suit, the publicity had worked its miracle.   People
were thoroughly convinced that the robot had done most of
the picture if not all of it.

The new King Kong left many viewers unsatisfied and
wondering where the $25 million budget had gone.   Even
without the original RKO picture as a comparison, Paramount's King Kong presented nothing that had not already
been explored on the screen "giant monster" films for decades.   In my opinion the new King Kong appears to be no
more than an incredibly expensive Godzilla film and leaves
no doubt that there is still only one King Kong.

Before completing King Kong, Dino De Laurentiis announced yet another sequel title, the obvious Son of Kong.
Before its release, scenes from his King Kong were incorporated into the television specials "The Big Party" and
"Life Goes to the Movies."   Behind-the-scenes color footage
of people crowding around the full-sized Kong mock-up at
the base of the World Trade Center was given the title,
The King Is Dead!, and made available to home movie
collectors.

The Anglo/Italian production of Queen Kong was still
not completed as Paramount's epic played its thousand
theatres.   Queen Kong was produced by Dexter Films at Shep-
perton studios in Great Britain.   Unlike the Paramount film,
this was an outright spoof with no pretentions of outranking
the RKO original.   The picture, directed by Frank Agrama,
is a reverse on the old Kong story.   Luce Habit (Rula Lenska), a female movie-maker, wants to shoot a film with her
star Ray Fay (Robin Askwith).   In the remote village of
Lazangawheretheydothekonga, Luce discovers the huge female
gorilla Queen Kong, who runs rampant once she is brought

back to London in pursuit of her beloved Ray Fay. In one
sequence the ape dreams that she is a normal sized anthropoid dancing with Ray. The climax of Queen Kong occurs
atop the Post Office Tower. Advance poster artwork for the
picture depicted Queen Kong fighting off planes, a nude Ray
Fay in one hand and a huge bra in the other.

Like Ape, Queen Kong incurred legal problems, this
time from both De Laurentiis and RKO, who sued on the
grounds that it marked an infringement of copyright and that
its terrible script would be detrimental to the reputation of
Paramount's King Kong. Yet even closer to the De Laurentiis
picture was a Chinese film released in 1977 long after the
furor over the giant ape had subsided. The Shaw Brothers
of Hong Kong got into the King Kong act with Mighty Peking
Man, virtually a remake of Paramount's remake. Evelyn
Kraft played the huge monster's human bride.

Another 1977 picture that made use of the famous ape
(here called King Dong) was titled The Winner of 10 Academy
Awards. It was released in color by Spectrum Films.
Chuck Vincent directed. Yet another attempt to cash in on
the Kong mania of the seventies was the retitling of Tarz
and Jane and Boy and Cheetah, an "X" rated Tarzan spoof
of 1975 which was directed by Itsa Fine and released in
color by Fine Productions. In 1977 the picture was recircu-
lated as Ping Pong, but its cheap ape suit appeared no taller
than the actor wearing it. That same year King Kung Fu
and the announced titles Attack of the Giant Apes, The Return of King Kong (Chinese), The New King Kong and
Kong Island left little doubt as to their source of inspiration.

The original King Kong was in its first year of release when already it was being spoofed in another form of
animation, the cartoon. No less than four cartoon parodies
of King Kong were released in 1933. King Klunk was a
Pooch the Pup short for Universal Pictures, directed by
Walter Lantz and William Nolan. Pooch ventures to a prehistoric island where the ape King Klunk falls in love with
his girlfriend, then battles a dinosaur which emerges from
the water, for her safety. Klunk is then brought to the city
for a reenactment of Kong's Empire State Building demise.
Parade of the Wooden Soldiers (Paramount), directed by
Dave Fleischer, spoofed Kong as toys come to life. Mickey
Mouse had his own King Kong misadventure in the Walt Disney cartoon The Pet Shop (United Artists). A caged gorilla
in Mickey's pet shop falls in love with Minnie Mouse, surely

as strange a relationship as Kong had with Ann Darrow. Inspired by a picture of Kong on the Empire State Building,
the gorilla carries Minnie to the top of a bird cage (simulating the skyscraper's dirigible mooring mast).   Mickey and a
squadron of the shop's birds defeat the ape and save Minnie.
(Hollywood Film Enterprises' home movie edition of this
cartoon was retitled Mickey the Gorilla Tamer.) Bob Clampett brought the giant ape Ping Pong to life from a picture
on a magazine cover in the 1933 Warner Brothers cartoon I
Like Mountain Music.

    Clampett brought another giant gorilla to life, this
time off a box of animal crackers, in the Warner Brothers
color cartoon Goofy Groceries (1940).   Another giant gorilla
breaks loose at a circus to fight the mighty Superman in the
Paramount color cartoon Terror on the Midway (1941), directed by Dave Fleischer.   King Kong made cameo appearances in other color cartoons, including the British Beatles'
feature Yellow Submarine (United Artists, 1968), directed by
George Dunning; The Family That Dwelt Apart, a Canadian
cartoon of the middle 1970s, based on E. B. White's story
in the New Yorker; the titles of The Strongest Man in the
World (Walt Disney Productions, 1975)--a sequel to Now You
See Him, Now You Don't directed by Vincent McVeety--and
the titles of The Pink Panther Strikes Again (United Artists,
1976), animated by Richard Williams; and Basketball Jones
(1976), by St. Johns and Talmadge.

    Amateur filmmakers have also used the King Kong
character for their own special effects movies.   During the
1960s, Jon Berg, now a professional puppet animator,
brought a gorilla to life in some very impressive stop-motion color footage.   In 1965 Steve Kaplan went into production on Kong!, an amateur version of the RKO picture, recreating its key scenes.   An amateur production titled Son
of Kong Returns surfaced in 1965.   The author shot four amateur films featuring giant gorillas in prehistoric settings:
The Earth Before Man (1957) in color, with a prehistoric
ape vs. woolly rhinoceros; The Time Monsters (1959), in
color, in which a giant ape battles a Ceratosaurus and is
observed on a time machine screen; Tor, King of Beasts
(1962), in which Carl Denham finds the giant ape Tor on a
lost plateau in this amateur version of King Kong; and Son
of Tor (1964), partly in color, an amateur Son of Kong, co-
starring Godzilla and other famous movie monsters.   (Tor
also appeared in Frankenstein in the Lost World, a novel
by myself first published in Germany as Frankenstein bei

den Dinosauriern (Vampir Horror-Roman, 1976). Atop a prehistoric plateau somewhere in Africa, Tor, King of Beasts,
captures the female assistant of the scientist seeking to destroy the Frankenstein Monster. Tor and his lost world are
destroyed during a traditional volcanic eruption.)

KING KONG LIVES

Before the original King Kong was released in 1933,
the story was run in an issue of the pulp publication Mystery
Magazine. It was this "King Kong" that had lapsed into the
public domain and fed the controversies surrounding the King
Kong remakes of the 1970s. "King Kong" was directed
toward a more general audience and consequently omitted
many of the film's monster sequences. Editor Forrest J
Ackerman wrote in the missing scenes when he reprinted
"King Kong" in his magazine Famous Monsters of Filmland,
issues no. 25 (October 1963), 26 (January 1964) and 27
(March 1964). They became part of the magazine's three-
part series, "The Kong of Kongs. "

The actual novel of King Kong was written by Delos
W. Lovelace and published in 1932 by Grosset and Dunlap.
There were some differences, such as Denham's final lines
("It was Beauty. As always, Beauty killed the Beast") to
police sergeant while looking down at the dead ape from the
parapet of the Empire State Building. In 1976, in the midst
of the Kong-mania aroused by Dino De Laurentiis' remake,
at least four reprints of the novel were in the book stores,
including The Illustrated King Kong from Grosset and Dunlap.
That year Grosset and Dunlap also issued a simplified version of the story King Kong; A Picture Book.

Mark of the Beast, a mid-1960s novel by John E.
Miller, published in England by Badger Books, had a scientist create an enormous ape in his laboratory. The cover
depicted a gorilla, obviously patterned physically after Kong,
rampaging through a metropolis. William Rotsler's novel
To the Land of the Electric Angel (Ballantine Books, 1976)
featured a King Kong robot, eight stories high, who snatches
up a woman and then battles fighter planes until its destruction in a futuristic Roman style arena. Rotsler wrote the
story long before De Laurentiis announced his own anthropoid robot.

My Side (Collier Books), "by King Kong as told to
Walter Wager, " was the huge ape's supposed autobiography,

loaded with obvious jokes and anachronisms. "Kong" reveals
that he was born on February 29, 1912, to a gorilla father
and human mother. He was named Stan Kong and grew to a
height of nearly 132 feet. The narrator goes on to tell how
the natives on his island were actually a shipwrecked Porgy
and Bess stock company. When the ship finally came with
its motion picture crew, Captain Englehorn was actually a
Nazi and Ann Darrow was in reality an American undercover
agent hunting down Communist spies. Kong, according to
"Kong," had been tricked by Denham into appearing in the
RKO movie under the pretext that he was to essay the role
of King Lear. And only the destructive scenes in New York
were performed by O'Brien's miniature dummy. Years after
the completion of King Kong, the ape went on to star in his
Japanese outing with Godzilla, enter politics and finally re-
tire.

Robert Bloch's short story "The Plot Is the Thing"
(1966) climaxed with the protagonist's being dragged off to
become Kong's "bride." "Fay Was a Darn Nice Girl," published in 1969 by the New York Times, was writer Arnold
M. Auerbach's alleged interview with the retired King on his
island home. Kong explains how he and not an animated miniature starred in King Kong and that only his death scenes
were simulated with a model. That same year the New York
Times printed "Portnoy's Mother's Complaint," by Russell
Baker. Mrs. Portnoy identifies with Fay Wray, whom she
resembled in her youth, and sees her husband as Kong.
Philip José Farmer's delightful "After King Kong Fell," first
published in Omega (Walker and Co., 1973), reveals that
King Kong was based on actual events. Written with an obvious love for the picture, the story is about a man who
was a child in the theatre the night that Kong escaped.
Kong's appearance in New York arouses the interest of two
unidentified superheroes of the 1930s, obviously Doc Savage
and the Shadow. The protagonist of the story had grieved
over Kong's death--and also for his beloved aunt who, with
her lover, had been crushed beneath the monster's corpse.
The story also described the lawsuits that resulted from
Kong's rampage, revealed how the ape apparently did have
sex with Ann Darrow and told how Denham, after another
voyage to Skull Island, was slain by the witch doctor who
had lost his towering god. A "King Kong" limerick by Gene
Gallatin appeared in Famous Monsters of Filmland no. 102
(October 1973).

Gallery magazine published a satire "Queen Kong" in
1975. Brandon French demonstrated his abilities to imitate

the styles of various writers in his retelling of the King Kong
plotline, "King Kong: As it might be told by Joseph Conrad,
Charlotte Bronte, Ernest Hemmingway [sic], Jonathan Swift,
Samuel Robertson, and William Faulkner in a celestial story
conference. " A collection of Kong type stories The Rivals of
King Kong, edited by Michel Parry, was set for publication
by Corgi Books in 1977. (Following The Rivals of King Kong
will probably be The Rivals of the Wolf Man and The Rivals
of Godzilla.)

The best of the many nonfiction books about the mighty
ape was The Making of King Kong (A. S. Barnes and Co. ,
1975), by Orville Goldner (a technician on the original King
Kong) and George E. Turner. The book covered virtually
every aspect of the RKO classic's production. The text was
supplemented by over 160 photographs and pieces of artwork
and remains a real credit to its authors and a lasting tribute
to the film.

The Making of King Kong was followed by a deluge of
Kong-related nonfiction books once the Paramount and Universal remakes became big news. Ape: The Kingdom of
Kong (Lorrimer Publishing, 1975), which is also known under
the title Ape: Monster of the Movies, treated movie simians
in general. The Girl in the Hairy Paw (Avon Books, 1976),
edited by Ronald Gottesman and Harry Geduld, King Kong
Story (1976), a French book edited by René Chateau, and
The King Kong Story (Phoebus Publishing Co. , 1977), by
Jeremy Pascall contained articles, stories, book covers,
comic strip pages and other Kong manifestations. Two different Japanese books, each titled King Kong, were similar
ventures. The Creation of King Kong (Pocket Books, 1976),
by Bruce Bahrenburg, appeared in bookstores just before
the release of the Paramount King Kong to extoll the questionable virtues of the remake. And King Kong, the Semple
script of that film, was published by Ace Books in 1977.

Grosset & Dunlap published the Kong-inspired Giant
Apes Coloring Book and Giant Apes Activity and Games Book
in 1976, both illustrated by Tony Tallarico. Periodicals
dedicated to Kong also rode with the publicity of the remake
film, among them Kong News (a newsletter sent out by Paramount while its King Kong was in production), Kong (Countryside Communications, 1976), King Kong! The Monster That
Made History poster magazine (Sportscene Publishers, 1977),
King of the Monsters (Cousins Publications, 1977) and a
Japanese King Kong magazine.

King Kong, a musical stage play that premiered in
South Africa and then moved to London in 1961, was not
about the famed gorilla.   It was a biography of the Zulu boxer Ezekiel Dhlamini who was known as "King Kong."   The
more traditional Kong did, however, appear several times
on stage, though not with impact of his Carl Denham booking.   Philip Morris used an ape-suited actor called King
Kong in his stage show Macabro expectáculo which played in
Mexico.   Maureen Stapleton played a character who fantasizes being carried off by Kong in The Secret Affairs of
Mildred Wild, a play by Paul Zindel presented in 1972 at
New York's Ambassador Theater.   The highlight of the musical Clams on the Half Shell (1975) at New York's Minskoff
Theater was a scene with Bette Midler sitting and singing in
Kong's giant hand, with the Empire State Building sinking in
the background, simulating their ascent.

King Kong's roars were first broadcast over the
radio on the night of February 10, 1933, in a special presentation written by Russell Birdwell, edited by H. N. Swanson and heard over the National Broadcasting Company.   Besides providing listeners with interviews with Cooper and
O'Brien, the show presented capsulized scenes from the upcoming motion picture King Kong.   In the 1970s, Kong also
was the basis for the "King Cub" radio commercials for Datsun
automobiles and some Arctic Circle stores commercials.

Kong's television appearances were more numerous.
He has been seen in various incarnations on "Super Circus"
(Gnik Gnok), "The Tonight Show," "Sinister Cinema," "Sonny
and Cher," "Horror Theatre" (Kong's son Ping Pong), Bob
Clampett's "Time for Beany" (Ping Pong, played on various
occasions by George Barrows and Walker Edmiston), "The
Ghost Busters" (Bob Burns as Tracy, the ape's head made
by Rick Baker; Forrest Tucker as Tracy's human partner
Kong), Japan's "Kikaider" (superhero vs. the missile-firing
Blue Kong, a type of combination ape-bulldog monster),
"Saturday Night," "Fright Night" (Los Angeles), "The 49th
Annual Academy Awards," "Donny and Marie," the special
"Halleluja, Horrorwood," and cartoon series like "Franken-
stein, Jr." and "The Underdog Show."

RKO licensed its simian superstar to Videocraft International in 1966 for a series of King Kong color cartoons
for television's children's market on the ABC network.   The
show premiered as an hour-long "movie" titled King Kong
which loosely followed the plotline of the 1933 film.   Dr.

Nelson, a scientist, and his two children discover Kong on
Mondo Island. Kong proves to be an amiable oaf, who saves
the family from an attacking carnivorous dinosaur. As per
the RKO movie, Kong is finally brought back to New York
where he climbs the Empire State Building. This time,
however, he climbs back down, surviving into a string of
fantastic adventures on the series. Kong's major adversary
in these cartoons was the insidious Dr. Who, who managed
to materialize as a flesh and blood character in the feature-
length movie Kingu Kongu no Gyakushu.

Another of television's giant ape cartoon shows was
"The Great Grape Ape," produced by Hanna-Barbera Productions. The hero, a huge purple ape wearing a jacket and
baseball cap, blunders through his misadventures, somehow
managing to defeat the villains. In one episode the Grape
Ape substitutes for the malfunctioning, forty-foot-tall "Ton-
zilla" gorilla robot that a scientist built to star in a new
monster movie. The robot's inventor rebuilds his creation
and has it capture the picture's female star, while Grape
Ape goes off to rescue her. There was some merchandising
on this character, including a comic book The Great Grape
Ape (September 1975) from Charlton Publications.

The finest King Kong footage ever made for television
appeared in a Volkswagen 411 commercial made by David
Allen. The commercial, titled "King Kong," depicts the
mighty ape (animated model) battling the airplanes in the famous Empire State Building sequence. The only real difference between this and the 1933 footage is that the commercial was shot in color. Instead of falling to his death,
Kong grabs one of the planes, tucks it under a hairy arm
and climbs back to the street. After tossing the craft into
the trunk of a huge Volkswagen 411, Kong and his miniature
"date" (played by Vickie Riskin, the daughter of Fay Wray)
drive off as the ape waves goodbye through an open window.

Dave Allen shot some test footage, quite similar to
that which appeared in the Volkswagen commercial, at Cascade Pictures in 1970 when Hammer Films was investigating
the possibilities in remaking King Kong. "I made it as a
portfolio piece," Allen said to me. "I quite keenly enjoyed
doing it. I wouldn't have done it if I weren't so overly enthusiastic about the original King Kong." When the Hammer
project was shot down like Kong himself, Allen cut his footage into a Cascade sample film that went out to various advertising agencies. The Volkswagen people, realizing that

1930s nostalgia was viable in America at the time, were interested in using Kong to promote their product. A number of production companies, thinking in terms of a gorilla-suited actor, bid for the Volkswagen project. When Volkswagen executives viewed Allen's sample in the Cascade reel, their decision had been made.

One close-up, showing Kong's hand working the shift, required a non-animated Kong. Gorilla impersonators George Barrows and Janos Prohaska were both considered for the job but the part eventually went to Rick Baker, years before the Paramount remake. Allen animated his foot-high Kong model with affection. "King Kong" was enthusiastically received by the viewers, but dismally by the advertising agency. The agency people felt that it conveyed a false impression of the Volkswagen 411's actual size. They also feared that viewers might believe that apes drove their automobiles. When an executive's daughter was literally frightened by the commercial, that only contributed to its being quickly pulled from the network programing. Fortunately at least some of Kong's appreciators were able to see this priceless piece of film.

Less imaginative television commercials utilizing King Kong were made for Gatorade, Dodge, Datsun (King Kab), Ford (Bob Burns as Kong), Kitty Salmon, the Woolworth stores, Ames Home Loan (Kong smashing a window and then turning to face the airplanes) and Yale Auto Loans.

A King-Kong comic strip was serialized in French newspapers in 1948, but the storyline did not follow the 1933 motion picture. Western Publishing Company (Gold Key) issued its own King Kong comic book in 1968. The story was based on the Grosset and Dunlap novel and the artwork, though fine in its own right, bore little resemblance to actual characters or scenes from the motion picture. (In 1977 a giant-sized reprint of this book was issued by Western.) Years before, Western (then under the Dell Comics banner) featured a King Kong-influenced story in Turok, Son of Stone no. 6 (December-February 1957). "The Giant Ape" was about a Kong-sized gorilla ruling a mesa desired by a tribe of cave people in a prehistoric valley of America's Southwest. Weakened by a poisoned arrow, the gorilla falls off a cliff. Western's Underdog comic book featured "King Gong" in its tenth issue (December 1976), a villainous mechanical giant ape who falls off the Umpire State Building upon sighting the heroine standing in the street.

One of the earliest (and best) comic book lampoons of King Kong was "Ping Pong!" in the sixth issue of Mad (August-September 1953), published by EC (Entertaining Comics). Drawn by Bill Elder, the excellent satire climaxes with Pong's transport to New York, where the unimpressed population is larger than he. When Mad changed from color comic book to the more sophisticated black and white magazine format, it frequently made use of the King Kong character. In particular, Mad no. 94 (April 1965) featured "Son of Mighty Joe Kong," written by Dick De Bartolo and drawn by Mort Drucker. James Garner, Doris Day and Dick Van Dyke are characters who find the titled ape in the African jungle and bring him to New York to star in his own Broadway dance routine. It is Doris Day (as Rae Faye) who climbs the Empire State Building when Kong refuses to marry her. She jumps; but Kong, signing an autograph, fails to catch her. Mad finally spoofed the De Laurentiis King Kong in its 192nd issue (July 1977) with "King Korn," written by Dick de Bartolo and illustrated by Harry North.

National Periodical Publications (DC Comics) has contributed to Kong's mythology. "The Gorilla Boss of Gotham City!" was featured in Batman no. 75 (February-March 1953). The brain of executed criminal George 'Boss' Dyke is transplanted into the head of the world's biggest gorilla. The gigantic monster creates a wave of crime and destruction. The story included the necessary scene of the giant ape, with the apparent figure of Batman tucked under one arm, ascending a television tower to confront an attacking Batplane.

The Boy of Steel met his own Konglike adversary in the Superboy story "Kingorilla!" in Adventure Comics no. 196 (January 1954). Kingorilla guards a giant Oriental idol in a lost jungle and tries to devour Superboy before the flying hero, apparently refusing to be another Fay Wray, knocks him unconscious.

National introduced its own Konglike continuing character in Superman no. 127 (February 1959). "Titano the Super-Ape!" told of a chimpanzee named Toto who is sent into space in an artificial satellite. When Toto is bathed in the radiation of two colliding meteors, one uranium and the other kryptonite, he becomes a giant chimp upon returning to Earth. The ape, now called Titano, has also acquired kryptonite-vision which makes him a deadly threat to the Man of Steel. Superman finally hurls Titano into the prehistoric past to live among creatures his own size.

Titano had mysteriously become a giant gorilla when he returned in another story titled "Titano the Super-Ape," in Superman no. 138 (July 1960). Titano is brought back to the twentieth century by a time-transporter, where he climbs the Daily Planet Building to suggest yet another Empire State Building image. Both "Titano the Super Ape!" tales were drawn by Wayne Boring. More allusions to King Kong were made in "Krypto Battles Titano!" in Superman no. 147 (August 1961). Titano battles three tyrannosaurs simultaneously before making friends with Superman's super-dog. An unusual digression from the Titano stories occurred in the Tales of the Bizarro World series in Adventure Comics no. 295 (April 1962). "The Kookie Super-Ape!" was illustrated by John Forte. It introduced a "Bizarro" duplicate of Titano (created from lifeless matter by means of a duplicator ray focused on the original ape) who becomes a professional wrestler. The Japanese film Kingu Kongu tai Gojira received some spoofing in "Jimmy Olsen's Monster Movie!" which Curt Swan illustrated for Superman's Pal, Jimmy Olsen no. 84 (April 1965). Newspaper reporter Olsen transports both Titano and the fire-breathing Flame Dragon of Krypton to battle each other for a new horror film.

"The Super Gorilla from Krypton," drawn by Wayne Boring for the Superman strip in Action Comics no. 238 (March 1958), featured King Krypton, a huge gorilla with the Man of Steel's powers. But the ape finally reveals himself as a scientist from Superman's home world, changed into a gorilla by a backfiring evolution machine. The Man of Steel himself aped the famous RKO character in "When Superman Was King Kong!" in Superman no. 226 (May 1970), drawn by Curt Swan. Clark Kent is affected by red kryptonite, which always affects him unpredictably, while attending a screening of King Kong. Bursting from his Kent disguise, Superman shoots up to become a growling giant, even carrying girlfriend Lois Lane to the top of the suspiciously familiar Metro Building to battle some fighter planes. He falls to the street unharmed and, after creating more havoc, regains his normal size. It is Titano, snatched from his current domain, a planet of giants, who dons Superman's costume to allow both a normal-sized Kent and the "Man" of Steel to appear briefly together.

National spoofed the 1933 movie with "King Klonk, the Killer Gorilla" in The Adventures of Jerry Lewis no. 85 (January-February 1965), written by Arnold Drake and drawn by Bob Oksner. After falling in love with Lewis, Klonk is

floated by four blimps from his jungle home to the United
States where, after performing a number of demeaning show
business routines, goes berserk.   Klonk combats a squad of
ape-suited policemen before floating back home.   Kamandi,
The Last Boy on Earth no. 7 (July 1973), written, drawn,
and edited by Jack Kirby, was a tribute to King Kong with
the titled young hero substituting for Ann Darrow.   Kamandi
is captured by the future world's animal-men and tied to a
stake and offered to an enormous talking gorilla called Tiny.
The ape regards Kamandi as a toy and, after reviving from
a temporary shot from a chemical shell, seeks him out in
the city, then carries him to the top of a skyscraper for a
reenactment, complete with biplanes, of the obligatory Empire State Building climax.   "Kongzilla!" was a parody of
two movie monsters, written by George Evans and drawn by
Frank Robbins, and published in the first issue of Plop!
(September-October 1973).   Kongzilla, a huge apelike monster with a reptile's hind legs and tail, stalks a young new-
lywed couple through the city streets.   But it is the husband
instead of the wife that Kongzilla finally abducts, proving to
be a female of this monstrous species.   In the winter of
1976, National reprinted several of their gorilla stories including "The Super-Gorilla from Krypton" and "The Gorilla
Boss of Gotham City!" in the first issue of Super-Heroes
Battle Super-Gorillas.

The Marvel Comics Group changed the King Kong
theme somewhat, though its inspiration was quite evident, in
"I Discovered Gorgilla! The Monster of Midnight Mountain!"
in Tales to Astonish no. 12 (October 1960).   Gorgilla is a
huge apelike missing link with a long furry tail.   When the
explorers who think to capture the brute are saved by Gorgilla from an attacking Tyrannosaurus, they let him remain
in his lost world.   But Gorgilla himself made the journey
to civilization in "Gorgilla Strikes Again!" in Tales to Astonish no. 18 (April 1961).   Stowing away aboard a ship,
Gorgilla reaches New York, hides within the city's sewers
and bursts free through the playing field of Yankee Stadium
(most likely an inadvertent enactment of a scene originally
planned for the 1933 King Kong).   Gorgilla's rampage through
the city is climaxed with a climb up, not the Empire State
Building, but the Statue of Liberty from which he is shot by
a bazooka.   Both Gorgilla tales were drawn by Jack Kirby.

Marvel's Nick Fury, Agent of SHIELD no. 2 (July
1968) featured a giant robot Kong, a prop for an intended
motion picture, which battles a real Tyrannosaurus on a

prehistoric island. Jim Steranko both wrote and illustrated
the story. Another King Kong spoof appeared in Not Brand
Echh no. 11 (December 1968). "King Konk," by writer Roy
Thomas and artist Tom Sutton, brought the giant gorilla to
civilization where he battles parodies of Marvel's comic
book heroes. Finally he leaps from the Empire State Building into the East River to swim back home. Thomas and
artist Gil Kane paid tribute to King Kong in "Walk the Savage Land!" in The Amazing Spider-Man no. 103 (December
1971). Newspaper publisher J. Jonah Jameson leads an expedition to a prehistoric realm to get a photo story on a
legendary monster called Gog. Jameson brings along blonde
and beautiful Gwen Stacy to give his story sex appeal. He
sounds the gong which brings the orange, scaly Gog out of
the jungle. Gog carries off Gwen and is soon combatting a
Tyrannosaurus in the followup issue's (January 1972) story,
"Beauty and the Brute," in which the creature is revealed
as a being from another planet. Gog's final stand on this
world was high above New York, each foot straddling a tower
of the World Trade Center (three years before Paramount's
King Kong), in "Gog Cometh!" The story was published in
the Kazar strip in the 18th issue (June 1973) of Astonishing
Tales, written by Mike Friedrich and drawn by Dan Adkins.

"Death Is a Golden Gorilla!" was another Kong tribute
by Roy Thomas, illustrated by George Perez for Fantastic
Four no. 171 (June 1976). A gigantic auric gorilla emerges
from a crashed space-ship and is soon crashing its way
through New York. A bystander makes a timely comment:
"I thought this was just a publicity stunt for one of those
new movies about King Kong!" This time the ape (named
Gorr) ascends the Baxter Building, headquarters of the
superhero group, the Fantastic Four. Defeated by the
heroes, Gorr shrinks to normal gorilla size before toppling
from the roof and being saved from death on the pavement
by the Fantastic Four.

Crazy, Marvel's black and white humor magazine,
featured another movie spoof, "Kink Konk," in issue no. 19
(August 1976), written by Len Herman. Ernie Colon adapted
some photographs from the 1933 movie to augment his artwork. Konk falls from his familiar skyscraper perch, being
unaccustomed to the shoes he is wearing ("... 'twas booties
that killed the beast!"). After the release of the Paramount
King Kong, "New TV Spinoffs for King Kong" was featured
in Crazy no. 24 (April 1977). Kong is shown in parodies
of currently popular television shows in this satire by Jim

Simon, Jayson Wechter and artist Murad Gumen. "Kink
Konk Goes on Television," by Len Herman and artist Alan
Kupperberg in Crazy no. 26 (June 1977), had the ape lampooning various popular television programs. He finally
climbs the "Neelson Tower Building" to reach the top in the
ratings, only to be shot down by critics.

Other comics publishers also realized the potential
in graphically portraying Konglike characters. Radio Comics'
Adventures of the Fly no. 10 (January 1961) included "The
World of the Giant Gorillas!" Superheroes the Fly and the
Black Hood find a tribe of Kong-type apes living in a prehistoric world in an Indian jungle. These apes, however,
possess nearly human intelligence through a quirk of evolution. One ape rescues the heroes from a brontosaur. The
Fly returns the favor by summoning a swarm of prehistoric
insects to save the gorillas from an ambushing herd of tyrannosaurs. A series called Mytek the Mighty, about a
Konglike gorilla robot, was featured in issues of the British
comic paper Valiant (Fleetway Publications) in 1965. Mytek
was built by Professor Boyce in the shape of the Akari ape-
god in order to pacify that warlike Central African tribe.
As might be expected, the robot falls under the control of a
wouldbe tyrant.

America's Best Comics, published by the American
Broadcasting Company in 1967, featured a story based on
the "King Kong" television cartoon series. Simply titled "King
Kong," it brought the good-natured gorilla to the city where
he saves it from some wild animals that had escaped from a
circus. The Friendly Ghost, Casper no. 129 (May 1960),
from Harvey Comics, presented "So This Is Ding Dong?"
With good witch Wendy clutched in one paw, Ding Dong
climbs the Empire State Building until his angry father,
Bing Bong, orders him down. "Sacrifice!" was a King Kong
spoof written by John Simons and drawn by Steve Hickman
for The Monster Times no. 7 (April 26, 1972). Kong carries Ann Darrow to his skull-shaped lair and disrobes her.
Then, before a perplexed Ann, he complacently eats the
clothes. A comic-strip version of "King Kong vs. Godzilla"
appeared in England's Legend Horror Classics (1975). Jules
Feiffer depicted Richard M. Nixon as Kong destroying the
Government in his "Feiffer" strip for the April 25, 1974,
issue of The Village Voice. And numerous newspaper comic
strips either spoofed or referred to the King while the De-
Laurentiis King Kong was still in the news.

Major Magazines' Cracked no. 139 (January 197[7])
featured "The Men Behind Kong," about the people who constantly groom the big ape to maintain his public image.
"King Kung" in the next issue of Cracked (March 1977)
spoofed the De Laurentiis picture with John Severin on the
art. Cracked no. 141 (May 1977) followed with "King Kong's
Boyhood," with the baby ape growing up in Africa, finding
life difficult due to his increasing size and inevitably entering the movies.

Sick no. 112 (October 1976), from Charlton Publications, reviewed the mythical book Loves of Kong, which was
supposed to be the ape's autobiography. "King Dong (or
Monkey Business in the Bush)," in the third issue of Cousins Publications' Goose, had the giant ape exposed as a costumed basketball player. Nevertheless his captured bride
bears him two healthy infant gorillas. Wallace Wood's
beautifully rendered Sally Forth comic strip, published in
The Overseas Weekly, spoofed the old fashioned horror
films from November 1976 through February 1977. The
lovely heroine encountered various incarnations of Lawrence
Talbot (whose lycanthropic form Ms. Forth mistook for a
"doggie"), the Mummy, Frankenstein's Monster, Dracula and
a huge Konglike gorilla. The evil Captain Meno exchanges
Sally's mind with that of the ape and soon the thinking, talking anthropoid is pursuing a growling naked woman through
New York's streets. Finally the Ape with Sally's mind
chases the woman with the ape's mind up the Empire State
Building to be attacked by biplanes from an antique airplane
show.

One of the most unusual Kong-inspired graphic story
projects occurred at Warren Publishing Company. Publisher
James Warren had acquired an unpublished painting by illus-
trator Frank Frazetta depicting a Kong-sized nude woman
atop the Empire State Building, fighting off biplanes while
holding a miniature gorilla in one hand. Sixteen of Eerie
Magazine's writers and artists were then challenged to
create a story based on this painting and including the
Frazetta scene. Eerie no. 81 (February, 1977) was graced
with the Frazetta painting on its cover while seven of the
stories inspired by it were published inside. Two of these
tales were especially related to the original King Kong plotline.

The first, "The Bride of Congo," written by Bill
Dubay and drawn by Carmine Infantino, begins at the

conclusion of the 1933 motion picture. Amy La Bido (the
Ann Darrow character) yet moons for the huge ape Congo,
even after her marriage to Chuck Gauntlet (substituted for
Jack Driscoll). Chuck unsuccessfully tries to impress Amy
by dressing up in a gorilla suit. When Amy learns that
Kong, though weak and battered, had survived the Empire
State Building fall, she gives him a transfusion of her rare
(type o-gargantua) blood which restores him to health. But
some of Congo's blood enters Amy's veins and causes her
to grow to the ape's size. With her gorilla-suited husband
in one hand, she goes on to live the scene depicted on the
Frazetta painting, until Congo himself ascends to fetch her.
Congo and Amy return to his domain on "Noggin" Island
where she bears him a healthy hairless ape. "The Giant
Ape Suit," by writer Roger McKenzie and artist Luis Bermejo, revealed that the thirty-foot-tall gorilla that fell from
the Empire State Building in 1933 was actually a robot invented and controlled by one Edgar Cooper. Over thirty
years later, a scoundrel named Reicher discovers Cooper's
other robot creation, a giant mechanical woman. Working
the female automaton from within, Reicher hopes to loot
New York until Cooper, inside the dilapidated ape robot,
pursues him up the Empire State Building, where both of
them are destroyed.

International Insanity no. 5 (March 1977) not only featured a pinup of a "nude" Kong, but also the story "A Date
with Kong," by Judy Brown and Frank Cirocco. The most
popular girl in school is escorted to her prom by a smaller-
than-usual Kong who falls from a rooftop after slipping on a
banana peel.

The sheet music from the original King Kong was
published during the film's initial release. (The selections
were "The Forgotten Island," "A Boat in the Fog," "Aboriginal Sacrifice Dance" and "King Kong March.") Max Steiner's score, condensed into the "King Kong Suite," became
part of Jack Shaidlin's album 50 Years of Movie Music
(Decca) in the early 1960s. More selections from King Kong
were featured on Max Steiner: The RKO Years (Max Steiner Music Society) and Now, Voyager (RCA, 1973), the latter
by Charles Gerbhardt and the National Philharmonic Orchestra. (The selections appeared under the titles "The Forgotten Island," "Natives," "Sacrificial Dance," "The Gate of
Kong" and "Kong in New York.") King Kong (United Artists
Records, 1975), by LeRoy Holmes, presented the entire
Steiner score, unfortunately with limited orchestration. (The

individual cuts were now called "Main Title," "At the Ship's
Rail/Mysterious Seas," "The Last Port of Call," "Approach-
ing Kong's Island/Love Theme," "Jungle Dance/Anne [sic]
Is Offered to Kong," "Rescue Team Follows Kong and Meets
Brontosaur," "And That Children, Is Why There Is No 6th
Avenue 'L' Today" and 'Death on the Empire State.")

   A fully orchestrated King Kong soundtrack album,
authorized by Steiner's estate, was performed by England's
National Philharmonic Orchestra conducted by Fred Steiner
and issued in 1977 by Entr-acte Recording Society. (The
cuts were listed as "Main Title; A Boat in the Fog," "The
Forgotten Island; Jungle Dance," "The Sea at Night," "Abo-
riginal Sacrifice Dance," "The Entrance of Kong," "The
Bronte; Log Sequence," "Cryptic Shadows," "Kong; The
Cave," "Sailors Waiting," "The Return of Kong," "King
Kong Theatre March," and "Kong Escapes; Aeroplanes; Finale.") King Kong, a soundtrack album of John Barry's
music from the Paramount remake film, was issued by the
Dino De Laurentiis Corporation in 1976. (Included on the
album were "The Opening," "Maybe My Luck Has Changed,"
"Arrival on the Island," "Sacrifice--Hail to the King,"
"Arthusa," "Full Moon Domain--Beauty Is a Beast," "Break-
out to Captivity," "Incomprehensible Captivity," "Kong Hits
the Big Apple," "Blackout in New York or How About Buy-
ing Me a Drink," "Climb to Skull Island," "The End Is at
Hand" and "The End.") The theme music from the Paramount King Kong was also issued on a single recording in a
new disco version. Todd Matshikiza's music and Pat Williams' lyrics from the play about Ezekiel Dhlamini were
made available on another King Kong (Decca) album.

   There were more frivolous King Kong records. "I
Go Ape" (RCA) was a late 1950s rock 'n' roll record using
the King written and recorded by Neil Sedaka. "King Kong
Stomp" was featured on the album Dracula's Greatest Hits
in the mid-1960s. "Science Fiction/Double Feature," on
The Rocky Horror Show and The Rocky Horror Picture Show
albums of the mid-1970s used the character. In 1956 Bobby
Pickett released his own "King Kong" (Polydor) record tribute to the 1933 film. In a cut also titled "King Kong" the
mighty ape fights a giant sea monster off the coast of Japan
on the album Sounds of Terror. A Bob Newhart comedy album from Warner Brothers Records featured the monologue
"The Night Watchman," in which the titled character's first
night on the job at the Empire State Building coincides with
Kong's famous climb.

A serious attempt at presenting the Kong story in the fashion of radio drama was the album King Kong (Golden Records), produced about 1965. Adapted by Cherney Berg and directed by Daniel Ocko, the story was presented in two parts, "Journey to the Island" and "The Capture, Triumph and Death of King Kong." Ocko played Captain Englehorn (who was the narrator), Nat Pollen played Driscoll, Ralph Bell was Denham and Elaine Rost played "Anne." The changes from the original King Kong plotline included Denham and Driscoll getting into a fistfight en route to Kong's island, his battling a Palaeoscincus (actually an armored herbivore instead of the flesh-eater described on the record) in place of the Tyrannosaurus and Driscoll and Anne getting married by Englehorn aboard his ship. The recording may have been played over some stations as a radio play.

That King Kong has achieved mythical status is reinforced by the fact that his image is recognizable to millions of persons throughout the world. His giant-sized image (12 feet tall) can be viewed in amusement parks and wax museums thanks to a model made available through Hollywood's Don Post Studios. Another attraction called "Kong, 8th Wonder of the World" graces a New Jersey Amusement Park; and there is even a King Kong Memorial dominated by a life-sized reproduction of the character. Kong's image has appeared in advertising for a King Con fantasy films convention, for Moore Fabrics, Ronrico rum, Artists Entertainment Complex, Libbey-Owens-Ford glass, Potrazebie, Inc. (Brooklyn Heights pottery studio), American Express, a Cincinnati delicatessen (Kosherilla), American Sound Company (Ampzilla), Strathmore paper products, the Fort Worth Star-Telegram, Steak & Brew (New York), Mother's Cookies, Darco East (Cleveland), The Monster Times, Dave Bromberg's Wanted Dead or Alive (Columbia) record album, Datsun (King Kab), and the television show, "Fernwood 2 Night."

In addition to all the other King Kong merchandise that had been appearing in stores for years, a new plethora of Kong-related products was unleashed in 1976 and 1977 in association with the Paramount remake. These included King Kong Viewmaster reels from the GAF Corporation, Slurpees, posters, keychains (containing horsehair from the giant Kong robot), iron-on transfers, T-shirts, Sedgefield Jeans, Schrafft's chocolate and peanut butter candy, a china bust from Jim Beam bourbon (including a King Kong cocktail), Halloween costumes and other paraphernalia. In Los Angeles both a King Kong restaurant and a King Kong Klub opened

about the same time as De Laurentiis' movie.   Certainly
1977 was the Year of the Ape.

As Carl Denham said in 1933, Kong was a "King and
a God."   But the mighty Kong found his Skull Mountain
throne threatened by an upstart from prehistory.   This usurp-
er arose from the waters off the shores of Japan and announced his presence with a blast of his destructive radioactive breath.   The world would soon recognize him as the
new King of the Monsters.

IX

GODZILLA, THE NEW KING

By the 1970s, King Kong, though acknowledged as the greatest of all the behemoth monsters, relinquished his throne. To a new audience mostly comprised of children and teenagers, the mighty Kong was nostalgia. A new king --or perhaps an emperor, considering the nation that spawned him--was crowned after starring in a highly successful series of actionful monster epics. The reigning monster of the 1970s roared and stomped his way out of Japan.

In 1973 a newspaper called The Monster Times, devoted to horror, science fiction and fantasy films, conducted a "monster poll" to determine who among all the screens horrors was most popular during that decade. To the editors' astonishment, the winner of the poll in the category "your favorite monsters of all time" was not the immortal Kong. Runnersup in the poll were, in descending order; the ever popular Dracula, Frankenstein Monster, King Kong and Wolf Man, with the Mummy and Black Lagoon Creature making impressive showings in the horror race. But the creature who took in the majority of votes was Japan's awesome reptillian superstar Godzilla, the so-called (and appropriately so in the seventies) King of the Monsters.

Godzilla is a towering 400-foot tall amphibious prehistoric monster from the Mesozoic era, the age of dinosaurs. He walks upon two stocky hind legs. His back is adorned with a series of ornate spikes, which sometimes glow and crackle with energy. This radiance often heralds the monster's blasts of fiery, radioactive breath, against which little devised by man can survive. Whatever escapes the destructive force of Godzilla's breath might be crushed beneath his stomping taloned feet or his swishing tail as his gigantic green bulk makes its way through Tokyo and other cities.

It seems unlikely that a skyscraping monster, just
one of myriad others to lumber through cities and reduce
them to rubble, should achieve the popularity Godzilla displayed in that 1973 poll. Yet Godzilla, like Kong, has more
than size and strength to endear him to audiences all over
the globe; the huge reptile has personality and style, enough
to keep him flourishing through a long string of movies which
began in 1954 and continue to this day. The number of Godzilla imitators who have roared and wrecked cities in his
wake further attests to the impact the spike-backed monster
has had upon the world.

Originally, Godzilla was to be the star of a single
picture, made, as were all the succeeding films using the
character, by the Japanese company Toho International. The
name of the film in Japan was Gojira, from the English word
"gorilla" and the Japanese "kujira," meaning "whale." Actually Gojira happened to be the nickname of a rugged employee
of Toho at the time; his nickname has since become a part
of the cinema's pseudo-mythology, as numerous moviegoers
assume wrongly that Godzilla was based upon Japanese legend.

Gojira was directed by Inoshiro Honda, who would go
on to direct most of the sequels in the giant reptile's career.
In 1956, Honda's monster epic was released in the United
States by Joseph E. Levine's Embassy Pictures. Apparently
Godzilla himself was not considered a strong enough leading
character to sell the film to American audiences. New footage was inserted with Raymond Burr playing American news-
paperman Steve Martin (his role played by a Chinese actor
in the Japanese version). Thus Godzilla, King of the Monsters, "starring" Raymond Burr, was unleashed upon the
United States.

Unlike King Kong, Godzilla did not come to life on
the screen via puppet animation. Except for a few scenes
in which a waist-up mechanical model was utilized, Godzilla
was portrayed by a very human actor, Haru Nakajima, who
donned the foam rubber reptile suit (made by Ryosaku Takasugi) in this film and all the sequels. The good-natured
Nakajima literally became the towering Godzilla as Toho's
special effects wizard Eiji Tsuburaya (1901-1970) set him
loose upon a startingly realistic miniature reproduction of
Tokyo. Tsuburaya, who began his career as a cameraman
in the silent "Hunchback" film Enmei-In no Semushi, was
truly a master of miniatures and scenes of grand scale

destruction. With Honda's low-key direction, low angles and slow-motion photography, Godzilla, in his first motion picture adventure, proved that a convincing dinosaur-style monster could be portrayed by a man in a costume.

Godzilla, King of the Monsters, or Gojira, has a standard giant-monster-on-the-loose plot, transcended only by Honda's direction and Tsuburaya's screen magic. An investigation is underway after a number of ships have been destroyed by some unknown force. The natives of Odo Island, however, believe that the ships were destroyed by a monster out of their legends--Godzilla. Since Odo Island is located near the site of the disasters, Steve Martin and paleontologist Dr. Yogami (Takashi Shimura) go there, discovering such oddities as a living trilobite and a number of huge radioactive footprints. Suddenly an enormous reptilian head rises impressively over the hillside giving movie audiences their first actual look at Godzilla.

Dr. Yogami later offers his theory to a meeting of scientists. Godzilla, says Yogami, is actually a prehistoric animal freed from its 100 million years or so of hibernation by repeated hydrogen bomb testing. Perhaps more bombs can destroy the monster, it is reasoned. But after a series of depth bombs are ineffectually exploded, the unharmed Godzilla rises from the waters outside Tokyo, then crashes his way into the city itself.

Creating more destruction and death than even King Kong, Godzilla levels the city. With his every step buildings crumble and topple. Trains are like toys when clamped in the monster's toothy jaws. A series of electrical towers are erected to halt Godzilla's progress but they, along with whatever other weapons the Japanese can hurl against him, fail to stop the monster. Before long Tokyo, once one of the greatest cities on Earth, is barely more than rubble and flames, with the awesome bulk of Godzilla looming over the smoke-clouded horizon.

For one scene during Godzilla's raid through Tokyo, the script called for the monster to react to a siren. Before the film went into actual production the studio executives considered the scene and decided that for Godzilla to so react he must have ears. Virtually no one even noticed the earlike additions to the Godzilla suit (which remained on the creature only in this film and the first sequel).

The giant Japanese sea monster Godzilla's first appearance, in Gojira (Toho, 1954), released in the United States as Godzilla, King of the Monsters.

With despair, Steve Martin watches the destruction being caused by Godzilla through his hotel room, resigning himself to the eventual doom of the entire world by this monstrous atavism to another age. But mankind has not yet lost. Earth's salvation results from a device called the Oxygen Destroyer, invented by a brilliant scientist named Dr. Sarazowa (Akihiko Hirata). The Oxygen Destroyer is capable of removing oxygen from the water and disintegrating

any living creatures in the vicinity.   Until now Sarazowa has
vowed not to reveal the secret of his discovery, lest it be
used by unscrupulous persons.   Finally, however, the scientist is persuaded to use the Oxygen Destroyer against Godzilla by his girlfriend Emyko (Momoko Kochi), whom he has
lost to a rival.

Near the submerged Godzilla, Dr. Sarazowa sets off
the Oxygen Destroyer.   Then, in order that his secret be
never divulged, the scientist cuts his own life rope and air-
line.   The waters begin to churn and bubble.   Seconds later
Godzilla's mighty form pierces the water's surface, then
sinks to the bottom of the sea.   As the water becomes more
violent, Godzilla's carcass is stripped of its flesh, after
which his skeleton dissolves to nothingness.

Gojira was one of the minor classics to emerge from
the 1950s, an era when creatures revived or created via
atomic power were commonplace.   In Japan the picture played
to basically an adult audience.   Most of Godzilla's attacks
were at night, Honda's scenes grim and somber while Tsuburaya made them spectacularly exciting.   And, at least in
the English language version, Burr's verbalized observations
lent the picture a feeling of despair.

The picture was an overwhelming success when first
released in Japan in 1954.   The Toho studio heads had not
expected such profits to result from a monster movie.   But
after they began to count their yen it was inevitable that they
consider making a sequel.   There was only one problem:
Godzilla had been irrevocably destroyed for all time, his
atoms scattered beyond any logical reassembling.   Of course
the dollar sign had more power than even Dr. Sarazowa's
Oxygen Destroyer.

Toho would make a sequel and it would be even more
spectacular than Gojira.   The celebrated King of the Monsters would stomp and destroy once again, and in order to
make the second film twice as spectacular it was given twice
the number of giant monsters.   Thus, in 1955, Toho again
employed the talented Honda and Tsuburaya and went into
production with a two-monster epic called Gojira no Gyakushyu ("Godzilla's Counterattack"), which would be released in
the United States by Warner Brothers four years later under
the somewhat misleading title of Gigantis, The Fire Monster.
(The film is also known as Godzilla no Gyakushyu, Godzilla
Raids Again, Counterattack of the Monster and The Return
of Godzilla.)

The new monster was named Angurus.   Like Godzilla, Angurus breathed fire like a dragon out of Oriental legend. But unlike the monster who first attacked Odo Island, Angurus was a quadrupedal reptile, armed with a spiny carapace on its back and a set of formidable horns surmounting the head. Again there was a human actor sporting a monster outfit. In the case of Angurus (as with all the succeeding Japanese four-footed monsters) the actor had to walk on his knees to compensate for his disadvantageous human frame.   Occasionally Angurus would rise up on his hind legs to do battle with his monstrous adversary or to smash through a building. But usually he was down on all fours with Honda careful to avoid showing the hind legs as much as possible.

The resurrection of Godzilla himself was simple and logical enough.   Godzilla was an animal; and where there is one there could certainly be another.   The new Godzilla, or Gigantis as he was rechristened for the American version, was not the Godzilla who had invaded Tokyo the year before, but rather another Godzilla that had survived from the so-called Age of Reptiles.

The original Gojira was presented with complete sobriety.   Had the prehistoric giant remained nothing more than scattered atoms his image would have remained that of a stupid, lumbering behemoth.   To survive through any number of sequels, however, and not go to the extinction of so many other city-rampaging prehistoric beasts, Godzilla would need personality.

In Gojira no Gyakushyu can be seen the beginnings of the Godzilla personality which would become firmly established in movie monster lore during the succeeding films of the series.   Takasugi's Godzilla costume was basically the same as it had appeared in the initial movie.   But there was some revamping, especially in the head, with the teeth protruding a bit more than usual and with "takes" approaching the comical.

The second Godzilla movie proceeds with two Japanese fliers discovering two prehistoric reptiles, later identified by the returning Dr. Yogami (Shimura again) by their scientific names Gigantis and Angurus, battling for supremacy on a remote Pacific island.   After the two fliers report what they have seen to the authorities, Yogami provides a brief lecture, which includes footage of Tokyo being leveled by the original Godzilla in the previous film.   Yogami

explains that both Gigantis and Angurus existed in an age of
flames and volcanoes and thrive upon fire.   An interesting
piece of film accompanying the doctor's lecture depicted two
brontosaurs fighting via the technique of model animation.
The jerky results were enough to convince Tsuburaya to remain with the monster costumes with which he was more
familiar.

Gigantis and Angurus continue their battle into another
Japanese metropolis, again reducing the city to rubble before
the renamed Godzilla finally kills his prehistoric enemy.
Now it is Gigantis vs. mankind as he lashes out against the
city without interference from Angurus.   As with his predecessor, Gigantis is bombarded with the fire power of the
Japanese armed forces, before escaping unscathed into the
sea.

The picture climaxes upon another island where Gigantis had been spotted by fliers.   Bombs again prove useless against the monster whose dark body stands out against
the snow and ice of the island.   Finally the snowy slopes
become the planes' target, crashing down to bury the impervious Gigantis beneath tons of freezing whiteness.

Before the release of the film to American audiences,
scenes were to be shot (as in the case of Godzilla, King of
the Monsters) to make the picture more appealing to United
States audiences.   According to Forrest J Ackerman, "So
successful was the original Godzilla in America that the sequel, Godzilla Raids Again, was shown in Japanese sectors
3 years before it became Gigantis the Fire Monster.   I saw
it in '56 when it was 4 minutes longer.   In the intervening
3 years, I as film agent for Ib J. Melchior (he scripted &
directed The Time Travelers) was involved in a plan to
shoot more footage showing Godzilla turning up in the Philip-
pine Islands and headed for the USA.   It was to have been
called "The Volcano Monsters" [Ackerman, Forrest J, "Monsters from Japan," Famous Monsters of Filmland no. 114
(March 1975), p. 27].   But this second Godzilla production
proved capable of standing on its own merits.   No one
seemed to mind the exclusion of an American star, with the
Godzilla figure powerful enough to negate the inclusion of
another Raymond Burr.

Godzilla remained frozen beneath the ice for seven
years.   During the interim, however, Honda and Tsuburaya
were busy creating a pantheon of Toho monsters, all

presented in the Godzilla style and intended for one picture
only, yet eventually to be incorporated into the Godzilla
stock company.   The first of these was Rodan.

Rodan (also known as Rodan, The Flying Monster)
went into production in 1956 under the Japanese title Radon
and was released the following year.   The King Brothers released the picture in the United States in 1958.   Unlike Gojira and Gojira no Gyakushyu this latest Japanese export was
made in color.

While Godzilla leveled the cities of Japan on the
ground, Rodan did the same from the air.   Rodan was another prehistoric monster, a winged reptile capable of flying
at supersonic speeds while leaving behind a smoky trail.
The creature somewhat resembled the extinct Pteranodon although its head (at least in the close-ups) was surmounted
by two horns.   Its wingspan measured an incredible 500
feet.   Again, as with most of Japan's giant monsters, Rodan
was played by a human actor, except in the long shots of
the creature in flight.

Actually there were two Rodans.   Before either of
them actually appeared on screen a number of giant insects
herralded their rebirth in the modern-day world.   The explosion of a hydrogen bomb again provides the catalyst for
horror.   The results of the atomic test are first manifested
by an earthquake which frees a number of enormous centi-
pedes in a mine in the volcanic mountains of Kyushu, a
Japanese province.   The quake also exposes two eggs from
which hatch two of the Rodan monsters, which quickly grow
to awesome adult proportions.

Once more two prehistoric monsters seek out a Japanese metropolis, this time Sasebo City (Tokyo still apparently not having been rebuilt since Godzilla's attack).   Audiences were again treated to the wizardry of Eiji Tsuburaya,
who equaled the masterful work he did on Gojira.   For
added effect Tsuburaya showed cars, shards of rooftops and
other debris flying into the air by the gales created by the
Rodans' wings.   The pterodactyl-like monsters did not even
have to touch a building to reduce it to rubble.

Again modern weaponry cannot destroy the twin horrors.   It becomes the task of the Earth itself to rebel
against these anachronistic monsters.   Both Rodans are
tracked to their "nest," an active volcano.   As the army

proceeds to bombard the volcano it begins to erupt, with both creatures called Rodan perishing in the spectacular holocaust. "Randan," a parody of the motion picture drawn by Will Elder, was featured in Humbug no. 11 (October 1958). After the monsters' volcanic destruction another creature emerges with a huge frying pan intended for the human spectators.

Varan, another prehistoric reptile that would inevitably cross-over into the Godzilla mythology, roared in Japanese theatres in 1958. In Japan his film was entitled Daikaiju Baran ("The Monster Baran," as he was known in his native country). Four years later the picture was playing in American movie houses as Varan the Unbelievable, released by Crown-International.

As in Godzilla's first adventure, footage was added to Daikaiju Baran with an American actor, though B-films performer Myron Healey's name had little marquee value. Healey played Commander James Bradley who is conducting experiments on a Japanese island to desalinate the water. Though the natives warn Bradley that the chemicals he uses might awaken a monster that sleeps beneath the water of a lagoon, the commander continues to experiment--with the expected results.

Varan, or Baran, is of the Godzilla mold, occasionally a biped but usually stomping about on all fours. Its head and back are armed by a row of high spikes. And, at least in the Japanese version of the film, this prehistoric monster can glide through the air by means of a membrane attached to its legs like some saurian flying squirrel. First Varan creates havoc on the island, then proceeds to do the same in the city of Onida. When the usual display of Japanese firepower proves useless, Varan is destroyed as a truck filled with a heavier concentration of the chemicals that revived him explodes. The unbelievable Varan proved to be one of Toho's less popular monsters and would only briefly cross the path of Godzilla.

Having already unleashed four species of gigantic reptile upon Japanese cities, Toho turned its attention to the world of insects. In 1961 the studio made Mosura, which was released in color in the United States as Mothra the next year by Columbia Pictures. Mosura was based upon the short story "Shukan Asahi," by S. Nakamura. Emi and Yumi Ito, who in their off-screen lives are

professional singers known as the Peanuts, portrayed the
Aelinas, two-inch tall princesses who guard a monstrous
egg which exists on Infant Island.   An expedition of scientists discovers the two girls, who are promptly captured,
taken back to Japan and exhibited like circus sideshow freaks.
The audience could predict what was to follow.

The two miniature women gone, the sacred egg
hatches, releasing an immense insect larva which destroys
every ship in its path as it swims toward Japan on a rescue mission.   Once in Tokyo (which finally had been rebuilt
since Gojira) the huge caterpillar spins a cocoon, later to
emerge as a monster moth.   Once more Tokyo crumbles beneath the force of Mothra's wings, as the creature finally
saves the two tiny girls, waits for them to climb aboard its
back and then flies back to their island home, for once providing a happy ending to a monster fairy tale.   Eventually,
Mothra, along with Godzilla and Rodan, would round out
Toho's monster triumvirate.

Godzilla, however, was still the King of Toho's monster menagerie.   In 1963 he made his first comeback in almost a decade in a film pitting him against the greatest of
the American giant monsters Kingu Kongu tai Gogira or
King Kong vs. Godzilla (covered in the previous chapter).
The film was made in color, as would be all of Godzilla's
succeeding films, and allowed the reptile to attack Tokyo
once more.

Since the old Godzilla costume had long since deteriorated, a new one was built for his encounter with the giant
gorilla King Kong.   A few modifications were made in the
costume's design.   The elongated canine fangs of the original were shortened to match the other teeth in Godzilla's
mouth; and the ears that were apparent in the first two
Godzilla films were eliminated in favor of a sleeker, more
reptilian appearance.   This was the beginning of the new approach to the Godzilla films, which would now, as decided
by the Toho executives, be made for a more youthful audience.   The film was made tongue-in-cheek and Godzilla's
appearance was altered to make him less frightening and
more lovable to children.   For the first time Godzilla was
portrayed with an almost anthropomorphic personality; he
virtually laughs as he singes King Kong's hide with his
flaming breath and continues to battle his simian adversary
with the style and grace of a human wrestler.

The Godzilla in Kingu Kongu tai Gojira is plainly the afore-mentioned "Gigantis." He is discovered in an iceberg, the result of the freezing climax of Gojira no Gyakushyu. Once more new footage was shot for American distribution using Caucasian actors. In one amusing scene an American paleontologist tries to explain the nature of Godzilla by pointing to illustrations of the carnivorous Tyrannosaurus and the plated and spiked Stegosaurus in a popular children's book about prehistoric animals. Godzilla, he stated profoundly, was a combination of both these dinosaurs. To explain the absurdity of such a statement is not within the scope of this book; but it did bring about a number of chuckles from even some of the youngest would be paleontologists in the audience.

Toho brought to life another monster in a film of its own before overlapping his career with Godzilla's. Manda was a sea serpent of the usual gigantic size who made his appearance near the climax of Kaitei Gunkan ("Underwater Warship"), a color epic filmed in 1963 and released in the the United States by American International two years later under the title Atragon. (The picture is also known as Atoragon and Atoragon--Flying Supersub.) Manda is a legendary monster that threatens the lost Mu empire, which is out to destroy the world. The serpent is finally destroyed by the fabulous flying submarine Atragon.

The last of the Godzilla stock company of monsters to be introduced in an unrelated film was Baragon, another quadrupedal prehistoric reptile which came up on its hind legs when the actor inside (Godzilla emoter Haruo Nakajima) wearied of crawling about on his hands and knees. Baragon had a glowing horn between his eyes and a pair of earlike attachments that flared out from his head. Like Godzilla, Baragon could fire deadly blasts from his mouth. He was the co-star of the color Furankenshutain tai Baragon ("Frankenstein vs. Baragon"), which was made in 1964 and released two years later in the United States by American International as Frankenstein Conquers the World.

The Frankenstein Monster in this version of Mary Shelley's concept is the result of his living, disembodied heart, which is stolen from a German laboratory during World War II and taken to Hiroshima. After the atomic horror that destroyed the city, the heart continues to regenerate new tissue, until, by the mid-1960s, it has grown into a complete humanoid organism of gigantic size. Coincidentally an earthquake frees Baragon (he remained nameless in the

American dubbed version) from hibernation. The two monsters inevitably meet and battle to the death during a raging
forest fire. The skyscraping Frankenstein finally kills Baragon as the ground splits and swallows them both.

Before Furankenshutain tai Baragon went into produc-
tion, Toho announced two other Frankenstein titles in 1965:
Frankenstein vs. The Giant Moth, in which the artificially
created horror was to fight Mothra, and Frankenstein vs.
King Kong, neither film being made. The Frankenstein/
Baragon match was originally announced as Frankenstein vs.
the Giant Devilfish with scenes shot (but not used) of the
Frankenstein Monster struggling with an enormous octopus.
This same "devilfish" would, however, appear in the sequel
Sanda tai Gailah.

Furankenshutain no Kaiju--Sanda tai Gailah ("Frankenstein Monsters--Sanda vs. Gailah") was the original title of
the sequel before its shortening. The picture was given a
United States release by UPA as The War of the Gargantuas.
According to the original Japanese version, the green gar-
gantua called Gailah (meaning "sea") was the result of the
regenerating severed hand of Frankenstein, which had crawled
into the ocean. Sanda (meaning "mountain") was the regene-
rated hand that had been cut from Frankenstein during the
previous film's earthquake. Since both monsters bore only
a slight resemblance to the Frankenstein Monster of the
earlier film, producer Henry G. Saperstein deleted any
Frankenstein references for the American release. The
murderous Gailah and the benevolent Sanda battle each other
with the usual Tsuburaya visuals, until both of them are
destroyed by a volcanic eruption. Honda directed.

Another Toho title, The Frankenstein Brothers,
emerged in 1966, with Tab Hunter announced as the star.
Whether this was a new film altogether or simply an alternate title for Sanda tai Gailah is not known.

Godzilla's next adventure was also filmed in 1964.
In Japan the picture was called Mosura tai Gojira [also
known as Godzilla tai Mothra and Godzilla vs. the Giant
Moth] and the theme of the picture is easily made evident
by the translation "Mothra vs. Godzilla. " Mothra, the first
Toho monster to crossover into Godzilla's series, was a
superstar in Japan. Apparently American International Pictures, which released the movie in the United States, felt
otherwise. Perhaps to capitalize on an RKO science fiction

picture of 1951 called The Thing (From Another World), AIP
issued Mosura tai Gojira as Godzilla vs. the Thing.   Mothra
was not even depicted in the film's American advertising.
In place of the giant winged insect was an obtrusive question
mark with the catchlines, "What is it ... how much terror
can you stand?"

With the ever-increasing emphasis on comedy in the
series, yet another Godzilla costume was built with more
attempts made at presenting him in a less frightening and
more comical light.   The eyes were larger, hooded, almost
humanly fiendish in appearance and were capable of looking
forward.   Though still a villain, the great reptile was already showing signs of his eventual reformation.

A hurricane washes ashore a huge egg, the so-called
"thing" of the American title.   The egg glows and vibrates,
obviously containing some unknown form of life.   Soon the
egg becomes the target of carnival promoters and scientists
who vie for its possession.   As the egg is being photographed by the press, the ground begins to stir.   A familiar
reptilian tail snakes out of the sand and moments later Godzilla, who had apparently also been washed ashore during the
hurricane, rises to his awesome height.   Once again the
mighty Godzilla lashes out against the cities of mankind,
amassing a huge deathtoll and defying Japan's armed forces.

The hope for mankind's survival seems to be in
Mothra, the giant monster god of Infant Island.   The Aelinas
(the Ito sisters, as always) agree to send Mothra to combat
Godzilla.   Meanwhile the huge saurian smashes the giant in-
cubator which has been set up to hatch the egg.   But the
egg is Mothra's and the winged creature is not about to permit its falling into Godzilla's claws.

The battle between Godzilla and Mothra was another
Tsuburaya spectacle and foreshadowed the comedy clashes
that were to follow in future Godzilla epics.   Godzilla was
portrayed as a nasty oaf, clumsily stumbling and rolling
beneath the torrential force of Mothra's wings.   In one hilarious sequence which startled viewers familiar with the
Godzilla of old, Mothra flaps her expansive wings and pulls
the spike-backed saurian by the tail.   Godzilla's front claws
desperately tear at the dirt as Mothra drags him along.
Finally with a blast of his flaming breath, Godzilla sets
Mothra's wings smoking, after which the giant moth gently
settles down to shelter her egg and die.

The chanting of the Aelinas, along with that of the natives on Infant Island, hatches Mothra's eggs. Two huge caterpillars emerge to avenge the death of their mother. Working as a team the larvae begin their attack, spraying the prehistoric reptile with the silky substance used in making cocoons. Entangled by the weblike strands, Godzilla falls into the sea to an apparent death.

This would be the final "death scene" for Godzilla on the screen. It was also the last time that the King of the Monsters would be portrayed as a villain. Viewers, especially children, had grown too fond of the scaly protagonist and it was decided by the head of Toho International that Godzilla's adventures should be made strictly for the younger generation. The actual transitional film in which Godzilla's role switched from villain to a weird sort of superhero was the 1965 production Sandai Kaiju Chikyu Kessen which Continental released in America as Ghidrah, The Three-Headed Monster. (Other titles for the film include The Biggest Fight on Earth, The Greatest Battle on Earth, Chikyu Saidaino Kessen and Monster of Monsters, Ghidorah. Titles for 8mm home movies edited from the film include Battle of the Monsters and Ghidrah (Monster of Monsters).)

As with the old Wolf Man films made by Universal during the 1940s, there was no turning back. Audiences who were accustomed to seeing their monster hero sharing screen credit with some other famous creature wanted to see more. And so, Sandai Kaiju Chikyu Kessen, a multi-monster extravaganza, revived one of the Mothra caterpillars and the presumably destroyed Rodan, the latter appearing more comical to fit the mood of the new film, with a slightly longer neck and lacking his old sky-writer's exhaust.

In addition to Toho's "big three" the studio introduced the predacious King Ghidrah (or Ghidorah in the Japanese version of the film), a monster from outer space with enormous batlike wings and three horned dragon heads surmounting serpentine necks and each with lightning blast breath capable of instantaneous destruction. Within minutes Ghidrah can decimate a city the size of the eternal target Tokyo. In size Ghidrah dwarfs even the towering Godzilla.

Ghidrah is introduced to earthlings when a brilliant meteorite crashes to free an alien life essence. Fire blasts into the sky, after which a three-headed ghostly form begins to take on solidity. Within seconds Ghidrah is flapping his leathery wings and anxious to destroy.

As with a number of the later Godzilla films, Sandai
Kaiju Chikyu Kessen included a virtually unrelated subplot,
this time involving a gang of thugs out to murder a lovely
prophetess (played by Eiko Wakabayashi) claiming to be a
Martian. The prophetess, Princess Salno, predicts a number of disasters, which come true when Rodan (only one of
them) is freed from the mountain that has imprisoned him
all these years and Godzilla rises from the sea to destroy
a ship with his incendiary breath.

Before long both Godzilla and Rodan are battling each
other, causing enough Tsuburaya-created destruction to please
the series- fans. The monsters fight in the slapstick style
that was now officially a main ingredient of the Godzilla
series. In one amusing scene during the battle Godzilla
holds his scaly belly and simulates uproarious laughter as he
briefly bests his winged adversary. Later the wormlike
Mothra swings his head in the manner of a spectator to a
tennis game as Godzilla and Rodan batter a boulder back
and forth at each other.

With Ghidrah on the rampage, the tiny Aelinas sisters
decide that only the combined might of Godzilla, Rodan and
their own Mothra can save the world from the alien monster.
Sandai Kaiju Chikyu Kessen was the pivot point of the Godzilla series, in which Japan's three resident monsters officially evolved heroic stature. The Aelinas ask Mothra to
stop the battle between Godzilla and Rodan and to ask them
to save mankind and the world by teaming up against Ghidrah.
Mothra, the Aelinas explain, knows how to converse in monster language! The caterpillar sprays both monsters in his
cocoon and forces them to listen. Godzilla replies with a
loud growl. ("Godzilla! Watch your language!" gasps one of
the miniature women in the English-dubbed version.) Neither
Godzilla nor Rodan care much for the human race, which has
been fighting them with missiles, tanks and fighter planes for
many years now (Godzilla and Rodan apparently forgetting who
the aggressors were in their earlier motion pictures). But
eventually the monsters realize that their existence is also
threatened by the presence of Ghidrah. The precedent had
been firmly established: Godzilla, Rodan and Mothra were
now Earth's greatest champions with Ghidrah (who would also return in upcoming films in the series) the perennial villain.

The final clash occurs on Mount Fuji, where Godzilla
had previously tangled with the Japanese version of King

Kong. Against one of Earth's monsters Ghidrah might have
triumphed. Now, chewed, battered, burned and covered
with Mothra's sticky cocoon material, a defeated Ghidrah
can only flap his wings and fly out into space. For the
first time in any Godzilla film, the flame-breathing reptile,
along with Mothra and Rodan, leaves in peace.

With Godzilla the most bizarre superhero of all,
there was no longer any need to explain his return from an
apparent death. He simply made his appearance and, when
his size and power were no longer required, he would lumber away. Though Godzilla and Rodan had reformed, they
would briefly return in their destructive incarnations in the
1905 sequel Kaijû Daisenso ("Invasion of Astro-Monsters")
[also known as Battle of the Astros, Godzilla Radon King-
Gidorah, Invasion of Planet X, and Invasion of Astro-Mon-
sters], which would be released as Monster Zero in the
United States by Maron Films five years later.

Kaijû Daisenso incorporated space opera into the Godzilla series, with two astronauts, one played by American
actor Nick Adams, rocketing to a new planet (called Planet
X by terran scientists) which has moved into our solar system. The astronauts learn that the inhabitants of Planet X
have been cataloguing monsters with individual numbers.
Currently these alien humanoids are being plagued by the
designated Monster Zero, which Earth knows as Ghidrah.
The leaders of Planet X request to borrow Earth's Godzilla
and Rodan in hopes of ridding their world of the Ghidrah
menace.

Godzilla and Rodan are both placed in suspended animation with sedatives fired from alien spacecraft on Earth.
Then, encircled by energy cocoons and resembling two
saurian fetuses, the Earth monsters are transported via
flying saucers to the mountainous terrain of Planet X, where
they resume their war against Ghidrah. Soon, however, the
residents of Planet X reveal their true intentions--to use all
three monsters (Ghidrah having been under their control all
along) against the Earth people, finally occupying our planet
and stealing its water supply. Once again Godzilla and Rodan, accompanied by Ghidrah, are on the rampage on Earth,
killing and wrecking everything in their paths. Through the
efforts of the military power and science of Earth, and after
some spectacular footage of spaceships warring in futuristic
dogfights, the aliens are defeated, with Godzilla and Rodan
(this time without the aid of Mothra) vanquishing Ghidrah
and resuming their roles of heroes and villain.

There was less spectacle in the 1966 followup picture Nankai no Dai Ketto ("Big Duel in the North Sea"), or Godzilla vs. the Sea Monster as it was retitled by Continental when released in America three years later. (In England the film became Ebirah, Horror of the Deep while German audiences saw it under the misleading title Frankenstein und die Ungeheuer aus dem Meer--"Frankenstein and the Monster from the Sea.") For this epic Rodan was given a rest, while Mothra (in moth form again) and Godzilla encounter not only enormous birds but also a gigantic crab called Ebirah. (Almost all Japanese film monsters have names.) Ebirah lives in the waters off the island of Letchi, inhabited by a band of would-be tyrants with plans to rule the world. When a group of native slaves tries to escape from their megalomaniacal masters they are gobbled up by Ebirah.

By now it was obvious that the only logical way to get rid of one Japanese monster was by employing the services of another. Since the Letchi natives are really immigrants from Infant Island, it is not too difficult to summon their monster deity Mothra. Godzilla is discovered slumbering in a vast cavern and soon both he and the giant moth are once again battling a monster adversary to save the world. They succeed. The film was the first Godzilla epic that did not use the abilities of Honda; Jun Fukuda directed.

Ebirah, like Varan and Manda, was not among Toho's more popular creations. He also would appear in but one more Godzilla film, yet not in the next one, 1967's Gojira no Musuko, also directed by Fukuda. Older fans of the Godzilla films of the 1950s cringed when they learned that the American title, when the picture was issued the next year by American International, was Son of Godzilla. (In Germany it was improperly named Frankensteins Monster jagens Godzillas ("Frankenstein's Monster Hunts Godzillas.")

The plot and direction of Gojira no Musuko made no pretentions at being anything other than kiddie fare. A group of scientists sponsored by the United Nations Food Planning Committee labors on Sollgell Island to control the weather and convert deserts, frozen tundras and jungles into food-producing lands. The initial experiments to lower the temperature backfire, the soaring climate resulting in overgrown plants, huge preying mantises (unnamed, surprisingly) and a monster spider, given the menacing name of Spiega. Another result of the upsurge in temperature is the hatching of a giant reptile egg. The infant saurian disturbingly

resembles something out of a medical book on human freaks
and whines like a human baby. The creature is the son of
Godzilla. (The argument over whether or not Godzilla is
actually of the female sex still rages among the monster's
more dedicated fans. Toho has never revealed if Godzilla
himself/herself laid the egg or if the egg somehow managed
to survive since prehistoric times. Perhaps this will remain one of the great unsolved mysteries of the monster
films genre.)

Minya, as Godzilla's offspring would come to be
known, is menaced by Spiega and the giant mantises, when
his fire-breathing parent charges to the rescue. Again Godzilla triumphs, this time not only for the safety of the
world but also for his own heir. Until now Godzilla has
tried to shirk off the pesky Minya as he gets in his parent's
ponderous way or tries to hitch a ride on his tail. But in
the final scenes of the movie Godzilla turns, embraces and
accepts his whimpering son. The scene is both bizarre and
tender, with strong audience identification as father and son
unify the Godzilla family in a bond of saurian love. Even
as this touching union occurs, snow begins to fall as a result of another temperature control experiment used to combat the monsters that had menaced the island. Both Godzilla and his offspring are forced into hibernation by the
sudden coldness, leaving audiences with little doubt that the
series would continue.

Honda returned to direct Kaijû Sôshingeki ("Attack of
the Marching Monsters") [also, Kaiju Sokogeki], a 1968 film
which American International Pictures released the next year
as Destroy All Monsters [also, Operation Monsterland]. The
movie featured not only Toho's three most popular behemoths,
Godzilla, Rodan and Mothra, but also a number of other
monsters, some of which had been literally taken out of
storage. Among the supporting horrors who appeared in
this multi-monster spectacular were Gorosaurus (from Kingu
Kongu no Gyakushu), Minya, Spiega, Manda, Ghidrah, Baragon, a more comical looking Angurus, and the unbelievable
Varan, finally shown to Americans gliding with his winglike
membranes. (Unfortunately for Varan fans, this monster's
costume had already deteriorated to the point that his appearance was limited to two brief shots.) To cut down on
the cost of filming an epic with such an all-star cast, stock
footage was used from such earlier Toho monster movies as
Furankenshutain tai Baragon, Sandai Kaiju Chikyu Kessen
and Radon.

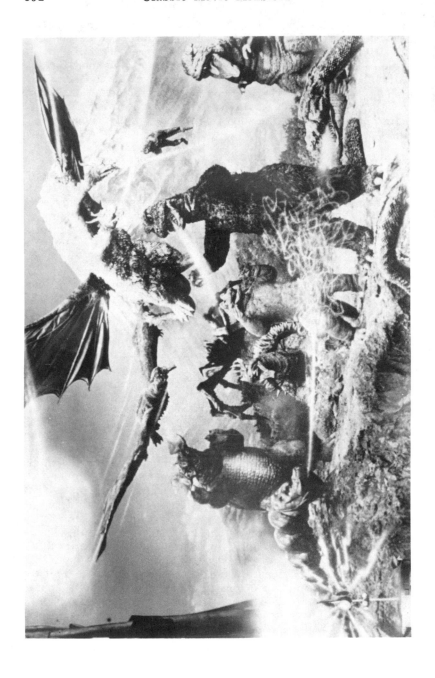

The story is set in the not-too-distant future of 1999.
All of Earth's monsters are now confined to a body of land
called Monster Island, a kind of Lion Country Safari for
monsters, with special electronic devices designed to keep
Godzilla, Minya, Rodan, Mothra, Angurus (here called Angi-
las), Gorosaurus, Manda, Spiega and Varan from either
swimming or flying back to civilization.   This Monster Island plot device would eventually prove convenient for the
Toho writers.   Now whenever Godzilla's aid was needed to
save the world he could be easily reached, returning to
Monster Island after his work was completed.

Beneath Monster Island (also known as Ogasawara Island) a group of scientists observe the activities of the behemoths on monitor screens, while scientists study the marine life swimming about the island.   But the forces guarding
the various monsters are not effective against a group of
invading aliens called Kilaaks, who use gas to subdue the
creatures and compel them to follow their own orders.
Soon Rodan is invading Moscow, Gorosaurus is breaking
through the streets of Paris beneath the Arc de Triomphe,
Mothra (in caterpillar form) is on the crawl against Peking,
London is under Manda's attack, Baragon charges through
Paris and Godzilla is crunching his way through New York.

It is soon discovered that the Kilaaks have also im-
bedded mini-transceivers in the necks of the human inhabitants of Ogasawara Island, transforming them into science-
created zombies.   While the Earth people are preoccupied
with the rampaging monsters, the Kilaaks operate from a
secret subterranean base in Japan.   Their goal is to destroy
the Earth's space program.   Soon Tokyo (which had obviously been rebuilt again since a Toho monster's last attack)
becomes the target of Godzilla, who is promptly joined by
Manda, Rodan and Mothra.

A Japanese scientist finally deduces that the main
control transmitter of the Kilaaks is located on the moon.
Rocketing to the moon, Earthmen destroy the Kilaaks' lunar
headquarters, after which the aliens assume their true forms
of minuscule spores.   No longer under the Kilaaks' power,

Opposite: From left to right, Mothra [as caterpillar], Baragon, Rodan [flying], Spiega [spider], Angurus, Minya, Ghidrah [three-headed, flying], Godzilla, Varan [background],
Manda [serpent], and Gorosaurus in Toho's multi-monster
extravaganza, Kaijû Sôshingeki (1968), seen in the United
States as Destroy All Monsters.

Godzilla and the other invading monsters prepare to attack
their former alien masters.

The final scenes of Kaijû Sôshingeki take place upon
the familiar monster stomping grounds of Mount Fuji. Indeed it is a weird sight as Godzilla, Minya, Angurus, Varan,
Manda, Rodan, Mothra, Spiega, Baragon and Gorosaurus as-
semble for the attack. Yet the adamantine Kilaaks are still
not defeated. Calling upon one final monster, they see
Ghidrah appear in the sky and swoop down to battle the
Earth's mightiest monsters. In one of Tsuburaya's more
spectacular monster battles, Godzilla and company descend
upon Ghidrah in full force. Even little Minya contributes to
the foray, choking one of the space monster's necks with a
radioactive smoke ring. In the past Ghidrah was defeated
by the team of Godzilla and Rodan alone; against this squad
of behemoths there is no way he can survive.

After the defeat of Ghidrah, Godzilla finds the Kilaaks'
base of operations, smashing it with a mighty kick, permit-
ting the cold air to change them into tiny spores. Once
again mankind has been saved by monsters that once threatened to destroy it. In the final shot of the picture we see
that all the monsters have resumed their idyllic existences
on Monster Island.

Kaijû Sôshingeki was Eiji Tsuburaya's last Godzilla
film. He died shortly afterwards during the filming of the
1969 Toho Godzilla entry Oru Kaijû Daishingeki ("All Monsters Attack"), a film which first played in the United States
two years later as Godzilla's Revenge [also, Terror of God-
zilla] courtesy of United Productions of America (UPA).
Perhaps it was due to Tsuburaya's death that Oru Kaijû
Daishingeki relied mostly upon stock footage (from Furankenshutain tai Baragon, Nankai no Dai Ketto, Gojira no Musuko
and Kingu Kongu no Gyakushu) with the new monster scenes less
spectacular than usual. There are no new scenes of monsters ripping through cities; most of the action takes place
on Monster Island. With Tsuburaya no longer at the special
effects helm, Inoshiro Honda directed a unique entry into the
series, one centering more upon story and characterization
than upon spectacle.

Opposite: Godzilla and son Minya pit their individual powers
against Spiega the monster spider in the excellent children's
fantasy, Oru Kaiju Daishingeki (Toho, 1969), released in the
United States as Godzilla's Revenge.

Oru Kaijû Daishingeki is actually a children's fantasy set not in the super-scientific Tokyo so often destroyed by the Japanese monsters but rather the smoggy, industrial, off-screen Tokyo. A young boy is constantly pestered by a neighborhood bully named Gabera and finds solace only in his daydreams. Surrounded by models of Godzilla and other monsters, the boy periodically fantasizes visiting Monster Island. There periodically he watches Baragon, Spiega, Ebirah, the giant mantises and birds, and observes as Godzilla himself battles monster after monster for survival. Godzilla's son Minya is also present. Like the boy, Minya is constantly chased by a scaly, tailless monster called, like the human bully, Gabera. Periodically Minya shrinks down to the boy's size and speaks to him, commenting on his father's battles with the other monsters and expressing verbally his fear of Gabera. Godzilla finally inspires Minya to shoot back up to monster size and face Gabera. After the coup de grace is administered to Gabera by Godzilla himself, the boy returns to his own world. There, inspired by the dawning bravery of Minya, he finds the courage to face and defeat his own version of Gabera.

The film is a thoroughly delightful fantasy for children with enough monster action to please fans of the more traditional Godzilla films. Honda's direction of the boy in the real world is sensitive with an understanding of a child's problems. His direction is also cagey; we are never told whether or not Godzilla or Monster Island actually exist within the universe of this film or if they--along with everything else in the seemingly endless Godzilla film saga--are merely fantasies alive on the screen and in a boy's active imagination. Unfortunately Oru Kaijû Daishingeki was marketed as a standard Godzilla opus, dumbfounding an unreceptive older audience unable to comprehend what Honda's ingenious picture was all about. To many such viewers the film, with its talking and size-changing Minya, remains the most ridiculous Godzilla adventure of all instead of one of the finest children's monster fantasies ever made.

Both Honda's and Tsuburaya's talents were missed in Gojira tai Hedora ("Godzilla vs. Hedorah"), a 1971 Godzilla vehicle directed by Yoshimitsu Banno and released in America the next year by AIP under the title Godzilla vs. the Smog Monster. (In Germany the picture was inappropriately retitled Frankensteins Kampf gegen die Teufelmonster--"Frankenstein's Struggle Against the Devil Monster.")

The picture was directed by Yoshimitsu Banno with special effects by Shokei Nakano.

Hedorah is a shapeless garbage heap created from the waste material of Japanese industry. His appearance in Gojira tai Hedora not only marked Toho's first attempt at relevance in a standard Godzilla film (Oro Kaijû Daishingeki notwithstanding) but also heralded a long line of unlikely new behemoths that would soon be appearing in the series. The so-called Smog Monster first appears in the water, a red-eyed blob that feeds on pollution and is capable of burning its victims with its acid touch. Soon Hedorah has grown to such proportions that it destroys two ships in the harbor, then focuses its crimson eyes upon the city. There, inhaling the acrid smoke polluting the skies, the pile of living sludge grows to a height of 200 feet and commences to evolve. Now able to fly like some filthy flying saucer, Hedorah soars through the skies, destroying living things by excreting sulfuric acid smog, releasing poisonous mud and disintegrating men to fleshless bones by scarlet rays shot from its eyes.

A young boy named Ken Yano (Hiroyuki Kawase) dreams that the city will be saved by Godzilla, which shortly afterwards the giant reptile does on Mount Fuji. Since his last appearance Godzilla has learned a new stunt; by curling his tail under him and blasting an exhaustlike flame from his mouth, the huge saurian actually propels himself through the air. The two monsters are soon engaged in a titatic struggle. Yet it is a human being, Ken's father Dr. Yano (Akira Yamauchi), who discovers the secret of destroying the Smog Monster. With a huge electrical machine Dr. Yano literally dehydrates the sludge creature, transforming it into a lifeless pile of mud and crusted filth. A miniature Hedorah rises out of the mound, only to be seized by Godzilla and destroyed by his fiery breath. Again Godzilla has saved the world.

The great days of Godzilla had passed. In his adventure with the Smog Monster there was less spectacle than ever before. Godzilla and Hedorah battled mostly in open areas where no miniature cities existed to raise the film's budget. Most assuredly Gojira tai Hedora was a programmer, a quickie vehicle to keep the character before the public. But the film was a success, promising yet more appearances by the spike-backed prehistoric monster.

Godzilla tai Gaigan (Godzilla vs. Gigan) was cranked
out the same year as Gojira tai Hedora and directed by the
the returning Jun Fukuda, who would also direct the next
two sequels.   By now the monsters themselves were the
real stars of the Godzilla films, their names taking prefer-
ence above those of the human players. · (A 1972 issue of
Japanese Film Quarterly lists the first four cast members
as "Godzilla, Anguirus, Gigan and King Ghidra. ")

Kotaka (Hiroshi Ishikawa), a cartoonist, discovers an
insidious plot originating at an amusement park called International Children's Land.   Among the strange attractions at
the park is a huge mechanized structure called Godzilla
Tower.   A small boy named Kubota is the head of this play-
land who apparently intends to use the sounds on two reels
of tape to stimulate the brains of the creatures on Monster
Island.   Both Godzilla and Angurus are aroused from their
hibernation on the island.   Soon Kotaka discovers that Kubota
and his associate have actually been possessed by aliens who,
once again, are bent upon conquering Earth via remote-con-
trolled monsters.   By now the aliens should have realized
the futility in such ambitions.

Ghidrah and Gigan, a new addition to Toho's monster
rostrum, are summoned from their current preying grounds
in the Hunter Nebula.   Gigan is an alien monster with great
hooklike claws, one red visorlike eye, horns surmounting the
head and neck, a bird beak, a dorsal fin and a type of buzz-
saw stomach.   Before long Tokyo again crumbles as the
Earth's champions Godzilla and Angurus pit their might
against the villainous Ghidrah and Gigan.   (Godzilla also engages his enemies in a verbal battle, for in this film the
King of Monsters has somehow gained the ability to speak
Japanese!)   The heroic Kotaka uses a laser to destroy Godzilla Tower, the aliens' headquarters, while Earth's monster
team vanquishes the two foreign monsters.

Two years later Godzilla would again be summoned
to save his planet in Gojira tai Megaro, which Cinema
Shares released in the United States as Godzilla vs. Megalon.   The print that I saw had no credits save for the film
title itself, as though Cinema Shares realized that the majority of viewers were too young to be concerned with such
trivialities.   Perhaps the releasing company was right; I
saw the movie at a Saturday afternoon kiddie matinee with
an audience that cheered each appearance of the mighty saurian and became absolutely enthralled over his every blast of

destructive breath. By 1976, when the picture first went into American release, Godzilla had assumed the superheroic niche once dominated on the screen by comic book heroes and cowboys. No one in the theatre even seemed to notice the absence of credits. (Germany calls the film King-Kong, dä Monen aus dem Weltall.)

Seatopians, survivors of the ancient Mu empire (last seen in Toho's Kaitei Gunkan) can no longer tolerate the nuclear bombs exploded by the scientists of the surface world. Already two-thirds of Seatopia has been destroyed by such nuclear testing. In retaliation the subterraneans summon Megalon, a monstrous insect who utilizes its drill-like head and appendages to dig up to the Earth's surface and attack Japan.

Two scientists have invented a silver-and-red robot colorfully christened Jet Jaguar. (Originally the robot's name was to have been Red Baron; it was dropped since the name had already been preempted by the German World War I flying ace.) In one fantastic scene Jet Jaguar, now under his own control, shoots up to the height of the standard Toho monster, surprising even his creators. The explanation is simple enough; the robot had been equipped with a self-preservation device and the only way to survive against Megalon was by growing to giant size!

Rocketing through the air like Superman, Jet Jaguar reaches Monster Island, where Godzilla, Rodan and Angurus are living their peaceful existences. Communicating via sign language with the famous reptile, Jet Jaguar elicits Godzilla's aid. Soon both of them are in a slapstick battle against Megalon and, returning from the previous movie to lend physical support to the huge insect, the alien Gigan. In some delightfully absurd scenes Godzilla uses claw signals to communicate with his robot partner, assumes the poise of a martial arts expert and leaps at his opponents feet first in defiance of every law of gravity. With the defeat of both Megalon and Gigan, Jet Jaguar shakes Godzilla's paw in thanks, after which the reptile heads back toward Monster Island. Jet Jaguar, the threat of Megalon ended, shrinks back to his normal height and again submits to the control of his creators. The robot was an impressive character but did not return for a sequel.

Yet Godzilla did in 1975's Gojira tai Mechagojira (Godzilla vs. Mechagodzilla), which introduced two new monsters to the Toho stock company. The first of these is the legendary King Seeser, a bipedal, shaggy lion monstrosity. According to the beliefs of the Okinawans, two monsters will someday appear--King Seeser included--to save them from danger. A previously lost cave harbors a wall painting of the two battling monsters along with an effigy of King Seeser.

The second of the new monsters offered audiences two Godzillas for the price of one admission. Mechagodzilla rises from Mount Fuji to create havoc in Tokyo (a city which by all rights should have been vacated considering the number of monster attacks it has suffered since 1954). He is a cyborg, a silvery metallic robot in the image of Godzilla himself, built from "space titanium" and controlled by the perpetrators of so many recent villainies in the Japanese science fiction movies, invaders from another planet. Once more the fate of Earth rests in the claws of its monsters.

The human hero and heroine of Gojira tai Mechagojira follow the instructions carved into the King Seeser statue, taking it to a shrine in the Azumi Castle and allowing the rising sun to shine upon it. A beam of light streaks from the statue's eye, hitting a seaside rock from which emerges the living King Seeser. Presently Godzilla gets the message that his help is needed. Again vacating Monster Island, leaving behind Angurus and its other resident creatures, Godzilla joins King Seeser in Tokyo to thrash it out with his gleaming mechanical counterpart. Before the alien invaders and their base of operations are destroyed, Godzilla overcomes the deadly Mechagodzilla, pushing it into the sea. The film was released in America as Godzilla vs. the Bionic Monster in 1977; in Germany as King Kong gegen Godzilla.

Mechagodzilla was far from destroyed, however. The robot returned to the screen along with Godzilla and the saurian's initial director, Inoshiro Honda, for a direct sequel made in 1976, Terror of Mechagodzilla (also known as Revenge of Mechagodzilla). Yes, once more the story pivoted about an alien plot to conquer the world, this time the invaders originating from the "Third Planet in the Black Hole in Space." Maintaining the series' present format of introducing new monsters, Terror of Mechagodzilla unveiled Titanosaurus, a bipedal dinosaur with a horned head, fishlike tail, finned back and an elongated neck that made him even more skyscraping than Godzilla himself. (Actually the name is ludicrous to paleontologists. Indeed there is a dinosaur of the genus Titanosaurus. It was discovered in 1877, almost a century before Godzilla's latest adversary appeared

upon the screen. The actual Titanosaurus was a sauropod
dinosaur, long-necked and quadrupedal, bearing no similarity
to the creature in Terror of Mechagodzilla.) Godzilla was
again to encounter some stiff competition.

A bathyscaphe sent to retrieve the wreckage of Mechagodzilla is destroyed by the monster Titanosaurus. A scientist named Dr. Mafune had been ousted from the academic
society after he discovered the living dinosaur because of his
desire to control it. Now living in the mountains with his
lovely daughter, Dr. Mafune continues his dinosaur-control-
ling experiments. Enter the aliens, who finance the scientist, then salvage and reconstruct Mechagodzilla, improving
it with Mafune's control invention. When another bathyscaphe
investigates the disappearance of the first, the remote-con-
trolled Titanosaurus attacks the craft and is repelled only by
a supersonic wave oscillator built by the Ocean Exploitation
Institute and Interpol. Later Mafune's daughter, Katsura,
destroys the oscillator but is killed in the process. Her
corpse is then returned to life by the aliens as a cyborg.

Despite all the science fiction turns in the plot, this
was Godzilla's film. Soon he is traversing the ocean to attack his mechanized duplicate and this other monster from
the prehistoric past. Against both Mechagodzilla and Titanosaurus, however, Godzilla, the Earth's guardian, is apparently doomed. Then, the oscillator is finally repaired, its
vibrations rendering Titanosaurus inoperative. Now it is
Godzilla vs. Mechagodzilla once more. When the Interpol
agent enters the aliens' lair and destroys both Dr. Mafune
and his cyborg daughter, the mind-control device is also
destroyed. On his own, Mechagodzilla proves no match for
the living monster that inspired his creation.

Godzilla has proven to be the movies' most enduring
monster. He has an unprecedented 15 authorized films to
his credit, a distinction to which not even the Wolf Man, Invisible Man and Mummy can lay claim. And while such im-
mensely popular horrors as Mr. Hyde may have skulked
through more individual films than the great Japanese reptile, these films did not comprise a single series. With the
exception of the original Gojira, none of Godzilla's motion
pictures has achieved classic status; yet they continually
provide youthful audiences with unpretentious escapism as
these lovable Toho behemoths clash in some of the most preposterous and entertaining battles ever filmed.

In 1977, however, Toho decided that another overhaul of their colossal sea monster might be in order.   Most assuredly considering the success of the Paramount remake of King Kong, Toho announced that Godzilla would return to his former, menacing image in a spectacular high-budgeted remake in full color of their original Gojira.   Thus it was that Toho issued advance publicity for what may become the greatest film yet to star the flame-breathing saurian--Godzilla 1980.

Godzilla may be the newcomer to the movie monster pantheon; but to an entire new generation of horror, science fiction and fantasy buffs, he (or she) is most certainly the King (or Queen) of the Monsters.

GODZILLA RAIDS AGAIN

Toho International did not limit its reptilian leading monster to motion picture appearances.   Godzilla has taken his King of the Monsters status into Japanese television in at least three different series, all involving superheroes and gigantic adversaries.   For the "Ultra Q" series Godzilla was revamped with a new head sporting fangs and hair and renamed Gomesu (also known as Gometius).   A second Toho series "Ultra Man," made during the mid-1960s and featuring a skyscraping superhero who defends the Earth from enormous monsters, featured a disguised Godzilla.   A mad scientist creates a monster called Kira (played by Godzilla with a flaring frill protecting his neck) to be greater than the Loch Ness monster.   There is a battle between hero and monster with Kira going through the familiar Godzilla routines.   Ultra Man finally tears off Kira's neck frill (dispelling any doubts as to just who this monster really was) and the science-spawned creature, weakened by this injury, falls over dead.   Godzilla's fans saw through the deception. The latest Toho series featuring Godzilla was "Zone Fighter," in which the King of the Monsters and the titled hero combine their strength and powers to defend the Earth against Ghidrah, Gigan and an entire zoo of new monstrosities created for the show.

American television has generally ignored the famed saurian, though Godzilla has been spoofed on "Sinister Cinema," "Cos" (Godzilla doing a foot powder commercial) and the cartoon series "The Flintstones" ("Son of Rockzilla") and "Frankenstein, Jr." ("Gadzooka").

Godzilla has also invaded a small number of films
outside the Toho canon. Hollywood Boulevard (New World
Pictures, 1976), a spoof of exploitation films, was made in
color and directed by Joe Dante and Allan Arkush. It featured a female "Godzinna" on an outdoor set of a movie
studio. "Godzinna" was portrayed by Rob Short who built
this fairly accurate Godzilla suit which made its first appearance at a science fiction convention masquerade. Short
frequently appears as Godzilla at parties and other functions.
In 1977, John Belushi wore Short's costume to host the television network premiere of Godzilla vs. Megalon and also in
a mock interview on the show "Saturday Night." In the latter appearance he stomped on a miniature city for the benefit of his fans.

Amateur film-makers have not ignored Godzilla. The
Fire Monsters (1959) was my color version of Gojira
no Gyakushyu, only set in Chicago and using animated models
for the monsters. I used Godzilla again to battle another
famous movie monster in Son of Tor (1964). Britain's Delta
SF Film Group created its own color film called Son of Godzilla in 1963. And in 1969 Marvin Newland filmed one of
the most unusual Godzilla opuses of all, the animated cartoon Bambi Meets Godzilla. Bambi is seen frolicking in the
woods until Godzilla's huge hind foot squashes him against
the ground; the entire film lasts a total of 30 hysterical seconds
and was seen in the film Fantastic Animation Festival (1977).

An authorized Godzilla novel based on the first two
movies and written by Shigeru Kayama was published in
Japan. A 27-meter Godzilla robot was written into the
American novel To the Land of the Electric Angel (1976).
There have been numerous picture books published in Japan
devoted to Godzilla and other Japanese monsters including
his Daiei competitor Gamera. The books abound in photographs of the various creatures and, for the hard core Japanese monster devotees, cutaway shots of the creatures displaying their hypothetical internal organs. "Ballad of Godzilla," a poem by Richard Morgana, was published in Famous Monsters of Filmland no. 102 (October 1973).

The first authorized Godzilla comic books were published in Japan and are rare items for American collectors.
During the mid-1970s the Marvel Comics Group was ready
to negotiate with Toho for a black and white Godzilla, King
of the Monsters comic magazine. When rival company Atlas
Comics (Seaboard Periodicals) offered Toho more money to

produce the book, Marvel put its sample Godzilla pages into storage and used Bob Larkin's cover painting for the fifth issue (February 1975) of Monsters of the Movies magazine. Ironically, Atlas went out of business, leaving the Godzilla project in limbo. Marvel finally secured the rights for a Godzilla, King of the Monsters comic book, the first issue of which was dated August 1977. In "The Coming!," written by Doug Moench and drawn by Herb Trimpe, Godzilla bursts free from his long confinement in an iceberg and attacks the North American continent. He is fought by the agents of SHIELD, an organization of superagents.

The Monster Times, aside from determining the popularity status of the Japanese saurian, has kept his image before his demanding public. In addition to publishing articles devoted to the character, The Monster Times has starred Godzilla in a number of special features. The Big G Speaks was a series of comic strip style columns lampooning humorist Will Rogers, with Godzilla spouting his folksy (and destructive) solutions to today's problems. "The Monsters That Devoured Canarsie," by Dean Latimer, was a comic strip spoof of Godzilla, Ghidrah, Mothra, Rodan, King Kong and other giant monsters in The Monster Times no. 26 (September 1973). Various articles in the paper have been purportedly written by Godzilla, while the 23rd issue (June 1973) was devoted almost entirely to the spike-backed creature.

Cartoonist Scott Shaw created his own Godzilla-inspired monstrosity in "The Incredible, Edible Invasion of Earth!" for his You-All Gibbon, the Junk-Food Monkey comic strip. The story, which appeared in the second issue (1977) of Mike Friedrich's "ground level" comic book Quack!, introduced Dogzilla, a towering Japanese spike-backed canine wrecking a city in search of his "bionic bone."

A number of Godzilla records have been issued in Japan, featuring music and songs about the big saurian and his monster entourage and also his titanic roar. In America the song parody "Waltzing Godzilla" was part of the Dracula's Greatest Hits album. The Firesign Theatre spoofed Godzilla and the whole Japanese monster movie genre on the comedy album Not Insane (Columbia, 1972).

In Japan, Godzilla is a celebrity of the first rank, as famous as such movie screen superstars as Toshiro Mifune. The monster's scaly image on virtually any merchandised

item is enough to guarantee a sale. Even in the United
States, Godzilla, Ghidrah, Rodan, Baragon and Mechagodzilla
enter the home in form of model kits, toys, T-shirts and
the like. Variations on the Godzilla name and character
have even invaded the advertising world with some success:
Detroit radio station WWWW has publicized itself with a pic-
tured monster called "Quadzilla," while a California distributor of stereo equipment has promoted its product via a radio
commercial starring its own "Quadzilla" creature.

Where there is success there is often imitation.
With Godzilla proving himself to be one of the most successful monsters ever to stomp a city, it is not surprising that
a rival monster would build up his own following of fans at
a competing studio. Godzilla's main contender to the throne
of Emperor of the Japanese Monsters was also a prehistoric
reptile who enjoyed a similar though less enduring career.

GAMERA VS. GODZILLA

By 1966 the mighty Godzilla had already established
himself as a top box office draw in Japan. Daiei Motion
Pictures, which would become Toho's most serious rival in
the production of films about huge beasts rampaging through
mankind's cities, analyzed the Godzilla phenomenon and set
out to create their own saurian superstar. That year Daiei
released its historic Daikaiju Gamera (or simply Gamera),
which was released in the United States a few years later
by American International Pictures under the title Gammera
the Invincible.

Gamera (or Gammera as his name was spelled in this
singular case) is an enormous prehistoric turtle. Like Godzilla he can destroy whatever gets in his way by blasts of
flaming breath; his deafening roar also seems to have been
borrowed from Toho's King of the Monsters. The invincible
Gamera, like Godzilla, is actually a human actor in a rubber monster suit, and as with Angurus and Baragon, the
actor often finds it more comfortable to stomp and lumber
on two legs rather than crawling about on hands and knees.
When it suits him Gamera pulls his head and limbs into his
impenetrable shell, fires out flaming jets which enable him
to spin, rise and fly through the air like a living flying
saucer. (Not until he met the Smog Monster in 1971 was
Godzilla to perform such an aerodynamically improbable
stunt.)

The giant prehistoric turtle Gamera in his debut in Daikaiju Gamera (Daiei, 1966), released in the United States as Gammera the Invincible [in subsequent movies the American spelling reverted to "Gamera"].

Unlike the Toho monsters, such Daiei giants as Gamera somehow lack a logic of conception and design.   Preposterous though Godzilla and his Toho cousins may be, they work within the constructs of their own make-believe world; once we suspend our disbelief and accept that world (in which prehistoric monsters could attain such scientifically impossible sizes, could breathe fire and could survive into our modern world) the concept of Godzilla seems logical enough.

Gamera, however, and his Daiei contemporaries seem a trifle off, oftentimes more the product of some electronics or machine shop rather than an out-of-whack Nature.   Living creatures are often depicted with laser beams and jet exhausts, with heads in the shape of oversized hand tools or bodies mimmicking man-made aircraft.   In Gamera's case the presence of only a minimal number of teeth in his gaping jaws gives one the impression that his designer never once opened a natural history book or considered the fact that the giant turtle's mouth should bear some resemblance to that of an authentic prehistoric reptile.   The two huge tusks in the lower jaw serve no function at all and come dangerously close to impaling the eyes every time Gamera shuts his mouth.   Nevertheless, the oftentimes erroneous aspects of the Daiei monsters seemingly go unnoticed by the juvenile audiences for which the movies were intended, with the ancient turtle rivaling the celebrated Godzilla in popularity.

Daikaiju Gamera parallels the original Gojira (Godzilla) in many ways.   Both films were shot in black and white and incorporated American actors (Albert Dekker and Brian Donlevy for Gammera the Invincible) in footage shot for United States release.   Gamera, like Godzilla, has been in hibernation since prehistoric times, the former frozen solid at the arrival of the Ice Age and freed as a result of a nuclear explosion.   In Daikaiju Gamera, his first in an impressively long list of feature-length films, the giant turtle was an outright menace, just as his spiny precursor had been in his premiere Toho adventure.

Gamera is freed from his millions of years of slumber when United States SAC aircraft destroy an enemy plane carrying a nuclear bomb over the Arctic.   Presently Gamera, angered at having been thrust into a twentieth-century world, destroys a ship, the Arctic research base and is soon plowing through another Japanese city.   Gamera thrives on fire and consumes the flames resulting from his attack while the Japanese military forces are unable to drive him

away. Explosive charges finally flip the turtle over, trap-
ping him on his back. A newly invented freezing bomb renders the monster even more helpless. Yet the resourceful
Gamera is not without his own unique defense; raising his
body temperature, Gamera melts the ice, then becomes a
reptilian flying saucer and zooms away.

    Noriaki Yuasa's direction and Yonesaburo Tsukiji's
special effects of the actor in the Gamera suit devastating
the miniature sets are in direct imitation of the Toho product. But the climax of Daikaiju Gamera is completely atypi-
cal of Godzilla's studio. Pooling their resources, the major governments of the world put their "Plan Z" into effect.
Gamera is baited with a trail of flaming oil into the nose-
cone of a spaceship, which promptly blasts off on a one-way
journey to the planet Mars.

    Yet Gamera--like Godzilla--did not conclude his ca-
reer after but a single picture. In the climax of Daikaiju
Gamera the shelled reptile was not destroyed and his trek
through outer space could well be interpreted as merely a
cliffhanger. Within the same year Gamera returned, both to
Earth and to the movies, in the first of many sequels Gamera tai Barugon ("Gamera vs. Barugon"), which AIP-TV
released in the United States as War of the Monsters. (The
movie is known misleadingly as Godzilla--Der Drache aus
dem Dschungel in Germany to capitalize on the Toho monster
king's name.)

    Barugon is not to be confused with Toho's Baragon,
though it seems as if the possibility of such confusion was
not entirely unintended by Daiei. Like Baragon, Barugon is
a quadrupedal reptile with a sharp horn surmounting the
snout. Yet while the Toho monster's horn glowed bright in
the darkness, Barugon's similar ability was shifted to the
spines protecting its back.

    Gamera tai Barugon was directed in color by Shigeo
Tanaka and included some mismatching black-and-white footage from the first Gamera film. A meteor strikes the
Mars-bound rocket ship containing the imprisoned turtle, de-
flecting the craft's course back to Earth. Gamera is back
on his own turf to encounter the first of his many monstrous
adversaries.

    The picture, however, was mainly concerned with
Barugon. An enormous opal is taken from a cave on a

primitive island. The opal, however, is actually a strange
egg and soon out hatches baby Barugon who promptly grows
to dinosaurian proportions. Soon the adult Barugon is rampaging through the city streets, blasting buildings apart with
his dragonlike breath, destroying whatever touches his lengthy
clublike tongue and freezing whatever comes within range of
the colorful rainbows generated by his glowing dorsal spines.
Finally Gamera is attracted to the monster by the radiance
of its rainbow and is engaging Barugon in a conflict that
ends in the turtle's being turned over on its back and frozen.
The world is now at Barugon's mercy.

Barugon's only weakness is water and helicopters constantly bathe him in tranquilizing sprays. Inevitably, however, this fails and it is Gamera's task first to thaw himself out and they soar into the sky in pursuit of Barugon.
Still not the hero he would become in later films, Gamera
does his share for Japanese urban renewal as he fights the
dinosaur-like reptile and forces him into the sea, where,
powerless, he sinks to the bottom. In his own way Gamera
has saved the world.

Gamera tai Barugon, like the second Godzilla movie,
was generally a serious picture with none of the nonsense
that would characterize the later films in the giant turtle's
series. The actual silliness commenced with the second sequel, Gamera tai Gyaos ("Gamera vs. Gyaos"), which like
all the succeeding Gamera epics, was made in color, directed by Noriaki Tyasa and issued in the United States by
AIP-TV (as The Return of the Giant Monsters; the picture
is also known as Gamera vs. Gaos and in Southeast Asia as
Boyichi and the Super-Monster.) Gamera was not the only
giant monster to return. The picture introduced Gyaos, a
Rodan-style bat-winged horror equipped with laser beam
breath. Gyaos' physical design was typical of the Daiei
monsters, with eyes seemingly misplaced on its angular
head and a mouth that dropped open like a trapdoor. Nevertheless he proved a more than capable foe of Gamera, now
an heroic defender of Earth. Gyaos could emit a yellow
smog fire repellent from his chest to combat the turtle's
flame breath. Their battle was augmented in the film by
scenes from Gamera's first two motion pictures and the
shelled saurian's own theme song.

Gamera's movie career was just beginning. In 1968's
Gamera tai Uchi Kaijû Bairusu ("Gamera vs. the Outer Space
Monster Viras") [also, Gamera tai Viras] the turtle briefly

returned to his villainous role, as a band of invading squid-like aliens control his will and use him to lash out against humanity. The plot was familiar to Godzilla fans who had watched the Toho sea monster similarly manipulated by aliens that same year in Kaijû Sôshingeki (Destroy All Monsters). (Perhaps not so coincidentally AIP-TV released Gamera tai Uchi Kaijû Bairusu as Destroy All Planets.) Since the Gamera adventures were made for children it is not surprising that two young boys succeed in severing the bond that holds the turtle's mind. Once again Gamera plunges into battle, this time against the gigantic cephalopod Viras. For a while Gamera seems doomed as Viras rams the tip of his dagger shaped head into the turtle's back. But Gamera survives, killing Viras and heroically departing to return in the next sequel.

Gamera came back to his fans in Gamera vs. Guiron (1969), issued to American television as Attack of the Monsters. The story was an unusual one considering the youthful market at which it was aimed. Beautiful alien women kidnap two Japanese boys and take them via flying saucer to their home world on the opposite side of the sun. There they plan to eat the boys' brains! On the alien planet the boys observe as Guiron, the aliens' protector, whose head is actually a gigantic knife blade, battles a whitish extraterrestrial version of Gyaos, cleanly slicing off the winged monster's head. Gamera, now established as a guardian of children, streaks through space to rescue the boys with his heroic theme song blaring in the background, but not before fighting Guiron and imbedding his cranium blade into the ground.

Gamera tai Daimaju Jaiga, or Gamera vs. Jiger, was the 1970 entry to the series, seen in America as Gamera vs. Monster X. (Southeast Asia knows the picture as Monsters Invade Expo '70 while in Germany the picture was misleadingly retitled Frankensteins Dämon bedroht die Welt-- "Frankenstein's Demon Threatens the World.") This latest Gamera opus was as much a travelogue as it was a fantasy, given the timely setting of Japan's Expo '70. Gamera battles a horned dinosaur type of female monster called Jiger on a rocky island. Jiger's weapons include a deadly heat ray, which she uses to temporarily defeat Gamera. Then, using jets that shoot from beneath her horny neck shield, Jiger streaks off the island. Soon she is rising from the sea, destroying a ship and invading Expo '70 (which has already been given enough documentary-style footage in the film to

make a separate short subject apart from the Gamera movie)
in pursuit of a mysterious statue.

Gamera arrives in time to save not only the world
and humanity but also Expo '70, though not before getting
paralyzed and then impregnated by Jiger. Now the host of
a Jiger egg, Gamera remains helplessly motionless as the
infant offspring hatch and feed off the turtle's blood. It
again becomes the mission of two small boys to enter Gamera's body and destroy Jiger's offspring. An electric
charge reviving Gamera, Daiei's champion of Earth kills the
female who had gotten him into monstrous trouble in the final climactic battle.

Gamera tai Shinkai Kaijû Jigura, or Gamera vs. Zigra, was made by Daiei in 1971 with the giant turtle again
thrashing with a prehistoric monster. Zigra was a sleek,
silvery flying fish that resembled a futuristic aircraft as
much as it did a living, breathing creature from our own
Earth's past. Like so many of Zigra's contemporaries he
shoots death rays from his toothy beaked mouth. The battle
between Gamera and Zigra, as with the earlier conflicts in
the giant turtle's series, are comical while being exciting,
yet never become the burlesque bashes characterizing the
later Godzilla movies. Gamera grasps the metallic-looking
Zigra, overturns him and rides the creature across the
water like a surfboard. Later Zigra pins the rocks hurled
by Gamera onto the pointed armor encasing his head. In a
final act of heroism Gamera unleashes his all-out attack
against Zigra and tosses him from the shore back into the
sea, never to emerge again.

In 1971 the film Gamera vs. Leoman was announced
as going into production, but whether or not it was ever
completed remains a mystery. Still, the prehistoric turtle
has amassed a respectable number of screen credits, not
as many as Godzilla whose series has survived into the
latter 1970s, but enough to give the Toho superstar some
serious competition. Although the two monsters never actually met on screen, Gamera utilized all of his monstrous
tricks in trying to wrest the King-of-the-Monsters crown
from Godzilla's scaly head. Godzilla may have won this
battle for popularity, but Gamera, the jet-propelled turtle
from Earth's prehistoric past, certainly met defeat fighting
to the last. Of such an effort a monster need not be
ashamed.

BESIDES THE MOTION PICTURES,

plays, radio and television programs, novels and short
stories, comic books and records that chronicle the life his-
tories of Godzilla, King Kong, the Wolf Man, Mummy and
their infamous brethren, merchandise bearing their images
have become familiar items in retail stores the world over.

The Wolf Man and King Kong have been reworked into costumes and patches; the Mummy and the Wolf Man have
leered at us from rings, bubble bath dispensers, Glo-Heads,
and Nestlés' "Spook Group" flavors; there have been Black
Lagoon Creature and Wolf Man paint-a-statues; Creature,
Mummy and Wolf Man bendable figures, swizzle sticks,
spoons and Horrorscope Viewers; mechanical toys in the
form of Godzilla, Baragon, King Kong, the Phantom of the
Opera and Wolf Man; puzzles of Mr. Hyde, the Mummy,
Quasimodo, Wolf Man, Phantom and Creature; glow pictures,
toy figures, iron-ons, stick-on stamps, buttons, photo printing sets, paint-by-number sets, candy, wallets, pencil
sharpeners and wall plaques of the Mummy, Phantom, Creature and Wolf Man; T-shirts and games boasting the Wolf
Man, Godzilla and Kong; and model kits, masks, calendars,
greeting cards, trading cards, posters and play money featuring the Wolf Man, Kong, Hyde, Creature, Phantom and
Mummy.

The monsters are definitely a part of our culture,
these men turned beast by the quaff of a bubbling drug or
exposure to the beams of a full moon, horrors that stiffly
walk from millenia-old coffins or haunt the darkest catacombs
of an opera house, or behemoths born in another age only to
awaken to vent their anger against an alien man-made world.
We might use our silver bullets, our torches, our biplanes
and oxygen destroyers and for a while it will seem as
though we've purged the Earth of their awesome presences.
Yet despite the seemingly permanent destructions we deal
them, the werewolves, mummies and gargantuan apes and
lizards somehow manage to return for another sequel. And
for that, those of us who so highly revere these monsters
can indeed be thankful.

INDEX

Abbott, Bud 27-30, 37, 45, 99-102, 147-9, 185-6, 258, 271-2, 324

Abbott, Richard 80

"Abbott and Costello" 38, 121, 184, 273

Abbott and Costello in Africa see Africa Screams

Abbott and Costello Meet Dr. Jekyll and Mr. Hyde 100-2, 272

Abbott and Costello Meet Frankenstein (Abbott and Costello Meet the Ghosts) xi, 19, 27-30, 34, 36, 39, 147, 185, 260, 272

Abbott and Costello Meet the Invisible Man 148-50

Abbott and Costello Meet the Mummy 185-7

Abbott et Costello contre Frankenstein (Abbott et Costello et les monstruos) see Abbott and Costello Meet Frankenstein

Abrams, Leon 179

Ackerman, Forrest J (Spencer Strong, K. Vazau Virlup) xii, 19, 40, 43, 219, 253, 358, 380

Adachi, Shinsei 154

Adams, Jane 22

Adams, Julia 263-4

Adams, Neal 44

Adams, Nick 389

Adamson, Al 66

Addams, Dawn 103

Addobati, Giuseppe 245

Adkins, Dan 367

Adult Version of Dr. Jekyll and Mr. Hyde, The 122

Adult Version of Jekyll and Hide, The 107, 110

Adult Version of The Hunchback of Notre Dame, The 225

Adventure Unlimited see White Pongo

Adventures of Jerry Lewis, The 184, 365

"Adventures of Rin-Tin-Tin, The" 292

Adventures of the Spirit, The 37, 203, 248

Africa Screams 324-5

"After King Kong Fell" 359

Agar, John 102, 266, 268, 354

Agrama, Frank 355

Aguirre, Javier 224

Ainuda, Satoru 326

Alazraki, Benito 34

Alland, William 259-60

Allen, David 362-3

Allen, Irwin 292

Allman, Sheldon 39

Almanaque Lobisomem 42

Almanaque Múmia 195

Along the Moonbeam Trail 285

Amazing Transparent Man, The 154

Ames, Ramsay 177

Ancira, Carlos 34

Andersen, Dick 36

Andrei, Franco 106

Andrews, John 31

Andru, Ross 160

Angel, Heather 56

Angus, Robert 248

Ankers, Evelyn xv, 9-10, 146

Ankhesenamon 164-5

Annett, Paul 67

Anobile, Richard J.　123
Aparo, Jim　255
Ape (A*P*E)　342-5, 356
"Ape Call"　324
Ape: Monster of the Movies
　(Ape: The Kingdom of Kong)
　360
Arkush, Allan　403
Armstrong, Robert　298, 311,
　315, 321
Arnold, Jack　259, 263-6, 268
Arrants, Rod　344
asesino invisible, El　155
Asher, William　31
Ashton, Roy　62, 67, 187, 191,
　246-7
Ashwell, Lena　80
Askwith, Robin　355
Aspi　218
Assignment Terror　see　El
　hombre que vino Ummo
Atoragon (Atoragon--Flying
　Supersub)　see　Kaitei Gun-
　kan
Atorthy, P.　217
Atragon　see　Kaitei Gunkan
Attack of the Giant Apes　356
Attack of the Mayan Mummy
　see　La Momia
Attack of the Monsters　see
　Gamera tai Guiron
Attack of the Puppet People
　103, 278
Atwill, Lionel　23
Aubert, Lenore　29
Auerbach, Arnold M.　359
Augen der Mumie, Die　198
Aukin, Liane　246
Aured, Carlos　202
Aveco, Greg　183
Aztec Mummy, The　see　La
　Momia
Aztec Mummy vs. the Human
　Robot, The　see　La Momia
　contra el Robot humano

Babcock, Dwight V.　179
Baby Kong　343
Badshah Dampati　221
Baggot, King　84
Bahrenburg, Bruce　360
Baker, Rick　281, 340, 343-4,
　347, 349-50, 355, 363
Baker, Roy Ward　109
Baker, Russel　359
Balderston, John L.　165
Baledon, Rafael　165
"Ballad of Godzilla"　403
Ballbusch, Peter　96
Bambi Meets Godzilla　403
Bamo, Yoshimitsu　396-7
Bandmann, Daniel E.　78-9
Bara, Theda　210
Barbera, Joseph　114, 155
Barbour, Bruce　184
Barker, Lex　154
Barnabas, Quentin and Dr.
　Jekyll's Son　122
Barr, George　281
Barrault, Jean-Louis　117
Barrier, Edgar　241
Barrows, George　329, 361, 363
Barry, John　371
Barrymore, John　85-9, 91-2,
　94-5, 98, 106, 143
Bart, Lionel　119, 209
Barthelme, Donald　253
Barton, Charles T.　27, 324
Basketball Jones　357
Bass, Miles　31
Basserman, Albert　84, 144
Bates, Ralph　110-11
Batman and Robin　153
Battista, Vincenzo　208
Battle of the Astros　see　Kaiju
　Daisenso
Battle of the Monsters　see
　Sandai Kaiju Chikyu Kessen
Bava, Mario　343
Beach Boys　43
Beach Girls and the Monster,
　The　280
"Beany and Cecil"　291
Beast, The　see　King Kong
　(1933 film)
Beast Must Die, The　67
Beast with the Red Hands, The
　40, 122
"The Beatles"　225
Beatty, Clyde　324
Beauty and the Beast　31
"Beauty and the Brute"　367
Beck, John　332-3
Becker, Denise　209
Beebe, Ford　140, 146

Beery, Wallace 288-9, 291, 293
Beggs, Lee 198
Bei Vollmond Mord see Ly-canthropus
Bell, Ralph 372
Bellamy, Ralph xv, 9
Belushi, John 403
Benham, Harry 83-4
Bennet, Spencer G. 153
Benny, Jack 121
Benson, John 253
Benveniste, Bob 39
Beranger, Clara S. 85-7
Berendt, Allan 31-2
Berg, Cherney 372
Berg, Jon 357
Bergman, Ingrid 96
Bermejo, Luis 370
Bernhard, Jack 326
Bertin, Louise (Angélique) 208
Bertrand, Sergeant 61-2
Berwick, Irvin 279
Beswick, Martine 110-11
Betty Boop, M.D. 114
Bey, Turhan 174-5
Bezaire, Bruce 128
Big G Speaks, The 404
"Big Party, The" 355
Biggest Fight on Earth, The see Sandai Kaiju Chikyu Kessen
Bikini Beach 31
Bionic Kong, The 343
Birdwell, Russell 361
Bissell, Whit 59
Black Dragon of Manzanar see G-Men vs. the Black Dragon
Black Scorpion, The 305
Black Zoo 329
Blaisdell, Jackie 277
Blaisdell, Paul 276-9
Blake, Alfonso Corona 34-5
Blake, Dennis 199
Blakley, Susan 343
Blanche of Nevers see The Duke's Daughter; or The Hunchback of Paris
Bloch, Robert 41, 253, 359
Blom, August 82
Blond Gorilla see White Pongo

Blood 31-2
Blood from the Mummy's Tomb 193-4
Blood of Dracula's Castle 66
Blood of Frankenstein see Dracula vs. Frankenstein (1971)
Blood of the Werewolf see I Was a Teenage Werewolf
"Blood Relatives" 40-1
Blood Suckers, The see Dr. Terror's Gallery of Horrors
Blue Angel 202
Blue Demon 34-6, 64, 201-2
Bluemke, Ralph C. 183
"Bob Cummings Show" 121
Body Disappears, The 153
Bolognese, D. 208-9
Bolton, John 64
Bonafede, Carl 43
Boni, F. de 208
Bono, Cher 346
Bono, Sonny 121
Bonomo, Joe 214-5
Bonzo Dog Band 43
Bookworm, The 114
Bookworm Turns, The 114
Boring, Wayne 365
Bose, Amal 99
Bourgoise, Anicet 207
Boy Who Cried Werewolf, The 67
Boyichi and the Super-Monster see Gamera tai Gyaos
Brahm, John 54
Brain of Frankenstein, The see Abbott and Costello Meet Frankenstein
Brannon, Fred C. 153
Bresslaw, Bernard 103
"Bride of Congo, The" 369-70
Brides of Dr. Jekyll, The see El secreto del Doctor Orloff
Bridges, Jeff 346
Briefer, Dick 227
Briscoe, Don 37
Brocal, Jaime 128
Brocani, Franco 340
Brodrick, Susan 111
Bromberg, J. Edward 145
Brown, Dr. Barnum 284
Brown, Bob 125
Brown, Himan 116, 251

Brown, Judy 370
Browning, Rico 261, 263, 266-7, 269, 271, 280
Bruce, Virginia 143
Brute Force 284, 291
Brzezinski, Anthony 107, 114
Buchanan, Larry 279
Buchanan and Accles 274
Buck, David 194-5
Buck, Frank 324
Bucklige und die Tänzerin, Der 210
Bucklige von Soho, Der 224
Buddy's Lost World 291
Burch-Pfeiffer, Charlotte 207
Burgeois, Gerard 197
Burke, John 184, 194, 252
Burman, Ellis 248
Burman, Tom 67
Burns, Bob 36-8, 121, 202-3, 279, 343, 361, 363
Burr, Raymond 375, 378, 380
Buscema, John 274
Bushman 321
Busino, Orlando 42
Butler, Robert 155
Byrd, Larry M. 39
Byrd, Ralph 153
Byron, Arthur 162

Cabanne, Christy 170
Cabot, Bruce 300
Cagliostro see The Mummy (1932)
Cagney, James 222-3, 228, 245
Cahn, Edward L. 277
Calderón, René 201
Calvin, Tony 110
Cameron, Lon 123
Campana, Fabio 209
Campbell, Clay 99
"Campus Club" 279
Candidate, The 248
Capellani, Albert 210
Cappell, Barbara 50
Cardi, Pat 112
Cardona, René 155, 202, 248, 290
Cardoz, Johnny 64
Carew, Arthur Edmund 238
Carey, John 127

Carlson, Richard 263
Carnarvon, Lord 164
Carpenter, John 271
Carr, J. Comyne 80
Carr, John Dickson 293
Carradine, John 19, 22, 106, 146, 151
Carreras, Enrique 245
Carreras, Michael 191-3
Carry On Screaming 199
Carson, Johnny 121
Carter, Howard 164
casa degli orrori, La see House of Dracula
casa del terror, La 32-3, 200
Casey, Bernie 112
Cassidy, Jack 252
castillo de los momias de Guanajuarto, El 202
castillo de los monstruos, El 32, 271-2
Castrillo, Don 160
Ceri-Bibi 240
Chabelo y Pepito contra los monstruos 34, 183, 271
Chakrabarty, Amiya 221
Chaney, Lon 8, 11, 14, 18-9, 175, 204, 209-14, 216-8, 221-7, 229, 232-4, 236-40, 243-7, 251-4
Chaney, Lon, Jr. x, xv, 1, 7-18, 21-7, 29, 32-3, 37, 39, 42, 45-6, 54, 56, 64-6, 105, 173-8, 180-2, 184-5, 195, 200, 216, 218, 225-6, 232
Chang 295, 297, 311
Chang, Wah Ming 324
Chapman, Ben 261, 263, 266
charro del los calaveros, El 65
Chesterton, G. K. 156
Chikyu Saidaino Kessen see Sandai Kaiju Chikyu Kessen
Children of the Night 43
Chivra, Alex 6
Christine, Virginia 187
Cianelli, Eduardo 171
Cimino, G. T. 209
Citizen Kane 319
"City in the Sea" 280
City in the Sea see War-Gods of the Deep

Clampett, Bob 30, 113, 152,
    291, 357, 361
Clams on the Half Shell 341,
    361
Clark, Fred 192
Clarke, Gary 59
Clarke, Warren 225
Clavillazo 32, 272
Clemens, Brian 109
Climax, The xviii, 244
Clive, Colin 134
Closed Mondays 340
"Cobra and Mr. Hyde!, The"
    125
Cocharne, George 288
Cockrum, Dave 274
Coe, Peter 181
Cohen, Herman 58-9, 103,
    327, 329
"Colgate Comedy Hour, The"
    37, 159, 271-2
Collete, Hazel Ruth 319
Colline des desirs, La see
    The House on Bare Mountain
Collins, Edwin J. 210
Colon, Ernie 367
"Colonel March of Scotland
    Yard" 157
Comfort, Lance 103
Comic, The 106
"Coming!, The" 404
"Coming of the Hulk, The"
    124
"Concrete Jungle!, The" 125
Congo Pongo see White
    Pongo
Conklin, Chester 233
Conrad, Jess 329
Conried, Hans 160
Conway, Booth 210
Conway, Gary 61
Cook, Peter 113
Cooper, Merian C. 282, 294-
    300, 304, 311-12, 314-15,
    319-20, 326, 361
Cordeau, Sonya 246
Corman, Roger 279, 343
Corrigan, Ray "Crash" 278,
    325-6, 329
"Cos" 402
Cosby, Bill 44
Costello, Lou 27-30, 37, 45,
    99-102, 147-50, 185-6, 258,

271-2, 324
Count Down see Son of Dracu-
    la
Counterattack of the Monster
    see Gojira no Gyakushyu
Cozzi, Luigi 183
Crabbe, Buster 326
Crabtree, Arthur 103
Crain, William 112
Cravenna, Alfredo B. 150
Crawford, Katherine 159
Creation 293-4, 296-7, 313
Creation of King Kong, The
    360
Creature, The 274
"Creature, The" 275
"Creature from the Amazon"
    274
Creature from the Black Lagoon
    (film) 257-61, 263-66, 268,
    271, 275, 279, 281; (novels)
    273
"Creature from the Black La-
    goon, The" 274-5
Creature from the Haunted Sea,
    The 279
Creature from the Lagoon see
    Creature from the Black La-
    goon (film)
Creature of Destruction 279
"Creature of Uang-Ni, The"
    330-1
Creature Walks Among Us, The
    (The Creature Walks with a
    Brain) 268-71, 275
Crimes in the Wax Museum
    see Nightmare in Wax
"Crimes of Two-Face!, The"
    125
Cristadoro, Charles 324
Cruze, James 82-3
Cry of the Werewolf 57
Cuny, Alain 221
Curse of Frankenstein, The
    187
Curse of the Allenbys, The
    see She-Wolf of London
Curse of the Aztec Mummy,
    The see La maldición de la
    momia
Curse of the Mummy's Tomb,
    The (film) 191-3, 195;
    (novel) 195

Curse of the Pharaoh see
Pharaoh's Curse
Curse of the Werewolf, The
61-4, 67
Curtis, Alan 147
Curtis, Dan 37, 112, 117
Cushing, Peter 67, 109, 187-
9, 193

Daikaiju Baran 382
Daikaiju Gamera 405-8
Daitozoku 292
Damon, Mark 31
"Dance of the Sacred Ape,
The" 313
Dancer of Paris, The 217
Dane, Oscar 78
Danet, Jean 221
Danforth, Jim 293, 341, 343-
4, 351
Daniels, Harold 64
Dans les griffes de Dracula
see La noche de Walpurgis
Dante, Joe 403
Darasingh 331
Dargomyshchky, Aleksandre
208
"Dark Shadows" 37-8, 117,
122
Dark Star 271
Darling of Paris, The 210
"Date with Kong, A" 370
Daughter of Dr. Jekyll 102-3
Daughter of the Werewolf see
Cry of the Werewolf
Davenport, Basil 156
Davis, Mannie 114
Davis, Miles 129
Davis, Sammy, Jr. 112
Dawley, Herbert M. 284-5,
287
Dawn, Jack 95
Dawn, Norman 291
Dawson, Maurine 39
Day, Dennis 121
Day, John 148
Day I Vanished, The 152
Deacon, Richard 186
Deacon Brodie; or, The Double
Life 69
Dean, Ivor 110
"Death Is a Golden Gorilla!"

367
"Death O'Clock" 227
De Bartolo, Dick 364
De Brulier, Nigel 215
Dekker, Albert 407
Delannoy, Jean 221
De Laurentiis, Dino 155, 341-7,
349-50, 354-6, 358, 364,
368-9, 371
Deleon, Jack 39
Delgado, Marcel 282, 286-7,
290, 293, 296-7, 315-16,
318-20
Delgado, Miguel M. 36
Delgado, Roger 193-5
DeMarne, Denis 107
Demicheli, Tulio 48
De Mond, Albert 95
Demonio Azul, El 64
Denning, Richard 263
Denny, Reginald 102
De Palma, Brian 248-9
"Descent into the Maelstrom,
A" 280
Destination Inner Space 280
Destiny see The Wolf Man
(1941 film)
Destroy All Monsters see
Kaijû Sôshingeki
Destroy All Planets see Ga-
mera tai Uchi Kaijû Bairusu
Deux Nigauds contre Franken-
stein see Abbott and Cos-
tello Meet Frankenstein
Deux Nigauds contre le Dr.
Jekyll et Mr. Hyde see
Abbott and Costello Meet Dr.
Jekyll and Mr. Hyde
Deux Nigauds et l'homme in-
visible see Abbott and Cos-
tello Meet the Invisible Man
Devarona, Joanna 344
Devil Wolf of Shadow Mountain
64
Devil's Brood, The see House
of Frankenstein
Dezuniga, Tony 126
Dhanwan 217
Dhlamini, Ezekiel ("King Kong")
361, 371
Dick and the Demons 32
Dick Tracy vs. Crime, Inc.
(Dick Tracy vs. Phantom

Empire) 153
Dierkes, John 102
Dieterle, William 218
Diller, Barry 341
Dillman, Bradford 66
"Dinner with Drac" 43-4
Dinosaur and the Missing Link,
    The 283-4
Dirty Dr. Jekyll see Naughty
    Dr. Jekyll
Ditko, Steve 330
Dix, Robert 66
Dr. Black and Mr. White 112
Dr. Black Mr. Hyde 112-3
Dr. Breedlove see Kiss Me
    Quick
Dr. Devil and Mr. Harc 113
"Dr. Elmer and Mr. Fudd"
    127
"Dr. Grisley's Experiment"
    127
"Dr. Jackal and Mr. Hyde"
    124
Dr. Jekyll 84
"Dr. Jekyll" 129
Dr. Jekyll and His Weird Show
    81
Dr. Jekyll and Madame Hyde
    84
Dr. Jekyll and Miss Hyde 112
Dr. Jekyll and Mr. Blood see
    The Man with Two Heads
"Dr. Jekyll and Mr. Cummings"
    121
Dr. Jekyll and Mr. Hyde
    (Stevenson novel) see The
    Strange Case of Dr. Jekyll
    and Mr. Hyde; (films)
    (1897) 81; (1908) 81-2;
    (1910) see Den Skaebnesvan-
    gre Opfindelse; (1912) 82-4;
    (1913) 84; (1915) 84, 95;
    Arrow (1920) 84; Lipow
    (1920) 84-5; Paramount
    (1920) 85, 88-9, 98, 106;
    Pioneer (1920) 88-9; (1925)
    89; (1932) 89-97, 105-6,
    115-6, 123; (1941) 40, 95-7,
    122, 125; (1960) see The
    Two Faces of Dr. Jekyll;
    (1971 announced) 112; ama-
    teur 114; (television movie)
    see The Strange Case of

Dr. Jekyll and Mr. Hyde;
    (plays) Sullivan 75-9, 82, 85,
    91, 94; Dane 78; Bandmann
    78-9; Poole 79; vaudeville
    79; Forepaugh & Fish 79-81;
    Fletcher 80; Tanner 80;
    Carr 80; Thomas 80; Ash-
    well & Pocock 80; Abbott
    80-1
"Dr. Jekyll and Mr. Hyde"
    (comics) Classic Comics &
    Classics Illustrated, A Star
    Presentation 123; Legend
    Horror Classics, Supernatur-
    al Thrillers, Marvel Classic
    Comics 124; (Pendulum
    Press) 124; also see "The
    Strange Case of Dr. Jekyll
    and Mr. Hyde" (comics);
    (radio) "Lux Radio Theatre"
    115; "Weird Circle" 115,
    128; "CBS Radio Mystery
    Theater" 116-7; (records)
    129; (records of radio shows)
    128; (television) "Suspense,"
    "Climax," "Matinée Theatre"
    117; NBC musical 119-21; al-
    so see "The Strange Case of
    Dr. Jekyll and Mr. Hyde"
    (radio, TV)
Dr. Jekyll and Mr. Hyde Done
    to a Frazzle 84
Dr. Jekyll and Mr. Mouse 114
Dr. Jekyll and Mistress Hyde
    112
Dr. Jekyll and Mrs. Hyde (1953)
    see Abbott and Costello Meet
    Dr. Jekyll and Mr. Hyde;
    (1972) 112; (1976) 113
Dr. Jekyll and Sister Hyde 107,
    109-11, 128
Dr. Jekyll and the Werewolf
    52, 111
"Dr. Jekyll Was Right" 127-8
Dr. Jekyll's Hide 95
"Dr. Jekyll's Hyde" 121
"Dr. Jekyll's Jest" 127
"Dr. Jerk-ll and Mr. Hyde"
    126
"Dr. Jerkyll and Mr. Bugs"
    127
Dr. Jerkyll and Mr. Hyde see
    The Nutty Professor

Dr. Jerkyll's Hide 113
"Dr. Jimmy" 120
Dr. Orloff and the Invisible
  Man 152
Dr. Pyckle and Mr. Pride 89
Dr. Rock and Mr. Roll 106
Dr. Sexual and Mr. Hyde 107,
  114
"Dr. Spektor and Mr. Hyde"
  126-7
Dr. Terror's Gallery of Hor-
  rors 65
Dr. Terror's House of Hor-
  rors 64-5
Dr. Yekyll see El hombre y
  la bestia
The Doctor's Horrible Experi-
  ment see Le Testament du
  docteur Cordilier
"Don Adams' Screen Test"
  252
Don Juan 86
Donat, Robert 95
Donlevy, Brian 407
"Donny and Marie" 361
Dottor Jekyll 106
Dottor Jekyll, Il see El
  hombre y la bestia
Double Trouble 248
Douglas, Kirk 119-21
Doyle, Sir Arthur Conan 285-
  7, 289-90, 292
Dracula 2, 40, 65, 85, 89,
  133, 164-5, 167, 245
Dracula en de Werewolf see
  La marca del Hombre Lobo
Dracula jagt Frankenstein see
  El hombre que vino del
  Ummo
Dracula (The Dirty Old Man)
  65, 106
Dracula vs. Frankenstein
  (1970) see El hombre que
  vino del Ummo; (1971) 47,
  66
Dracula's Castle see Blood
  of Dracula's Castle
Drake, Arnold 41-2, 126, 184,
  365
Dreadstone, Carl 273
Drucker, Mort 364
Duality of Man, The 82
Dubay, Bill 369

Duce, Sharon 251
Duke's Daughter; or, The Hunch-
  back of Paris, The (The
  Duke's Bequest, The Hunch-
  back and the Swordsman,
  The Duke's Daughter; or, The
  Duke's Device, The Duke's
  Signal) 207, 210
Dunning, George 357

Earth Before Man, The 357
Ebirah, Horror of the Deep see
  Nankai no Dai Ketto
Eddy, Nelson 244, 251
Edmiston, Walker 361
Edwards, George 224
Edwards, Gus 217
Edwards, J. Gordon 210
Edwards, William 65
Egyptian Mummy, The 198
Eighth Wonder, The 326
Eighth Wonder of the World,
  The see King Kong (1933
  film)
Eisner, Michael 341
Elder, Bill (Will) 364, 382
Elder, John 67
Ellenstein, Robert 225
Elliott, B. Ron 107
Ellison, Ralph 156
Endore, Guy 61
English, John 153
English, Marla 275
Enmascardo de Oro contra el
  asesino invisible, El see
  El asesino invisible
Enmei-in no Semushi 217, 375
Ensign Pulver 105
"Enter: Mr. Hyde" 128
Equiluz, Enrique L. 45
Erik the Great see The Last
  Performance
Ermelinda 208
Erotic Dr. Jekyll, The 113
Errol, Leon 147
Esmeralda (films) (1905) 209;
  (1922) 210; (operas) Mazzu-
  cato, Dargomyshchky 208;
  Battista see Ermelinda;
  Campana, Thomas 209
Esmeralda, La 208
Esmeralda--Dancer of Paris

217
espectro del Estrangulador, El
    248
Esposito, Mike 160
Essex, Harry 260, 281
Evanier, Mark 127
Evans, George 366
Evans, Robert J. 222
Everett, Bill 124, 273
Evolution 285
Experiment in Evil see Le
    Testament du docteur Corde-
    lier
Eyer, Richard 154
Eyes of the Mummy, The see
    Die Augen der Mumie

Fabian, Mary 235
Fabian, Victor 37
Face of the Screaming Were-
    wolf see La casa del ter-
    ror
Falk, Peter 343
Family That Dwelt Apart, The
    357
fantasma da opera, O 254
Fantastic Animation Festival
    403
Fantastic Puppet People, The
    see Attack of the Puppet
    People
Fantastique see The Scarab
Farmer, Philip José 359
"Fay was a Darn Nice Girl"
    359
Fearn, John Russell (Vargo
    Statten) 273
Fee, Melinda 157-8
Feiffer, Jules 368
Fejos, Paul 240
Ferguson, Frank 28
Ferrer, Mel 105
Feval, Paul 207
Fiander, Lewis 110
Fields, Sidney 100
Fields, Suzanne 340
Film Firsts, Chapter II 291
Filmland Monsters 278
Fils de King Kong see Na-
    bonga
Fine, Itsa 356
Finger, Bill 254

Finley, William 249-50
Fire Monsters, The 403
Fish, George F. 79-81
Fisher, Terence 61, 103-4,
    187, 245
Flash Gordon 139-40
Flashman contre les hommes in-
    visibles (Flashman) 152
Fleisher, Dave 114, 356-7
Fleisher, Max 114, 285
Fleming, Victor 95
Flesh Gordon 340
Fletcher, Bramwell 54, 162
Fletcher, Charles Leonard 80
"Flintstones, The" 121, 402
Florey, Robert 133
Foch, Nina 57
Foran, Dick 171, 175
Ford, John 320
Ford, Wallace 171, 175
Forepaugh, Luella 79-81
Forte, John 365
"49th Annual Academy Awards,
    The" 361
Foster, Suzanna 241-4, 251
Fowler, Gene, Jr. 58-9
"Fractured Flickers" 216
Francis, Freddie 31, 64, 67
Franco, Jesus (Jess) 106
Frankenstein 2, 49, 89, 133-4,
    139, 165, 176, 217, 224,
    245, 248
Frankenstein and the Curse of
    Dr. Jekyll 123
Frankenstein bei den Dinosauri-
    ern see Frankenstein in the
    Lost World
Frankenstein Conquers the World
    see Furankenshutain tai
    Baragon
Frankenstein contre l'homme in-
    visible see Frankenstein 1970
"Frankenstein Gang, The" 42
Frankenstein in the Lost World
    357-8
"Frankenstein, Jr." 361, 402
Frankenstein Meets the Mummy
    183
Frankenstein Meets the Wolf
    Man x, xviii, 15-9, 48-9
Frankenstein 1970 103
Frankenstein Slept Here 39-40,
    81, 159, 183

Frankenstein und die Unge-
   heuer see Mankai no Dai
   Ketto
Frankenstein vs. King Kong
   336, 385
Frankenstein vs. the Giant
   Devilfish see Furankenshu-
   tain tai Baragon
Frankenstein vs. the Giant
   Moth 385
Frankenstein's Bloody Terror
   see La marca del Hombre
   Lobo
Frankensteins Dämon bedroht
   die Welt see Gamera tai
   Daimaju Jaiga
Frankensteins Kampf gegen die
   Teufelmonster see Gojira
   tai Hedora
Frankensteins Monster jagens
   Godzilla see Gojira no
   Musuko
Frankestein, el Vampiro y Cia
   (also, Frankestain, el Vam-
   piro y compañía) 33-4
Frantics 43
Franz, Arthur 148
Frawley, William 149
Frazetta, Frank 369
"Freaks of Fear!" 228
Freedberg, Bruce 41
Freleng, Friz 113
French, Brandon 359-60
Freund, Karl 164, 167, 169
Friedlander, Louis 139
Friedman, Seymour 98
Friedrich, Gary 36
Friedrich, Mike 367, 404
"Fright Night" 361
Frost, R. Lee 30
Fry, J. R. 209
Fry, William Henry 209
Frye, Dwight 224
Fuchs, Gaby 50
Fukuda, Jun 390, 398
Fulton, John P. 6, 36, 100,
   135-46, 151-2, 158
"Funny Side, The" 38, 252
Furankenshutain tai Baragon
   384-5, 391, 395
furia del Hombre Lobo, La
   49-50, 53
Furneaux, Yvonne 189-90

G-Men vs. the Black Dragon
   199
"Gadzooka" 402
Galbo, Andy 36
Gallatin, Gene 359
Gallery of Horrors see Dr.
   Terror's Gallery of Horrors
Gamera see Daikaiju Gamera
Gamera tai Barugon 408-9
Gamera tai Daimaju Jaiga 410-
   11
Gamera tai Gyaos 409
Gamera tai Shinkai Kaijû Jigura
   410-11
Gamera tai Uchi Kaijû Bairusu
   (Gamera tai Viras) 409-10
Gamera vs. Gaos see Gamera
   tai Gyaos
Gamera vs. Guiron 410
Gamera vs. Jiger see Gamera
   tai Daimaju Jaiga
Gamera vs. Leoman 411
Gamera vs. Monster X see
   Gamera tai Daimaju Jaiga
Gamera vs. Zigra see Gamera
   tai Shinkai Kaijû Jiguru
Gammera the Invincible see
   Daikaiju Gamera
Gardiner, Bob 340
Garrett, Eliza 340
Garrett, Grant 100
Garzon, Carlos 64
Gaskill, Charles L. 84
Gautier, Theophile 199
Gay, Ramon 200
Geduld, Harry 360
Gekkoh Kamen 326-7
Gemini Man, The (film) 158-9;
   (record) 159
"Gemini Man, The" 159
Gemora, Charles 311, 324-5,
   329
Genius at Work 305
"Genocide Spray!" 41
Gentleman Jekyll and Driver
   Hyde 97
Gerani, Gary 64
Gerbhardt, Charles 370
"Get Smart" 38, 184, 225
Ghidrah (Monster of Monsters)
   (Ghidrah, The Three-Headed
   Monster) see Kaiju Chikyu
   Kessen

"Ghost Busters, The" 38, 121, 184, 252, 361
Ghost of Dragstrip Hollow 278
Ghost of Frankenstein, The 15-16, 26
Ghost of Slumber Mountain, The 284-7
Ghost Party see Hillbillys in a Haunted House
Ghoul, The 134, 169
Ghoul in a Girls' Dormitory (The Ghoul in School) see Lycanthropus
Ghouls, Les 36
"Giant Ape, The" 363
"Giant Ape Suit, The 370
Giant Apes Activity and Games Book 360
Giant Apes Coloring Book 360
Gibson, Buz 312
Gibson, Walter 121
Gigantis, the Fire Monster see Gojira no Gyakushyu
Gilbert, John 7
Giles, David 251
Gilling, John 193
Giordano, Dick 254
Girl and the Gorilla, The see Nabonga
Girl in the Hairy Paw, The 360
Girl Who Stole the Eiffel Tower see Paris When It Sizzles
Girolami, Marino 104
Gladir, George 42
Glut 201
Go and Get It 288
Godzilla--Der Drache aus dem Dschungel see Gamera tai Barugon
Godzilla, King of the Monsters (film) see Gojira; (comic book) 403-4
Godzilla 1980 402
Godzilla no Gyakushyu see Gojira no Gyakushyu
Godzilla Radon King-Gidorah see Kaiju Dai Senso
Godzilla Raids Again see Gojira no Gyakushyu
Godzilla tai Gaigan 398
Godzilla tai Mothra see Mo-
sura tai Gojira
Godzilla vs. Gigan see Godzilla tai Gaigan
Godzilla vs. Megalon see Gojira tai Megaro
Godzilla vs. the Sea Monster see Nankai no Dai Ketto
Godzilla vs. the Smog Monster see Gojira tai Hedora
Godzilla vs. the Thing see Mosura tai Gojira
Godzilla's Revenge see Oru Kaiju Daishingeki
"Gog Cometh!" 367
Gojira 375-80, 382-3, 401-2, 407
Gojira no Gyakushyu 378-81, 384, 403
Gojira no Musuko 390-1, 395
Gojira tai Hedora 396-8, 405
Gojira tai Mechagojira 399-400
Gojira tai Megaro 398-9, 403
Goldman, Bo 344
Goldner, Orville 360
Gone with the Wind 301
Gonzáles, Arturo 52
Goodbar, Rick 36
Goodkind, Saul A. 140
Goodman, Evelyn 123
Goodwins, Leslie 179, 305
Goofy Groceries 357
Gordon, Bert I. 103, 152
Gordon, Keire 329
Gorgo 190
Gorilla see Nabonga
"Gorilla Boss of Gotham City!, The" 364, 366
Görünmiyen Adam Istanbulda 150
Gottesman, Ronald 360
Gough, Michael 103, 246, 328-9
Goulart, Ron 124, 160
Govar, René 48
Graham, Gerrit 249
Graham, Ron 36
Grainger, Sam 274
Grandenetti, Jerry 123
Grant, John 272
Grass 294
Great Grape Ape, The 362
"Great Grape Ape, The" 362
Great Joe Young, The see

Mighty Joe Young
Great Moments from the Phan-
    tom of the Opera   239
Great Piggybank Robbery, The
    30
Greatest Battle on Earth, The
    see Sandai Kaijû Chikyu
    Kessen
Green Hell   173
Grey, Nan   142
Griffith, D. W.   284
Grodin, Charles   346
"Groovie Goolies, The"   38,
    121, 184
Guardamagna   106
Guild, Nancy   149
Guillerman, John   347, 352
Guiol, Fred   198
Guitty, Madeleine   53
Gulliver's Travels   295
Gumen, Murad   368
Guy-Blanché, Alice   209
Gwangi   320-2
Gwynne, Fred   121

H. G. Wells' New Invisible
    Man see El hombre que
    logro ser invisible
Haden, Sara   26
Hafeesjee   218
Hale, Richard   273
"Half-Invisible Man, The"   156
Halfback of Notre Dame, The
    217
Hall, Jon   144-7, 280
Hall, Sam   38
"Halleluja, Horrorwood"   39,
    121, 184, 273, 361
Halliday, Andrew J.   207
Hampshire, Susan   119
Hanna, William   114, 155
"Happy Days"   159
Haram Alek   30, 183
"Hard Times"   41
Harding, Kay   181
Hardwicke, Sir Cedric   141,
    144, 218
Hare Remover   113
Hargan, Patrick   160
Harishchandra   218
Harmon, Hugh   113
Harmon, Jim   104, 203

Harolde, Ralf   293
Harper, Jessica   249
Harrigan, William   138
Harris, Jack H.   104, 340,
    344-5
Harris, Michael   183
Harris, Robert H.   59
Harrison, Marguerite   294
Harryhausen, Ray   xi, 320-1,
    341
Haunted Hotrod, The see
    Ghost of Dragstrip Hollow
Haunted Mountain   251
Haunted Tomb   36
Have You Got Any Castles?
    240
Haven, James C.   264
Hawn, Goldie   346
Haydock, Ron   36, 175-6
Hayward, Louis   98-9
Head of Janus, The see Der
    Januskopf
Healey, Myron   382
Healy, Annesley   210
Heck, Don   125
Hell's Creatures see La mar-
    ca del Hombre Lobo
"Hellzapoppin'"   252
Helm, Fay   10
Henderson, Lucius   82
Henley, William Ernest   69
Henry's Night Inn   155
Hercules, Prisoner of Evil   64
Hercules vs. Maciste in the
    Vale of Woe   64
Herman, Len   367-8
Hevener, Jerold T.   84
Hewetson, Alan   124
Hewitt, David L.   65-6, 340
"Hey, Hey, Hey--It's Fat Al-
    bert"   30
"Hey Wolfman"   38
Hickman, Bob   259
Hickman, Steve   368
Hicks, Arnold   123
Highlights of Horror   216, 239
Hill, Craig   49
Hillbillys in a Haunted House
    65
Hines, Leonard   169
Hirata, Akihiko   377
Hobart, Rose   92
Hobbes, Halliwell   92

Hobson, Valerie 6
Hodgson, Leland 146
Hoffman, Herman 154
Holloway, Stanley 119
"Hollywood and the Stars" 313
Hollywood Boulevard 403
Hollywood Party 324
Hollywood Review of 1929
  217, 240
"Hollywood: The Selznik Years"
  313
Holmes, Herbert 94
Holmes, LeRoy 370
"Holmes and Yo Yo" 252, 273
Holt, Seth 193
hombre invisible, El 160
hombre invisible ataca, El
  151-2
Hombre Lobo, El see La
  marca del Hombre Lobo
hombre que logro ser invisible,
  El 150-1
hombre que vino del Ummo, El
  48-9, 201
hombre y la bestia, El 97-8
homem lôbo, O 66
Homolka, Oscar 143
Honda, Inoshiro 333, 336-7,
  375-6, 368, 380, 385, 390-1,
  395-6, 400
Hopkins, Miriam 92
Hor Balevana 339
Horrible Hyde 84
"Horripilate Host" 254
"Horror Hall of Fame--A Mon-
  ster Salute, The" 39, 225
Horror High 112
"Horror Movie" 41
Horror of Dracula 187
Horror of Party Beach, The
  279-80
"Horror Theater" 184, 252,
  361
horrores del Bosque Negro,
  Los see La loba
Horrors of the Black Museum
  103
House of Dracula xi, 19, 22-
  6, 97, 260
House of Frankenstein xi,
  xviii, 19-22, 24, 26, 43,
  48-9, 54, 224, 260
House of Fright see The Two

Faces of Dr. Jekyll
"House of Horror" 225
House of the Black Death 64-5
House on Bare Mountain, The 30
How to Make a Monster 59, 61,
  278
Howard, John 56, 143
Hoyos, Kitty de 65
Hoyt, Arthur 288
Hoyt, Henry O. 286, 290, 293-
  4
Hubbard, John 175
Hudson, Earl 285
Huebsch, Edward 98
Huesch, Paolo 64
Hughes, Lloyd 288
Hugo, Victor 204, 205, 207-11,
  214, 222, 224-8
Hugo the Hunchback 209
Hull, Cortlandt B. 26
Hull, Henry 4-6, 13
Hunchback, The 209
Hunchback of Cedar Lodge, The
  224
"Hunchback of Hollywood and the
  Movie Murder, The" 227
Hunchback of Notre Dame, The
  (Hugo novel) see Notre-Dame
  de Paris; (films) (1923) 11,
  89, 209-17, 227, 229, 232-4,
  236, 239, 253; (1923 an-
  nounced) 217; (1939) 218-21,
  225; (1953) see Badshah
  Dampati; (1956) see Notre-
  Dame de Paris; (plays) 208
"Hunchback of Notre Dame, The"
  (comics) Classic Comics
  226-7; Classics Illustrated,
  Almanaque Estorias de terror,
  The Monster Times 227;
  (prose story) 216; (radio)
  224; (television) "Robert
  Montgomery Presents" 224-5;
  BBC 225
"Hunchback of Notre Doom, The"
  227
Hunchback of Soho, The see
  Der Bucklige von Soho
Hunter, T. Hayes 169
Hurndall, Richard 109
Hurst, Brandon 85, 215
"Hyde--And Go Seek!" 126
Hyde and Go Tweety 113

Hyde and Hare   113
Hyde and Sneak   114

"I Discovered Gorgilla! The
    Monster of Midnight Moun-
    tain!"   366
"I Go Ape"   371
I Like Mountain Music   357
I Married a Werewolf   see
    Lycanthropus
I, Monster   107-9
I Was a Teenage Frankenstein
    59, 61, 327
I Was a Teenage Gorilla   see
    Konga
I Was a Teenage Mummy   183
I Was a Teenage Werewolf
    58-60, 66, 327
Idle Roomers   57
Illustrated King Kong, The
    358
"(I'm in Love with) The Crea-
    ture from the Black Lagoon"
    275
"(I'm in Love with) The Invisi-
    ble Man"   160
I'm Sorry, the Bridge Is Out,
    You'll Have to Spend the
    Night   39, 183
Im-Ho-Tep   see   The Mummy
    (1932 film)
Impatient Patient   240
inafferrabile Mr. Invisible, L'
    see   El invencible hombre
    invisible
Incredible Dr. Jekyll, The
    see   The Erotic Dr. Jekyll
"Incredible, Edible Invasion of
    Earth!, The"   404
Incredible Hulk, The   124-5
Incredible Werewolf Murders,
    The   see   The Maltese Bippy
Infantino, Carmine   369
Invasion of Astro-Monsters (In-
    vasion of Planet X)   see
    Kaijû Daisenso
invencible hombre invisible, El
    (The Invincible Mr. Invisible)
    152
Invisible Agent   xviii, 144-5
Invisible Boy, The   154
Invisible Dr. Mabuse, The   see

Die unsichtbaren Krallen des
    Dr. Mabuse
Invisible Fluid, The   153
Invisible Horror, The   see   Die
    unsichtbaren Krallen des Dr.
    Mabuse
Invisible Mad, The   156
Invisible Man, The   (Wells
    novel) 130-5, 138-9, 141,
    144, 146, 150, 155-6; (Cliff's
    Notes) 156; (Ellison, Littrell
    books) 156; (John novel) 158;
    (films) (1910) 132; (1933)
    xii, 132-9, 142, 148, 159,
    240; (1959 announced) 151;
    (1961) see Los Invisibles;
    (1975 TV film) 157-8
"Invisible Man, The"   (comic
    book) 160; (comics) Superior
    Stories 159;   Classics Illus-
    trated 159-60;   Supernatural
    Thrillers, Marvel Classic
    Comics 160;   (prose story)
    156;   (records) 160;   (tele-
    vision) Matinee Theatre,
    British series 157;   Univer-
    sal series 159
Invisible Man from Space, The
    151
Invisible Man in Mexico, The
    see   El hombre que logro
    ser invisible
"Invisible Man Murder Case,
    The"   156
Invisible Man on Bikini Beach,
    The   151
"Invisible Man ... or ... What
    Ever Did His Wife See in
    Him?, The"   160
Invisible Man Returns, The
    xviii, 140-2, 144-5, 148,
    150
Invisible Man's Revenge, The
    146-7, 150
Invisible Men
"Invisible Mr. Mann, The"   160
Invisible Monster, The   153
Invisible Mouse, The   155
Invisible Teenager, The   152-3
Invisible Terror, The   see
    Der Unsichtbare
Invisible Thief   see   Les In-
    visibles

Invisible Woman, The xviii,
142-4
Invisible Woody, The see
Operation Meatball
Invisibles, Les 132
Invisibles, Los 151
Irving, Sir Henry 80
Isabell, A Dream 183
Isabella, Tony 274
Ishikawa, Hiroshi 398
Ising, Rudolf 113
It Came from Outer Space
258-9, 281
Ito, Emi and Yumi (The Pea-
nuts) 382-3, 386
(It's a) Monster's Holiday 43

Jack, Wolfman 38
"Jack Benny Show" 121
Jackman, Fred 294
Jacobs, Dick 43, 275
Jacobs, Jack 42
Jahn, Michael 158
Jamboree see The Son of
Kong
Janowitz, Hans 84
Januskopf: Eine Tragödie am
Rand der Wirklichkeit, Der
(Der Januskopf) 84-5
Jarrott, Charles 117
Jay, Griffin 177
"Jeepers' Creepers" 203
Jekyll and Hyde see Den
Skaobnesvangre Opfindelse
Jekyll and Hyde Cat 114
Jekyll and Hyde Portfolio, The
112
"Jekyll and Hyde '69" 123-4
"Jekyll-Hyde Heroes, The"
126
Jekyll's Inferno see The Two
Faces of Dr. Jekyll
Jewel of the Seven Stars, The
193
"Jimmy Olsen's Monster Movie!"
365
Johann, Zita 166-8
Johns, Margo 329
Johnson, Ben 322
Johnson, Brad 41
Johnson, Noble 167, 301, 316
Johnston, William 122

Jones, Dean 152
Jones, Russ 169, 184
jorobado de la morgue, El 224
Joy, Charlie 84
Julian, Rupert 233, 235
"Jungle Rhythms" 313
Jungle Witch (The Jungle Wo-
man) see Nabonga
Juran, Nathan H. 67

Kaijû, Daisenso 389
Kaijû Soshingeki (Kaiju Soko-
geki) 336-7, 391-3, 395,
410
Kaitei Gunkan 384, 399
Kane, Bob 125, 345
Kane, Gil 367
Kaplan, Steve B. 114, 183,
357
Kaptan, Atif 150
Karama, Issa 30
Karloff, Boris xi, xiii, 2, 8,
15, 19, 31, 37, 43, 91, 100-
01, 133, 157, 163-70, 175-6,
187, 189, 217, 244
Katalion, Buck 38
Katch, Kurt 180
Katzman, Sam 57
Kawase, Hiroyuki 397
Kayama, Shingeru 403
Kellard, John 80
Kellaway, Cecil 171
Kelly, Tim 39
Kennedy, Douglas 154
Kent, Gary 64
Kenton, Erle C. 19, 22
Kerruish, Jessie Douglas 54
Kerry, Norman 215, 238, 239
Kevan, Jack 27, 259, 279
"Kid Who Made Monsters, The"
184
Kiernan, Joe 160
"Kikaider" 361
Kimberley, Maggie 193-5
King, Frank 169
King, Jack 291
King, Thomas C. 208
King Ape see King Kong
(1933 film)
"King Cub" 361
"King Dong or (Monkey Business
in the Bush)" 369

"King Gong" 363
King Is Dead, The 355
"King Klonk, the Killer Gorilla"
365-6
King Klunk 356
King Kong (films) [see following several entries also]
(1933) xi, 282, 287-8, 290-1,
294-316, 320-22, 324, 326-7,
333-4, 336, 339-45, 352,
355-63, 366-8, 370-1, 373;
(1962) 331; (Hammer intended remake) 341, 362; (Barkett intended remake) 341;
(Corman, Japanese announced)
342; (Korean) see Ape;
(Universal) see The Legend
of King Kong; (1976) 341-
56, 358, 360, 363-4, 367-9,
371, 373, 402
King Kong (books) Lovelace
novel 358; Japanese, Semple
360; (magazine) 360; (play)
361; (records) Holmes 370-
1; Steiner, Barry, Matshikiza, Williams 371; Golden
372; King-Kong 363
"King Kong" (comics) 363,
368; (limerick) 359; (story)
342; (sheet music) 370;
(television) cartoon series
337, 361-2; commercial
347, 362-3
King Kong; A Picture Book 358
"King Kong: As it might be
told by Joseph Conrad,
Charlotte Bronte, Ernest
Hemingway, Jonathan
Swift, Samuel Robertson,
and William Faulkner in a
celestial story conference"
360
King-Kong, dä Monem aus dem
Weltall see Gojira tai Megaro
King Kong Escapes see Kingu
Kongu no Gyakushu
"King Kong: Fact or Fantasy"
353
King-Kong Frankensteins Sohn
see Kingu Kongu no Gyaku-
shu
King Kong gegen Godzilla see

Gojira tai Mechagojira
King Kong in Africa 343
"King Kong Stomp" 371
King Kong Story 361
King Kong Story, The 361
"King Kong Suite" 370
King Kong: The Legend Reborn
see King Kong (1976 film)
King Kong! The Monster That
Made History 360
King Kong vs. Frankenstein
331-2
King Kong vs. Godzilla see
Kingu Kongu tai Gojira
"King Kong vs. Godzilla" 368
King Kong vs. Prometheus see
Prometheus vs. King Kong
King Kong vs. the Ginko see
King Kong vs. Frankenstein
"King Kong's Boyhood" 369
"King Konk" 367
"King Korn" 364
"King Kung" 369
King Kung Fu 356
King of Kings, The 301
King of the Dead, The see
The Mummy (1932 film)
King of the Monsters 360
"Kingorilla!" 364
Kingsley, Arthur 210
Kingu Kongu no Gyakushu 336-
9, 362, 391, 395
Kingu Kongu tai Gojira 333-6
369-40, 365, 383-4
Kingukongu no Gyakushu see
Kingu Kongu no Gyakushu
"Kink Konk" 367
"Kink Konk Goes on Television"
368
Kirby, Jack 41, 124-5, 227-8,
255, 273, 366
Kiss Me Quick 183
Klimovsky, Leon 50, 52
Klug, Paul 61
Knight, Charles R. 286-7,
304-5
Knowles, Patrick 9, 16
Knox, Alexander 98
Knox, Elyse 174-5
Kobayashi, Tsuneo 151
Kochi, Momoko 378
Kong (film) see King Kong
(1933); (periodical) 360

Kong! 357
Kong Island 356
Kong News 360
Konga (film) 327-30; (novel,
   comic book) 330
Konga--Frankensteins Gorilla
   see Konga (film)
Konga's Revenge 331
Kongorilla 343
"Kongzilla!" 366
"Kookie Super-Ape!, The" 365
"Kopykats, The" 38
Kosleck, Martin 181
Kraft, Evelyn 356
Krauss, Henri 210
"Krofft Supershow, The" 273
"Krypto Battles Titano!" 365
Kupperberg, Alan 368

Laemmle, Carl 211, 232-3
Laemmle, Ernst 239
Lamont, Charles 100, 148,
   185
Land of the Living Mummy
   203
Landers, Lew 56
Landis, John 340, 345
Landon, Michael 59-60
Lane, Ben 37
Lane, Charles 143
Lane, Mike 151
Lanfield, Sidney 95
Langdon, Verne 256
Lange, Jessica 346, 349
Lantz, Walter 155, 294, 356
Larkin, Bob 404
Last Performance, The 240
Latimer, Dean 404
Lattuado, Alberto 155
Laughton, Charles 204, 218-
   9, 221, 225
Laurel, Stan 89
"Laurel and Hardy" 121, 184
Lawrence, Jody 98
Le Borg, Reginald 177
Leder, Paul 344
Lederman, D. Ross 153
Lee, Christopher 103-4, 108-
   9, 112, 128, 187-9, 190-1,
   245
Lee, Stan 124-5, 228, 273-4
Legend of King Kong, The

343-4
Legend of the Werewolf 67
Legend of the Wolfman, The
   43
Leiber, Fritz 241
Lemon Grove Kids Meet the
   Monsters, The 203
Lemont, John 327
Lenska, Rula 355
Leon, Valerie 193-4
Leonard, Sheldon 148
Lépire, Charles 132
Leroux, Gaston 230-3, 240,
   245, 248-51, 253-4
Let the Good Times Roll 59
"Letter to an Angel" 253
Levesque, Michel 66
Levin, Henry 57
Lewis, Al 121
Lewis, Jeffrey 207-8
Lewis, Jerry 96, 105, 365-6
Lewis, Robert Michael 157
Lewis, Sheldon 88-9
"Life Goes to the Movies" 355
Life in Hollywood 214
Light, Mike 340
"Lights! Camera! Marty! 39,
   184
Liszt, Franz 208, 240-1
"Litter to a Werewolf" 40
Little, Rich 38
Littrell, Dennis 156
"Lizard's Leg and Owlet's Wing"
   37
loba, La 65
Locke, Edward 244
Lockhart, Gene 128
Lockhart, June 26
Lollobrigida, Gina 220-1
Lom, Herbert 245-6, 250
"Lon Chaney's Gonna Get You
   If You Don't Watch Out" 217
London, Jack 325-6
"Lonely One, The" 330
Lord, Del 57, 198
Lorre, Peter 37, 144
Loscalzo, Vincent 37
Lost Atlantis 294
Lost Continent 291-2
Lost Island, The 324
Lost Valley, The see The Val-
   ley of Gwangi
Lost World, The (Doyle novel)

285-6, 289, 292, 340;
(films) (1925) 286-94; (1960)
292-3; (comic books) 293
"Lost World, The" 293
Lost World of Sinbad, The
   see Daitozoku
Loup des Malveneurs, Le 53
Loup-garou, Le 53, 208
Love, Bessie 288, 293
"Love Comes to Mockingbird
   Heights" 272-3
Lovelace, Delos W. 358
Loves' Mockery see Der
   Januskopf ...
Loves of a Hunchback, The
   210
Lowe, Edward T. 19, 22
Lowery, Robert 177
Lowther, George 116
Loy, Mino (S. Lee Donan)
   152
Lubin, Arthur 240, 243
Lubitsch, Ernst 198
Lucchetti, Rubens Francisco
   (Vincent Lugosi) 40
luchadoras contra la momia,
   Las 201
Ludwig, Edward 305
Lüftü, Akad 150
Lugosi, Bela xv, 6, 8-10,
   15, 17-18, 28, 37, 39, 56,
   85, 140, 164, 301
Lycanthrope, Le see Lycan-
   thropus
Lycanthrope, The 36
Lycanthropus 64
Lyon, Francis 280

Macabro expectáculo 184, 361
McCabe, Norman 113
McCallum, David 157-9
McCarthy, Kevin 116, 252
McCarty, Gene 184
McFadden, Bob 184
Machard, Alfred 7
Mack, Helen 316
Mack, Max 84
McKenzie, Roger 370
McKimson, Robert 113
McKuen, Rod (Dor) 184
McRae, Henry 1
McVeety, Vincent 357

Mad Ghoul, The 232
"Mad, Mad, Mad Monsters"
   31, 106, 151, 183, 222, 271,
   339-40
Mad Monster, The 53-5
Mad Monster Party? 31, 106,
   151, 183, 222, 271, 339
"Madame Jekyll of Metropolis!,
   The" 126
Magic Memories 290
Making of King Kong, The 360
maldición de la momia, La
   200-1
Malediction des Pharoans, Le
   see The Mummy (1959 film)
Maltese Bippy, The 65
Mamoulian, Rouben 89, 91-3,
   95-6, 99, 123
"Man from Transilvane!, The"
   41
Man Made Monster 8, 9, 14
Man of a Thousand Faces 222-
   3, 245
"Man of 1000 Faces 500 Bodies
   and 348 Voices Growls and
   Shrieks, The" 222
Man Upstairs, The see Il vi-
   cino di casa
"Man Who Lost Face, The"
   160
Man with Two Heads, The 107
"Man Without a Body, The"
   157
Mancini, Henry 275
Mandell, Mel 119
Maneely, Joe 227
Mankowitz, Wolf 30, 103
Mann, Hank 84
Manners, David 165-6
"Mannie Get Your Ghoul" 42
Manphibian, The 274
Man's Genesis 284
Mansfield, Bob 112
Mansfield, Martha 87
Mansfield, Richard 75-80, 82,
   85-6, 91-2, 94
Marau, Jean 53
marca del Hombre Lobo, La
   45-8, 50, 53
March, Fredric 90-6, 99,
   105-6, 113-5, 123, 128
Margano, Richard 403
Margheriti, Antonio 64

Mark, Michael 20
Mark of the Beast 358
"Markheim" 69, 116
Marshall, E. G. 116
Marston, John 316
Martin, Dick 65
Martin, Edwin L. 144
Martin, Sobey 199
Marzials, T. J. H. 209
Máscaras do pavor, As 40,
  253
Massey, Ilona 18, 144
Massie, Paul 103
"Master Plan of Mr. Hyde!,
  The" 125
Matchless 155
"Mate for Konga, A" 331
Mathews, Kerwin 67
Matshikiza, Todd 371
Matthews, Lester 6, 98
May, Joe 140, 142
Mayer, Louis B. 88
Mayerik, Val 160
Mazzucato, Alberto 208
"Meet the Creature" 275
Meet the Ghosts see Abbott
  and Costello Meet Franken-
  stein
Megowan, Don 269-70
Mein Gott, Frankenstein see
  Abbott and Costello Meet
  Frankenstein
Melchior, Ib J. 380
"Men Behind Kong, The" 369
Mentasti, Martin 152
Mesina, Rudy 160
"Mess America Contest, The"
  184
Meyer, Russ 183
Meyerbeer, Giacomo 208
Mickey the Gorilla Tamer see
  The Pet Shop
Mickey's Gala Premiere 217
Midler, Bette 361
"Midnight Special" 252
Mighty Gorga, The 340
Mighty Joe Young xi, 312,
  321-4, 339
Mighty Mouse Meets Jekyll and
  Hyde Cat see Jekyll and
  Hyde Cat
Mighty Peking Man 356
Miller, John E. 358

Miller, Linda 337
Miller, Patsy Ruth 213-4
Millhauser, Bertram 146
Milligan, Andy 31, 66, 107
Mils Mascaras 202
"Milton the Monster" 184
mio amico, Jekyll, Il 104
Miss Jekyll and Madame Hyde
  84
Mr. Invisible see El invencible
  hombre invisible
Mr. Joseph Young of Africa
  see Mighty Joe Young
Mr. Super Invisible (Mister
  Unsichtbar) see El invenci-
  ble hombre invisible
misterio della piramide, Il see
  Abbott and Costello Meet the
  Mummy
Mistresses of Dr. Jekyll see
  El secreto del Doctor Orloff
Mistri, Babubhai 331
Modern Dr. Jekyll, The see
  Dr. Jekyll and Mr. Hyde
  (1908 film)
Moench, Doug 160, 404
momia, La (La momia azteca)
  199-200
momia contra el robot humano,
  La (La momia azteca ...)
  200
momias de Guanajuato, Las
  202
Momie, La 198
Momie du roi, La 197
"Monkees, The" 38, 121, 184
Monster Among the Girls see
  Lycanthropus
"Monster from the Lost Lagoon!,
  The" 273
Monster from the Surf see
  The Beach Girls and the
  Monster
Monster Gorilla, The see
  Gekkoh Kamen
"Monster Mash" 43
"Monster Minuet" 43
"Monster Motion" 43
"Monster Movie Ball" 128, 160
"Monster Muddled" 121
Monster of Monsters, Ghidorah
  see Sandai Kaiju Chikyû
  Kessen

Monster of Piedras Blancas,
  The 279
Monster of the Opera see Il
  vampiro dell'opera
Monster of the Wax Museum,
  The see Nightmare in Wax
Monster Rumble 37, 61
"Monster Squad" 38, 159
Monster Zero see Kaijû Dai-
  senso
Monsters Crash Pajama Party
  65
Monsters from an Unknown
  Planet see Terror of Me-
  chagodzilla
"Monster's Holiday" 43
Monsters Invade Expo 70 see
  Gamera tai Daimaju Jaiga
"Monster's Secret!, The" 274
"Monsters That Devoured Car-
  narsie, The" 404
Monstre au filles, Le see
  Lycanthropus
monstruos del terror, Los see
  El hombre que vino de Ummo
Montana, Bull 288
Montgomery, Thomas 333
Monti, Maura 280
Moon of the Wolf 66
Moore, Dennis 180
Moore, John J. 119
Moore, Steve 64
Moore, Terry 322
Morales, Nela 65
Moran, Peggy 171-2
Moreau, Gabriel 132
Morell, Andre 194-5
Moretti, Wayne 37
Morgan, Ralph 153
Morgan, A Suitable Case for
  Treatment (Morgan!) 313
Morris, Chester 134-5, 275
Morris, Philip 184, 361
Morrow, Gray 47
Morrow, Jeff 269
Morrow, Sonora 41
Mortimer, Edmund 7
Mortimer, Win 124
Moss, Howard 41
Most Dangerous Game, The
  298, 300
Mosura 382-3
Mosura tai Gojira 385-7

Mothra see Mosura
"Mouse Factory, The" 38,
  184, 225
Movie Star Mickey see Mick-
  ey's Gala Premiere
Muir, Gavin 148-9
mujer murcielago, La 280
mujer y el monstruo, La see
  Creature from the Black
  Lagoon (film)
Mullin, Scott 183
Múmia 195
Mumia, El 198
Mummies' Dummies 199
Mummy, The (films) (1900)
  198; (1908) 198; (1911) 197;
  (1912) 198; (1932) xi, xii,
  40, 54, 139, 162-70, 175-7,
  182, 187, 245; (1957) see
  La momia; (1959) 187-91,
  193, 195; (novel) 273;
  (comics) 169
"Mummy, The" 44
Mummy and the Curse of the
  Jackals, The 201
Mummy Love 198
Mummy of King Ramsees see
  La Momie du roi
Mummy Strikes, The see La
  momia
Mummy vs. the Were-Jackal,
  The see The Mummy and
  the Curse of the Jackals
Mummy's Boys 198
Mummy's Curse, The xi, 179-
  82
Mummy's Ghost, The 168,
  177-80
Mummy's Hand, The (film)
  168, 170-3, 177, 180;
  (comic) 184
Mummy's Revenge, The see
  La venganza de la momia
Mummy's Shroud, The 193-5
Mummy's Tomb, The 173-7,
  180, 182, 203, 232
Munkell, Hans 50
"Munsters, The" 19, 38, 121,
  272-3
Munsters and the Great Camera
  Caper, The 122
Murayama, Mitsuo 154
"Murder in Movieland" 254-5

Murderer Invisible, The 133
Murdering Mite, The see
    Tomei-Ningen to Haiotoko
Murnau, F. W. 84-5, 210
Murphy, Ben 159
My Friend, Dr. Jekyll (My
    Pal, ...) see Il mio
    amico, Dr. Jekyll
My Side 358-9
Mysterious Dr. Jekyll, The
    114
"Mysterious Mr. Hyde!, The"
    125
Mystery of Life 285
Mytek the Mighty 368

Nabonga (Nabob) 325-6
Nacht der Vampire see La
    noche de Walpurgis
Necropolis 340
Naish, J. Carrol 19, 224
Nakajima, Haru 375, 384
Nakamura, S. 382
Naldi, Nita 86
Nanbanji no Semushi-Otoko
    222
Nankai no Dai Ketto 390, 395
Napierkovska, Stacia 210
Naschy, Paul (Jacinto Molina)
    45-53, 202, 224, 248
Nassour, Edward 294
Naughty Dr. Jekyll 112
Nav Jawan 218
Neilan, M. 288
Neill, Roy William 15, 19
Nelson, Bill 227
Nelson, Lori 268
Neuss, Alwin 82
New Invisible Man, The (film)
    see El hombre que logro
    ser invisible; (TV film)
    see The Gemini Man
"New Invisible Man, The" 157
New King Kong, The 356
"New TV Spinoffs for King
    Kong" 367
New York Dolls 44
Newell, Michelle 225
Newfeld, Sigmund 326
Newfield, Samuel 53, 291, 326
Newhart, Bob 371
Newland, Marvin 403

Niece of Dr. Jekyll, The 112
"Night Gallery" 121, 252, 273
Night of the Beast see House
    of the Black Death
Night of the Howling Beast 53
Night of the Jackass 128
"Night of the Pentagram" 43
Night on Bare Mountain see
    The House on Bare Mountain
"Night Watchman, The" 371
"Nightmare" 184, 252
"Nightmare, A" 41
Nightmare in Wax 248
Nigro, Carmen (Ken Roady) 311-
    2
"Nine Hairy Horrors" 41
"9th St. Bridge" 44
"No Place for Hyde" 126
No Place Like Homicide see
    What a Carve-Up!
"No Werewolf" 43
noche de Walpurgis, La 50-2
noche del Hombre Lobo, La 48
Nodel, Norman 160
Nolan, William 356
North, Harry 364
Norton, Edgar 93
Norvis, Nervous 324
Not Insane 404
Notre Dame (opera) 209; (film)
    210
Notre-Dame de Paris (Hugo
    novel) 204-10, 216-7, 222,
    224-7, 229; (films) (1911)
    210; (1913) see Notre Dame;
    (1956) 220-2, 227; (opera)
    209; (play) 207
Notre Dame; or, The Gipsy
    Girl of Paris 207-8
Now You See Him, Now You
    Don't 155, 357
Nueller, Chris 259
Nuit des loups-garous, La see
    La noche de Walpurgis
Nussbaum, Raphael 151
Nutty Professor, The 105
Nympho Werewolf 66

O'Brien, Darleen 299, 319
O'Brien, Willis 282-8, 290,
    292-3, 296-9, 305, 307, 312,
    315-6, 319-22, 326, 331-3,

359, 361
Ocko, Daniel 372
O'Connolly, James 320
O'Connor, Una 135
Octa-Man 287
Oda, Motoyoshi 154
O'Driscoll, Martha 23
Of Mice and Men 8, 54
"Ogre's Ode, The" 42
O'Hara, Maureen 218
Oksner, Bob 42, 126, 184,
　365
Oland, Warner 5
"Old Weird Harold" see "9th
　St. Bridge"
Oliver, Stephen 66
Olivier, Sir Laurence 116
O'Neal, Patrick 155
Operación Terror see El
　hombre que vino del Ummo
Operation Meatball 155
Operation Monsterland see
　Kaijū Sôshingeki
Orgy of the Dead 31, 186
Orlando, Joe 184
O'Rourke, Mickey 324
Ortiz, Jose 128
Oru Kaijû Daishingeki 394-7
O'Shea, Daniel 341
Ouspenskaya, Maria xv, xvii,
　9, 11, 16
Owen, Dean 330
Owen, Dickie 191, 193
Owens, Buck 43

Pacheo, Lauro 65-6
Paco and Agapito 34
Pacto diabólico (Pact with the
　Devil) 106
Palance, Jack 118-9
Palmer, Tony 112
Panama, Norman 65
"Panic in the Night!" 255
Panik um King Kong see
　Mighty Joe Young
"Panorama Pacific" 121, 203
Parade of the Wooden Soldiers
　356
Paris When It Sizzles 105
Parker, Eddie (Edwin) 100-1,
　176, 185-6
Parry, Michel 360

Pascall, Jeremy 360
Pastell, George 189, 191, 329
Patti, Adelina 209
Pearce, Alice 160
"Peerless Power of the Silver
　Surfer, The" 228
Pennock, Christopher 117
Perez, George 367
"Personality Crisis" 43
Pet Shop, The 356-7
Peterson, Pete 305
Petherbridge 251
Petrie, Daniel 66
Petronius 2
Pevney, Joseph 222
Phantom see Phantom of the
　Paradise (film)
Phantom Creeps, The 139-40
Phantom from Space 151
Phantom of Hollywood, The 252
Phantom of Lot 2, The see
　The Phantom of Hollywood
Phantom of Paris, The 240
Phantom of the Fillmore see
　Phantom of the Paradise
　(film)
Phantom of the Horse Opera
　245
"Phantom of the Kensington
　Theatre, The" 253
Phantom of the Opera, The
　(Leroux novel) 230-3, 248-51,
　253-4; (films) (1925) 216,
　230, 232-40, 244-5, 253;
　(1943) 240-5, 248-9, 251-2,
　254; (1962) 245-8; (1974
　announced) 248; (play) 250-1
"Phantom of the Opera, The"
　(comics) 254; (prose story)
　253; (radio) 251; (records)
　256
"Phantom of the Opera's Friend,
　The" 253
Phantom of the Organ, The
　255-6
Phantom of the Paradise (film)
　248-50; (novel, record) 250
Phantom of the Paradise, Part
　II 250
"Phantom of the Sewers" 255
"Phantom of the Soap Opera"
　255
Phantom Ruler, The see The

Invisible Monster
Pharaoh's Curse   199
Philbin, Mary   235, 239-40
Pichel, Irving   91
Pickett, Bob   39, 43-4, 371
"Pickman's Model"   273
Piel, Harry   150
Pierce, Arthur C.   305
Pierce, Jack   5-6, 13, 24, 31-
   2, 36, 165-6, 171, 175-6,
   179, 203, 243
Ping Pong   see   Tarz and Jane
   and Boy and Cheetah
"Ping Pong!"   364
Pink Panther Strikes Again,
   The   357
Pipitone, Nino   199
Piscopo, Dick   274
Plague of the Werewolves   67
Platt, Kin   124
"Plot Is the Thing, The"   41,
   253, 359
Pocock, Roger   80
Poe, Edgar Allan   140, 237-8,
   258, 280
"Poisen to Poisen"   160
Polidouris, Basil   201
Pollen, Nat   372
Pool, Howard   79
"Porky Pig and Daffy Duck
   Meet the Groovie Goolies"
   39, 252
Porky's Movie Mystery   152
Portello, Rafael Lopez   199-
   200
"Portnoy's Mother's Complaint"
   359
Post, Don   31, 39, 183, 203,
   228, 248, 271, 273, 344, 372
Powell, Eddie   193-5
Price, Stanley   153
Price, Vincent   30, 140, 142,
   147
Primitive Man, The   see
   Brute Force
Prinz, LeRoy   324
Prize Pest   113
Prohoska, Janos   363
Prometheus vs. King Kong
   332-3
Pronzini, Bill   156
Putnam, Nina Wilcox   165

Quasimodo!   209
Quasimodo, the Deformed; or,
   The Man with the Hump and
   the Belle of Notre Dame   207
Quasimodo's Monster Magazine
   42, 226
Quayle, Anthony   128
Queen Kong   343, 355-6
"Queen Kong"   359
Queen Kong: The Illegitimate
   Son of You Know Who   343,
   345
"Queen of Horror"   274
Quine, Richard   105
Quinn, Anthony   220-1, 227
Quirk, Billy   198

Radon   381-2, 391
Radot, Guillaume   53
Rains, Claude   xv, 9, 134-6,
   138-40, 142, 148, 151, 157,
   159, 240, 242-5, 247, 251,
   254, 292
Ramadal   154
Rambaldi, Carlo   346-7, 349
"Randan"   382
Randegger, A.   209
Ratanbai   217
Rathbone, Basil   19, 106, 117,
   251
Rats Are Coming! The Were-
   wolves Are Here!, The   66
Raven, Mike   109
Ravo de Jalisco, El   202
"Real Phantom of the Opera,
   The"   255
Reason, Rhodes   337
Redondo, Nestor   124
Reed, Oliver   62-3
regreso del monstruo, El   see
   Revenge of the Creature
Reicher, Frank   300, 316
Reid, Janey   216
Reiner, Carl   106
Reinl, Harold   154
Reisner, Charles   217
Rendezvous   26, 95, 139, 182,
   244, 266, 313
Rennie, Michael   48, 292
Renoir, Jean   117
retorno de Walpurgis, El   52-3
Return from the Past   see   Dr.

Terror's Gallery of Horrors
Return of Chandu, The 301
Return of Godzilla, The see
    Gojira no Gyakushyu
"Return of Konga" 330
Return of Konga, The 331
Return of the Giant Monsters
    see Gamera tai Gyaos
"Return of the Monster!, The"
    274
Return of the Teenage Werewolf
    61
Return of the Vampire, The
    56-7
Return of the Wolfman 37
Return to Manhood see Nan-
    banji no Semushi-Otoko
Return to the Lost World 292
Revenge of King Kong see
    Kingu Kongu no Gyakushu
Revenge of Mechagodzilla see
    Terror of Mechagodzilla
Revenge of Rendezvous 26, 95,
    182, 244-5
Revenge of the Creature 266-
    8, 275
Revenge of the Teenage Were-
    wolf 61
Reyes, Effren 154
Richmond, Bill 105
Rickard, Jack 42
Rintoul, David 67
Riskin, Vickie 362
Ritch, Steven 57-8
Rivals of Godzilla, The 360
Rivals of King Kong, The 360
Rivals of the Wolf Man, The
    360
Robbins, Frank 366
Robertson, John S. 85-6, 240
Robinson, Glen 347
robo de las momias de Guana-
    juato, El 202
robot humano, El see La
    momia contra el robot hu-
    mano
Robot Monster 291
Robot vs. the Aztec Mummy,
    The see La momia contra
    el robot humano
Rock, Joe 198
Rocky Horror Picture Show,
    The 160, 371

Rocky Horror Show, The 160,
    371
Rodan (Rodan, The Flying Mon-
    ster) see Radon
Rodrigues, Moacir 254
Roland, Jeanne 192
Romain, Yvonne 63
Romero, Cesar 155
Rose, Ruth 297
Rosen, R. Michael 127
Ross, Arthur 260
Ross, Harry 54
Ross, Joe E. 121
Ross, Marilyn 127
Rossi, Rafaello 66
Rost, Elaine 372
Rostaing, Bjarne 250
Rothacker, Watterson 285, 287
Rotsler, William 258
Rouben Mamoulian's Dr. Jekyll
    and Mr. Hyde 123
"Route 66" 37, 184, 225-6
"Rowan and Martin's Laugh-In"
    184
Royer, Mike 127
Ruanova, Fernando 245
Russell, Kent 155
Ryder, Alfred 225

"Sabrina, the Teenage Witch"
    38, 121
Sachs, Norman 119
"Sacrifice!" 368
Salazar, Alfredo 65, 201
Salter, Hans J. 10, 275
Salvador, Jaime 34, 106, 151
Samson in the Wax Museum
    see Santo en el museo de
    cera
Samson vs. the Vampire Women
    see Santo contra las mujeres
    vampiras
Sanda tai Gailah 385
Sandai Kaijū Chikyu Kessen
    388-9, 391
Sangster, Jimmy 187
"Santa Claus Lane Parade, The"
    252
Santo 34-6, 201-2, 222, 248
Santo contra el Estrangulador
    248
Santo contra las mujeres

vampiras   35
Santo contra los monstruos de
  Frankenstein   see   Santo y
  Blue Demon contra los
  monstruos
Santo en el museo de cera   34,
  105, 222, 248
Santo en la venganza de la
  momia   202
Santo y Blue Demon contra
  Dracula y el Hombre Lobo
  36
Santo y Blue Demon contra los
  monstruos   34-5, 201
Santos, Jesse   126
Saperstein, Henry G.   385
Sato, Torajiro   222
"Saturday Night"   361
Satyricon   2
Savo, Jimmy   313
Scarab, The   104-5
Scardon, Paul   84
"Scared Silly!"   41-2
Scarlet Claw, The   19, 25
Schaffenburger, Kurt   126
Schayer, Richard   165
Schlock   281, 340, 344-5, 347
Schmidt, Franz   209
Schoedsack, Ernest B.   282,
  294-5, 297-8, 300-1, 311-2,
  315, 319-20
Schubert, Bernard   179
schwarze Mann, Der   7
"Science Fiction/Double Fea-
  ture"   160, 371
"Scooby Doo/Dynomutt Hour"
  121
"Scooby Doo--Where Are You?"
  38
Scram, Arthur N.   52
"Scream Screen Scene: The
  Mummy"   169-70
"Scream Test"   253
Screaming   see   Carry On
  Screaming
Sea Beast, The   86
Sea Monster   see   Destination
  Inner Space
Sears, Heather   246
Secret Affairs of Mildred Wild,
  The   361
"Secret Horror of Dr. Jekyll,
  The"   122

secreto del Doctor Orloff, El
  106
Sedaka, Neil   371
Sedgwick   233
Selby, David   37
Selig, William   81-2
Selznik, David O.   296
Semple, Lorenzo, Jr.   346, 360
Sennett, Mack   217
sensacional y extraño caso del
  hombre y la bestia, El   see
  El hombre y la bestia
Seven Year Itch, The   266
Severin, John   369
sfida du King Kong, La   see
  White Pongo
Shado Kalo   99
Shadow of the Werewolf   see
  La noche de Walpurgis
Shaidlin, Jack   370
Shane, Arnold   341
Shannon, Frank   139
Sharkey, Jack   122
Shaw, Scott   404
She Creature, The   275-9
Shea, Thomas E.   80
Sheinberg, Sid   341
Shepard, Bill   349
Sherlock Meets the Phantom
  251
Sherriff, R. C.   133-4, 138
Sherwood, John   268
She-Wolf of London   26
Shields, Arthur   102
Shimura, Takashi   376, 379
"Shock Theater"   xii, 38, 159,
  203, 252-3
Shocker, Dan   123
Shokei, Nakano   397
Sholem, Lee   199
Short, John   36
Short, Rob   403
"Shukan Asahi"   382
"Silver Threats Among the Gold"
  40
Simon, Allen   226
Simon, Jim   367-8
Simons, John   368
Sims, Willard   40
Sing, Baby, Sing   95
"Sinister Cinema"   38, 121, 159,
  184, 225, 273, 361, 402
Siodmak, Curt (Kurt)   xiii-xviii,

8, 10, 15, 19, 38, 45, 140, 142, 144, 145
Six Inches Tall see Attack of the Puppet People
Skaebnesvangre Opfindelse, Den 82
Skeates, Steve 128
Skinner, Allen 183
Slave of the Vampire, The 37
Slaves of the Invisible Monster see The Invisible Monster
Slesar, Henry 156
Sloan, Blanding 324
Sloan, Edward Van 162, 165
Smart, Ralph 157
Smith, Dick 118-9, 225
Smith, Paul J. 114, 245
Snow, Marguerite 82
Snow Fire 114
Snowden, Leigh 270
"So This Is Ding Dong?" 368
Soffici, Mario 97
Solares, Gilberto Martínez 32
Soler, Julian 32
Son of Dr. Jekyll, The 98-9
"Son of Dr. Jerkyll, The" 127
Son of Dracula 31, 183
Son of Godzilla (1963 amateur) 403; (1968) see Gojira no Musuko
Son of Kong 355
Son of Kong, The 305, 315-9, 324-6, 339, 357
Son of Kong Returns, The 357
"Son of Mighty Joe Kong" 364
"Son of Rockzilla" 402
Son of Tor 357, 403
Sondergaard, Gale 146
Songs Our Mummy Told Us 184
"Sonny and Cher Comedy Hour, The" 38, 121, 159, 184, 225, 361
Soul, Peter 183
Sounds Galactic 43
Souza, Edward de 246
"Space: 1999" 121
Special Effects 324
Spiegle, Dan 126
"Spike Jones Show" 128, 184
Spooks 99
Spry, Burl H. 207
Stacy, Terry 122

Stallings, Charles 212
Stansbury, Hope 31
Stapleton, Maureen 361
Steckler, Ray Dennis 203
Stein, Herman 275
Steiner, Fred 271
Steiner, Max 301-3, 315, 343, 370-1
Stephani, Frederick 140
Steranko, Jim 367
"Steve Allen Show, The" 159
Stevens, Alex 37
Stevens, Craig 100
Stevens, Onslow 22, 25, 97
Stevens, Richie 44
Stevens, Stella 105
Stevenson, R. L. (actor) 95
Stevenson, Robert Louis 68-70, 72-4, 76, 78-82, 84-6, 89, 91, 94-9, 102-3, 105-9, 111-7, 119, 121-4, 126-9
Stewart, Bob (Bhob) 253
Stockwell, Dean 66
Stoker, Bram 65, 85, 187, 193
Stokes, Slim 184
Stone, Lewis 288, 293
"Storm Before the Calm!" 128
Story of Dracula, Frankenstein and the Wolfman, A (A Story of Dracula, Werewolf, Frankenstein, A Story of Dracula, the Wolfman and Frankenstein) 44
Stouffe, Larry N. 112
Strange, Glenn 19, 24, 28, 37, 39, 54-5, 260-1, 271-2
Strange Case of Dr. Jekyll and Mr. Hyde, The (Stevenson novel) 68-76, 78, 80-2, 84, 97, 99, 103, 105-9, 112-7, 119, 121-4, 128-9; (play) 80; (records) 128; (spoofs) 122; also see Dr. Jekyll and Mr. Hyde (plays)
"Strange Case of Dr. Jekyll and Mr. Hyde, The" (comics) 123, 124; (radio) "Theatre Guild on the Air" 115-6, 128; "Theatre Royale" 116; (television) Curtis 117-9; commercial 121; (Gibson story) 121-2; see also 'Dr. Jekyll and Mr. Hyde" (comics,

radio, TV)
Strange Case of Dr. Jekyll and
    Mr. Hyde and Other Stories,
    The 121
Strange Case of ... !#*%?,
    The see The Maltese Bip-
    py
Streisand, Barbra 346
Strickfaden, Ken 143
Strock, Herbert L. 59
Strongest Man in the World,
    The 357
Struss, Karl 91, 93
Stuart, Gloria 138
Stuart, Roy 121
Stuart, Sidney 40
Study in Identity, A 112
Subotsky, Milton 107-9
Sullivan, Thomas Russell 75-
    6, 78-9
"Super Circus" 361
"Super Gorilla from Krypton,
    The" 365-6
Superbestie Dr. Jeckyll 123
Super-Heroes Battle Super-
    Gorillas 366
"Super-Hip, the Sickest Super-
    Hero of 'em All" 42
Superzan 202
Surf Terror see The Beach
    Girls and the Monster
Sutherland, A. Edward 143
Sutton, Tom (Sean Todd) 228,
    367
Swan, Curt 126, 365
Swanson, H. N. 361
Swift, Alan 151
Swift, Jonathan 295
Symonds, Henry R. 288
Szabo, Sandor 122

Tails of Horror see Spooks
Takasugi, Ryosaku 375, 379
Talarico, Tony (Tony William-
    sune) 127, 360
Talbot, Gloria 102
Tanner, Edwin 80
Tarz and Jane and Boy and
    Cheetah 356
Tarzan and King Kong 331
Tashlin, Frank 113, 240
Taurog, Norman 248

Teenage Frankenstein, The 37
Teenage Frankenstein Meets the
    Teenage Werewolf, The 61
Teenage Jekyll and Hyde 114
Teenage Werewolf, The 61
Tenney, Del 280
Terror Is a Man 36
Terror of Godzilla see Oru
    Kaijū Daishingeki
Terror of Mechagodzilla 400-1
Terror of New York City, The
    36
Terror of the Deep see Desti-
    nation Inner Space
Terror of the Kirghiz see
    Hercules, Prisoner of Evil
Terror of the Mummy see The
    Mummy (1959 film)
Terror on the Midway 357
Terrors of the Unknown 184
Testament du docteur Cordelier,
    Le 117
Thalberg, Irving 212, 222
Theory of the Evil Satan see
    Konga
Thesiger, Ernest 169
Thing, The see Destination
    Inner Space
Thing with Two Heads, The 347
"Things of Wax" 126
Thomas, Arthur Goring 209
Thomas, Eugene 80
Thomas, Gerald 199
Thomas, Harry 278
Thomas, Roy 36, 367
Thorndike, Sybil 210
Three Stooges 57, 99, 198-9
Three's a Crowd 113
Thursday Meets the Wolfman
    40, 183
Tim, Tiny 121
"Time for Beany" 361
Time Monsters, The 357
Tin Tan 32, 245
Tinieblas 202
"Titano the Super-Ape!" (1959)
    364; (1960) 365
"To Tell the Truth" 19
To the Land of the Electric
    Angel 358, 403
Tokyo Ninja Butai 151
"Tom Slick" 38
Tômei Kaijin 151

Tomei Ningen 154
Tomei Ningen Arawaru 154
Tomei-Ningen to Hai-Otoko 154
"Tonight Show" 121, 361
Tor, King of Beasts 357
Tore ng Diyablo 65-6
Tormented 152
Torrance, Ernest 216
Toten Augen des Dr. Dracula see La marca del Hombre Lobo
Tourneur, Jacques 280
Townsend, Bud 248
Tracy, Spencer 40, 95-7, 113, 115, 117, 122, 125
Travers, Henry 138
Trevor, Austin 329
Trimpe, Herb 404
Trowbridge, Charles 173
Tsuburaya, Eiji 336-7, 375-6, 378, 380-1, 395-6
Tsukiji, Yonesaburo 408
Tucker, Forrest 361
Tunnel Under the World 183
Turner, George E. 360
Turner, Lana 96
Tutankhamen 164-5, 173, 197
Tuttle, Tom 66
Tuttle, William 66, 252
12 Plus 1 112
Twisted Brain see Horror High
Two Faces of Dr. Jekyll, The 103-4
200 Motels 112
Two Lost Worlds 291-2
Tyasa, Noriaki 409
Tyler, Tom 168, 170-3, 175, 177

Ugly Duckling, The 103
Ulhas 221
Ulmer, Edgar G. 102, 154
"Ultra Man" 273, 402
"Ultra Q" 402
"Uncle Croc's Block" 38
Uncle Walt 217
"Underdog Show, The" 361
Undying Monster, The 54-6
Unholy Hour see Werewolf of London

Universal Pictures Presents Dracula, The Mummy plus Other Stories 169
Unknown Island 326-7
Unknown Purple, The 153
Unseen, The 153
Unsichtbare, Der 151
Unsichtbarer geht durch die Stadt, Ein 150
unsichtbaren Krallen des Dr. Mabuse, Die 154

Valley of Gwangi, The (The Valley Where Time Stood Still) 320
Vampire des Dr. Dracula, Die see La marca del Hombre Lobo
vampiro dell'opera, Il 245
Van, Billy 38
Vance, William 114
Van Dyke, Dick 106
Vanishing Cream 152
Vanishing Shadow, The 139
Varan the Unbelievable see Daikaiju Baran
Varney, Gabriel 253
Veidt, Conrad 85, 240
Velle, Gaston 132
venganza de la momia, La 202
"Vengeance" 273
"Vengeance Crude" 274
Verdugo, Elena 20-1, 224
vicino di casa, Il 30, 183
Villamonte, Ricardo 274
Vincent, Chuck 356
Vinton, Will 340
Volcano Monsters, The see Gojira no Gyakushyu
Voodoo Woman 278
Vovins, Henry 209
"Voyage to the Bottom of the Sea" 263, 292

Wager, Walter 358
Waggner, George 12, 244
Wakabayashi, Eiko 388
'Walk the Savage Land!" 367
Walker, Stuart 7
Walking Dead, The 105
Wallace, Edgar 224, 282, 297

Wallman, Jeffrey 156
"Waltzing Godzilla" 404
Wang, Peter 40
War Eagles 319-20
War of the Gargantuas, The
   see Sanda tai Gailah
War of the Monsters see Ga-
   mera tai Barugon
War of the Primal Tribes see
   Brute Force
War-Gods of the Deep (War-
   Lords...) 280
Warner, J. B. 7
Warren, Bill 112, 127, 353
Warren, James xii, 369
Warren, Jerry 33, 200
Warren, Val 31
"Way Out" 225
"Wayne and Shuster Take an Af-
   fectionate Look at the Mon-
   sters" 39
We Want Our Mummy 198-9
Wechter, Jayson 368
Weeks, Stephen 107
Wein, Len 126
Wells, H. G. [Herbert George]
   130-3, 139, 141, 144, 146,
   150, 155-7, 159-60
Welt ist mein!, Die see Ein
   Unsichtbarer geht durch die
   Stadt
"Werewolf" 43
Werewolf, The (1913) 1-2;
   (1932) 7; (1956) xi, 57-9
Werewolf and the Yeti, The
   53
Werewolf in a Girls' Dormitory
   see Lycanthropus
Werewolf of London 2-3, 7, 13,
   26, 38, 40, 49-50
Werewolf of London 273
Werewolf of Paris, The (novel)
   61-2; (film) see The Curse
   of the Werewolf
Werewolf of Washington, The
   66-7
Werewolf vs. the Vampire Wo-
   man, The (film) [The Were-
   wolf's Shadow] see La
   noche de Walpurgis (novel)
   52
Werewolves on Wheels 66
Werner, Tom 61

West, Adam 121
West, Roland 153
Westcott, Helen 100
Westmore, Bud 27, 100, 186,
   222, 245, 259-61
Westmore, Wally 93
Whale, James 133-4, 139, 141-
   2
What a Carve-Up! 169
"What Are the Loch Ness and
   Other Monsters All About?"
   39, 121
"Whatever Happened to Farley
   Fairfax?!!" 225
Wheeler, Bert 198
When Dinosaurs Ruled the Earth
   293, 343
When Quackel Did Hyde 84
"When Superman Was King Kong!"
   365
White, Glen 210
White, Jules 99
White Pongo 326
White Wolf, The 2
Whitten, Leslie H. 66
Who, The 129
Who Killed Cock Rubin? see
   The Maltese Bippy
Widderburn Horror, The see
   House of the Black Death
"Wide World of Adventure" 353
Wilder, W. Lee 151
Wilk, L. 209
William, Warren xv, 9
Williams, Hugh 115
Williams, Pat 371
Williams, Paul 249
Williams, Richard 357
Willis, Matt 56
Wilson, Clarence 316
Wilson, Ian 246
Windsor, Marie 186
Winkler, Henry 159
Winner of 10 Academy Awards,
   The 356
Winters, David 345
Witney, William 153, 199
Wnoroski, Jim 32
Wolf Boy 67
Wolf Man, The (1915, 1918,
   1924) 7; (1941) xii-xviii, 1-
   2, 7-15, 26-7, 37-8, 40, 43-
   4, 50, 53, 56, 61, 175, 240,

299; (1961) see The Curse of
    the Werewolf
Wolf Man, The (The Were-wolf)
    see Der schwarze Mann
"Wolf Men, The" 19, 30
"Wolfbane" 43
Wolfman 30
"Wolfman" 42-3
WolfMan, The 42
Wolfman, The 273
"Wolfman, The" 44
Wolfman, Marv 125, 274
Wolfman Jack 38
Wolfman of Count Dracula,
    The see La marca del
    Hombre Lobo
"Wolf-Man of Metropolis, The"
    41
Wolfman's Cure, The see
    House of Dracula
Wolfmensche des Dr. Dracula,
    Der see La marca del
    Hombre Lobo
Wolheim, Louis 87
Women of the Prehistoric
    Planet 305
Wong, Victor 316
Wood, Edward J. 31
Wood, Wallace 169, 369
Woolsey, Robert 198
World of Abbott and Costello,
    The 30, 187
"World of the Giant Gorillas!,
    The" 368
Worsley, Wallace 210, 212
Wray, Fay 298, 300, 306-9,
    311, 343, 359, 362
Wrestling Women vs. the Az-
    tec Mummy, The see Las
    luchadoras contra la momia
Wylie, Philip 133

Xirinius 124

Yamauchi, Akira 397
Yarbrough, Jean 27, 65
Yellow Submarine 357
York, Duke 57
Young, Harold 173
Young Dracula see Son of
    Dracula
Younger, Henry 192

Yuasa, Noriaka 408
Yuge, Tarou 151

Zacherle, John (Zacherly) 43,
    252-4
Zappa, Frank 112
Zavitz, Lee 301
Zegri, Armando 43
Zegri, Joana 43
Zindel, Paul 361
Zohar, Uri 339
"Zone Fighter" 402
Zucco, George 54, 171, 177
Zukor, Adolph 85, 88